Amazon Redshift:
The Definitive Guide
Jump-Start Analytics Using
Cloud Data Warehousing

Rajesh Francis, Rajiv Gupta, and Milind Oke

Beijing · Boston · Farnham · Sebastopol · Tokyo

Amazon Redshift: The Definitive Guide

by Rajesh Francis, Rajiv Gupta, and Milind Oke

Published by O'Reilly Media, Inc., 1005 Gravenstein Highway North, Sebastopol, CA 95472.

O'Reilly books may be purchased for educational, business, or sales promotional use. Online editions are also available for most titles (*http://oreilly.com*). For more information, contact our corporate/institutional sales department: 800-998-9938 or *corporate@oreilly.com*.

Acquisitions Editor: Aaron Black	**Indexer:** Sue Klefstad
Development Editor: Sara Hunter	**Interior Designer:** David Futato
Production Editor: Christopher Faucher	**Cover Designer:** Karen Montgomery
Copyeditor: Piper Editorial Consulting, LLC	**Illustrator:** Kate Dullea
Proofreader: Stephanie English	

October 2023:   First Edition

Revision History for the First Edition

2023-10-02:   First Release

See *http://oreilly.com/catalog/errata.csp?isbn=9781098135300* for release details.

978-1-098-13530-0

[LSI]

Table of Contents

Foreword

In today's data-driven world, organizations are constantly looking to extract actionable business insights from the vast amount of data at their disposal and turn it into a competitive advantage by offering seamless experiences to their customers and streamlining business operations. The ability to efficiently store, manage, and enable access to data assets for all users in the organization in a secure and governed fashion is a critical requirement that requires rethinking the traditional data architectures. Cloud data warehousing has emerged as a central pillar of this modern data architecture in the past decade.

Amazon Redshift, developed by Amazon Web Services (AWS), has been at the forefront of this revolution ever since it was launched as the first cloud data warehouse in 2013, empowering businesses to scale their data warehousing and do it cost effectively unlocking the full potential of their data . Tens of thousands of organizations have adopted Amazon Redshift as the foundational data store for their modern data strategy to serve a wide spectrum of analytics requirements. As a data leader, I am thrilled to introduce this comprehensive guide to Amazon Redshift, which is written for both seasoned data professionals and those new to the world of cloud data warehousing.

In *Amazon Redshift: The Definitive Guide*, the authors take a solutions architecture approach and offer practical insights, best practices, and real-world examples that will enable you to harness the full power of this service. The authors have extensive experience building solutions for hundreds of customers of all types, from startups to global organizations. In particular, they've helped projects ranging from migrations from other data warehouses to Amazon Redshift and run then with high performance at scale, to delivering new analytics use cases such as real time analytics leveraging Redshift streaming ingestion and zero-ETL, building predictive analytics solutions using Redshift ML, and even go beyond to offer analytics as a service using powerful capabilities such as Redshift data sharing.

The book starts by laying the foundations of modern data strategy, explaining the fundamental concepts of data warehouse and architecture of Amazon Redshift. From there, the authors dive deep into key features of the service with relevant examples for data modeling, loading and transforming data including streaming ingestion, performance optimization, scaling, and security best practices. You will also find in-depth coverage of integration with other AWS services like Amazon SageMaker, Amazon Aurora ensuring you can leverage the broader AWS ecosystem to build robust and scalable data applications.

What sets this book apart is its practical approach. The authors have drawn upon their experience as solutions architects working with Amazon Redshift to provide real-world use cases that will help you build a scalable data architecture with best practices. From an executive seeking to make informed decisions about your organization's data strategy, to a data engineer responsible for curating and managing data, or a data analyst looking to get business insights from your data, this book has something to offer for all types of readers.

As we continue to navigate an increasingly complex data landscape, building a data strategy around Amazon Redshift can help you simplify your data architecture. Beyond managing data, Amazon Redshift can be a catalyst for innovation in your organization to help you derive meaningful insights at scale and speed. I have seen the transformative impact that Amazon Redshift can have on businesses, and I'm confident that this book will empower you to achieve similar success on your data journey.

I commend the authors for their initiative and effort to create this comprehensive guide to Amazon Redshift. This book has information that will help readers starting their data modernization journey on cloud or readers who are just seeking to understand data architecture patterns. I encourage you to learn and apply the principles and techniques outlined in this book to drive your organization to become data-driven, and improve customer experience.

— Neeraja Rentachintala
Director, Amazon Redshift Product Management

Preface

Welcome to the world of data warehousing and Amazon Redshift! In this book, we embark on an exciting journey that explores the powerful capabilities of Amazon Redshift and its role in modern data warehousing. Whether you are a data professional, architect, IT leader, or simply someone curious about data management and analytics, this book is designed to provide you with comprehensive insights into modern data warehousing patterns using Amazon Redshift.

Data plays a pivotal role in modern business operations, serving as a valuable asset that fuels informed decision making to drive growth. In today's digital age, businesses generate and collect vast amounts of data from various sources, including customer interactions, market trends, social media, devices, and operational processes. By harnessing and analyzing this data, businesses can gain competitive advantage by identifying patterns and correlations to make data-driven decisions and drive innovation. As the volume, velocity, and variety of data continue to grow exponentially, it has become increasingly crucial for businesses to have efficient and scalable data warehousing solutions that can handle the demands of today's data-driven world.

Amazon Redshift, a fully managed, cloud-based data warehousing service, has emerged as a leading solution in the industry, empowering organizations to store, analyze, and gain actionable insights from their vast datasets. With its flexible architecture, high-performance processing capabilities, and integration with other Amazon Web Services (AWS), Amazon Redshift provides a platform for building robust and scalable data warehouses.

Amazon Redshift has been at the forefront in the Gartner Database Management System (DBMS) Magic Quadrant, and this book will provide extra insight on how to successfully implement your analytical solutions on this data warehousing service from AWS. Amazon Redshift has evolved from a standalone analytical query engine to an AI-powered data warehouse service leveraging machine learning (ML) at the core of its features like automatic workload management, Autonomics, and Code-Whisperer in Query Editor.

In this book, we delve into the fundamental concepts and principles of data warehousing, covering topics such as data modeling; extract, transform, and load processes; performance optimization; and data governance. We explore the unique features and advantages of Amazon Redshift, guiding you through the process of setting up, configuring, and managing your Redshift clusters. We will also discuss best practices for data loading, schema design, query optimization, and security considerations.

This book is equally apt for personnel completely new to data warehousing or those who are looking to modernize their current on-premise solutions by leveraging the power of the cloud. The chapters have been organized to first introduce the Amazon Redshift service and the focus shifts toward migration in Chapter 9. But we encourage readers interested in migration to Amazon Redshift to review Chapter 9 earlier as they see fit.

We have used our personal experience with Amazon Redshift, along with our interactions with customers using Amazon Redshift, which is a privilege we earn from our day jobs. Also being close to the actual product teams and engineering teams building out this service has assisted us in sharing some interesting pieces throughout the book.

We took almost an entire calendar year to put this book together. AWS is ever evolving its services based on customer feedback, every few months rolling out new features, and we are looking forward to seeing how soon this book gets "outdated," or should we say, we are rooting for it!

As you progress through each chapter, you will gain a deeper understanding of how to leverage the power of Amazon Redshift to build a modern data warehouse that can handle large volumes of data, support complex analytical queries, and facilitate real-time insights. We provide practical examples, code snippets, and real-world scenarios to help you apply the concepts and techniques to your own data warehousing projects.

It is important to note that this book assumes no prior knowledge of Amazon Redshift or data warehousing concepts. We start with the basics and gradually build upon them, ensuring that readers of all levels can benefit from this comprehensive guide. Whether you are just beginning your data warehousing journey or seeking to enhance your existing knowledge, this book will serve as a valuable resource and reference.

Without further ado, let's embark on this exciting journey into the world of data warehousing with Amazon Redshift. May this book serve as a trusted companion, equipping you with the knowledge and tools necessary to build scalable, high-performance data warehouses and transform your organization's data into a strategic asset.

Happy reading, and may your data endeavors be successful!

Conventions Used in This Book

The following typographical conventions are used in this book:

Italic
> Indicates new terms, URLs, email addresses, filenames, and file extensions.

`Constant width`
> Used for program listings, as well as within paragraphs to refer to program elements such as variable or function names, databases, data types, environment variables, statements, and keywords.

`Constant width bold`
> Shows commands or other text that should be typed literally by the user.

`Constant width italic`
> Shows text that should be replaced with user-supplied values or by values determined by context.

> This element signifies a tip or suggestion.

> This element signifies a general note.

> This element indicates a warning or caution.

Using Code Examples

Supplemental material (code examples, exercises, etc.) is available for download at *https://resources.oreilly.com/examples/0636920746867*.

If you have a technical question or a problem using the code examples, please send email to *bookquestions@oreilly.com*.

This book is here to help you get your job done. In general, if example code is offered with this book, you may use it in your programs and documentation. You do not need to contact us for permission unless you're reproducing a significant portion of the code. For example, writing a program that uses several chunks of code from this book does not require permission. Selling or distributing examples from O'Reilly books does require permission. Answering a question by citing this book and quoting example code does not require permission. Incorporating a significant amount of example code from this book into your product's documentation does require permission.

We appreciate, but generally do not require, attribution. An attribution usually includes the title, author, publisher, and ISBN. For example: "*Amazon Redshift: The Definitive Guide* by Rajesh Francis, Rajiv Gupta, and Milind Oke (O'Reilly). Copyright 2024 Rajesh Francis, Rajiv Gupta, and Milind Oke, 978-1-098-13530-0."

If you feel your use of code examples falls outside fair use or the permission given above, feel free to contact us at *permissions@oreilly.com*.

O'Reilly Online Learning

 For more than 40 years, *O'Reilly Media* has provided technology and business training, knowledge, and insight to help companies succeed.

Our unique network of experts and innovators share their knowledge and expertise through books, articles, and our online learning platform. O'Reilly's online learning platform gives you on-demand access to live training courses, in-depth learning paths, interactive coding environments, and a vast collection of text and video from O'Reilly and 200+ other publishers. For more information, visit *https://oreilly.com*.

How to Contact Us

Please address comments and questions concerning this book to the publisher:

O'Reilly Media, Inc.
1005 Gravenstein Highway North
Sebastopol, CA 95472
800-889-8969 (in the United States or Canada)
707-829-7019 (international or local)
707-829-0104 (fax)
support@oreilly.com
https://www.oreilly.com/about/contact.html

We have a web page for this book, where we list errata, examples, and any additional information. You can access this page at *https://oreil.ly/amazon-redshift-definitive-guide*.

For news and information about our books and courses, visit *https://oreilly.com*.

Find us on LinkedIn: *https://linkedin.com/company/oreilly-media*.

Follow us on Twitter: *https://twitter.com/oreillymedia*.

Watch us on YouTube: *https://youtube.com/oreillymedia*.

Acknowledgments

We would like to acknowledge the entire Amazon Redshift customer base, the various AWS teams working on developing this service, the product managers, the engineers, the solutions architects field teams, and also the product marketing teams. Without support from all these teams, this endeavor would simply not have been possible!

CHAPTER 1

AWS for Data

It is a capital mistake to theorize before one has data.
—Sherlock Holmes

Data is ubiquitous and powers everything we do today. Who would have thought you could generate data just by walking and monitor your steps in real time on your wrist as you call your friend? From mobile phones, smartwatches, and web clicks to the Internet of Things (IoT), we are generating various types of data in abundance, and organizations are faced with the challenge of deriving meaning out of all of this data to deliver insights. You have to analyze this data to present unbiased information in a simple way for leaders to make business decisions. Data is the underlying force that fuels the insights and predictions that lead to better decision making and innovation. Although challenging, it is imperative that you harness this data and reinvent your business to stay relevant now and in the future. Amazon Redshift is a fully managed, petabyte (PB)-scale data warehouse service in the cloud that powers a modern data architecture to store data from all sources in a centralized or decentralized architecture. It enables you to query data across your data warehouses, data lakes, and operational databases to gain faster and deeper insights not possible otherwise.

In this chapter, we will cover the core tenants of the Amazon Web Services (AWS) for data framework including what makes "Data-Driven Organizations" successful, the core tenants of a "Modern Data Strategy", and what goes into building a "Modern Data Architecture". Finally, we'll dive into some popular ways organizations are using "Data Mesh and Data Fabric" to satisfy their needs for each analytics user group in a scalable way.

Data-Driven Organizations

Data-driven organizations treat data like an asset; they make it available and accessible not just to business users, but to all who need data to make decisions so they can make more informed decisions. These organizations recognize the intrinsic value of data and realize the value that good data brings to the organization and its economic impact. They democratize data and make it available for business decision makers to measure the key performance indicators (KPIs). The saying "You can't improve what you don't measure," attributed to Peter Drucker, is all the more relevant for today's businesses.

Most businesses have a range of KPIs that they regularly monitor to drive growth and improve productivity. These KPIs could range from the common ones like growth, sales, market share, number of customers, and cost of customer acquisition to more domain-specific ones like sell through, capacity utilization, email opt-out rates, or shopping cart abandonment rates. A good KPI is specific, measurable, and impactful to overall business goals and could vary from business to business.

Though some attributes like employee morale, confidence, and integrity of an organization cannot really be measured, there is a lot that can get measured and monitored for progress. Having access to this data means leaders can employ strategies to move the business in a certain direction. For example, after acquiring a power tool company, a manufacturer was flying blind until their IT team integrated the data into the core enterprise resource planning (ERP) system. The executive remarked that it was like turning the lights on for them to see where they were headed on the road with this business.

In his book *Infonomics* (Gartner, Inc.), Doug Laney talks about how it is essential for organizations to go beyond thinking and merely talking about information as an asset to actually valuing and treating it as one. He argues that information should be considered a new asset class in that it has measurable economic value and should be administered like any other type of asset. Laney provides a framework for businesses to monetize, manage, and measure information as an actual asset. He talks about how monetizing is not all about selling data, or exchange of cash. It is about realizing the value of information and thinking more broadly about the methods used to have an impact on your customers and generate profits. It is about working backward from your customers' requirements and interests and aligning your business and operational strategy to fulfill the priorities of your customer. Analytics helps organizations make better decisions and enables key strategic initiatives. It also helps you improve relationships with both your customers and your business partners.

At AWS re:Invent 2021, Adam Selipsky talked about how Florence Nightingale analyzed soldier mortality rates from the Crimean War. Nightingale, a nurse, used data and analytics to gain an insight that the majority of soldiers had not died in combat, but instead from preventable diseases caused by poor sanitary conditions in the hospital. Nightingale analyzed the data she collected and created a simple but powerful visualization diagram (Figure 1-1) depicting the causes of soldier mortality. This Rose Chart, also known as a polar area chart, allowed multiple comparisons in one diagram showing mortality rates for each month from diseases, wounds, and other causes. This visual helped Nightingale convince Queen Victoria and generals that more men had died from disease than from wounds, especially in winter, and highlighted the need for hospital reform and care for soldiers. This is a great example of the storytelling impact of data; it really changed the conversation to help save lives.

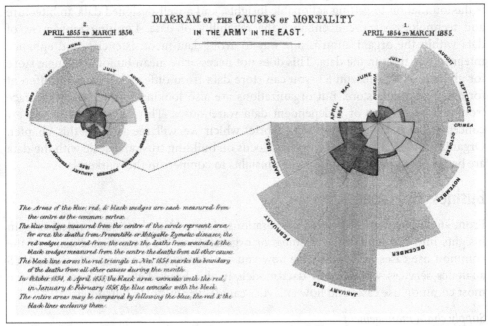

Figure 1-1. Florence Nightingale's Rose Chart for causes of mortality

Today, you may expect to have real-time insights and prefer to access the data as soon as it lands. There are many inspiring examples of data-driven companies focusing on and adapting to changes in their customers' preferences by using analytics. Dow Jones, a global news provider, increased response rates by 50% to 100% for mail communication by using analytics and making data accessible. Magellan Rx modernized its data warehouse and is able to improve patient outcomes by bringing drugs to market sooner and reduce operational costs by 20%. Moderna is using Amazon Redshift for simple, cost-effective data warehousing to avoid silos and establish a single source of truth for data across the organization. Nasdaq migrated its growing data warehouse to a more modern data lake architecture and was able to support the jump from 30 billion records to 70 billion records a day because of the flexibility and scalability of Amazon Simple Storage Service (S3) and Amazon Redshift. Netflix uses data to create blockbuster hit series like *House of Cards*. Their managers have collected and analyzed data from the digital transformation of media and entertainment to build lucrative markets where none previously existed. Coco Cola Andina, which produces and distributes products licensed by The Coca-Cola Company within South America, increased the productivity of its analysis team by 80% by creating a data lake that became the single source of data generated by SAP ERP and other legacy databases.

A common theme with these successful data-driven companies is the democratization of data and placing insights in the hands of decision makers. Having reliable data is the foundation to getting actionable insights, and a well-designed data architecture and technology stack can enhance the reliability of data. Limiting movement of data within the organization is one way to avoid data inconsistencies, and enhance integrity and trust in the data. This does not necessarily mean building a single store for all data. With Amazon S3, you can store data from different sources in different formats in a single store. But organizations are also looking to query data in place from source systems or independent data warehouses. This has given rise to new concepts like data mesh and data fabric, which we will see later in this chapter. Organizations that are data driven and focus on building trust and scale with the data are better positioned to gain real-time insights to compete in the marketplace.

Business Use Cases

From small businesses to global corporations, data and analytics are critical to gain insights into the state of the business or organization. We have picked some of the common use cases to demonstrate how you can derive business insights using AWS analytics services with specific data models in this book. Let's look at some of the most common use cases and how analytics can deliver business outcomes.

Supply chain management
> With the impact of ecommerce on traditional brick-and-mortar retailers, companies have to use analytics to transform the way they define and manage supply chains. Using data and quantitative methods, demand and supply planners can improve decision making across the supply chain cycle. Manufacturers and retailers can apply statistical methods to improve supply chain decision making to have the product at the right time at the right place for their consumers. They can analyze inventory and plan their supply based on demand signals. A good example is Amazon, which processes 51,000 daily queries to drive supply chain excellence using Amazon Redshift (*https://oreil.ly/-Veb6*).

Finance
> Financial and banking organizations help their customers make investment decisions and provide money management solutions. Today, many banks use artificial intelligence (AI) and machine learning (ML) to identify fraud, predict

customer churn, and proactively engage to prevent fraud or churn. For example, you may have had your credit card disabled at some point while you were on a vacation or visiting a new place. This is ML working behind the scenes to detect unusual activity and block a possible fraud transaction before it is too late. Having the right data available and easily accessible makes this possible.

Customer relationship management (CRM)

Implementing a data warehousing data model for CRM can enable businesses to consolidate customer data from multiple touchpoints, such as sales, marketing, and customer support. By analyzing this data, businesses can gain insights into customer behavior, preferences, and satisfaction levels. This information can be used to personalize marketing campaigns, improve customer service, and foster long-term customer relationships.

Education

Analytics in education can make a big difference in student experience and outcomes. The traditional educational method of classroom teaching has its challenges for today's children immersed in a digital world. Schools are dealing with high dropout rates, ineffective outcomes, and outdated syllabi. Moving to a personalized learning approach would mean students can take advantage of flexibility and learn at their own pace. This also means adopting hybrid learning with online learning management solutions with the ability to provide customized content for learners. Data from student interactions with online learning environments combined with data from test scores can be used to analyze and provide insights into where the student might need additional help. With AI and machine learning, educators could predict the outcomes of individual students and take proactive steps to provide a positive outcome and experience.

Healthcare industry

Data plays a crucial role in the healthcare industry, revolutionizing the way patient care is delivered, medical research is conducted, and rising costs are controlled with operational efficiency. Healthcare organizations can unlock valuable insights that drive evidence-based decision making by harnessing the power of data to improve patient outcomes and enhance overall healthcare delivery. By identifying patterns, trends, and correlations in large datasets, healthcare professionals can gain a deeper understanding of diseases and treatment effectiveness based on patient response. With predictive analytics, these organizations can detect diseases early and administer personalized medicine for at-risk patient groups. These organizations can also detect fraudulent claims by analyzing claims data and identifying patterns of fraudulent activities.

New Business Use Cases with Generative AI

Generative AI and data warehousing can complement each other to enhance various aspects of data analysis and decision-making processes. Next, we will outline some ways in which generative AI can be integrated with data warehousing:

Code generation

Generative AI models can be trained on vast code repositories and programming languages to generate code completions and suggestions. When developers are writing code, the AI model can provide real-time suggestions that help programmer efficiency by suggesting or writing snippets. This can also help reduce errors and improve overall developer productivity to bring products to market quicker.

Natural language generation

Data warehousing often involves extracting insights and presenting them in a meaningful way to stakeholders. Generative AI models can generate human-readable reports or narratives based on the data stored in the warehouse. This can also be summarizing or automated generation of descriptive analytics, making it easier for decision makers to understand and interpret the data or the content of a report.

Synthetic data generation

To train a machine learning model, the quality of data determines the accuracy of the prediction. Generative AI models can be used to generate synthetic data that mimics the characteristics of real-world data. This synthetic data can be combined with actual data in a data warehouse to expand the dataset and create more comprehensive and diverse training sets for machine learning models. It helps overcome data scarcity issues and improves the accuracy and robustness of analytical models.

Anomaly detection

Generative AI models, such as Generative Adversarial Networks (GANs), can be employed for anomaly detection in data warehousing. By training the GAN on normal data patterns, it can learn to identify anomalies by comparing the generated data with the actual data stored in the warehouse. This can help you detect unusual patterns and outliers for you to identify potential fraudulent transactions or operations.

Data imputation and augmentation

Incomplete or missing data can affect the accuracy of data analysis and decision making. Generative AI techniques can be used to impute missing values by learning the underlying patterns in the available data. By training a generative model on the existing data, it can generate plausible values for missing data points, filling in the gaps and improving the integrity of the data warehouse. You can augment existing datasets in a data warehouse generating new synthetic samples based on the existing data, and create a larger and more diverse dataset for training analytical models. This can improve the performance and generalization ability of machine learning algorithms and enable better predictions and insights.

Recommendation systems

Generative AI techniques can enhance recommendation systems by generating personalized recommendations for users. By leveraging user behavior data stored in a data warehouse, generative models can learn user preferences and generate personalized recommendations for products, services, or content. This helps businesses improve customer engagement and drive sales or user satisfaction.

Integrating generative AI with data warehousing expands the capabilities of data analysis, enhances data quality, and enables advanced analytics and decision-making processes. However, it's essential to ensure ethical considerations, privacy, and security when generating and utilizing synthetic data.

Modern Data Strategy

The concept of data gravity was first coined by Dave McCrory in 2010. In his analogy, he compares data to a planet and talks about data mass that is built when organizations collect data in one place. Applications and services are attracted to this mass because proximity to data leads to better performance and throughput. This accelerates growth of data, and eventually it becomes almost impossible to move data around. Data generated by IoT, smart devices, cloud applications, and social media is continuing to grow exponentially. You need ways to easily and cost-effectively analyze all of this data with minimal time-to-insight, regardless of the format or where the data is stored.

Data is at the center of every application, process, and business decision. It is the cornerstone of almost every organization's digital transformation. It fuels new experiences and leads to insights that spur innovation. But building a strategy that unlocks the value of data for your entire organization is not an easy and straightforward journey. Data systems are often sprawling, siloed, and complex, with diverse datasets spread out across data lakes, data warehouses, cloud databases, software as a service (SaaS) applications, IoT devices, and on-premises systems. Many organizations are sitting on a treasure trove of data, but don't know where to start to get value out of it. Companies struggle to get a handle on where all their data sits, how to connect and act on that data effectively, and how to manage access to that data. And as data volumes grow, this only gets more difficult. The inability to use data effectively can hinder rapid decision making and sustained innovation.

To harness the value of their data, organizations need more than a single database, data lake, data warehouse, or business intelligence service. The reality is that each organization has multiple use cases, types of data, and users and applications that require different tools. And these needs will evolve over time. To truly unlock the value of your data to drive timely insights and innovation, you need to implement an end-to-end data strategy that makes working with data easier at every step of the data journey for everyone who needs it in your organization. An end-to-end data strategy combines tools, resources, and processes for ingesting, storing, and querying data, analyzing data, and building machine learning models, and ultimately helping end users develop data-driven insights. This end-to-end data strategy must have:

A comprehensive set of capabilities for any data use case
> A comprehensive set of tools that accounts for the scale, variety of data, and many purposes for which you want to use it now and in the future

An integrated set of tools to easily connect all your data
> The ability to integrate data stored and analyzed in different tools and systems to gain a better understanding of your business and predict what will happen

End-to-end data governance
> Governance of all your data to securely give data access when and where your users need it

With these three pillars (shown in Figure 1-2), you can store the ever-increasing data at scale, access that data seamlessly, and manage who has access to the data with security and governance controls.

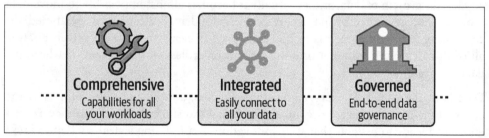

Figure 1-2. Pillars of end-to-end modern data strategy

AWS provides you with the capabilities you need for an end-to-end data strategy with built-in intelligence and automation in its data services. Let's dive a bit deeper into each of these pillars and learn what it entails.

Comprehensive Set of Capabilities

To understand your business and scale with changing workloads, streamline processes, and make better decisions, you need to build data strategies that can meet your needs now and in the future. It takes more than just a single data lake, data warehouse, or business intelligence tool to effectively harness data. You need a comprehensive set of tools that accounts for the scale, variety of data, and many purposes for which you want to use it.

You can modernize your data architecture at various stages of the data journey, and that means breaking free from legacy databases and moving to fully managed and purpose-built data services. If you are running legacy, on-premises data stores or self-managing databases in the cloud, you still have to take care of management tasks such as database provisioning, patching, configuration, and backups. By transitioning to managed services on AWS cloud or other hyperscalers, you can benefit from the cloud providers' experience, maturity, reliability, security, and performance for hosting and managing your applications.

For an end-to-end data strategy, you need to store data in databases optimized for your type of workloads, integrating from multiple sources and enabling access to business decision makers using the tool of their choice to act on the information. As shown in Figure 1-3, AWS provides a comprehensive set of data capabilities to store, integrate, act, and govern for various types of data workloads. A one-size-fits-all approach to modernizing the analytics platform can eventually lead to compromises, so AWS offers purpose-built engines to support diverse data models, including relational, key-value, document, in-memory, graph, time series, wide column, and ledger databases. These sets of capabilities help you access data wherever it resides, analyze it, and act on the insights.

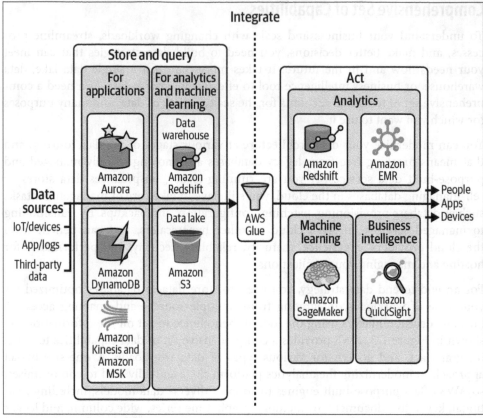

Figure 1-3. End-to-end data strategy

These data services and analysis tools are optimized for specific types of workloads, and AWS provides tools to integrate and govern the data stored in the purpose-built data services:

AWS Glue
> A serverless, scalable extract, transform, and load (ETL) and data integration service that makes it easier to discover, prepare, move, and integrate data from multiple sources for analytics and machine learning.

Amazon DynamoDB
> A fully managed, serverless, key-value NoSQL database designed to run high-performance applications at any scale. DynamoDB offers built-in security, continuous backups, automated multiregion replication, in-memory caching, and data import and export tools.

Amazon EMR

A big data solution for PB-scale data processing on the cloud with capabilities for interactive analytics and machine learning using open source frameworks such as Apache Spark, Apache Hive, and Presto.

OpenSearch

A distributed, community-driven, Apache 2.0-licensed, open source search and analytics suite used for a broad set of use cases like real-time application monitoring, log analytics, and website search.

Amazon Simple Storage Service (Amazon S3)

An object storage service offering high scalability, data availability, security, and performance. You can store and protect structured and unstructured data for use cases such as data lakes, cloud native applications, and mobile apps.

Amazon QuickSight

A serverless service for users that helps you meet varying analytic needs from the same source of truth through modern interactive dashboards, paginated reports, embedded analytics, and natural language queries.

Amazon Kinesis

Makes it easy to collect, process, and analyze real-time, streaming data so you can get timely insights and react quickly to new information. Amazon Kinesis offers capabilities to cost-effectively process streaming data at scale, along with the flexibility to choose the tools that best suit the requirements of your application.

Amazon Redshift

A fully managed, PB-scale data warehouse service in the cloud. With Amazon Redshift, you can modernize your data warehouse on the cloud with compliance, security, and governance, and leverage the scaling feature to meet your variable requirements. You can securely ingest, combine, and run historical, real-time, or predictive analytics on all your data using a serverless or provisioned deployment option.

Amazon SageMaker

A fully managed service to prepare data and build, train, and deploy machine learning models for any use case with fully managed infrastructure, tools, and workflows.

These services are tightly integrated and can talk to each other to leverage data from each other.

Integrated Set of Tools

The most impactful data-driven insights come from getting a full picture of your business and your customers. This can be achieved only when you connect the dots between your different data sources across multiple departments, services, on-premises tools, and third-party applications such as business intelligence (BI) systems or statistical modeling tools. Typically, connecting data across different data sources requires data replication or complex ETL pipelines, which can take hours, if not days. That's just not fast enough to keep up with the speed of decision making. ETL needs to be easier and in many cases, eliminated.

Great business leaders see opportunities to transform their business all along the value chain. But making such a transformation requires data that enables decision makers to get a full picture of the business and single source of truth. This necessitates breaking down data silos and making data accessible and shared in a secure way to unlock the value of data across the organization.

To make decisions quickly, you need new data stores that will scale and grow as your business needs change. You also want to be able to connect everything together, including your data lake, data warehouse, and all the purpose-built data stores into a coherent system that is secure and well governed.

That consolidated view can be achieved in many ways: federated querying, low/no-code data synchronization, or tradition ETL using serverless or server-based execution. Amazon Redshift provides options for each of these, with tight integration with other AWS services. The zero-ETL feature between Amazon Aurora and Amazon Redshift enables you to near real-time synchronize transactional data into your data warehouse. Amazon Redshift allows for querying data from your Amazon S3 data lake, and the federated query feature allows querying data securely and directly from operational databases. For analytics workloads, where you want to isolate compute, you may build ETL pipelines to extract, transform, and load data into a target data store. The tight integration with AWS Glue allows you to easily create spark-based jobs in AWS Glue Studio for execution using a serverless framework. For more details on Amazon Redshift data transformation strategies, see Chapter 4, "Data Transformation Strategies".

For exposing your data to data analysts and data scientists, Amazon Redshift has simplified the access path. In the past, machine learning has been limited to highly skilled data scientists or programmers with deep skills in programming languages such as Python, R, etc. With tight integration with Amazon SageMaker, Amazon Redshift data analysts can use Amazon Redshift ML to run machine learning work-loads from within the data warehouse or data lake without having to select, build, or train an ML model. For more details on Amazon Redshift machine learning, see Chapter 6, "Amazon Redshift Machine Learning". In addition, business analysts can use tools like Amazon QuickSight to autodiscover their Amazon Redshift data warehouse and connect to the data stores to quickly produce impactful dashboards with business insights. For more details on the different options for getting to your Amazon Redshift data warehouse, see Chapter 2, "Getting Started with Amazon Redshift".

End-to-End Data Governance

Establishing the right governance lets you balance control and access and gives people within your organization trust and confidence in the data. It encourages innovation, rather than restricts it, because the right people can quickly find, access, and share data when they need it.

To spur innovation, organizations should endorse the concept of data security as meaning how you can set your data free in a secure manner, rather than meaning how you can secure data and limit access to your users. With end-to-end data governance on AWS, you have control over where your data sits, who has access to it, and what can be done with it at every step of the data workflow.

For data engineers and developers, AWS has fine-grained controls, catalogs, and metadata within services like AWS Glue and AWS Lake Formation. AWS Glue enables you to catalog data across data lakes, data warehouses, and databases. AWS Glue comes with data quality rules that check for data freshness, accuracy, and integrity. With AWS Lake Formation, you can govern and audit the actions taken on the data in your data lake on Amazon S3 and data sharing in Amazon Redshift. If you have a data lake on Amazon S3, you can also use Amazon S3 Access Points to create unique access control policies and easily control access to shared datasets.

Data scientists can use governance controls in SageMaker to gain end-to-end visibility into ML models, including training, version history, and model performance all in one place.

Finally, Amazon DataZone is a data management service to catalog, discover, share, and govern data. It makes it easy for data engineers, data scientists, product managers, analysts, and other business users to discover, use, and collaborate with that data to drive insights for your business.

In summary, it is becoming increasingly clear that harnessing data is the next wave of digital transformation. Modernizing means unifying the best of data lakes and purpose-built data stores and making it easy to innovate with ML. With these three pillars—comprehensive, integrated, and governance—your modern data strategy with AWS can help you build an architecture that scales based on demand and reduce operational costs.

Modern Data Architecture

When you embark on a modern data strategy, you have to think about how to handle any amount of data, at low cost, and in open, standards-based data formats. The strategy should also let you break down data silos, empower your teams to run analytics or machine learning using their preferred tool or technique, and manage who has access to data with the proper security and data governance controls.

To execute a modern data strategy, you need a *modern data architecture*. You may have heard about data warehouses, data lakes, and data mesh, and you may also be considering one of these strategies. A *data warehouse* enables you to store structured data and enable fast query access on a large mass of data. A *data lake* is a central repository where you store all structured and unstructured data and have it easily accessible. A *data mesh* allows you to access data in place while decentralizing ownership and governance of data. A modern data architecture needs to support all of these aspects to gain business insights from the ever-increasing data mass.

AWS modern data architecture is built on a model that includes purpose-built data stores to optimize for scale, availability, performance, and cost. It enables integrating a data lake, a data warehouse, and purpose-built stores, enabling unified governance and easy data movement. Amazon Redshift and Amazon S3 form the core for your modern data architecture, with tight integration with other purpose-built services.

In the modern data architecture shown in Figure 1-4, there are three different patterns for data movement: inside-out, outside-in, and around the perimeter.

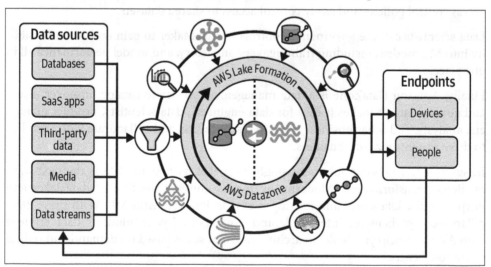

Figure 1-4. Modern data architecture using purpose-built services

Inside-out data movement

A subset of data in a central data store is sometimes moved to a purpose-built data store, such as Amazon Redshift for online analytical processing (OLAP) workloads, Amazon OpenSearch Service cluster, or Amazon Neptune cluster to support specialized analytics such as search analytics, building knowledge graphs, or both. In the context of Amazon Redshift, you may use Amazon Redshift for your central data store where other services like AWS Glue or other Amazon Redshift data warehouses can access the data through data sharing. Alternatively, you can consume data from an Amazon S3 data lake into Amazon Redshift by loading it via the COPY command or directly querying it as an external Amazon S3 schema.

Outside-in data movement

Organizations start with data stores that best fit their applications and later move that data into a central data store for collaboration. For example, to offload historical data that is not frequently accessed, you may want to UNLOAD this data from Amazon Redshift to your Amazon S3 data lake. A gaming company might choose Amazon DynamoDB as the data store to maintain game state, player data, session history, and leaderboards. This data can later be exported to an Amazon S3 data lake for additional analytics to improve the gaming experience for its players.

Around the perimeter

There are also scenarios where the data is moved from one specialized data store to another. For example, you can use the federated query capability of Amazon Redshift to query data directly from operational data stores like Amazon Aurora or use Amazon Redshift ML capability to run a model that will trigger a process in Amazon SageMaker.

You can innovate at various stages of the modern data strategy by moving away from building tightly coupled monolithic applications. Instead, you can build modular applications with independent components called microservices. These native, purpose-built, integrated AWS services are well suited for building modular applications while leveraging new emerging technologies like ML and AI.

Role of Amazon Redshift in a Modern Data Architecture

Amazon Redshift powers the modern data architecture and enables you to store data in a centralized or decentralized architecture and break down data silos by enabling access to all data in your organization. With a modern data architecture, you can store and access data within the data warehouse tables in structured columnar format and open file formats in your Amazon S3 data lake. The capability to query data across your data warehouse, data lake, and operational databases with security and governance helps unify and make data easily available to your business users and other applications.

Some of the key capabilities of Amazon Redshift and the benefit of tight integration to native services are shown in Figure 1-5.

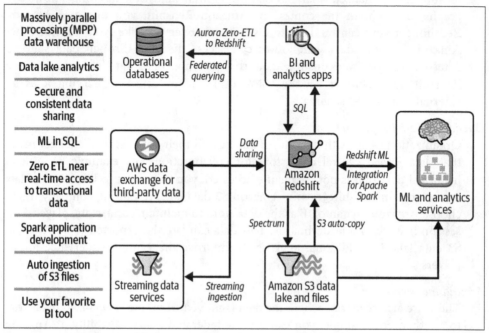

Figure 1-5. Amazon Redshift in a modern data architecture

We will discuss the features in detail in later chapters, but here is a brief summary of each:

Massively parallel processing (MPP) data warehouse

Amazon Redshift is based on MPP architecture, which enables fast run of the complex queries operating on large amounts of data by distributing the query processing to multiple nodes and virtual processing units within each node of your data warehouse. An MPP architecture has the added benefit of co-locating like data in processing units through the use of distribution keys, therefore making analytics processing more cost performant. In Chapter 2, "Getting Started with Amazon Redshift", you will learn more about the importance of MPP architecture.

Separation of storage and compute

With the Redshift architecture generation 3 (RA3), Amazon Redshift has separation of storage and compute, which helps you to scale storage or compute independently based on the requirements of your workloads. In Chapter 2, you will learn more about the architecture of Amazon Redshift and how to get started.

Serverless

Amazon Redshift offers a serverless option, so you can run and scale analytics without having to provision and manage data warehouses. With Amazon Redshift serverless, you don't have to choose a node type or the number of nodes you need for a specific workload; instead, you set an initial configuration for compute unit, which is measured in Redshift Processing Unit (RPU). Amazon Redshift automatically provisions and scales data warehouse capacity to meet the requirements of demanding and unpredictable workloads, and you pay only for the capacity you use. Amazon Redshift serverless is compatible with the provisioned cluster, so you can migrate your applications from a provisioned cluster to serverless without changing your existing analytics or BI applications. In Chapter 2, "Getting Started with Amazon Redshift", you will learn more about creating an Amazon Redshift serverless data warehouse.

Data lake analytics

Amazon Redshift can efficiently query and transform structured and semistructured data from files in Amazon S3 without having to load the data into Amazon Redshift tables. Amazon Redshift queries external S3 data with only the required data sent to your Amazon Redshift data warehouse. In Chapter 3, "Setting Up Your Data Models and Ingesting Data", you will learn more about how to query and transform data from Amazon S3.

Secure and consistent data sharing

Amazon Redshift data sharing allows you to share live data between data warehouses internal within your organization or with external partners. This feature allows you to extend benefits of a single data warehouse to multiple data warehouse deployments without the need to copy or move it. This enables you to access and query data where it is stored by sharing data across organizational boundaries and different data domains where data mass is accumulated. In Chapter 7, "Collaboration with Data Sharing", you will learn more about Amazon Redshift data sharing and how you can use this for collaboration with internal and external stakeholders.

Machine learning using SQL

Amazon Redshift ML makes it easy for data analysts and database developers to create, train, and apply machine learning models using familiar Standard Query Language (SQL) commands in Amazon Redshift data warehouses. With Amazon Redshift ML, you can reduce ML model development time by using SQL-based prediction model creation and taking advantage of integration with Amazon SageMaker (*https://oreil.ly/aG8L1*), a fully managed machine learning service, without learning new tools or languages. In Chapter 6, "Amazon Redshift Machine Learning", you'll learn more about the types of machine learning problems you can solve using Amazon Redshift ML.

Zero-ETL

Amazon Aurora supports zero-ETL integration with Amazon Redshift to enable near real-time analytics using Amazon Redshift on transactional data. Using log-based replication, transactional data written into Aurora is available in Amazon Redshift within a few seconds. Once data is available in Amazon Redshift, you can query data as is or apply transformation rules using either SQL or stored procedures. In Chapter 3, you'll learn more about how to set up zero-ETL integration with Amazon Redshift.

Spark application development

With Apache Spark integration (*https://oreil.ly/tkSCj*), you can build Apache Spark applications in a variety of languages such as Java, Scala, and Python, and the connector is natively installed on Amazon EMR (previously called Amazon Elastic MapReduce), AWS Glue, and SageMaker. These applications can read from and write to your Amazon Redshift data warehouse without compromising on the performance of the applications or transactional consistency of the data, as well as performance improvements with pushdown optimizations. In Chapter 3, you'll learn how to take advantage of the Spark connector for ingestion and in Chapter 4, "Data Transformation Strategies", you'll learn how to use the Spark connector for data transformation.

Auto ingestion of Amazon S3 files

You can set up continuous file ingestion rules to track your Amazon S3 paths and automatically load new files into Amazon Redshift without the need for additional tools or custom solutions. Using a COPY command is the best practice for ingestion of data into Amazon Redshift. You can store a COPY statement into a copy job, which automatically loads the new files detected in the specified Amazon S3 path. In Chapter 3, we will describe the different options for loading data and how to configure auto ingestion.

Query transactional data using federated query

With federated queries, you can incorporate live data as part of your BI and reporting applications. With this feature, you can query current real-time data from external databases like PostgreSQL or MySQL from within Amazon Redshift and combine it with historical data stored in data warehouses to provide a combined view for your business users. In Chapter 4, you'll learn how to set up a federated source and query that data in real time for use in reporting and transformation.

Use your favorite BI tool

You can use your BI tool of choice to query your Amazon Redshift data warehouses using standard Java Database Connectivity (JDBC) and Open Database Connectivity (ODBC) connections or using APIs and provide business insights. Amazon QuickSight (*https://oreil.ly/ZgXHL*) is an AWS native service to create modern interactive dashboards, paginated reports, embedded analytics, and natural language queries on multiple data sources including Amazon Redshift. In Chapter 2, you'll learn about the many ways you can connect your client tools to Amazon Redshift.

Discover and share data

Amazon Redshift also supports integration with Amazon DataZone (*https://oreil.ly/HtHqd*), which allows you to discover and share data at scale across organizational boundaries with governance and access controls. In Chapter 7, "Collaboration with Data Sharing", you will learn how Amazon DataZone gives you federated data governance where the data owners and subject matter experts of that dataset can enforce security and access controls on their relevant data assets.

Real-World Benefits of Adopting a Modern Data Architecture

Results of research conducted by many analysts show us that organizations who make data accessible even by a few percentage points will see a significant increase in net income. According to Richard Joyce, senior analyst at Forrester (*https://oreil.ly/VFZJu*), "Just a 10% increase in data accessibility will result in more than $65 million additional net income for a typical Fortune 1000 company." Analytics can explore new markets or new lines of business through insights that can have an impact on the top line and cost of operations.

Here are some real-world examples:

- Intuit migrated to an Amazon Redshift–based solution in an effort to make data more accessible. The solution scaled to more than 7 times the data volume and delivered 20 times the performance over the company's previous solution. This resulted in a 25% reduction in team costs, 60% to 80% less time spent on maintenance, 20% to 40% cost savings overall, and a 90% reduction in time to deploy models. This freed up the teams to spend more time developing the next wave of innovations.

- Nasdaq decreased time to market for data access from months to weeks by consolidating the company's data products into a centralized location on the cloud. They used Amazon S3 to build a data lake, allowing them to ingest 70 billion records per day. The exchange now loads financial market data five hours faster and runs Amazon Redshift queries 32% faster.

- The Expedia Group processes over 600 billion AI predictions per year with AWS data services powered by 70 PB of data. Samsung's 1.1 billion users make 80,000 requests per second, and Pinterest stores over an exabyte of data on Amazon S3.

- Toyota migrated from an on-premises data lake and now collects and combines data from in-vehicle sensors, operational systems, and data warehouses at PB scale. Their teams have secure access to that data when they need it, giving them the autonomy and agility to innovate quickly. Now Toyota can do things like monitor vehicle health and resolve issues before they impact customers. Philips built a secure and HIPAA-compliant digital cloud platform to serve as a base for application suites that could store, interpret, unify, and extract insights from customers' data from different sources.

Reference Architecture for Modern Data Architecture

Now that you understand the benefits of a modern data architecture and the value of storing data in both a data lake and a data warehouse, let's take a look at a reference architecture for a data warehouse workload using AWS analytics services. Figure 1-6 illustrates how you can use AWS services to implement various aspects of your modern data architecture from collecting or extracting data from various sources and applications into your Amazon S3 data lake to how you can leverage Amazon Redshift to ingest and process data, to how you can use Amazon QuickSight and Amazon SageMaker to analyze the data.

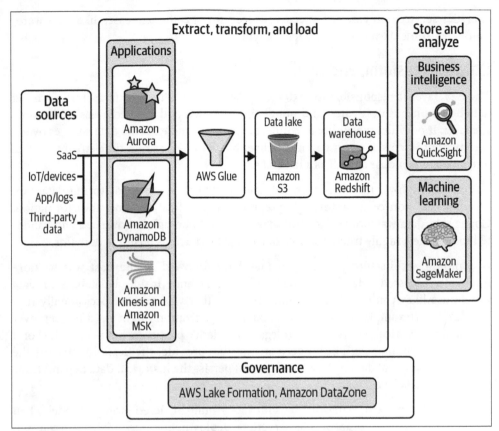

Figure 1-6. Modern data reference architecture

Data Sourcing

The modern data architecture enables you to ingest and analyze data from a variety of sources. Many of these sources such as line of business (LOB) applications, ERP applications, and CRM applications generate highly structured batches of data at fixed intervals. In addition to internal structured sources, you can receive data from modern sources such as web applications, mobile devices, sensors, video streams, and social media. These modern sources typically generate semistructured and unstructured data, often as continuous streams.

The data is either temporarily or persistently stored in Amazon S3 as a data lake in open file formats such as Apache Parquet, Avro, CSV, ORC, and JSON, to name a few. The same data from your Amazon S3 data lake can serve as your single source of truth and can be used in other analytical services such as Amazon Redshift, Amazon Athena, Amazon EMR, and Amazon SageMaker. The data lake allows you to have a single place to run analytics across most of your data while the purpose-built analytics services provide the speed you need for specific use cases like data warehouse, real-time dashboards, and log analytics.

Extract, Transform, and Load

The ETL layer is responsible for extracting data from multiple sources, transforming data based on business rules, and populating cleansed and curated areas of the storage layer. It provides the ability to connect to internal and external data sources over a variety of protocols. It can ingest and deliver batch as well as real-time streaming data into a data warehouse as well as a data lake.

To provide highly curated, conformed, and trusted data, prior to storing data, you may put the source data through preprocessing, validation, and transformation. Changes to data warehouse data and schemas should be tightly governed and validated to provide a highly trusted source of truth dataset across business domains.

A common architecture pattern you may have followed in the past was to store frequently accessed data that needed high performance inside a database or data warehouse like Amazon Redshift and cold data that was queried occasionally in a data lake. For example, a financial or banking organization might need to keep over 10 years of historical transactions for legal compliance purposes, but need only 2 or 3 years of data for analysis. The modern architecture provides the flexibility to store the recent three years of data in local storage, and persist the historical data beyond three years to the data lake.

Following this pattern, Amazon Redshift has a built-in tiered storage model when using the RA3 node type or the serverless deployment option. The storage and compute are separated where the data is stored in Amazon Redshift Managed Storage (RMS) so you scan scale your compute independent of storage. Amazon Redshift manages the hot and cold data by hydrating the frequently used blocks of data closer to the compute, replacing less-frequently used data. With this architecture, while you can still persist the historical data in your data lake to run analytics across other analytics services, you do not have to offload as much, if any, data from your data warehouse.

Storage

The data storage layer is responsible for providing durable, scalable, and cost-effective components to store and manage vast quantities of data. The data warehouse and data lake natively integrate to provide an integrated cost-effective storage layer that supports unstructured and semistructured as well as highly structured and modeled data. The storage layer can store data in different states of consumption readiness, including raw, trusted-conformed, enriched, and modeled.

Storage in the data warehouse

The data warehouse originated from the need to store and access large volumes of data. MPP–based architectures were built to distribute the processing across a scalable set of expensive, highly performant compute nodes.

Historically, the data warehouse stored conformed, highly trusted data structured into star, snowflake, data vault, or denormalized schemas and was typically sourced from highly structured sources such as transactional systems, relational databases, and other structured operational sources. The data warehouse was typically loaded in batches and performed OLAP queries.

Amazon Redshift was the first fully managed MPP-based cloud data warehouse, supporting all the functions of a traditional data warehouse, but has evolved to have elastic storage, reducing the amount of compute nodes needed, store semistructured data, access real-time data, and perform predictive analysis. Figure 1-7 shows a typical data warehouse workflow.

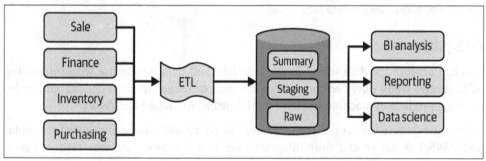

Figure 1-7. Typical data warehouse workflow

Storage in the data lake

A data lake is the centralized data repository that stores all of an organization's data. It supports storage of data in structured, semistructured, and unstructured formats and can scale to store exabytes of data. Typically, a data lake is segmented into landing, raw, trusted, and curated zones to store data depending on its consumption readiness. Because data can be ingested and stored without having to first define a schema, a data lake can accelerate ingestion and reduce time needed for preparation before data can be explored. The data lake enables analysis of diverse datasets using diverse methods, including big data processing and ML. Native integration between a data lake and data warehouse also reduces storage costs by allowing you to access any of the data lake data you need to explore and load only that which is most valuable. A data lake built on AWS uses Amazon S3, as shown in Figure 1-8, as its primary storage platform.

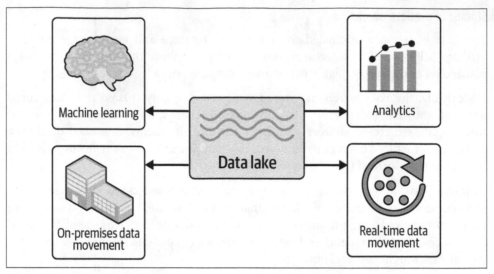

Figure 1-8. Use cases for data lake

Analysis

You can analyze the data stored in the data lake and data warehouse with interactive SQL queries using query editors, visual dashboards using Amazon QuickSight, or by running prediction machine learning models using Amazon SageMaker.

When using these services, there is no need to continually move and transform data, and AWS has native and fully integrated services for core use cases rather than a collection of partially integrated services from other vendors.

Comparing transactional databases, data warehouses, and data lakes

While a transaction database, a data warehouse, and a data lake may all be organized into a similar collection of data stored and accessed electronically through simple *Structured Query Language* (SQL), let's take a closer look at key differentiating characteristics of each of these.

A transactional database is a system where the underlying table structures are designed for fast and efficient data inserts and updates on individual rows. The data model is typically highly normalized, and the storage is designed to store a large number of transactions. To support a high transaction volume on particular rows of data, all the data in a row is physically stored together on disk (row-based storage). This type of database is used for building online transaction processing (OLTP) systems. Online purchases, sales orders, stock trades, and banking credits or debits are some of examples of use cases for a transactional database.

A data warehouse is a database optimized to analyze relational data coming from transactional systems and LOB applications and semistructured non-relational data from mobile apps, IoT devices, and social media. Data is cleaned, enriched, and transformed so it can act as the "single source of truth" that users can trust. The data structure and schema are optimized for fast summarizing of large quantities of data or large batch processing. The results are used for reporting and analysis. Some examples of analytical use cases include analyzing year-over-year retail and online sales, trend analysis for customer purchase preferences, and determining top 10 profitable products.

The key differentiating characteristics of transactional databases and data warehouses are listed in Table 1-1.

Table 1-1. Data warehouse versus database

Characteristics	Data warehouse	Transactional database
Suitable workloads	Analytics at scale, reporting, big data	Transaction processing, operational reporting
Data source	Data collected and normalized from many sources	Data captured as-is from a single source, such as a transactional system
Data capture	Bulk write operations typically on a predetermined batch schedule	Optimized for continuous write operations as new data is available to maximize transaction throughput
Data normalization	Denormalized schemas, such as the star schema or snowflake schema	Highly normalized, static schemas
Data storage	Optimized for simplicity of access and high-speed query performance using columnar storage	Optimized for high throughout write operations to a single row-oriented physical block
Data access	Optimized to minimize I/O and maximize data throughput	High volumes of small read operations

A data lake also stores relational data from LOB applications and semistructured data, but it can also store completely unstructured data. The structure of the data or schema is not defined when data is captured. This means you can store data without initial design and create a catalog on top of the data based on business user query requirements.

As organizations with data warehouses see the benefits of data lakes, they require a platform that enables both use cases. They are evolving their warehouses to include data lakes and enable diverse query capabilities.

Table 1-2 includes key differentiating characteristics of data warehouses and data lakes.

Table 1-2. Data warehouse versus data lake

Characteristics	Data warehouse	Data lake
Data	Relational data from transactional systems, operational databases, JSON with streaming ingestion, and line of business applications	All data, including structured, semistructured, and unstructured
Schema	Often designed prior to the data warehouse implementation but also can be written at the time of analysis (schema-on-write or schema-on-read)	Written at the time of analysis (schema-on-read)
Price/ performance	Fastest query results using local storage	Query results getting faster using low-cost storage and decoupling of compute and storage
Data quality	Highly curated data that serves as the central version of the truth	Any data that may or may not be curated (i.e., raw data)
Users	Business analysts, data scientists, data architects, and data engineers	Business analysts (using curated data), data scientists, data developers, data engineers, and data architects
Analytics	Batch reporting, BI, and visualizations, machine learning	Machine learning, exploratory analytics, data discovery, streaming, operational analytics, big data, and profiling

Data Mesh and Data Fabric

Data mesh and data fabric are two approaches to implementing a modern data architecture in a distributed and complex environment. They share some common principles such as the use of distributed architectures and the importance of data quality and governance. However, they have different goals and approaches to data management. Data mesh is focused on decentralization and autonomy of data domains, while data fabric is focused on integration and consistency of data across different sources and systems. Data fabric is a top-down technology solution, whereas data mesh is a bottom-up approach focusing more on teams and processes and less about architecture enforcement.

Data Mesh

In a data mesh architecture, data is organized around business capabilities or domains, and each domain is responsible for its own data management, quality, and governance. The data is treated as a product, with data teams responsible for creating and maintaining data products that can be consumed by other teams. The goal of data mesh is to improve the agility and scalability of data management in a complex and rapidly changing environment by reducing dependencies and improving collaboration between teams.

Data mesh encourages distributed teams to own and architect their domain-oriented solution independently how they see fit; refer to Figure 1-9, which depicts domains for Sales, Marketing, Finance, R&D, and their own teams. This architecture then asks each team to provide data as a product via a self-service infrastructure platform, as shown in the last slab of Figure 1-9. For the data mesh to maintain global interoperability, the oversight is the responsibility of a federated governance team, as shown in the top slab of the figure.

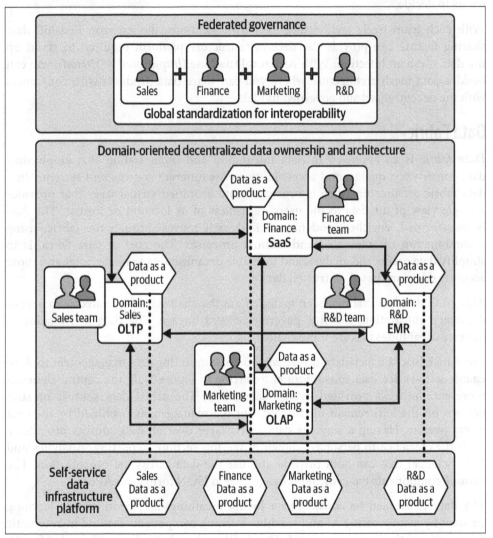

Figure 1-9. A data mesh architecture

This domain-oriented data ownership and architecture allows the ecosystem to scale as needed. Providing data as a product enables easy discovery across many domains. A self-service infrastructure platform enables the various domain teams to create data products as well as to consume data products by abstracting the complexity. The federated governance teams are responsible for defining global standardization rules for interoperability of the entire data mesh ecosystem and more importantly, to balance what needs global standardization and what should be left for the domain-oriented teams to decide.

With each team freely architecting their own solutions, the Amazon Redshift data sharing feature can provide the data infrastructure platform required to stand up the data mesh architecture. With Amazon DataZone (*https://oreil.ly/HtHqd*), you can build a data mesh architecture where you can share data products with consumers with the decentralized and governed model.

Data Fabric

Data fabric is an approach to data integration and orchestration that emphasizes data consistency, quality, and accessibility across different sources and systems. In a data fabric architecture, data is organized into a unified virtual layer that provides a single view of the data to the users, regardless of its location or format. The data is transformed, enriched, and harmonized as it moves through the fabric, using a combination of automated and manual processes. The goal of data fabric is to simplify data access and analysis and to enable organizations to make faster and more accurate decisions based on trusted data.

Alongside the data that has been gathered are the challenges associated with access, discovery, integration, security, governance, and lineage. The data fabric solution delivers capabilities to solve these challenges.

The data fabric is a metadata-driven method of connecting data management tools to enable self-service data consumption. Referring to Figure 1-10, the central elements represent the tools provided by the data fabric. The actual data sources or silos (shown on the left) remain distributed, but the management is unified by the data fabric overlay. Having a singular data fabric layer over all data sources provides a unified experience to personas (shown in the top section: Reporting, Analytics and Data Science) that can both provide and use the data across the organization. The various components typically interchange data in JSON format via APIs.

The data fabric can be considered a living, breathing, and continuously learning element by incorporating AI and machine learning components that aid in automatic discovery and the lineage processes. The challenge here is to obtain agreement for the unified management from the various departments and teams owning and maintaining their individual datasets.

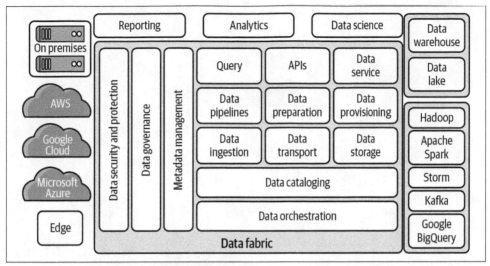

Figure 1-10. A data fabric consists of multiple data management layers (Image source: Eckerson Group)

Amazon Redshift's integration with AWS Lake Formation (*https://oreil.ly/9Gi-I*) can be used to provide ease of access, security, and governance. In Chapter 8, "Securing and Governing Data", you'll learn how to set up access controls when working with AWS Lake Formation. And, Amazon SageMaker (*https://oreil.ly/C0ChL*) can be leveraged to build the machine learning capabilities of the data fabric architecture on AWS. In Chapter 6, "Amazon Redshift Machine Learning", you'll learn how Amazon Redshift is tightly integrated with Amazon SageMaker.

Summary

In this chapter, we covered how organizations can become data-driven by building a modern data architecture using the purpose-built AWS for data services. A modern data strategy will help you drive your roadmap to migrate your data workloads to the cloud, and we saw how Amazon Redshift is the foundation for the modern data architecture.

The remaining chapters explore how you can use Amazon Redshift to transform your data workloads to the cloud, democratize data, and provide business insights to all your users. You will also learn how you can implement some of the modern architectures like data mesh using Amazon Redshift and leverage the tight integration with other AWS native analytics services.

CHAPTER 2

Getting Started with Amazon Redshift

Amazon Redshift enables you to run analytics for your business without having to provision servers or infrastructure, making it easy to get started. It includes a web-based query editor in the AWS console to start loading and analyzing your data without having to install software. Amazon Redshift is also compatible with your favorite query editors like DBeaver, SQL WorkbenchJ, and Toad using *Java Database Connectivity* (JDBC) or *Open Database Connectivity* (ODBC) drivers provided.

In this chapter, we will provide an Amazon Redshift architecture overview, describing the key components of the platform. Next, we'll provide steps on how you can "Get Started with Amazon Redshift Serverless" and begin querying "Sample Data" with a few button clicks. We'll also describe "When to Use a Provisioned Cluster?" and how you can "Estimate Your Amazon Redshift Cost" for both serverless and provisioned data warehouses. Then, we'll talk about "AWS Account Management", describing how you can create a single account or manage multiple accounts in your organization. Lastly, we'll cover some options for "Connecting to Your Amazon Redshift Data Warehouse" and how to manage user access.

Amazon Redshift Architecture Overview

What's in a name? That which we call a rose by any other name would smell just as sweet.
—Romeo and Juliet

William Shakespeare uses this line in his play *Romeo and Juliet* to convey that the naming of things is irrelevant.

There are many theories about how and why the name *Redshift*. We discovered that the term was coined based on the astronomical phenomenon Red Shift, which is a concept in physics for astronomers. It means the wavelength of light is stretched as it expands, so the light is shifted toward red, the color at the longest wavelength end of the visible spectrum of light.

Because data is ever expanding, Amazon Redshift provides a platform to store and analyze data and scale it seamlessly. Being the first fully managed, PB-scale cloud data warehouse, Amazon Redshift is an architectural shift from on-premises data warehousing solutions, which require upfront capital investment, effort to scale, and full-time resources to operate.

Amazon Redshift data warehouse service is ANSI SQL compatible and built for OLAP workloads that store your data in compressed columnar format. This service is available as a provisioned or serverless data warehouse.

Figure 2-1 illustrates a *provisioned* cluster. With the newest generation of node type RA3 (*https://oreil.ly/m-WgQ*), you can scale compute and storage independently based on your workloads. The storage for this node type is *Amazon Redshift Managed Storage* (RMS), which is backed by Amazon S3.

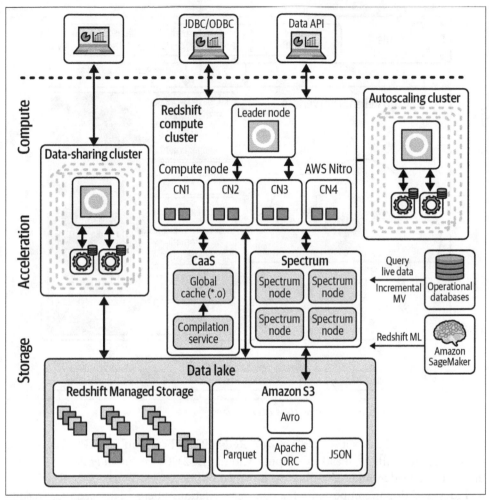

Figure 2-1. Amazon Redshift architecture

The *serverless* architecture (see Figure 2-2) automates many of the operational activities to monitor and scale Amazon Redshift. Amazon Redshift serverless leverages a machine learning-based workload monitoring system to automatically scale compute resources to meet the demands of your workload. Also, as your demand evolves with more concurrent users and new workloads, your data warehouse scales automatically to provide consistent query execution times. Finally, the getting started experience with Amazon Redshift serverless is also simpler; you're charged only when it is in use. Coupled with the data-sharing capabilities of RMS, a department can use serverless to start analyzing data in an isolated data warehouse with zero impact to that shared data. Since you are not paying for idleness, your team does not need to reach out to an administrator to pause or resume your data warehouse.

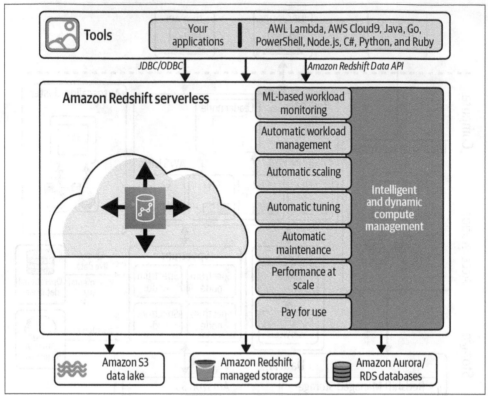

Figure 2-2. Amazon Redshift serverless architecture

Both provisioned and serverless Amazon Redshift are based on an MPP framework consisting of multiple Elastic Compute Cloud (EC2) (*https://oreil.ly/2816C*) nodes including a leader node and one or more compute nodes. Amazon Redshift also includes additional components for code compilation, query plans caching, results caching, data lake access, Concurrency Scaling (CS), machine learning, federated query, and data sharing. We will cover these in detail in subsequent chapters.

With Amazon Redshift, you can get started in minutes and analyze your data using either a serverless or a provisioned data warehouse. We will start with how you can create a serverless data warehouse and work with a sample dataset to run queries.

Get Started with Amazon Redshift Serverless

Both Amazon Redshift serverless and provisioned have many of the same functional capabilities like loading and querying structured and semistructured data, federating to operational databases in PostgreSQL and MySQL, and querying data in your data lake. In addition, both serverless and RA3 provisioned data warehouses are built on top of RMS, allowing both to access data that was produced in other Amazon Redshift data warehouses whether they are provisioned or serverless. While there are considerations for when you may choose one over the other for your workload, it's clear that serverless is the easiest way to get started with Amazon Redshift.

Creating an Amazon Redshift Serverless Data Warehouse

Amazon Redshift serverless is separated into workgroups and namespaces to manage storage and compute resources separately. The namespace is a collection of database objects that include databases, schemas, tables, users, user permissions, and AWS Key Management Service keys for encrypting data. Other resources grouped under namespaces include datashares, recovery points, and usage limits. The workgroup is a collection of compute resources and include Amazon RPU base capacity, virtual private clouds (VPC) subnet groups, security groups, and limits.

To get started with Amazon Redshift serverless, you can configure the storage (namespace) and compute (workgroup) properties using the AWS console, the AWS CLI, or Amazon Redshift serverless APIs.

To deploy an Amazon Redshift serverless data warehouse using the AWS console, navigate to the Create Workgroup (*https://oreil.ly/fDs-g*) page and choose your configuration options. In the first section, you will choose the workgroup name. Next, you will decide the initial compute capacity by choosing the base RPU capacity. This is the compute capacity used when Amazon Redshift serverless starts processing your workload, but it can scale up automatically based on your workload needs. You can choose a little as 8 RPUs or as many as 512 RPUs with a default of 128. For more details on determining the best RPU size for your use case, see "Amazon Redshift Serverless Compute Cost" on page 51.

Finally, you will select the security configuration (see Figure 2-3). This determines where your data warehouse will be deployed in the context of your network configuration. By default, the serverless data warehouse will be deployed in the default VPC, subnets, and security group. You can use the default settings or customize each one. For a more detailed discussion on considerations on network configuration, see "Private/Public VPC and Secure Access" on page 59.

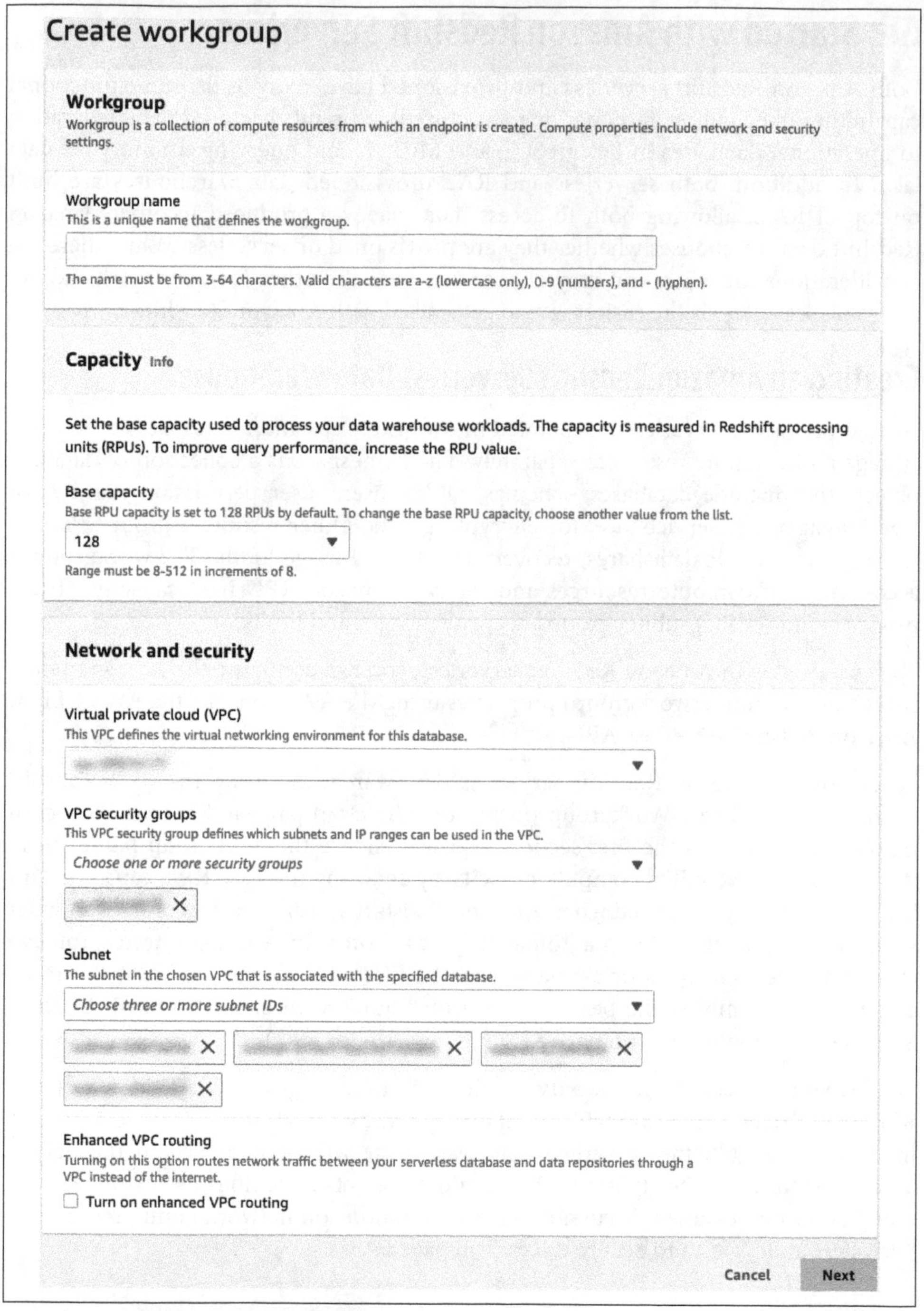

Create workgroup

Workgroup

Workgroup is a collection of compute resources from which an endpoint is created. Compute properties include network and security settings.

Workgroup name
This is a unique name that defines the workgroup.

[   ]

The name must be from 3-64 characters. Valid characters are a-z (lowercase only), 0-9 (numbers), and - (hyphen).

Capacity Info

Set the base capacity used to process your data warehouse workloads. The capacity is measured in Redshift processing units (RPUs). To improve query performance, increase the RPU value.

Base capacity
Base RPU capacity is set to 128 RPUs by default. To change the base RPU capacity, choose another value from the list.

[128   ▼]

Range must be 8-512 in increments of 8.

Network and security

Virtual private cloud (VPC)
This VPC defines the virtual networking environment for this database.

[▼]

VPC security groups
This VPC security group defines which subnets and IP ranges can be used in the VPC.

[Choose one or more security groups   ▼]

[✕]

Subnet
The subnet in the chosen VPC that is associated with the specified database.

[Choose three or more subnet IDs   ▼]

[✕] [✕] [✕]

[✕]

Enhanced VPC routing
Turning on this option routes network traffic between your serverless database and data repositories through a VPC instead of the internet.

☐ Turn on enhanced VPC routing

Cancel   **Next**

Figure 2-3. Workgroup name and security configuration

Next, create a new namespace (Figure 2-4) or attach your workgroup to an existing namespace. The namespace will contain your database objects.

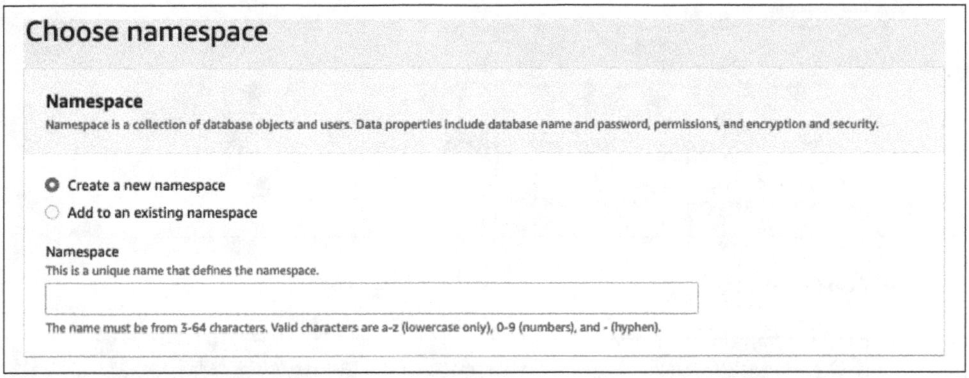

Choose namespace

Namespace
Namespace is a collection of database objects and users. Data properties include database name and password, permissions, and encryption and security.

◉ Create a new namespace
◯ Add to an existing namespace

Namespace
This is a unique name that defines the namespace.

[   ]

The name must be from 3-64 characters. Valid characters are a-z (lowercase only), 0-9 (numbers), and - (hyphen).

Figure 2-4. Namespace

If creating a new namespace, you will be prompted to specify the permissions and admin credentials (Figure 2-5). Similar to a provisioned cluster, permissions are defined via Identity and Access Management (IAM) roles the workgroup can assume to access other resources within your AWS environment. In the next example, we created an IAM role `RedshiftRole`, assigned it the `AmazonRedshiftAllCommandsFul lAccess` policy, and made it the `default`.

The permissions defined in the IAM role associated to your Redshift data warehouse affect which AWS services the Amazon Redshift service can access, such as reading and writing to Amazon S3. This should not be confused with permissions assigned to a database user, database group, or database role.

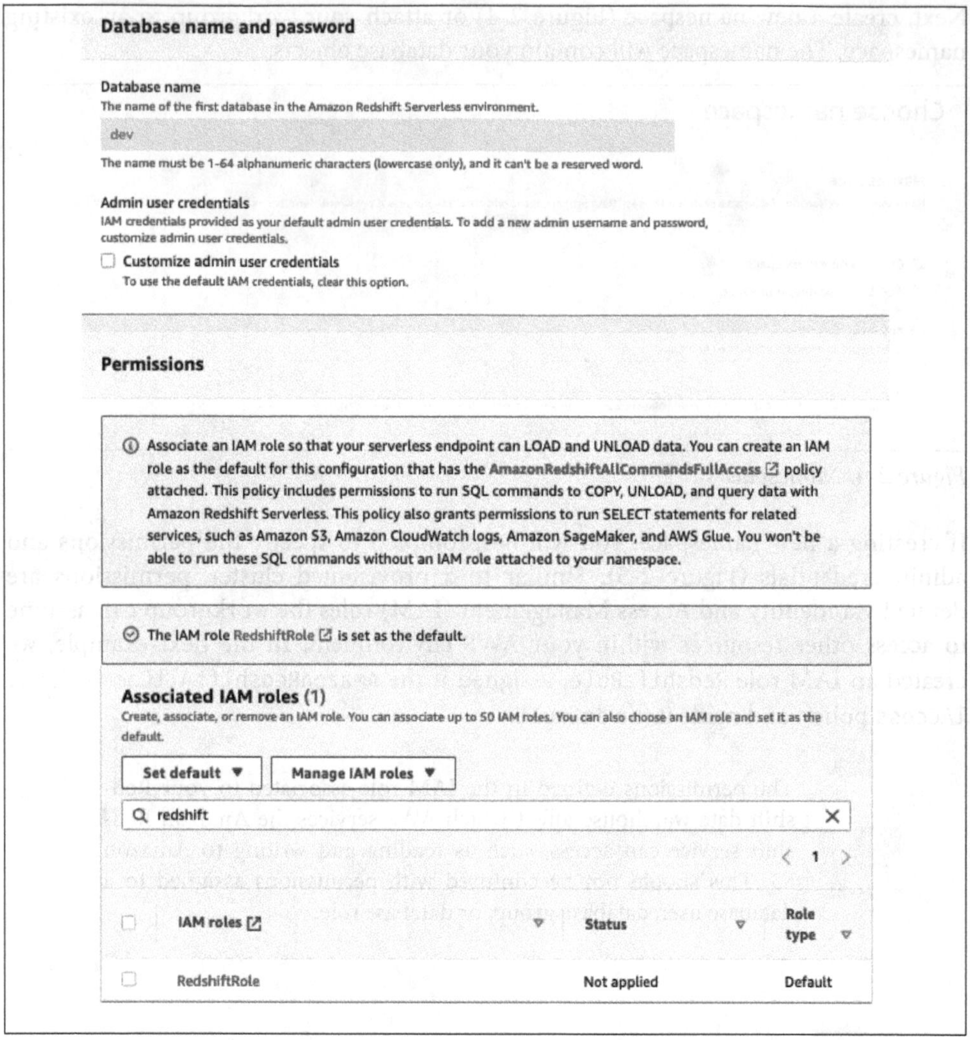

Database name and password

Database name
The name of the first database in the Amazon Redshift Serverless environment.

dev

The name must be 1-64 alphanumeric characters (lowercase only), and it can't be a reserved word.

Admin user credentials
IAM credentials provided as your default admin user credentials. To add a new admin username and password,
customize admin user credentials.

☐ **Customize admin user credentials**
   To use the default IAM credentials, clear this option.

Permissions

ⓘ Associate an IAM role so that your serverless endpoint can LOAD and UNLOAD data. You can create an IAM
    role as the default for this configuration that has the **AmazonRedshiftAllCommandsFullAccess** ☐ policy
    attached. This policy includes permissions to run SQL commands to COPY, UNLOAD, and query data with
    Amazon Redshift Serverless. This policy also grants permissions to run SELECT statements for related
    services, such as Amazon S3, Amazon CloudWatch logs, Amazon SageMaker, and AWS Glue. You won't be
    able to run these SQL commands without an IAM role attached to your namespace.

⊘ The IAM role RedshiftRole ☐ is set as the default.

Associated IAM roles (1)
Create, associate, or remove an IAM role. You can associate up to 50 IAM roles. You can also choose an IAM role and set it as the
default.

| Set default ▼ | Manage IAM roles ▼ |

| 🔍 redshift | ✕ |

‹ 1 ›

☐	IAM roles ☐	▽	Status	▽	Role type	▽
☐	RedshiftRole		Not applied		Default	

Figure 2-5. Permissions and admin credentials

Finally, for your new namespace, specify if you would like to customize the encryption and logging (Figure 2-6).

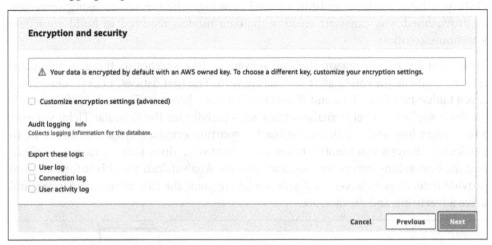

Figure 2-6. Encryption and logging

Once complete, your workgroup list (Figure 2-7) can be retrieved by navigating to the Redshift Workgroups (*https://oreil.ly/G8Mdn*) page, where you can retrieve information such as the workgroup endpoint and JDBC and ODBC URL. For options to connect to your workgroup, see "Connecting to Your Amazon Redshift Data Warehouse" on page 58.

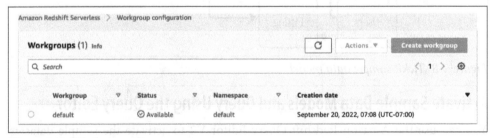

Figure 2-7. Workgroup list

 Configurations of 8 or 16 RPU support Amazon RMS capacity of up to 128 TB. If you're using more than 128 terabytes (TB) of managed storage, you can't downgrade to less than 32 RPU.

Sample Data

Once you have Amazon Redshift up and running, whether you're using serverless or provisioned, you can start creating the data models required to build your data warehouse solution.

When you create an Amazon Redshift serverless data warehouse, three sample datasets are available for you to start interacting with. The first dataset, `tickit`, consists of seven tables: two fact tables and five dimensions, as shown in Figure 2-8. This sample database application helps analysts track sales activity for the fictional Tickit website, where users buy and sell tickets online for sporting events, shows, and concerts. In particular, analysts can identify ticket movement over time, success rates for sellers, and the best-selling events, venues, and seasons. Analysts can use this information to provide incentives to buyers and sellers who frequent the site, attract new users, and drive advertising and promotions.

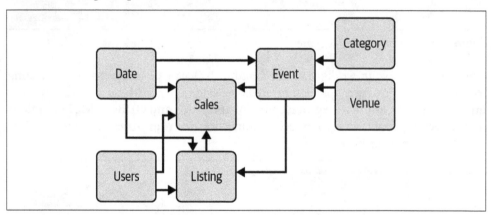

Figure 2-8. Tickit sample data model

Activate Sample Data Models and Query Using the Query Editor

You can use the Amazon Redshift Query Editor V2 to activate the sample datasets and start querying. See "Querying a Database Using the Query Editor V2" on page 67 for more details on how to get started using the Query Editor V2. Once authenticated, expand the `sample_data_dev` database. Then click on the folder icon next to each schema to open sample notebooks (Figure 2-9). This will create the sample data model tables, data, and the queries relevant to the sample data models. Query Editor V2 supports a notebook as well as an editor interface. When you activate the dataset, the sample queries will also be opened in the notebook interface, and you can query the data.

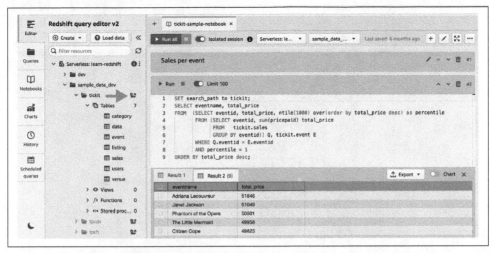

Figure 2-9. Query tickit *sample dataset*

Once you activate the sample dataset, you can start querying the data. From the queries provided in the notebook, try the following sample queries using the tickit data.

The first query (Example 2-1) finds the total sales revenue per event.

Example 2-1. Total sales revenue per event

```
SELECT e.eventname, total_price
FROM (
  SELECT eventid, sum(pricepaid) total_price
  FROM   tickit.sales
  GROUP BY eventid) Q, tickit.event E
WHERE Q.eventid = E.eventid
QUALIFY ntile(1000) over(order by total_price desc) = 1
ORDER BY total_price desc;
```

The second query (Example 2-2) retrieves total sales quantity for a date.

Example 2-2. Total sales quantity for a date

```
SELECT sum(qtysold)
FROM   tickit.sales, tickit.date
WHERE  sales.dateid = date.dateid
AND    caldate = '2008-01-05';
```

You can also open the query editor interface by clicking the + button and choosing the "Editor" menu option (see Figure 2-10).

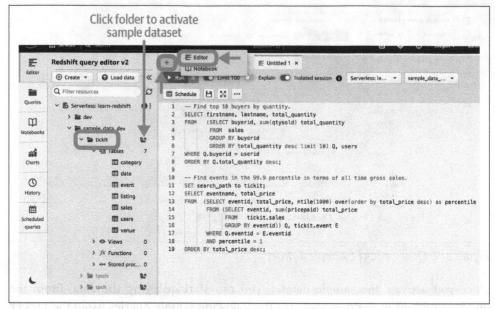

Figure 2-10. Query `tickit` sample dataset in editor mode

Try entering the following queries in the editor and run it to see the result. This query (Example 2-3) retrieves total sales quantity for the top 10 buyers.

Example 2-3. Total sales quantity for top 10 buyers

```
SELECT firstname, lastname, total_quantity
FROM    (SELECT buyerid, sum(qtysold) total_quantity
         FROM  tickit.sales
         GROUP BY buyerid
         ORDER BY total_quantity desc limit 10) Q, tickit.users
WHERE Q.buyerid = userid
ORDER BY Q.total_quantity desc;
```

This query (Example 2-4) finds events in the 99.9 percentile in terms of all time gross sales.

Example 2-4. Events in the 99.9% of sales

```
SELECT eventname, total_price
FROM  (SELECT eventid,
       total_price,
       ntile(1000) over(order by total_price desc) as percentile
      FROM (SELECT eventid, sum(pricepaid) total_price
            FROM   tickit.sales
            GROUP BY eventid)) Q, tickit.event E
     WHERE Q.eventid = E.eventid
```

```
        AND percentile = 1
ORDER BY total_price desc;
```

The other two datasets are tpch, and tpcds, which are standard benchmark datasets from tpc.org. The TPC-H (*https://www.tpc.org/tpch*) and TPC-DS (*https://www.tpc.org/tpcds*) datasets are decision support benchmarks. These consist of a suite of business-oriented ad hoc queries and concurrent data modifications. The queries and the data populating the database have been chosen to have broad industry-wide relevance. The benchmark provides a representative evaluation of performance as a general-purpose decision support system.

These data models are available in the sample_data_dev database with respective schemas tpch and tpcds. You can activate these data models and access the related objects for each schema by clicking on the folder icon next to the schema names as you did earlier for the tickit schema. This will open all the queries in a notebook interface (Figure 2-11). Now you can try running the sample queries. The first query returns the amount of business that was billed, shipped, and returned.

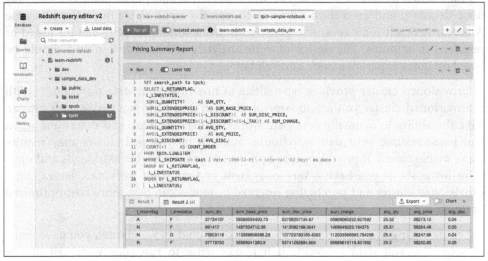

Figure 2-11. Query tpch sample dataset

When to Use a Provisioned Cluster?

Amazon Redshift provides a second deployment option where you can have additional controls over your data warehouse. The key consideration when setting up your Amazon Redshift data warehouse is to choose a configuration and architecture that is best suited for your workload to give you the the best out-of-the-box performance.

According to an article from Jeff Bezos, the founder of Amazon, from November 23, 2020:

> There are two types of decisions. There are decisions that are irreversible and highly consequential; we call them one-way doors [...] They need to be made slowly and carefully. I often find myself at Amazon acting as the chief slowdown officer: "Whoa, I want to see that decision analyzed seventeen more ways because it's highly consequential and irreversible." The problem is that most decisions aren't like that. Most decisions are two-way doors.

As mentioned by Bezos, choosing between serverless and provisioned is a two-way door decision, and even if you do not choose the optimal configuration, because Amazon Redshift is a pay-as-you-go cloud-based solution, capacity can be added or removed in minutes. The design of your analytics architecture can and should be based on quick experimentation and validation.

A provisioned cluster provides capabilities to fine-tune your data warehouse. With a provisioned cluster you are in control of when and how you resize your cluster, have the ability to manually configure workload management, and determine when you pause/resume your data warehouse. While a provisioned cluster may require more management, it provides more options to tune predicable workloads and optimize for costs. If you have a very consistent and constant workload, leveraging a provisioned cluster and purchasing reserved instances can be a more cost-optimized option.

When designing the architecture of your production data warehouse, you have many options. You will want to decide if it makes sense to run your workload in one Amazon Redshift data warehouse or split/isolate your workload in multiple Amazon Redshift data warehouses. You will also want to decide for the one or many data warehouses if it makes sense to use provisioned or serverless. In the following example, two different strategies are illustrated to support the same workload (Figure 2-12).

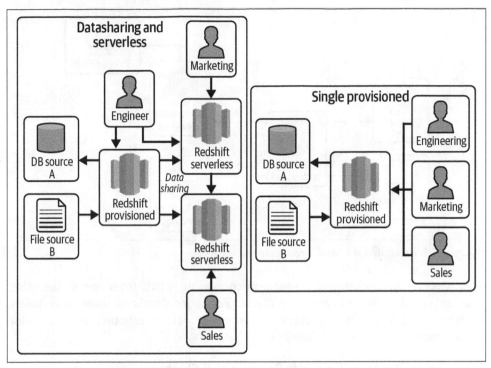

Figure 2-12. Amazon Redshift deployment options

In Chapter 1, "AWS for Data", you learned how a modern data architecture encourages distributed teams to own and architect their domain-oriented solution independently. In the following Amazon Redshift data mesh architecture (Figure 2-13), you can see an architecture that takes advantage of both a provisioned data warehouse and multiple serverless data warehouses. In this environment, you use a provisioned data warehouse (1) for data ingestion from multiple sources because the workload profile is consistent and runs during a large portion of the day. You can purchase reserved instances and have full control over predictable costs. In addition, you set up a serverless data warehouse (2), which can read from the data in the provisioned data warehouse using data sharing. Users in this serverless data warehouse read from the shared data as well and curate new datasets by loading their own data, joining to the shared data and aggregating data as needed. The users of this serverless data warehouse become the shepherds of data specific to their domain or department. Any data outside of their domain is accessible, but they are not dependent on that organization's processing needs. Finally, you set up another serverless data warehouse (3), which also reads from the provisioned data warehouse the curated datasets from the other serverless data warehouse (2) using data sharing. Each of these workloads have different profiles in terms of how much compute they need, when they run, and how long they need to be active.

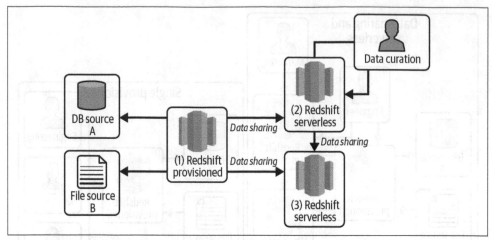

Figure 2-13. Redshift data mesh architecture

Regardless of the deployment option you choose, to switch from one to the other you can use the snapshot/restore processs. For more details on how to restore a snapshot from a provisioned cluster to serverless data warehouse, see the online documentation (*https://oreil.ly/a66BT*).

Creating an Amazon Redshift Provisioned Cluster

Deploying Amazon Redshift using the provisioned option means you'll be deploying a certain number of compute nodes of a certain node type, forming a cluster. To deploy an Amazon Redshift provisioned cluster, navigate to the Create Cluster (*https://oreil.ly/2xS0U*) page and chose your configuration options. You can also follow the steps described in the AWS documentation to create a sample Amazon Redshift cluster (*https://oreil.ly/ptbqk*).

In the first section, you will be choosing the cluster name and size (Figure 2-14). For more details on determining the best cluster size for your use case, see "Amazon Redshift Provisioned Compute Cost" on page 54.

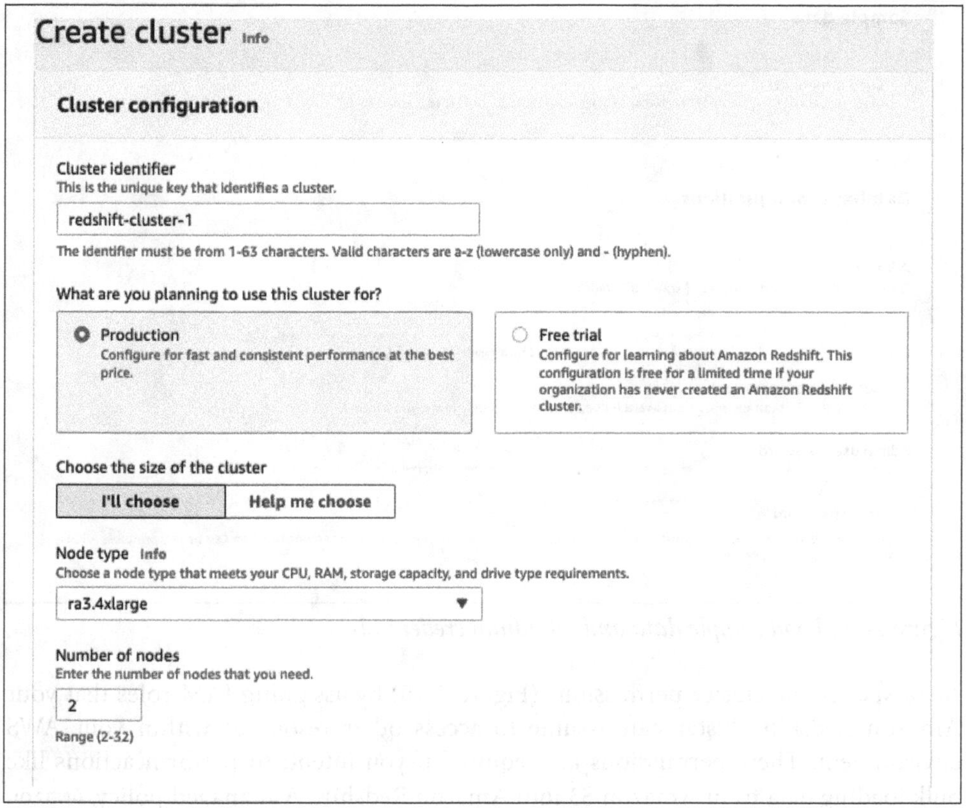

Figure 2-14. Cluster name and size

Next, you will decide if you want to load sample data (optional) and set admin credentials (Figure 2-15).

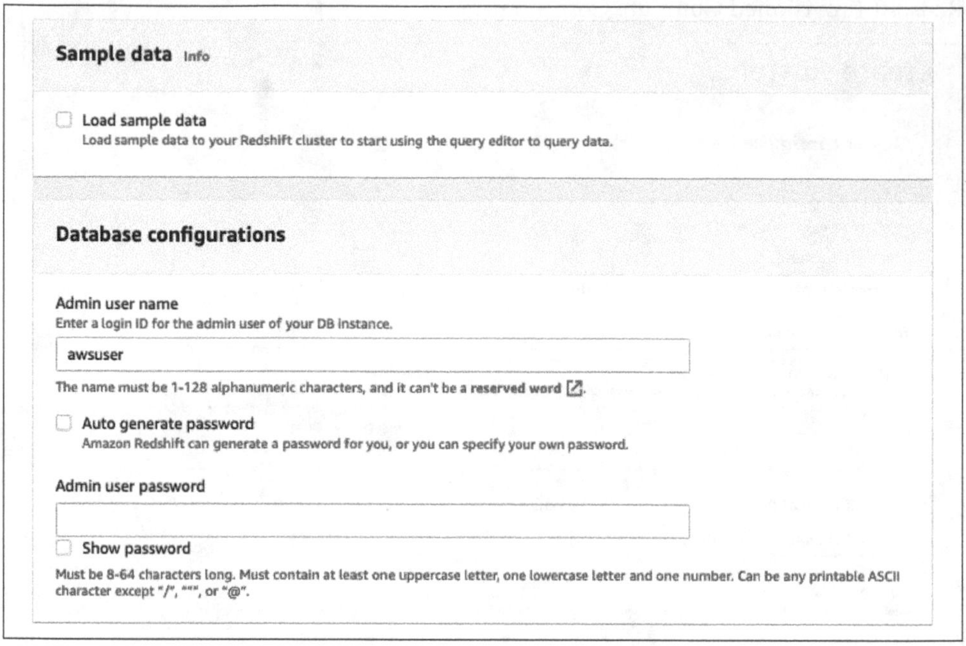

Sample data Info

☐ Load sample data
Load sample data to your Redshift cluster to start using the query editor to query data.

Database configurations

Admin user name
Enter a login ID for the admin user of your DB instance.

```
awsuser
```

The name must be 1-128 alphanumeric characters, and it can't be a reserved word ↗.

☐ Auto generate password
Amazon Redshift can generate a password for you, or you can specify your own password.

Admin user password

☐ Show password

Must be 8-64 characters long. Must contain at least one uppercase letter, one lowercase letter and one number. Can be any printable ASCII character except "/", """, or "@".

Figure 2-15. Load sample data and set admin credentials

Next, specify the cluster permissions (Figure 2-16) by assigning IAM roles that your Amazon Redshift cluster can assume to access other resources within your AWS environment. These permissions are required if you intend to perform actions like bulk loading data from Amazon S3 into Amazon Redshift. A managed policy, `Amazon RedshiftAllCommandsFullAccess`, is available to associate to your role containing the common services you may use. In the next example, we created an IAM role `RedshiftRole`, assigned it the `AmazonRedshiftAllCommandsFullAccess` policy, and made it the `default`. For more details on authorizing Amazon Redshift to access other Amazon services on your behalf, see the online documentation (*https://oreil.ly/zjIDn*).

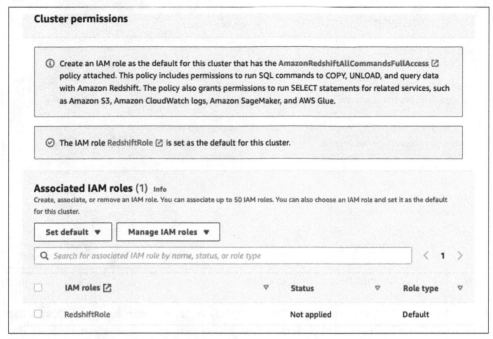

Figure 2-16. Cluster permissions

Lastly, set up the cluster additional configurations (Figure 2-17). These determine where your cluster will be deployed in the context of your network configuration. By default, the cluster will be deployed in the default VPC, subnets, and security group. You can use the default settings or customize each one. For a more detailed discussion on considerations on network configuration, see "Private/Public VPC and Secure Access" on page 59.

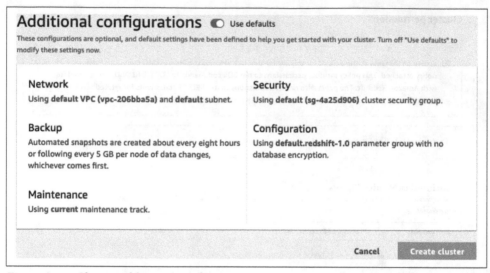

Figure 2-17. Cluster additional configurations

From the Redshift Clusters (*https://oreil.ly/Sgl51*) page, you can see your cluster list (Figure 2-18). Clicking on the cluster, you get to general information such as the cluster endpoint and JDBC and ODBC URL. For options to connect to your cluster, see "Connecting to Your Amazon Redshift Data Warehouse" on page 58.

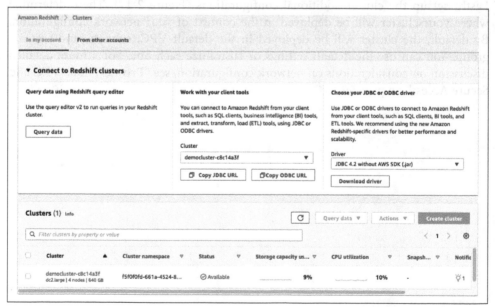

Figure 2-18. Cluster list

Estimate Your Amazon Redshift Cost

When estimating the cost of Amazon Redshift, the two main factors to consider are storage and compute. For the case of the RA3 node type and serverless, you must consider the managed storage separate from the serverless compute cost or the provisioned compute cost. If, however, you are using the DC2 node type, you need to consider only the provisioned compute cost, as all storage is local to the compute nodes.

Amazon Redshift Managed Storage

Amazon RMS is a compressed and columnar formatted data structure designed for optimal performance on analytics workloads. The storage is separated from the compute and is elastic in nature. You can scale from TB to PB of data. It can be shared between Amazon Redshift data warehouses whether they are RA3 provisioned or serverless. The shared data is available to consumers even if the Amazon Redshift data warehouse is not active. For example, if the primary owner of the data is a provisioned cluster, a consumer can access that data even if the provisioned cluster is paused. This functionality allows you to choose the appropriate compute for the workload without needing to move or transform the data. It also ensures the data is not duplicated, reducing maintenance and storage costs. Because you can easily move between different compute options and the storage is available even if the compute is not running, storage is priced independently. To estimate the cost of your storage when using an RA3 cluster or a serverless data warehouse, you can estimate the compressed storage needs multiplied by the storage prices per month. For example, let's say your storage usage is 10 TB. Based on the pricing of $0.024/GB month, your charge for storage would be $240:

```
$0.024*10*1000 = $240
```

For the most up-to-date details on Amazon Redshift Managed Storage pricing, see the online documentation (*https://oreil.ly/QsZE6*).

Amazon Redshift Serverless Compute Cost

For Amazon Redshift serverless, in addition to the RMS cost, there is one other key cost to consider: the compute. To facilitate Amazon Redshift billing, a unit of measurement called RPU was created (Figure 2-19) and represents the compute capacity that is used in a given time period. When you set up your workgroup, it is configured with a base capacity of 128 RPUs. This base is used when Amazon Redshift serverless wakes up from an idle state and will scale up when more compute is needed. You can modify the base capacity for your workgroup by editing the Amazon Redshift serverless configuration and modifying the Limits.

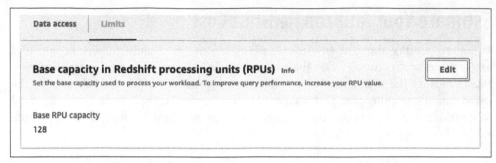

Figure 2-19. Amazon Redshift serverless base capacity

Each query is logged in the system, and you are charged only for the time period the serverless workgroup is running queries (with a 60-second minimum charge for transactions). For example, let's say you've used the default of 128 RPUs and within the hour you submit only 1 query, which runs for 90 seconds. Based on the us-west-2 pricing of $0.45/RPU hour, your charge for that query would be $1.44:

```
rate/sec = $0.45*128/60/60 = $0.016
secs = max(90,60) = 90
rate*secs = $0.016*90 = $1.44
```

Let's say this was actually a scheduled dashboard that triggers the execution of 3 simultaneous queries (15s, 30s, and 90s), the longest of which completes in 90 seconds. Let's also assume this is the only workload on the workgroup for the hour. You would still be charged only $1.44 because the workgroup was only up for those 90 seconds and the serverless workgroup was able to finish the job using the base capacity of 128 RPUs:

```
rate/sec = $0.45*128/60/60 = $0.016
secs = max(15,30,90,60) = 90
rate*secs = $0.016*90 = $1.44
```

Setting a different value for the base capacity

Let's say instead of 128 RPUs, you configure the workgroup to have the base capacity of 8 RPUs or 1/16 the compute. In all likelihood, that workload that completed in 90 seconds will take 16 times as long (1440 seconds) and the price would still be $1.44:

```
rate/sec = $0.45*8/60/60 = $0.001
secs = max(1440,60) = 1440
rate*secs = $0.001*1440 = $1.44
```

With a small base capacity configuration like 8 RPUs, workloads may take longer than 1440 seconds if the query uses a lot of memory because less will be available and you will have paging to disk. However, in some cases, the workload may take less time because the original 90 seconds may have contained overhead that doesn't need to be extrapolated.

Another consideration on choosing the base capacity is the minimum charge of 60 seconds. If you have a lot of queries that are less than 60 seconds and you have idle time between queries, the charge per query will be less on a smaller base capacity configuration.

In the following example, let's say you have a query that runs in 1 second on a 128 RPU base capacity configuration and 16 seconds on a 8 RPU base capacity configuration. If that is the only query run in the minute, they will each be subject to their respective minimum charge, resulting in 16 times difference in price:

```
8 RPU rate/sec = $0.001
secs = max(1,60) = 60
rate*secs = $0.060

128 RPU rate/sec = $0.016
secs = max(16,60) = 60
rate*secs = $0.960
```

High/frequent usage

In another example, let's say you have a streaming application that loads into your data warehouse at one minute intervals but the loads take only 5 seconds each (Figure 2-20). Because each transaction on the serverless workgroup is billed with a minimum of 60 seconds, even though each query finishes in 5 seconds, each is billed based on the 60 second minimum.

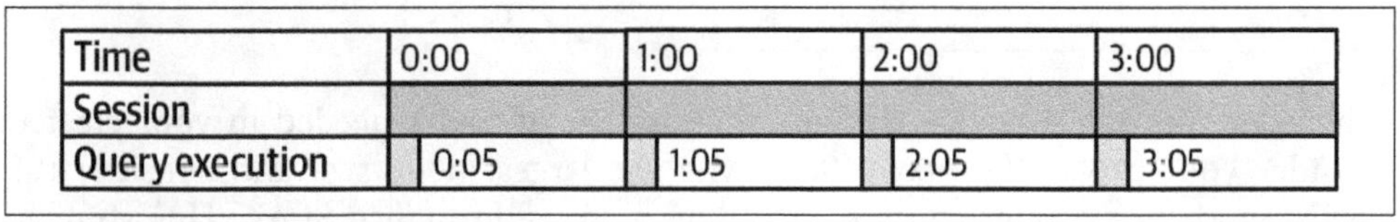

Time	0:00	1:00	2:00	3:00
Session				
Query execution	0:05	1:05	2:05	3:05

Figure 2-20. Streaming usage timeline

In this example, while the total query execution time was 5*60=300 seconds, the billed usage will be 60*60=3600 seconds when the 60 second minimum charge is applied. Based on the us-west-2 pricing of $0.45/RPU hour, your charge for this workload would be $57.60:

```
rate/sec = $0.45*128/60/60 = $0.016
secs = max(5,60)*60 = 60*60 = 3600
rate*secs = $0.016*3600 = $57.60
```

In each of these cases, it's a good idea to experiment on a base capacity configuration that meets your query service level agreements (SLAs) and budget requirements, keeping in mind that you are being charged only for the compute you are using.

For the most up-to-date details on Amazon Redshift pricing, including how much you can save with reserved capacity, see the online documentation (*https://oreil.ly/9kwzy*).

Amazon Redshift Provisioned Compute Cost

For an RA3 provisioned cluster, in addition to the storage cost, the key additional cost comes from the cluster size. The first step in planning your provisioned data warehouse is to determine the node type and the number of nodes you will need. When determining the size of your Amazon Redshift provisioned cluster, consider the steady-state compute that will satisfy the performance SLAs of your analytical processing needs. Each type of node is defined by a compute profile and gets progressively larger and more expensive so you can choose the node type and number of nodes best suited to meet your needs. The following table (Table 2-1) summarizes the allocated resources for each node for each node type as of 2023. You can get the latest compute profiles and read more about the different node types in the online documentation (*https://oreil.ly/hDesT*).

Table 2-1. RA3 node types

Node type	RMS	Memory	vCPUs
ra3.xlplus	32 TB	32 GB	4
ra3.4xlarge	128 TB	96 GB	12
ra3.16xlarge	128 TB	384 GB	48

When determining the node size and the number of nodes needed in your cluster, consider your processing needs. Start with the largest node size and consider the smaller node sizes when you are exceeding your performance SLAs. This strategy helps reduce network traffic when data shuffles between the nodes. For example, 2 nodes of the ra3.16xl is equivalent to 8 nodes of the ra3.4xlarge and 24 nodes of the ra3.xlplus node types in terms of vCPU and memory. If you start with the ra3.16xlarge node type and find that you are far exceeding your performance SLAs and your cluster CPU utilization is low, you can can resize your cluster to a smaller node type by leveraging the resize option. For more information on the resize option, see the online documentation (*https://oreil.ly/sRQdC*).

If you have not run your workload yet and need an initial cluster size, the Amazon Redshift console provides a tool (Figure 2-21) to help you choose the size of your cluster taking into consideration parameters such as the amount of storage needed as well as your workload.

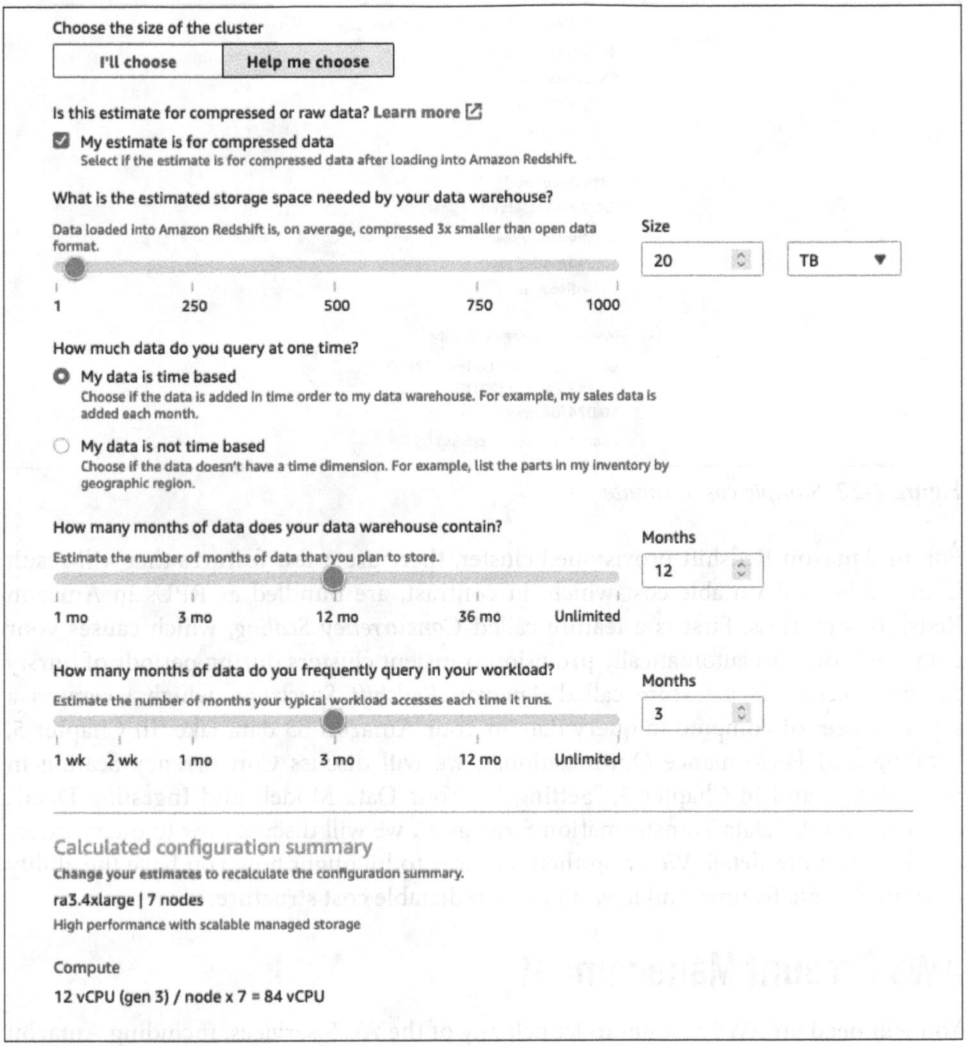

Choose the size of the cluster

| I'll choose | **Help me choose** |

Is this estimate for compressed or raw data? Learn more ☑

☑ My estimate is for compressed data
Select if the estimate is for compressed data after loading into Amazon Redshift.

What is the estimated storage space needed by your data warehouse?

Data loaded into Amazon Redshift is, on average, compressed 3x smaller than open data format.

Size
`20` ⬍ `TB` ▼

1   250   500   750   1000

How much data do you query at one time?

⦿ **My data is time based**
Choose if the data is added in time order to my data warehouse. For example, my sales data is added each month.

○ **My data is not time based**
Choose if the data doesn't have a time dimension. For example, list the parts in my inventory by geographic region.

How many months of data does your data warehouse contain?

Estimate the number of months of data that you plan to store.

Months
`12` ⬍

1 mo   3 mo   12 mo   36 mo   Unlimited

How many months of data do you frequently query in your workload?

Estimate the number of months your typical workload accesses each time it runs.

Months
`3` ⬍

1 wk 2 wk   1 mo   3 mo   12 mo   Unlimited

Calculated configuration summary

Change your estimates to recalculate the configuration summary.

ra3.4xlarge | 7 nodes
High performance with scalable managed storage

Compute
12 vCPU (gen 3) / node x 7 = 84 vCPU

Figure 2-21. Help me choose

A key aspect of Amazon Redshift pricing for a provisioned cluster is that it can either be billed on-demand, or you can purchase reserved instances, which give you a fixed cost and a deep discount. In the Help Me Choose tool, a summary of the cost for the compute is given (Figure 2-22).

You receive a 33% discount committing to a 1-year reservation and a 61% discount when committing to a 3-year reservation.

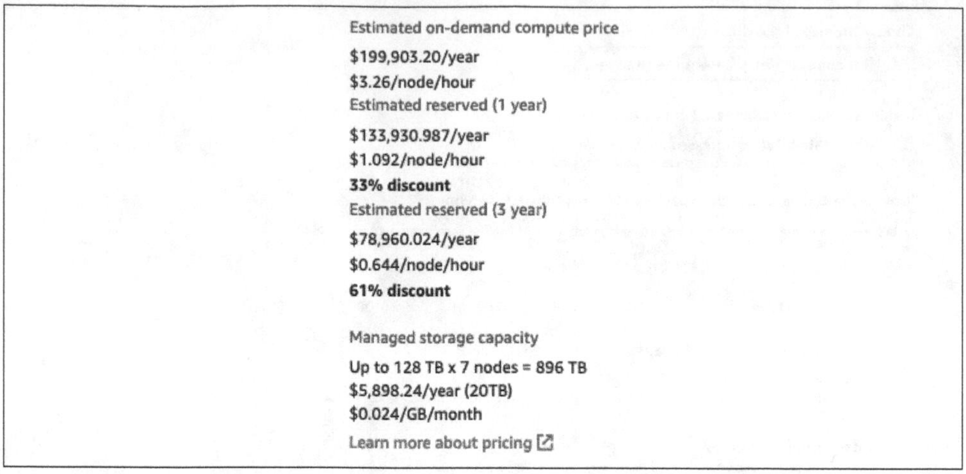

Estimated on-demand compute price

$199,903.20/year
$3.26/node/hour
Estimated reserved (1 year)

$133,930.987/year
$1.092/node/hour
33% discount
Estimated reserved (3 year)

$78,960.024/year
$0.644/node/hour
61% discount

Managed storage capacity

Up to 128 TB x 7 nodes = 896 TB
$5,898.24/year (20TB)
$0.024/GB/month
Learn more about pricing ☑

Figure 2-22. Sample cost estimate

For an Amazon Redshift provisioned cluster, there are a few features that will result in an additional variable cost which, in contrast, are bundled as RPUs in Amazon Redshift serverless. First is a feature called *Concurrency Scaling*, which causes your data warehouse to automatically provision transient clusters during periods of bursty activity. Second is a feature called *Amazon Redshift Spectrum*, which leverages a separate fleet of compute to query data in your Amazon S3 data lake. In Chapter 5, "Scaling and Performance Optimizations", we will discuss Concurrency Scaling in more detail, and in Chapter 3, "Setting Up Your Data Models and Ingesting Data", and Chapter 4, "Data Transformation Strategies", we will discuss how to query external data in more detail. We bring them up now to highlight how you have the ability to control these features and have a more predictable cost structure.

AWS Account Management

You will need an AWS account to launch any of the AWS services, including Amazon Redshift. An AWS account is owned by the root user that was used to create the account. Once you create your AWS account, you can create additional users using the *Identity and Access Management* (IAM) service and allocate permission to IAM users. We mention AWS accounts because like any other AWS service you launch, for Amazon Redshift you can establish boundaries by launching your data warehouse in different accounts; e.g., development versus production (see Figure 2-23).

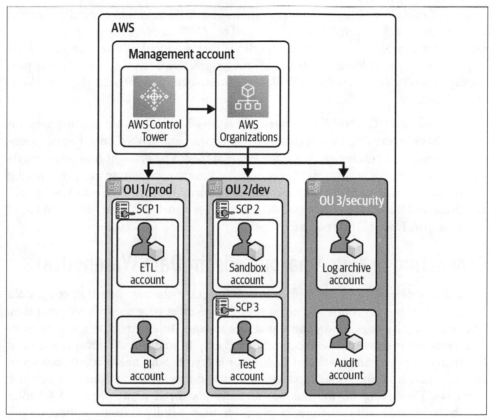

Figure 2-23. AWS Control Tower, AWS Organizations, and AWS accounts

AWS Organizations helps you collectively manage multiple AWS accounts, allocate resources, group accounts into organizational units (OUs), apply governance and security policies on OUs, and simplify billing for your organization by designating a management account for taking advantage of quantity discounts with a single bill. Other AWS accounts are member accounts.

Having a designated security OU with an isolated account for audit will allow your security team to quickly review all accesses across your entire organization. A separate logging account will allow you to centralize all log files, and troubleshooting end-to-end application problems is easy when you can correlate all your data together. Refer to "Set up a multi-account AWS environment using best practices for AWS Organizations" (*https://oreil.ly/tvrqD*) for a short video.

Instead of designing your AWS Organizations and AWS accounts manually, you can leverage the AWS Control Tower service. The AWS Control Tower is a separate service that provides a prescriptive experience that automatically sets up your AWS Organizations and AWS accounts based on best-practice blueprints. It also uses prepackaged service control policies (SCP) and governance rules for security, operations, and compliance.

You can use AWS Control Tower irrespective of whether you are starting new on AWS or have an existing multiaccount AWS environment. AWS Control Tower automates the setup of landings zone for the external files to be brought into your analytics environment, applies guardrails for ongoing governance, automates provisioning workflow, and also provides prepackaged dashboards for visibility across your OU, accounts, and guardrails. For more details, here's a short YouTube video, "What Is AWS Control Tower?" (*https://oreil.ly/7zyKO*).

Connecting to Your Amazon Redshift Data Warehouse

Once you've determined your deployment architecture, the next question you should ask yourself is how to control access to your data to meet your security requirements. The inherent challenge IT organizations face today is to ensure that access to your data platform is secure while also flexible and easy to manage. Administrators need the ability to provision access and tooling for everyone who needs access, but do so in a way that is in line with corporate policies and accessible via approved network pathways. Depending on the number of users you need to manage and whether you have existing infrastructure in place for user administration, authentication, and authorization, you may choose one strategy over another. Once connected, the identity of the user is stored within the Amazon Redshift metadata. That identity can be assigned to one or more groups, and roles for authorization and activity by that user will be logged for traceability. Amazon Redshift contains different features that enable secure and flexible access, and there are many considerations for choosing which options to leverage. In addition, there are multiple tools provided by AWS to access your Amazon Redshift data warehouse, with multiple options for how to leverage those security features.

Private/Public VPC and Secure Access

Whether you choose serverless or provisioned, Amazon Redshift is always deployed within a VPC and subnet. Depending on that choice, the data warehouse can be accessible by only internal resources or can be accessible by resources in the public internet. For more details on determining the best VPC strategy for your organization, read about VPC scenarios in the online documentation (*https://oreil.ly/ TKM1N*). Furthermore, when you connect to an Amazon Redshift data warehouse using tools based on JDBC or ODBC drivers, you are connecting via TCP/IP to a specific hostname and port number. Like any AWS service that is deployed to a VPC, you can control network traffic to Amazon Redshift by customizing inbound rules to the security group attached to your data warehouse. For more details on understanding security groups and setting inbound rules, see the online documentation (*https://oreil.ly/EArzG*). Finally, you may have a scenario where Amazon Redshift needs connectivity to an AWS service that runs outside your VPC or in another AWS account altogether. For these scenarios, a VPC endpoint may be suitable. Learn more about VPC endpoints in the online documentation (*https://oreil.ly/Rw5gK*).

The following sample architecture containing a private subnet with AWS Direct Connect (Figure 2-24) is commonly used by enterprise users because it contains controls that limit access to people within the corporate infrastructure or outside the infrastructure using a VPN service. To ensure a high-bandwidth and secure connection to the AWS cloud, the architecture leverages AWS Direct Connect. The virtual private gateway ensures that the data transferred is secure and encrypted. When set up correctly, resources within the AWS cloud such as the Amazon Redshift data warehouse and analytical tools are addressable via private IP addresses whether the user is on an internal or external client machine.

Within AWS, Amazon Redshift is deployed in a private subnet, which means it does not have direct internet connectivity and any access to the environment would have to originate from within the VPC or through the virtual private gateway. However, there are some AWS services that do not run within your AWS VPC. A key service used for COPY and UNLOAD commands in Amazon Redshift is the Amazon S3 service. To ensure that data transferred from Amazon S3 to Amazon Redshift goes through your VPC, the enhanced VPC routing feature is enabled and the private subnet is configured with a route table referencing a VPC endpoint to Amazon S3. To learn more about how to configure enhanced VPC routing, see the online documentation (*https://oreil.ly/yRMs-*).

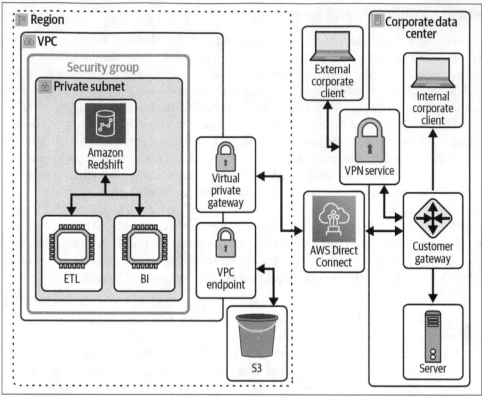

Figure 2-24. Private subnet with AWS Direct Connect

Stored Password

The easiest mechanism for maintaining users within your Amazon Redshift data warehouse is by creating a local user and storing a password within the Amazon Redshift metadata. This strategy is common to almost any database platform and can be done simply using the CREATE USER (*https://oreil.ly/Qmq49*) command. For example:

```
CREATE USER name PASSWORD 'password';
```

This strategy is typically used when you have very few users to maintain, but it can result in administrative overhead as your user population increases.

Temporary Credentials

The next concept to consider, which is only available for Amazon Redshift provisioned clusters, is temporary credentials. This strategy is possible based on the API function GetClusterCredentials (*https://oreil.ly/ABhoZ*). The API call will take as an input parameter, a DbUser and DbGroups parameter allowing you to join one or many database groups for authorization purposes. The API call also takes an AutoCreate parameter that, when set, will create a user if it doesn't already exist in the database. The API will return a temporary password for the user provided. Once the temporary password is retrieved, you can log in using that combination of username and temporary password.

To use the temporary credentials strategy for a provisioned data warehouse, a user needs to first be authenticated and associated to an IAM identity, either an IAM user or be logged in as an IAM role. That identity needs to have an IAM policy that allows the user to use the redshift:GetClusterCredentials action. To enable features such as creating new users and dynamically joining groups, you may add the redshift:CreateUser and redshift:JoinGroup privileges. To ensure that a user can't get a temporary password for any user or join a database group they shouldn't join, it is a good idea to scope down the policy and add a condition that ensures the username they are getting the temporary credentials for matches their identity. Here is a sample policy that grants a user access to the dev database and to join the marketing group. It also has a condition to ensure the aws:userid matches the DbUser, which is passed into the GetClusterCredentials API command:

```
{
  "Version": "2012-10-17",
  "Statement": [
    {
      "Effect": "Allow",
      "Action": [
        "redshift:GetClusterCredentials",
        "redshift:CreateUser",
        "redshift:JoinGroup"
        ],
      "Resource": [
        "arn:aws:redshift:*:123456789012:cluster:rs-cluster",
        "arn:aws:redshift:*:123456789012:dbuser:rs-cluster/${redshift:DbUser}",
        "arn:aws:redshift:*:123456789012:dbname:rs-cluster/dev",
        "arn:aws:redshift:*:123456789012:dbgroup:rs-cluster/marketing"
        ],
      "Condition": {
        "StringLike": {
          "aws:userid": "*:${redshift:DbUser}"
        }
      }
    }
  ]
}
```

```
    ]
  }
```

In addition to allowing users who are already logged into AWS via their IAM identity to query Amazon Redshift, this strategy has also been built into the JDBC and ODBC drivers. You simply indicate to the driver that you will use IAM to authenticate and pass it your IAM identity. Read more about how to configure a JDBC or ODBC connection to use IAM credentials in the online documentation (*https://oreil.ly/2nkuO*).

A simple way to pass the IAM identity is by passing an `AccessKeyID` and `SecretAccessKey`. See the following example JDBC URL:

```
jdbc:redshift:iam://examplecluster:us-west-2/dev?
    AccessKeyID=AKIAIOSFODNN7EXAMPLE&
    SecretAccessKey=wJalrXUtnFEMI/K7MDENG/bPxRfiCYEXAMPLEKEY
```

Federated User

The next concept to consider is a *federated user*. This strategy is possible based on the API functions `GetClusterCredentialsWithIAM` (*https://oreil.ly/Ygkg1*) for provisioned and `GetCredentials` (*https://oreil.ly/dlVqQ*) for serverless. Similar to the the API call `GetClusterCredentials`, these APIs will retrieve a temporary password for a user; however, instead of passing these APIs parameters for authorization, the API will read values based on the logged-in identity. In the case of serverless, it will retrieve the username from `aws:userid` and will retrieve the database roles from the principal tags `RedshiftDbRoles` to authorize the session. In the case of provisioned, it will only retrieve the username stored in the `aws:userid`. In both cases, by default it will create a user if one doesn't exist. Once the temporary password is retrieved, the user can login using that combination of username and temporary password.

Similar to `GetClusterCredentials`, to use the federated user, a user needs to first be authenticated and associated to an IAM identity, either an IAM user or be logged in as an IAM role. That identity needs to have an IAM policy that allows the user to use the `redshift:GetClusterCredentialsWithIAM` action for provisioned and `redshift-serverless:GetCredentials` action for serverless. Using the `Federated User` option, you do not need to have any additional permissions. In the case of serverless, you will need to ensure the IAM identity you use has the `RedshiftDbRoles` principal tag set if you want to enable role-based authorization. Here is a sample policy that grants a user access to the `dev` database:

```
{
    "Version": "2012-10-17",
    "Statement": [
        {
            "Effect": "Allow",
            "Action":
                "redshift-serverless:GetCredentials",
            "Resource":
                "arn:aws:redshift-serverless:*:123456789012:workgroup/rs-workgroup",
        }
    ]
}
```

Similar to the `GetClusterCredentials` API, the federated user functionality is built into the JDBC and ODBC drivers and is used by default when connecting to a serverless data warehouse when you indicate in the driver that you will use IAM to authenticate. Read more about how to configure a JDBC or ODBC connection to use IAM credentials in the online documentation (*https://oreil.ly/2nkuO*).

SAML-Based Authentication from an Identity Provider

Typically for enterprises and large-scale Amazon Redshift deployments, your user identities are not stored in IAM but instead in an identity provider (IdP) such as Okta, Azure Ad, or PingFederate. If that is the case, maintaining a separate directory in IAM or within the Amazon Redshift metadata is not a scalable solution. Also, there may be multiple groups a user can be a member of, and maintaining separate IAM roles for each group combination would be unmanageable. Native to the AWS platform is the ability to establish an IAM identity from an IdP using the `AssumeRole WithSAML` (*https://oreil.ly/WUg3v*) API command. When you leverage this strategy, an IAM role can be assumed that contains privileges to `GetClusterCredentials`. This functionality is built into the Amazon Redshift JDBC and ODBC drivers. In Figure 2-25, you can see how your SQL client will interact with your IdP and AWS services like AWS Security Token Service (AWS STS) and IAM prior to establishing a connection to Amazon Redshift.

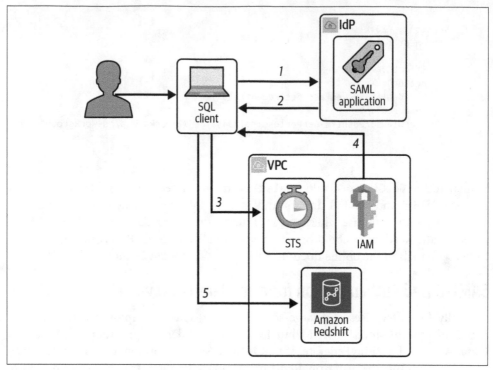

Figure 2-25. Security Assertion Markup Language (SAML) authentication

See the online documentation (*https://oreil.ly/RqO_P*) for a detailed look at the different IdPs and features supported, such as multifactored authentication.

For a step-by-step guide on how to set up an Okta IdP, see this blog post (*https://oreil.ly/mTqC3*) that uses the `OktaCredentialsProvider` plug-in. For scenarios where multifactor authentication is required, see this blog post (*https://oreil.ly/pQPST*) that also uses an Okta IdP, but leverages the `BrowserSamlCredentialsProvider` plug-in.

Whether you use Okta or another IdP, the steps required are:

1. Create a SAML application accessible to your users in your IdP.
2. Configure the application to reference the IAM role and pass the user and group information.
3. Download the application metadata from your IdP.
4. Establish an IdP within the AWS console using the metadata you just downloaded.

Native IdP Integration

When applications have a way to establish a trust relationship via an OAuth token, Amazon Redshift has additional plug-ins, such as the `BrowserAzureOAuth2Creden` `tialsProvider`. Instead of leveraging API commands or IAM to establish the trust relationship, the Amazon Redshift driver will make the initial request to the identity provider to validate the credentials and pop up a multifactor authentication prompt (if required) and receive the OAuth token. Next, the Amazon Redshift service will use the OAuth token to make further calls to the IdP to gather group authorization information. The native IdP architecture (Figure 2-26) outlines the flow with Microsoft Power BI and indicates how the native integration would work when using Azure Active Directory as the identity provider.

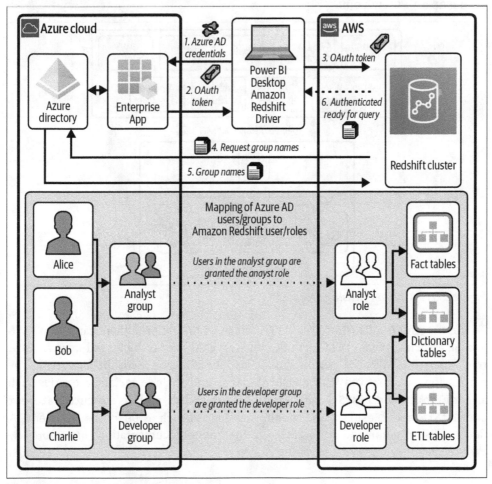

Figure 2-26. Native IdP architecture

For a detailed look at setting up native IdP integration with Power BI and active directory, see this blog post (*https://oreil.ly/fJFvP*).

Amazon Redshift Data API

Another way to connect to Amazon Redshift and query data is by using the Amazon Redshift Data API (Figure 2-27). Using this strategy, a user does not connect directly to Amazon Redshift but instead connects to a secure HTTP endpoint. You can use the endpoint to run SQL statements without managing connections. Calls to the Data API are asynchronous. Using this strategy, an application needs access to the internet, or if you are running an application from a private VPC, you can set up a VPC endpoint. See this online documentation (*https://oreil.ly/jaqge*) for more details on setting up a VPC endpoint.

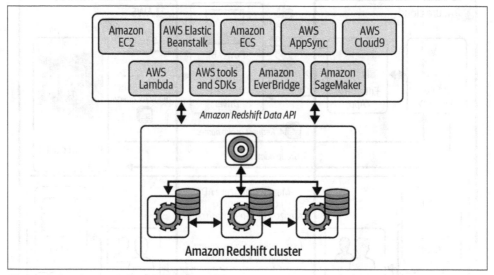

Figure 2-27. Amazon Redshift Data API

To use the Amazon Redshift Data API, users need to first be authenticated into AWS and be associated to an IAM identity, either an IAM user or be logged in as an IAM role. That role will need permissions to use the Amazon Redshift Data API. The permissions are prefixed with `redshift-data:` and include metadata queries such as `ListTables` and `ListSchemas`, execution commands such as `ExecuteStatement` and `GetStatementResults`, and monitoring queries such as `DescribeStatement`. A detailed list of command are available in the online documentation (*https://oreil.ly/PnVAL*).

When using the Amazon Redshift Data API, you have two options to authenticate. The first is by using temporary credentials where you call the API and pass the DbUser parameter and do not pass the SecretArn parameter. To learn more about using temporary credentials, see "Temporary Credentials" on page 61. Conversely, you may authenticate using a stored password by passing the SecretArn parameter but do not pass the DbUser. To learn more about using a stored password, see "Stored Password" on page 60.

In the following example, you can see how to leverage the Amazon Redshift Data API to execute a simple CREATE SCHEMA command using credentials stored within a secret:

```
aws redshift-data execute-statement \
    --database <your-db-name> \
    --cluster-identifier <your-cluster-id> \
    --secret-arn <your-secret-arn> \
    --sql "CREATE SCHEMA demo;" \
    --region <your-region>
```

For a more detailed guide on how you can use the Amazon Redshift Data API, see this blog post (*https://oreil.ly/qsFf6*).

Querying a Database Using the Query Editor V2

After you have established your authentication strategy, the next step is to query your data. Amazon Redshift offers two versions of query editor—the legacy query editor and Query Editor V2 (Figure 2-28) that you can use to author and run queries on your Amazon Redshift data warehouse. While the legacy query editor is still available to use, we recommend using Query Editor V2 as it has additional features allowing you to manage database objects, visualize results, and share your work with your team in addition to editing and running queries. It shows databases, schemas, and all objects in a tree-view panel for easy access of database objects.

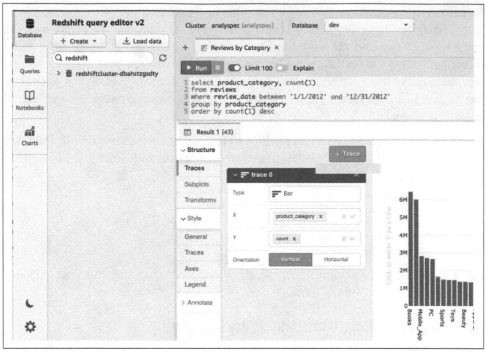

Figure 2-28. Query Editor V2

Query Editor V2 has two tab types (Figure 2-29), an Editor tab and a Notebook tab. The Editor tab will allow you to consolidate all queries in one page and trigger execution at the same time. The Editor will execute all the queries in sequence and produce the results in different result tabs. The SQL Notebook tab contains SQL and markdown cells, which you can use to organize, annotate, and share multiple SQL commands in a single document. Both editor scripts and notebooks can be saved and shared with your team for collaboration. In this book, we will use Query Editor V2 as this is the future direction for querying data in Amazon Redshift.

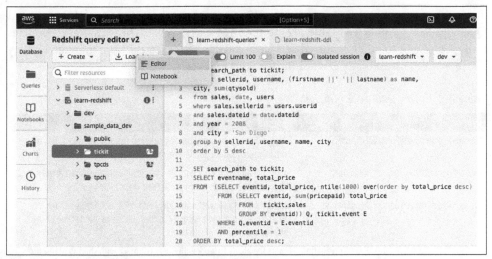

Figure 2-29. Query Editor V2 tab types

To access Query Editor V2 within the AWS console, click the link below the Query data button (Figure 2-30).

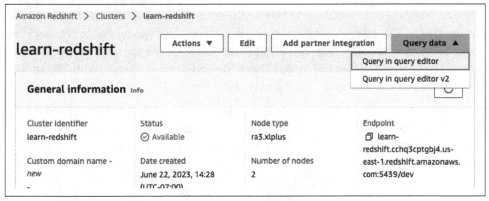

Figure 2-30. Query data

To enable users to access Query Editor V2, you can attach one of the AWS-managed Query Editor V2 policies (Table 2-2) to the IAM user or role. These managed policies also give access to other required services. You can also create a user-managed policy if you want to customize permissions for your end users.

Table 2-2. Query Editor V2 policies

Policy	Description
AmazonRedshiftQueryEditorV2FullAccess	Grants full access to Query Editor V2 operations and resources. This is primarily intended for administrators.
AmazonRedshiftQueryEditorV2NoSharing	Grants the ability to work with Query Editor V2 without sharing resources. Users can't share their queries with their team members.
AmazonRedshiftQueryEditorV2ReadSharing	Grants the ability to work with Query Editor V2 with limited sharing of resources. The granted principal can read the saved queries shared with their team but can't update them.
AmazonRedshiftQueryEditorV2ReadWriteSharing	Grants the ability to work with Query Editor V2 with sharing of resources. The granted principal can read and update the shared resources with their team.

To enable collaboration of queries between team members, you can tag the IAM principal. For example, if you have a group of users as a part of `marketing_group`, and you want them to collaborate between themselves by sharing their queries, you ensure their IAM role, `marketing_role`, is assigned the `AmazonRedshiftQueryEditorV2ReadSharing` policy. You can also tag the role with the tag `sqlworkbench-team` having the value of `marketing_group`. Now the end users logged in with the `marketing_role` can access Query Editor V2 with the ability to share their queries.

When using the query editor to connect to your Amazon Redshift data warehouse, you are prompted with a few options. You can connect as a "Federated user", use "Temporary credentials", with a "Database username and password", or through "AWS Secrets Manager".

> The temporary credentials option in the Query Editor V2 is available only when connecting to a provisioned cluster.

Federated user

When using the Query Editor V2 and the federated user option (Figure 2-31) is chosen, it will operate differently for a provisioned versus serverless data warehouse. For provisioned, Query Editor V2 will depend on the `GetClusterCredentials` used in the temporary credentials authentication method. However, instead of prompting for the user and group information, it will look for these values from two principal tags, `RedshiftDbUser` and `RedshiftDbGroups`, and will pass the values in those tags to the API call. Those principal tags can be set either directly in IAM or they can be passed from an IdP. To use this strategy, the IAM role passed from the IdP will also need to have permissions to use temporary credentials, as discussed previously. Using this strategy is both scalable and easy to use because the only input required from the end user is the database name. For a detailed walkthrough of how to set up federated user login with Okta, see this blog post (*https://oreil.ly/70qK6*).

Figure 2-31. Query Editor V2 federated user

In contrast, when federated user (Figure 2-31) is chosen for a serverless data warehouse, Query Editor V2 will leverage the `GetCredentials` API call used in the federated user authentication method. Similarly, the database username will be retrieved from the `aws:userid`, and the database roles will be retrieved from the `RedshiftD bRoles` principal tags.

Temporary credentials

The temporary credentials option (Figure 2-32) is similar to the federated user option in that the IAM identity will need to have permissions to use temporary credentials. One notable difference is that it is not dependent on principal tags, so in addition to the Database parameter, a user must enter the username and will not be automatically added to groups.

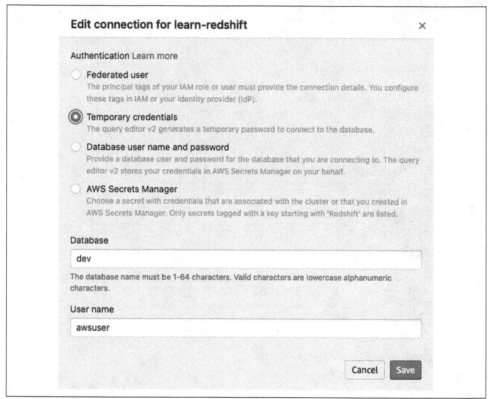

Figure 2-32. Query Editor V2 temporary credentials

Database username and password

With the password option (Figure 2-33), in addition to the Database and User name parameters, a user must supply a password. To make it easier in subsequent sessions, the password is saved within the Secrets Manager service and the IAM identity using the query editor will need to have permissions to read and write to Secrets Manager.

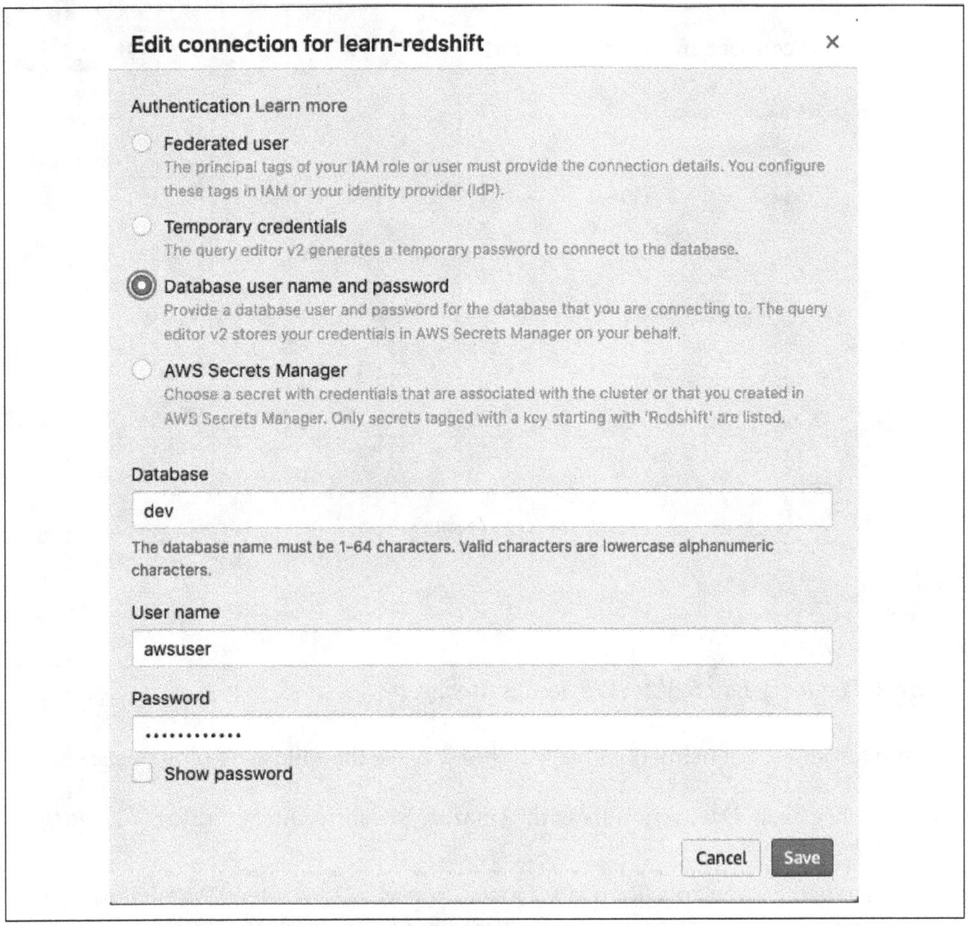

Edit connection for learn-redshift ×

Authentication Learn more

○ Federated user
   The principal tags of your IAM role or user must provide the connection details. You configure
   these tags in IAM or your identity provider (IdP).

○ Temporary credentials
   The query editor v2 generates a temporary password to connect to the database.

◉ Database user name and password
   Provide a database user and password for the database that you are connecting to. The query
   editor v2 stores your credentials in AWS Secrets Manager on your behalf.

○ AWS Secrets Manager
   Choose a secret with credentials that are associated with the cluster or that you created in
   AWS Secrets Manager. Only secrets tagged with a key starting with 'Redshift' are listed.

Database

```
dev
```

The database name must be 1-64 characters. Valid characters are lowercase alphanumeric
characters.

User name

```
awsuser
```

Password

```
............
```

☐ Show password

Cancel   Save

Figure 2-33. Query Editor V2 stored password

AWS Secrets Manager

With the AWS Secrets Manager option (Figure 2-34), the user only needs to specify a
predefined AWS secret. In this scenario, the secret would have been precreated by an
administrator so the IAM identity using the query editor does *not* need permissions
to write to Secrets Manager.

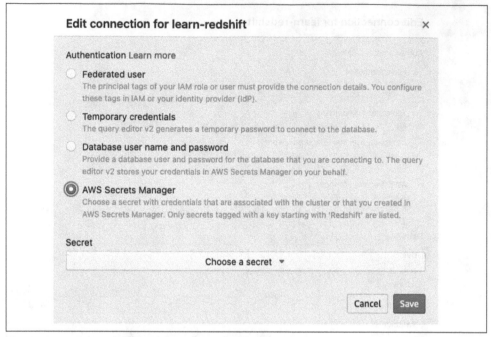

Figure 2-34. Query Editor V2 AWS Secrets Manager

For more examples of using the Query Editor V2, see the following blog posts:

- "Simplify Your Data Analysis with Amazon Redshift Query Editor V2" (*https://oreil.ly/wBMv-*)

- "Introducing Amazon Redshift Query Editor V2, a Free Web-based Query Authoring Tool for Data Analysts" (*https://oreil.ly/spxKw*)

- "Federate Access to Amazon Redshift Query Editor V2 with Active Directory Federation Services (AD FS): Part 3" (*https://oreil.ly/ihsKQ*)

Business Intelligence Using Amazon QuickSight

BI platforms of your choice can connect to Amazon Redshift using JDBC and ODBC drivers either packaged with those applications or that can be downloaded. Popular BI platforms that integrate with Amazon Redshift include MicroStrategy (*https://www.microstrategy.com*), Power BI (*https://powerbi.microsoft.com*), Tableau (*https://www.tableau.com*), and Looker (*https://www.looker.com*). For more information on connecting to Amazon Redshift using these drivers see "Connecting to Amazon Redshift Using JDBC/ODBC" on page 78.

AWS also provides a cloud native serverless BI service, Amazon QuickSight (*https://aws.amazon.com/quicksight*), which is tightly integrated with Amazon Redshift and does not require a driver to be set up. Amazon QuickSight has a pay-per-user pricing model, automatic scaling, and no servers to maintain. There are a number of live example dashboards available on the Amazon QuickSight Gallery (*https://oreil.ly/PX_nz*) for you to explore that demonstrate various features available in the tool.

In the following retail analytics example dashboard (Figure 2-35), you can see a number of key features of QuickSight. A few of these features include built-in machine learning algorithms to forecast and detect anomalies, customized narratives, and rich visualizations.

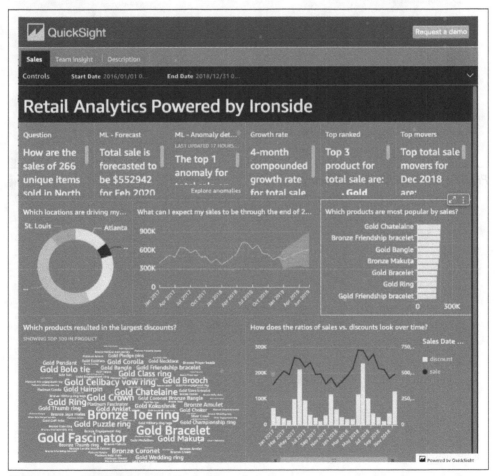

Figure 2-35. QuickSight example dashboard

Among the many QuickSight data sources (Figure 2-36), there are two options to connect to Amazon Redshift: Redshift Auto-discovered and Redshift Manual connect. With the connection in place, users can start building reports and dashboards with a few button clicks.

Figure 2-36. QuickSight data sources

When you leverage the Redshift Auto-discovered option, users select the Redshift Instance ID you want to connect to and enter the database, username, and password (Figure 2-37).

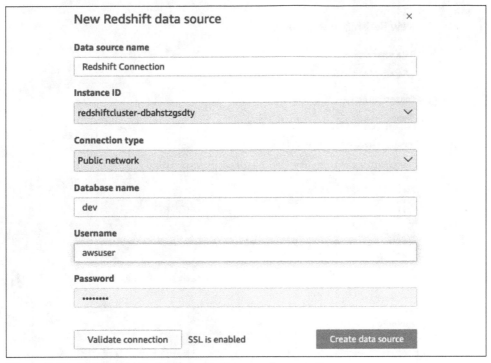

Figure 2-37. QuickSight Redshift Auto-discovered connection

When you leverage the Redshift Manual connect option, users enter the database server and port in addition to the database, username, and password (Figure 2-38).

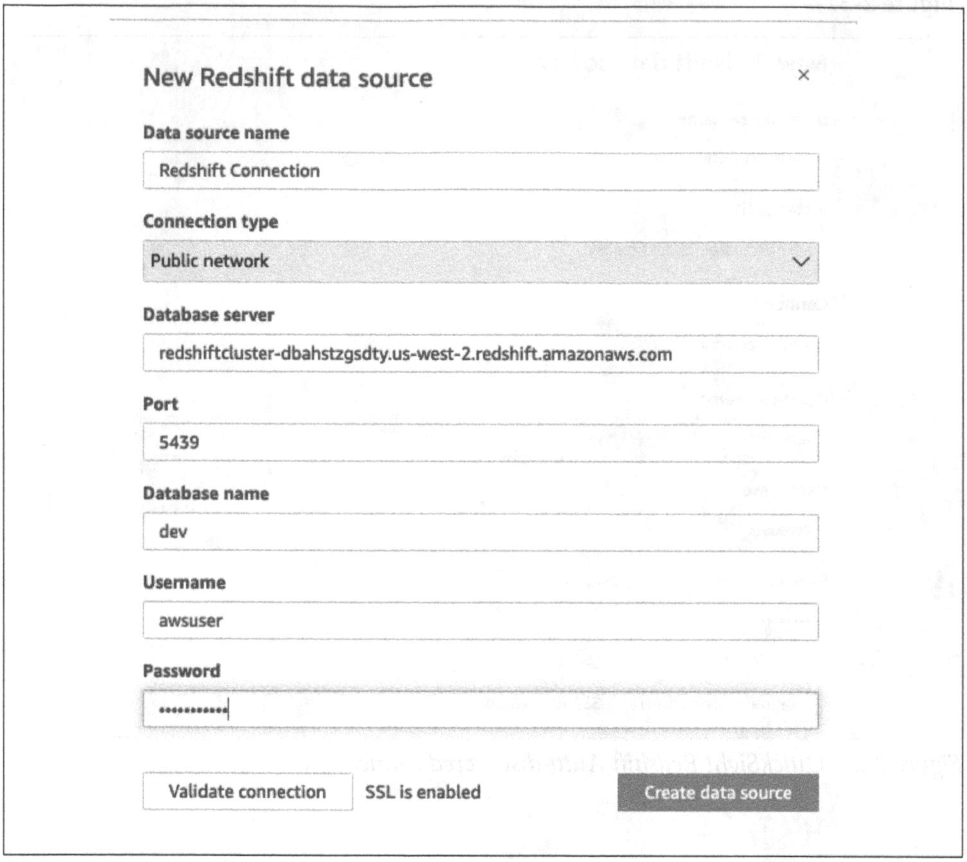

New Redshift data source ×

Data source name

Redshift Connection

Connection type

Public network ∨

Database server

redshiftcluster-dbahstzgsdty.us-west-2.redshift.amazonaws.com

Port

5439

Database name

dev

Username

awsuser

Password

•••••••••••

Validate connection   SSL is enabled   Create data source

Figure 2-38. QuickSight Redshift manual connect

Connecting to Amazon Redshift Using JDBC/ODBC

Many third-party BI and ETL tools access DB platforms through the use of JDBC and ODBC drivers. Amazon Redshift provides open source drivers for you to download and may already be packaged in your third-party tools. These drivers are updated by AWS frequently to work with new features being released in the product. While Amazon Redshift is also compatible with Postgres drivers, those drivers do not support all the features available in the Amazon Redshift drivers, such as IAM authentication. To configure your Amazon Redshift driver, you can obtain the connection URL by navigating to the Amazon Redshift console.

For a provisioned cluster, you can find the JDBC/ODBC URL (Figure 2-39) by inspecting the Cluster summary page.

Figure 2-39. Amazon Redshift provisioned JDBC/ODBC URL

For a serverless workgroup, you can find the JDBC/ODBC URL (Figure 2-40) by inspecting the Workgroup summary page.

Figure 2-40. Amazon Redshift serverless JDBC/ODBC URL

In the following example, using the open source Java tool SQL Workbench/J (*https://www.sql-workbench.eu*), we have set the client configuration (Figure 2-41) using the information gathered. With this tool, you can leverage the Extended Properties dialog to set optional parameters required for features like SAML-based authentication.

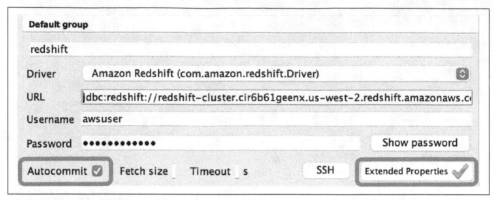

Figure 2-41. JDBC client configuration

Also notice the checkbox for Autocommit: this is an often overlooked setting and should be enabled in most use cases. Because Amazon Redshift follows Atomicity tenant of ACID (atomicity, consistency, isolation, durability) (*https://oreil.ly/ZRTMq*) compliance, it needs to maintain the state of the data across multiple user transactions. When disabled, Amazon Redshift will assume that every connection is the beginning of a new transaction and will not commit the transaction unless an explicit commit statement is executed. When overlooked, the system may unnecessarily use resources to keep track of multiple transaction states. If you find yourself in this situation, you can terminate idle connections using the PG_TERMINATE_BACKEND (*https://oreil.ly/WvQzN*) command.

For more details and options when configuring your JDBC driver, review this JDBC driver documentation (*https://oreil.ly/C7mcs*), and for more details and options when configuring your ODBC driver, review this ODBC online documentation (*https://oreil.ly/3Oto5*).

Summary

In this chapter, we showed you how Amazon Redshift is architected and how to get started. We compared the serverless and provisioned deployment options, showed you how to quickly query sample data, and showed you the different authentication and connection options.

In the next chapter, we will show you how to best model and load data from your data lake, operational sources, and real-time streaming sources.

CHAPTER 3

Setting Up Your Data Models and Ingesting Data

Now that you have set up your Amazon Redshift data warehouse, let's consider a data management strategy.

In this chapter, we will discuss a few options for your data management strategy and whether you should employ a "Data Lake First Versus Data Warehouse First Strategy". Next, we'll go into "Defining Your Data Model" and use the "Student Information Learning Analytics Dataset" to illustrate how to create tables and "Load Batch Data into Amazon Redshift" using a sample of this data in Amazon S3. However, in today's world, where speed to insights is critical to maintaining your competetive edge, we'll also show you how to "Load Real-Time and Near Real-Time Data". Lastly, we'll cover how you can "Optimize Your Data Structures".

Data Lake First Versus Data Warehouse First Strategy

In today's digital age, organizations are constantly collecting and generating large amounts of data. This data can come from various sources such as user interactions, sensor readings, and social media activity. Managing this data effectively is crucial for organizations to gain insights and make informed business decisions. One of the key challenges in managing this data is deciding on the appropriate data management strategy. Two popular strategies that organizations use are the *Data Lake first* strategy and the *Data Warehouse first* strategy. When you are considering your cloud-based data management strategy, whether you are migrating an on-premises data warehouse or loading new data, a question you should consider is whether you take a Data Lake first or a Data Warehouse first strategy.

Data Lake First Strategy

The Data Lake first strategy involves creating a centralized repository for all raw data, regardless of its structure or format. This data lake is typically built on a scalable storage platform, such as Amazon S3, and is designed to handle large volumes of data. The data is then ingested into the data lake in its raw form, and data scientists, analysts, and other stakeholders can use various data processing and analytics tools to extract insights from the data.

One of the main advantages of the Data Lake first strategy is that it allows for flexibility and scalability. Organizations can easily ingest new data sources, and the data lake can scale to handle large amounts of data. Additionally, maintaining the raw data in an untransformed format allows for more accurate insights and preserves the data integrity and data lineage.

However, one of the main disadvantages of the Data Lake first strategy is that it can be difficult to manage and govern the data effectively. You have to organize and maintain the files in buckets and partition appropriately for performance. Additionally, data scientists and analysts may have to spend a significant amount of time and resources preparing the data before they can extract insights.

Data Warehouse First Strategy

The Data Warehouse first strategy involves creating a centralized database for data that is optimized for querying and reporting. The data is extracted from various sources, transformed to fit a predefined schema, and loaded into the data warehouse. Data scientists, analysts, and other stakeholders can then use SQL or other query languages to extract insights from the data. This approach is often preferred when the primary focus is on analytics and BI, and this central data store is used to share data with other services or users.

One of the main advantages of the Data Warehouse first strategy is that it allows for better data governance and management. The structured data is easy to understand and find, making it easier for stakeholders to extract insights. Business analysts can analyze the data using ANSI SQL query language that is easy to use. The data is ready for consumption by decision makers as it is transformed and cleaned during the loading process, reducing the amount of time and resources needed to prepare the data for analysis.

However, one of the main disadvantages of the Data Warehouse first strategy is that organizations may have to spend more time and resources to extract and transform data from new data sources before providing access to business decision makers. Additionally, the transformation and cleaning process may lead to data loss or inaccuracies, which needs to be taken into consideration during the ETL design process. New innovations with zero-ETL strategy alleviates some of this problem in replicating data from source to target.

Deciding On a Strategy

Both the Data Lake first strategy and the Data Warehouse first strategy have their advantages and disadvantages. Organizations must consider their specific needs and goals when choosing a strategy. The Data Lake first strategy is best suited for organizations that need to handle large volumes of structured and unstructured data and require more flexibility and scalability to enable access to the data through a broader set of tools. On the other hand, the Data Warehouse first strategy is best suited for organizations that want to use SQL-based data management and data governance for structured and semistructured data.

The choice of a strategy could depend on the source of data and whether you want to replicate data from source to target at table level or at the application layer. When you extract data from a source system, typically you replicate at the physical layer at a table level. But, if the source system is a SaaS application like Salesforce, SAP, or ServiceNow, then you have the option of replicating data at the database table layer or at the application layer. Since these SaaS applications typically involve thousands of tables, they usually have extraction logic built in to apply the business rules for the native tables. For example, SAP has data extractors (SAP Business Warehouse extractors) that apply business logic to the source tables and extract data at a logical layer. A sales order transaction could be stored in 50 different tables within the SAP application, but the extractor will apply business logic to combine these tables to deliver a single denormalized sales data row that is easy to consume. If you want to centrally store this data for various type of workloads, such as big data processing, machine learning, or analytics for native and non-native AWS Analytics services, then building a data lake would make sense. If the workload is purely for analytics and BI, then it would be better to take a Data Warehouse first approach.

If the requirements dictate a table level replication, then you can either bring the raw data into the data lake or ingest data directly into a data warehouse such as Amazon Redshift. The approach you take with this scenario will depend on your business and technical requirements. Within the AWS cloud, if you want to share the raw data in the Amazon S3 data lake with other services like EMR, Athena, or SageMaker for business users and data scientists to consume, then taking a Data Lake first approach would make sense. With a lake first approach, you have the flexibility of keeping the data in its raw format and establishing governance on top of that data and sharing without having to go through another service. This comes with the additional complexity of having to maintain the raw files in Amazon S3 and partitioning for optimal storage and performance by storing and managing the buckets and partitions. Updates for these files can be done using Apache Hudi.

You will need to first evaluate the skills in your organization and your long-term strategy before you choose an approach. Amazon Redshift now supports native Spark integration to run EMR or AWS Glue code on Amazon Redshift. This integration enables you to write Python or Scala code and Amazon Redshift will take care of converting the code to native SQL code and run it within your Amazon Redshift data warehouse. With Amazon Redshift ML, you can run machine learning using SQL syntax and not have to code in Python or R languages. With these new features like data sharing, Amazon Redshift ML, native Spark integration, and AWS Data Exchange (ADX) integration, the need to build a data lake just to share data with other services could diminish further.

In the Data Warehouse first approach, you ingest the raw data directly into the Amazon Redshift data warehouse. This is done at the database table level using either the AWS Database Migration Service (DMS) or a data integration tool of your choice. This will be in line with the ELT approach, where you then read the raw data from within the data warehouse to transform and load for further analysis. With this approach, when you need to share data to other AWS native services, you can use the Amazon Redshift data sharing feature, and to share with non-native services for other use cases, you can use the UNLOAD command to offload data from Amazon Redshift to Amazon S3.

To summarize, the data lake versus Data Warehouse first strategy, a Data Lake first approach is useful when you want to maintain raw data to meet known and unknown requirements to future-proof your analytics application. This is to meet requirements of organizational-level decision makers, where it may be difficult to provide business value initially. Data lake is just a repository of data, and needs additional compute services to drive value. A Data Warehouse first approach is to store processed data in a purpose-built data store, and it usually is for a particular domain and scope of requirements. It is ideal for analysis of large data because it is well structured, easy to use, and easy to understand. Organizations often need both. Data warehouses have been around for years. Data lakes were born out of the need to harness big data and benefit from raw, granular structured and unstructured data. But there is still a need to create data warehouses for analytics use by business users.

Defining Your Data Model

When you launch Amazon Redshift, a default database is created. You can create your database objects under the default database or create additional databases to organize the objects under different databases. How you organize the database objects will depend on multiple factors, including application ownership, security requirements, ease of management, and cross-database query requirements.

This section describes how your Amazon Redshift data warehouse is organized and provides a starting point for understanding where to create your database objects. We will also cover the common data modeling strategies used to manage data.

Database Schemas, Users, and Groups

For Amazon Redshift, the database is the highest level in the hierarchy of database objects, and you can create multiple databases within a data warehouse. Within each database, you can have one or more schemas. Within each schema you create tables that store the data in a structured format, and other objects including views, procedures, and functions. By default, a database has a single schema, which is named "public." You can use schemas to group database objects under a common name.

Amazon Redshift supports both cross-schema and cross-database queries, and you could choose to organize database objects related to each application in separate schemas or separate databases. When organizing the database, consider if your queries have to go across databases. Cross-schema queries happen within the same database, and do not have any limitations. But cross-database queries have some limitations (*https://oreil.ly/2zPZV*) that you should consider. For performance, note that cross-database queries do not support result cache, and hence repeated queries have to go against the database. Concurrency scaling is also not supported for cross-database queries. Consider what percentage of queries have to go across databases before making a decision to organize objects in different databases.

The other factor to consider is the number of schemas or tables for your workloads or business area. If the number of schemas or table objects required exceeds the quotas or limits (*https://oreil.ly/wtKal*), then you might want to organize the data in separate databases.

For cross-database queries you use a two-dot (`database.schema.table`) notation to access a table outside of the current database. You can also create an external schema to reference using a one-dot (`externalschema.table`) notation. For more details on cross-database queries, you can refer to querying data across databases (*https://oreil.ly/-03Yn*).

When you have a multi-tenant architecture, you can refer to this blog (*https://oreil.ly/gaFz7*) to organize your database objects.

Star Schema, Denormalized, Normalized

Data warehouses have been built using the *star schema*, where there are one or more central fact tables that contain the measures to be analyzed, surrounded by dimension tables that provide the business context to the analysis. This layout looks like a star, thus the name. The star schema dimensions can be either denormalized as a single table with columns for every attribute of dimension or further normalized into separate tables, which makes the schema diagram look like a snowflake instead of a star and thus referred to as a snowflake schema (Figure 3-1).

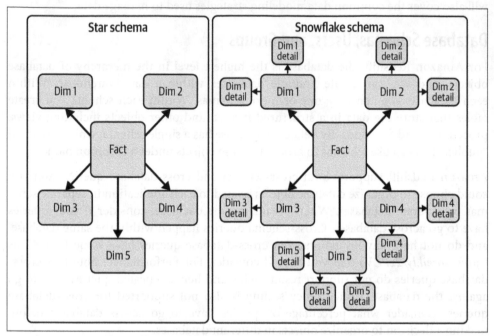

Figure 3-1. Star schema objects compared with snowflake schema objects

A star schema stores redundant data in dimension tables, whereas in a *snowflake schema*, the dimension tables avoid redundancy. However, this leads to increased query complexity and can impact query performance since more tables need to be joined for the analysis. A star schema data model or a denormalized data model is recommended when you create a data warehouse on Amazon Redshift.

On the other hand, storage requirements of a snowflake schema are lower as there is no redundancy and there is less risk of data integrity issues.

With advancements in storage media and dropping prices per TB, the storage aspect is less of a concern over query simplicity, and query execution often takes higher priority for modern data warehouses. This makes star schema a popular architecture for running analytics of very large datasets.

Let's look at a simple data model to understand the difference between normalized and a denormalized star schema. Sales orders are stored in a relational database using a normalized model. As you see in Figure 3-2, SalesHeader and SalesLineItem are stored in separate tables with a one-to-many relationship along with the master data tables Customer, Product, and Currency.

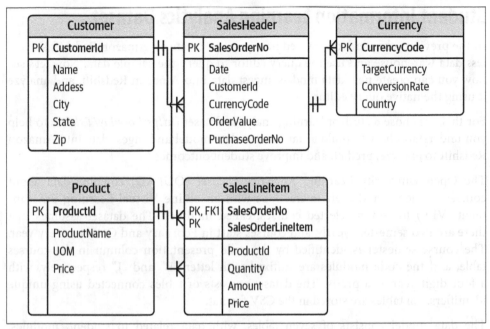

Figure 3-2. Denormalized OLTP schema data model in source database

For the star schema model in Figure 3-3, the SalesHeader and SalesLineItem tables are combined into one SalesFact table, and the data is also aggregated at the order level.

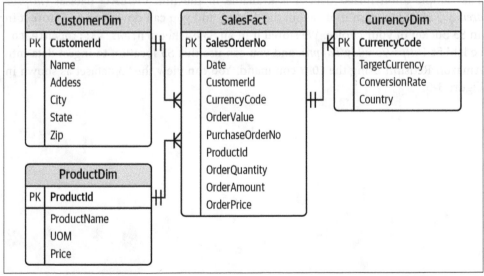

Figure 3-3. Star schema data model for data warehouse

Student Information Learning Analytics Dataset

In the previous chapter, you learned how you can create an Amazon Redshift serverless data warehouse and use the query editor to query the sample data. Now let's see how you can create new data models, ingest data into Amazon Redshift, and analyze it using the native query editor.

For this, we chose a student learning analytics dataset (*https://oreil.ly/TxkDS*) to help you understand how to build a star schema data model and ingest data into Amazon Redshift to analyze, predict, and improve student outcomes.[1]

The Open University Learning Analytics Dataset (OULAD) contains data about courses, students, and their interactions with an online Virtual Learning Environment (VLE) for seven selected courses, called modules. The dataset assumes that there are two semesters yearly, and courses start in February and October every year. The course semester is identified by the code_presentation column in the courses table, and the code modules are suffixed with letter "B" and "J," respectively, with a four-digit year as a prefix. The dataset consists of tables connected using unique identifiers. All tables are stored in the CSV format.

The data model consists of seven tables, with data related to student, modules, and activities, as shown in Figure 3-4, which shows the entity relationship. For the purposes of this book, we have modified this data model to store data for multiple schools instead of just one school. You can use the Data Definition Language (DDL) scripts shown in Example 3-1 to create the schema and database tables.

The sample anonymized dataset is available in the link OULAD dataset (*https://oreil.ly/TxkDS*) to learn more about the dataset, and you can download and store it in an S3 bucket of your choice. We stored it in an S3 bucket `arn:aws:s3:::openlearn-redshift` (*https://oreil.ly/Fdjqm*), and you can use this S3 location to ingest data into Amazon Redshift using the `COPY` command. You can view the S3 dataset as shown in Figure 3-5.

---

1 Kuzilek J., Hlosta M., and Zdrahal Z. Open University Learning Analytics dataset (*https://doi.org/10.1038/sdata.2017.171*), Sci. Data 4:170171 (2017).

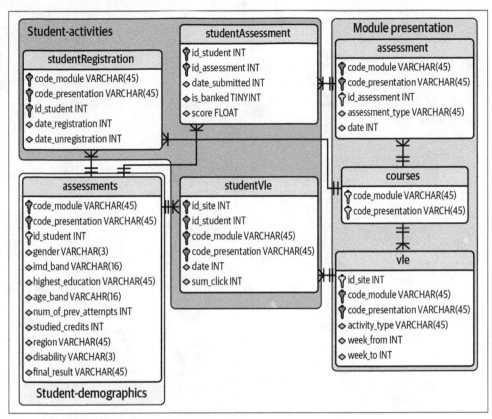

Figure 3-4. Student information system dataset

You can view the S3 dataset as shown in Figure 3-5, and you will use this as a source to ingest the sample dataset into Amazon Redshift using the COPY command. Similarly, you can find other publicly available datasets and create data models for these datasets to explore Amazon Redshift features.

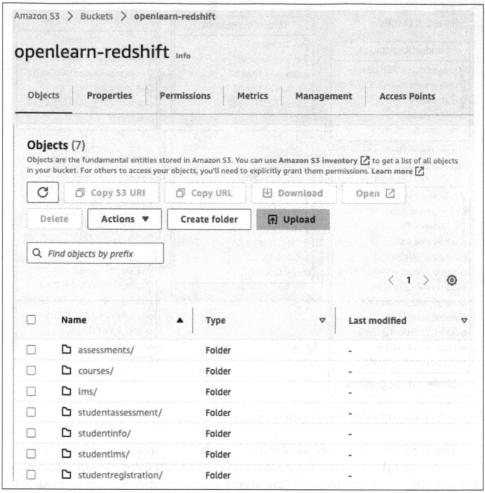

Figure 3-5. Review raw data in Amazon S3

Create Data Models for Student Information Learning Analytics Dataset

Next, let's create database tables to load data into Amazon Redshift. Connect to your Amazon Redshift data warehouse. Use the following script to create the schema and tables for your sample student information dataset (see Example 3-1).

Example 3-1. Load student information data

```
/* We'll use a modified version of the Open University Learning Analytics dataset */
/* to store data for multiple schools */
/* https://analyse.kmi.open.ac.uk/open_dataset */
/* https://analyse.kmi.open.ac.uk/open_dataset#rights */
/* Kuzilek J., Hlosta M., Zdrahal Z. Open University Learning Analytics dataset */
/* Sci. Data 4:170171 doi: 10.1038/sdata.2017.171 (2017). */

CREATE SCHEMA openlearn;

CREATE TABLE "openlearn"."assessments"
(
    code_module varchar(5),
    code_presentation varchar(5),
    id_assessment integer,
    assessment_type varchar(5),
    assessment_date bigint,
    weight decimal(10,2)
    )
DISTSTYLE AUTO
SORTKEY AUTO
ENCODE AUTO;

CREATE TABLE "openlearn"."courses"
(
    code_module              varchar(5),
    code_presentation        varchar(5),
    module_presentation_length integer
    )
DISTSTYLE AUTO
SORTKEY AUTO
ENCODE AUTO;

CREATE TABLE "openlearn"."student_assessment"
(
    id_assessment  integer,
    id_student     integer,
    date_submitted bigint,
    is_banked      smallint,
    score          smallint
    )
DISTSTYLE AUTO
SORTKEY AUTO
ENCODE AUTO;

CREATE TABLE "openlearn"."student_info"
(
    code_module          varchar(5),
    code_presentation    varchar(5),
    id_student           integer,
    gender               CHAR(1),
```

```
    region                varchar(50),
    highest_education     varchar(50),
    imd_band              varchar(10),
    age_band              varchar(10),
    num_of_prev_atteempts smallint,
    studied_credits       smallint,
    disability            char(1),
    final_result          varchar(20)
    )
DISTSTYLE AUTO
SORTKEY AUTO
ENCODE AUTO;

CREATE TABLE "openlearn"."student_registration"
(
    code_module          varchar(5),
    code_presendation    varchar(5),
    id_student           integer,
    date_registration    bigint ,
    date_unregistration  bigint
    )
DISTSTYLE AUTO
SORTKEY AUTO
ENCODE AUTO;

CREATE TABLE "openlearn"."student_lms"
(
    code_module          varchar(5),
    code_presentation    varchar(5),
    id_student           integer,
    id_site              integer,
    date                 bigint,
    sum_click            integer
    )
DISTSTYLE AUTO
SORTKEY AUTO
ENCODE AUTO;

CREATE TABLE "openlearn"."lms"
(
    id_site              integer,
    code_module          varchar(5),
    code_presentation    varchar(5),
    activity_type        varchar(20),
    week_from            smallint,
    week_to              smallint
    )
DISTSTYLE AUTO
SORTKEY AUTO
ENCODE AUTO;
```

When creating tables in Amazon Redshift, while there are many options to choose the distribution, sorting, and encoding for each table, in the previous example we did not specify these options, and the default of AUTO was used. In most cases, using AUTO will indicate that the Amazon Redshift service will monitor the actual usage of the table and automatically tune the table for you.

Load Batch Data into Amazon Redshift

Now that you created the data tables and have the data files available in Amazon S3, you can load the data into Amazon Redshift. There are multiple options to load data into Amazon Redshift.

- Using the COPY command
- Using AWS Glue or third-party ETL tools
- Manual loading using SQL commands
- Using the Query Editor V2

Using the COPY Command

The COPY command is the simplest and most efficient way to load data into Amazon Redshift. It allows you to load data directly from Amazon S3, Amazon DynamoDB, and Amazon EMR, as well as from external data sources such as CSV and JSON files. The COPY command automatically parallelizes the data load and can handle large amounts of data quickly and easily. This command reads multiple data files and can also split the files as necessary based on the number of slices in the target data warehouse to allocate the workload to all nodes and slices. It will also sort the rows and distribute data across node slices. A best practice is to compress the files when you store in Amazon S3 for faster reads. For ingestion of data, please note the differences between loading compressed files versus uncompressed files.

When you load compressed data as a single large file, Amazon Redshift serializes the load. But if you split the file into smaller files, the COPY command loads multiple files in parallel. This increases parallelism by dividing the workload among the nodes in your data warehouse. We recommend that you split your data into smaller files that are about equal size, from 1 MB to 1 GB after compression. For optimum parallelism, as a rule of thumb, make the number of the files a multiple of the number of slices in your data warehouse with the size between 1 and 125 MB after compression. For example, if you are loading a 1 GB file into a two-node ra3.4xlarge data warehouse that has 4 slices per node, divide the file into multiples of 8, so you can split the file into 8 files of 125 MB each for efficient load.

When you load all the data from a single large compressed file, Amazon Redshift is forced to perform a serialized load, which is much slower.

In contrast, when you load delimited data from a large uncompressed file, Amazon Redshift makes use of multiple slices. These slices work in parallel automatically. This provides fast load performance. Specifically, when Amazon Redshift loads uncompressed, delimited data, data is split into ranges and handled by slices in each node.

When loading compressed files, a good practice is to split your data into smaller files that are about equal size, from 1 MB to 1 GB after compression. For optimum parallelism, the ideal file size is 1 to 125 MB after compression.

Ingest Data for the Student Learning Analytics Dataset

To ingest the sample student learning analytics dataset, we use the recommended COPY command with the Amazon S3 bucket where we stored the sample data. The list of commands are as shown in Example 3-2, and you can use these commands and replace the S3 location and the region with appropriate values.

Example 3-2. Create schema and tables for student information data

```
COPY "openlearn"."assessments"
FROM 's3://openlearn-redshift/assessments'
iam_role default
delimiter ',' region 'us-east-1'
REMOVEQUOTES IGNOREHEADER 1;

COPY "openlearn"."courses"
FROM 's3://openlearn-redshift/courses'
iam_role default
delimiter ',' region 'us-east-1'
REMOVEQUOTES IGNOREHEADER 1;

COPY "openlearn"."student_assessment"
FROM 's3://openlearn-redshift/studentAssessment'
iam_role default
delimiter ',' region 'us-east-1'
REMOVEQUOTES IGNOREHEADER 1;

COPY "openlearn"."student_info"
FROM 's3://openlearn-redshift/studentInfo'
iam_role default
delimiter ',' region 'us-east-1'
```

```
REMOVEQUOTES IGNOREHEADER 1;

COPY "openlearn"."student_registration"
FROM 's3://openlearn-redshift/studentRegistration'
iam_role default
delimiter ',' region 'us-east-1'
REMOVEQUOTES IGNOREHEADER 1;

COPY "openlearn"."student_lms"
FROM 's3://openlearn-redshift/studentlms'
iam_role default
delimiter ',' region 'us-east-1'
REMOVEQUOTES IGNOREHEADER 1;

COPY "openlearn"."lms"
FROM 's3://openlearn-redshift/lms'
iam_role default
delimiter ',' region 'us-east-1'
REMOVEQUOTES IGNOREHEADER 1;
```

We are using the default keyword to use the default IAM role associated with the data warehouse. Amazon Redshift uses the IAM role that is set as the default (*https://oreil.ly/lRd6z*) and associated with the data warehouse when the command runs. You can run the DEFAULT_IAM_ROLE command to check the current default IAM role that is attached to the data warehouse.

Amazon Redshift sorts each batch of records in a single load based on sort key order. However, it does not resort existing records already stored for each COPY execution. If each batch of new data follows the existing rows in your table, your data is properly stored in sort order, and you don't need to run a vacuum. You don't need to presort the rows in each load because COPY sorts each batch of incoming data as it loads.

Building a Star Schema

You just ingested the data into a normalized student information data model to store the transactional records for course selections, grades, outcomes, and registrations for students. However, the business requirement is to enable school administrators and faculty to be able to measure course outcomes. As discussed in the previous chapter, a star schema model consisting of fact and dimension tables is the recommended data model for a data warehouse. The tables course_registration, course_outcome, and course_schedule have the data necessary to measure outcomes, so these tables could form the basis for the fact table.

There are many approaches to transform the data into your denormalized fact table. You can use an *extract-transform-load* (ETL) approach, which reads the source data, processes the transformations in an external application, and loads the results, or you can use an *extract-load-transform* (ELT) approach, which uses the data you just loaded and transforms the data in place using the power of the Amazon Redshift compute. In Chapter 4, "Data Transformation Strategies", we'll go into more details on deciding between these strategies. However, to complete this example, we will show how to use an ELT approach with the data that you just loaded.

Example 3-3 reads the normalized source tables and builds the `mv_course_out comes_fact` materialized view. The advantage of creating a materialized view is that it can be set to incrementally refresh data when the underlying tables are updated.

Example 3-3. Create a materialized view to denormalize

```
CREATE materialized view mv_course_outcomes_fact AS
SELECT
    co.student_id,
    co.course_id,
    co.semester_id,
    co.score,
    co.letter_grade,
    cr.date_registered,
    cr.date_dropped,
    cr.status,
    cs.staff_id,
    cs.lecture_days,
    cs.lecture_start_hour,
    cs.lecture_duration,
    cs.lab_days,
    cs.lab_start_hour,
    cs.lab_duration
FROM openlearn.course_registration cr
JOIN openlearn.course_outcome co
  ON cr.student_id = co.student_id AND
     cr.course_id = co.course_id AND
     cr.semester_id = co.semester_id
JOIN openlearn.course_schedule cs
  ON cr.course_id = cs.course_id AND
     cr.semester_id = cs.semester_id;
```

The student and faculty dimension tables can now be joined to the materialized view, which is the fact table to create a start schema model. Now when you look at the full star schema model, it will be as shown in Figure 3-6.

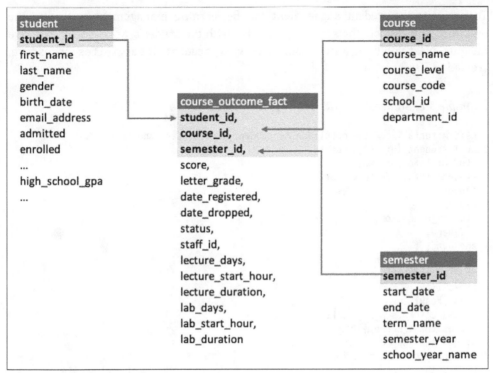

Figure 3-6. Full star schema model

Once you ingest the data, you can test the results by selecting data from the tables. Since we just created a materialized view to consolidate data from multiple tables, we can query this materialized view for efficient query performance. Let's test using a couple of queries (Examples 3-4 and 3-5).

Example 3-4. Find number of students who secured each grade

```
SELECT semester_id, course_name, letter_grade, count(*)
FROM openlearn.mv_course_outcomes_fact
GROUP BY semester_id, course_name, letter_grade;
```

Example 3-5. Determine if there is a correlation between lecture duration and grade

```
SELECT course_name, letter_grade, sum(lecture_duration), count(*)
FROM openlearn.mv_course_outcomes_fact
GROUP BY course_name, letter_grade
ORDER BY course_name, letter_grade;
```

To correlate the student engagement on the learning management system to the outcome, you can join the student_lms table with the student_assessment to derive insights. Next you'll see a materialized view, mv_student_lmsactivites_and_score, created in Example 3-6.

Example 3-6. Student activities `total_score` `mean_score`

```
CREATE materialized view openlearn.mv_student_lmsactivites_and_score AS
SELECT student_info.id_student,
  student_info.code_module,
  student_info.code_presentation,
  gender,
  region,
  highest_education,
  imd_band,
  age_band,
  num_of_prev_atteempts,
  studied_credits,
  disability,
  final_result,
  st_lms_clicks.sum_of_clicks,
  scores.total_score,
  scores.mean_score
FROM openlearn.student_info
  LEFT JOIN
    (SELECT code_module,code_presentation,id_student,sum(sum_click) AS sum_of_clicks
    FROM openlearn.student_lms
      GROUP BY code_module,code_presentation,id_student) st_lms_clicks
  ON student_info.code_module=st_lms_clicks.code_module
  AND student_info.code_presentation=st_lms_clicks.code_presentation
  AND student_info.id_student=st_lms_clicks.id_student
  LEFT JOIN
    (SELECT id_student, sum(score) AS total_score, avg(score) AS mean_score
    FROM openlearn.student_assessment
    GROUP BY id_student)  scores
    ON student_info.id_student = scores.id_student;
```

With this materialized view, you can gain many insights into student performance, as in Example 3-7, to analyze the impact of the student engagement on the result. Here you analyze the number of clicks for a student using the online learning management compared to the result or grade.

Example 3-7. Clicks versus result

```
SELECT code_module, final_result, sum(sum_of_clicks)
FROM  openlearn.mv_student_lmsactivites_and_score
GROUP BY code_module, final_result
ORDER BY code_module, final_result;
```

In Example 3-8, you see a query to analyze the percentage results by module to understand which modules students are scoring higher or lower, so the schools can proactively set up programs to increase student engagement for better outcomes.

Example 3-8. Percentage results by MODULE

```
SELECT code_module,
  sum( CASE final_result WHEN 'Pass' THEN 1 ELSE 0 END ) AS PassCount ,
    sum( CASE final_result WHEN 'Distinction' THEN 1 ELSE 0 END ) AS DistCount,
  sum( CASE final_result WHEN 'Fail'  THEN 1 ELSE 0 END ) AS FailCount,
  sum( CASE final_result WHEN 'Withdraws' THEN 1 ELSE 0 END ) AS WithdrawnCount,
    count(*) AS TotalCount,
        round(cast(PassCount AS numeric(10,4))/TotalCount, 2)*100 AS pct_PassCount
FROM  openlearn.mv_student_lmsactivites_and_score
GROUP BY code_module
ORDER BY code_module;
```

You can also query the tables directly to gain insights. Example 3-9 shows a query to find out the number of students who completed a course by performing any type of assessment but exams. You can try running this query.

Example 3-9. Students who finished a course performing any assessment but exams

```
select DISTINCT q.code_module, q.code_presentation, final_result
FROM openlearnm.student_info si
INNER JOIN
( SELECT * FROM openlearnm.student_assessment sa
    INNER JOIN openlearnm.assessments a
    ON sa.id_assessment = a.id_assessment) q
ON q.code_module = si.code_module
AND q.code_presentation = si.code_presentation
WHERE q.assessment_type = 'Exam';
```

Continuous File Ingestion from Amazon S3

Continuous ingestion of files landing in an Amazon S3 bucket into Amazon Redshift tables allows users to simplify their transformation pipeline. When you set up a COPY JOB, Amazon Redshift detects when new Amazon S3 files are added to the path specified in your COPY command. A COPY command is then automatically triggered, and the system keeps track of which files have been loaded and also determines the number of files batched together per COPY command. You can use this feature to automate the ingestion process without having to create an external data ingestion pipeline. For more details on continuous ingestion, you can refer to the online documentation (*https://oreil.ly/FNea8*).

The COPY job execution details (as in Example 3-10) are stored in the system tables for you to monitor the loads, and you can also use this to review historical job executions and load details. The sys_copy_job system table contains a row for each COPY JOB currently defined.

Example 3-10. Create a COPY job

```
<copy command>
JOB CREATE <job-name>
[auto on|off]
```

As shown in Example 3-11, to view the list of files loaded by a COPY JOB, you can run the following sample query replacing job_id:

Example 3-11. View a COPY job

```
SELECT job_id, job_name, data_source, copy_query,filename,status, curtime
FROM sys_copy_job copyjob
JOIN stl_load_commits loadcommit
ON copyjob.job_id = loadcommit.copy_job_id
WHERE job_id = <job_id>;
```

Using AWS Glue for Transformations

AWS Glue is one of the native serverless data integration services, commonly used to transform data using Python or Scala language and run on a data processing engine. AWS Glue makes it easier to discover, prepare, move, and integrate data from multiple sources for analytics, ML, and application development. It offers multiple data integration engines, which include AWS Glue for Apache Spark, AWS Glue for Ray, and AWS Glue for Python Shell. You can use the appropriate engine for your workload based on the characteristics of your workload and the preferences of your developers and analysts. Amazon Redshift supports Spark integration, which allows you to push down the Python or Scala transformation logic execution to Amazon Redshift layer by translating the Spark code to SQL code without moving the data out of the data warehouse.

Since AWS Glue V4, there's now a Amazon Redshift Spark connector with a new JDBC driver featured with AWS Glue ETL jobs. You can use it to build Apache Spark applications that read from and write to data in Amazon Redshift as part of your data ingestion and transformation pipelines. With the new connector and driver, these applications maintain their performance and transactional consistency of the data.

With AWS Glue (Figure 3-7), you can crawl an Amazon S3 data source to create a catalog, apply transformations, and ingest data into an Amazon Redshift data warehouse.

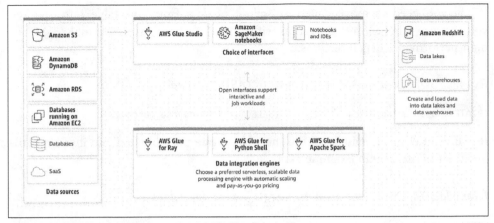

Figure 3-7. ETL integration using AWS Glue

Amazon Redshift integration for Apache Spark makes it easy to build and run Spark applications on Amazon Redshift using AWS Glue. This integration feature for Apache Spark adds pushdown capabilities for operations such as sort, aggregate, limit, join, and scalar functions so only the relevant data is moved from the Amazon Redshift data warehouse to the consuming Spark application in AWS for better performance. You can refer to this blog for more information (*https://oreil.ly/A309N*). In Chapter 4, "Data Transformation Strategies", you will learn how you can use AWS Glue Studio to create ETL transformations using a visual interface.

Manual Loading Using SQL Commands

Manually loading data into Amazon Redshift using SQL commands is a viable option, but it is generally not recommended for large datasets because it is time-consuming and error-prone. However, it can be useful for small datasets or for testing purposes. You can use SQL commands such as INSERT and CREATE TABLE to load data if using a COPY command is not an option. A multirow insert or bulk insert operation is recommended instead of a single INSERT statement.

Multirow inserts improve performance by batching up a series of inserts. The following Example 3-12 inserts two rows into a five-column table using a single INSERT statement. This is still a small insert, shown simply to illustrate the syntax of a multirow insert.

Example 3-12. Multirow insert

```
INSERT INTO openlearn.course_outcome values
(1, 1,1, 95,'A'),
(1, 2,2, 96,'B');
```

When you need to move data or a subset of data from one table into another, you can use a bulk insert operation with a SELECT clause, as in Example 3-13, for high-performance data insertions.

Example 3-13. Create table as statement (CTAS) with data

```
CREATE TABLE course_outcome_stage AS (SELECT * FROM course_outcome);
```

If you want to incrementally add to the table, create the table first and insert records based on a criteria as in Example 3-14.

Example 3-14. Create table as statement (CTAS) without data

```
CREATE TABLE course_outcome_stage AS (SELECT * FROM course_outcome WHERE 1<>1);

INSERT INTO course_outcome_stage
(SELECT * FROM course_outcome);
```

Using the Query Editor V2

For simple and quick data loads into Amazon Redshift, you can use the Query Editor V2 load data feature. You can upload a file directly from your desktop folder or upload the data file to an Amazon S3 location, and then within the Query Editor V2, choose the load data option as shown in Figure 3-8.

The Query Editor V2 will use the COPY command behind the scenes to load data from the Amazon S3 location you specify. The COPY command generated and used in the Query Editor V2 load data wizard supports all the parameters available to the COPY command syntax to copy from Amazon S3 through the wizard. You can set up data conversion parameters to accept invalid characters, set up date and time format, truncate data, handle exceptions like blank lines, missing columns, trailing white spaces, and other parameters. Choose the "Data conversion parameters" option under the "Advanced settings" section of the screen, shown in Figure 3-8. In addition, you can also set up load data operations like number of rows to analyze for compression analysis, auto update option for compression encoding, error handling, and statistics update options.

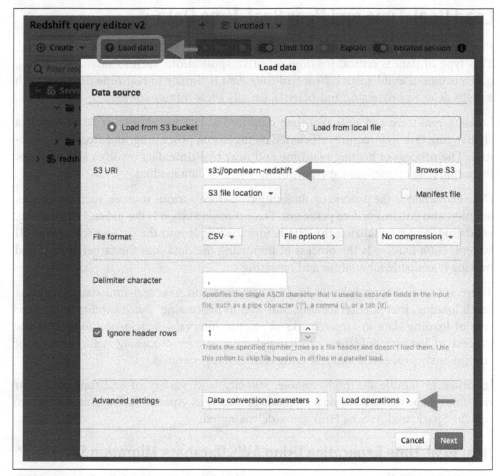

Figure 3-8. Upload the CSV files to Amazon S3 and load using Query Editor V2

 When you ingest data using the `COPY` command into an empty table, Amazon Redshift can analyze the data and optimize the compression type for each column. The `COMPUPDATE` parameter in the `COPY` command determines the action for compression.

Load Real-Time and Near Real-Time Data

Real-time data refers to data that is processed and analyzed as soon as it is generated. This type of data is critical for time-sensitive applications such as financial trading, transportation, and logistics. *Near real-time data* is similar to real-time data, but with a slight delay in processing and analysis, usually a few minutes or less.

Loading real-time and near real-time data into a data warehouse or BI system is a challenging task that requires efficient data ingestion, processing, and storage capabilities. The process of loading real-time and near real-time data involves several steps, including data extraction, data transformation, and data loading.

Data extraction is the process of obtaining data from various sources, such as sensors, log files, and streaming data platforms. *Data transformation* is the process of cleaning, validating, and normalizing the data before loading it into the data warehouse or BI system. *Data loading* is the process of importing the data into the target system and making it available for analysis and reporting.

There are several approaches to loading real-time and near real-time data, including batch loading, incremental loading, and stream processing. *Batch loading* is the process of loading data in large chunks at regular intervals. *Incremental loading* is the process of loading only new or changed data. *Stream processing* is the process of continuously processing and analyzing data as it is generated.

In order to handle the high volume, velocity, and variety of real-time and near real-time data, various big data technologies such as Apache Kafka, Apache Storm, Apache Spark, and Apache Flink are widely adopted.

Near Real-Time Replication Using AWS Database Migration Service

AWS DMS is a fully managed service that makes it easy to migrate databases to AWS. DMS can migrate your data to and from most widely used commercial and open source databases such as Oracle, MySQL, MariaDB, PostgreSQL (pgSQL), Microsoft SQL Server, and many more. One of the common use cases of DMS is migrating data to Amazon Redshift.

Before you begin your migration, it is important to plan and prepare your migration. This includes identifying the source and target databases, the amount of data to be migrated, and any specific requirements or constraints that need to be considered. You should also test your migration in a nonproduction environment to ensure that everything is working as expected.

Once you have planned and prepared for your migration, you can create a DMS replication instance. A replication instance is a DMS resource that you use to perform the actual migration. It is responsible for connecting to the source and target databases and for moving the data from one to the other.

After you create a replication instance, you can create a migration task. A migration task is a DMS resource that defines the specific details of the migration, such as the source and target databases, the data to be migrated, and any specific settings or options.

When you create a migration task, you can choose to perform a full load or a change data capture (CDC) migration. A full load migration will copy all of the data from the source database to the target, while a CDC migration will copy only the changes made to the source database since the last migration.

Once you have created a migration task, you can start the migration. DMS will begin moving data from the source database to the target. You can monitor the progress of the migration using the DMS console or the AWS CLI. For more details, refer to documentation on using Amazon Redshift data warehouse as a target (*https://oreil.ly/LN6gM*).

When the migration is complete, you can perform any necessary postmigration tasks, such as creating indexes or loading data into additional tables. You should also test the target database to ensure that all the data has been migrated correctly and that the target database is working as expected.

Amazon DMS provides a simple and easy way to migrate data to Amazon Redshift. By following the steps outlined in this chapter, you can plan, prepare, and perform your migration with confidence, knowing that your data will be moved quickly and securely to your new data warehouse.

Amazon Aurora Zero-ETL Integration with Amazon Redshift

Zero-ETL integration with Amazon Redshift enables an architecture pattern that eliminates the need for complex ETL jobs to move data for analysis. Zero-ETL integration with Amazon Redshift is available from Amazon Aurora to enable near real-time analytics and ML on petabytes of transactional data, whether that data is in the same account or a different account. Within seconds of transactional data being written into an Aurora database, the data is available in Amazon Redshift, so you don't have to build and maintain complex data pipelines to perform extract and load operations.

This zero-ETL integration (*https://oreil.ly/QNwc-*) also enables you to analyze data from multiple Amazon Aurora database clusters in the same new or existing Amazon Redshift data warehouse to derive insights across many applications or partitions. With near real-time access to transactional data, you can leverage Amazon Redshift's analytics capabilities such as built-in ML, materialized views, data sharing, and federated access to multiple data stores and data lakes to derive insights from transactional and other data. This architecture allows for faster time-to-insight and reduced costs, as data does not need to be loaded and transformed before being analyzed.

Additionally, it allows for near real-time analysis of data in the data warehouse without impacting the workloads in your transactional system.

To get started with zero-ETL, you will need to first ensure your Amazon Aurora database and Amazon Redshift data warehouse are configured correctly. For example, for Aurora you will need to be sure you are using the latest version and have logging enabled. Similarly, for Amazon Redshift, you will need to ensure you're on the latest version and have the required parameters set. See the online documentation (*https:// oreil.ly/meMEy*) for more details on the required configuration parameters.

Next, you'll set up the required permissions that enable your Amazon Aurora database to load your Amazon Redshift data warehouse. To complete this activity, you will need to ensure that your user has the `redshift:CreateInboundIntegration` permission.

Navigate to the Amazon Redshift console in your data warehouse resource policy and use the "Add authorized integration sources" option to specify the Amazon Resource Name (ARN) of the Amazon Aurora database (see Figure 3-9).

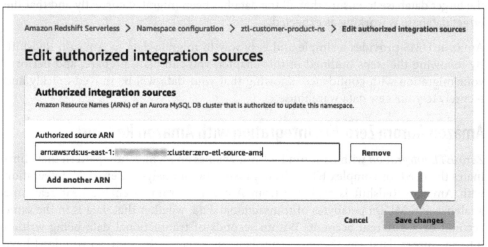

Figure 3-9. Edit authorized integration sources

Now, you're ready to create the zero-ETL integration. To complete this activity, you will need to ensure your user has the `rds:CreateIntegration` and `rds:Descri beIntegration` permission. Additionally, you may need the `rds:DeleteIntegration` permission if you ever need to delete the integration.

Navigate to the Amazon Relational Database Service (RDS) console and click on the "Zero-ETL integrations" menu item. Next, click on "Create zero-ETL integration" (see Figure 3-10). When creating the integration in the same account, select the Amazon Aurora database and the Amazon Redshift data warehouse from the prepopulated list and submit your request. You can monitor the creation of your zero-ETL integration by inspecting the status field in the Amazon RDS console. Your integration is ready when the status changes from Creating to Active.

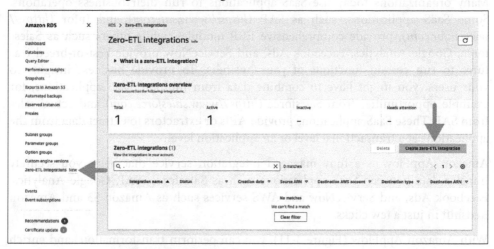

Figure 3-10. Create zero-ETL integration

Finally, you can start querying the data that has been loaded to Amazon Redshift. First, capture the `integration_id` for your zero-ETL integration from the Amazon RDS console or by executing the following SQL statement in Amazon Redshift:

```
SELECT integration_id FROM svv_integration;
```

Next, create a local database referencing the `integration_id`:

```
CREATE DATABASE <local_db_name> FROM INTEGRATION integration_id;
```

When complete, you'll be able to navigate and query all the objects that have been synchronized from your Amazon Aurora database in near real time. Each Amazon Aurora database/schema in your source will manifest as a different schema in the target Amazon Redshift data warehouse database.

To further process the data, you can consider materialized views and scripts or stored procedures that can be scheduled to run using the Amazon Redshift scheduler or by using external orchestration tools.

> If your Amazon Aurora database is in a different account from your Redshift data warehouse, you will need to perform additional configuration steps such as setting up an authorized principal and enabling cross-account access. For details on how to set up a cross-account integration, see the online documentation (*https://oreil.ly/ QNwc-*).

Using Amazon AppFlow

Many organizations today use SaaS applications to run their business operations. Some SaaS applications, such as SAP (*https://www.sap.com*) and Infor (*https://www.infor.com*), provide comprehensive ERP modules, while others such as Salesforce, Google Analytics, Facebook Ads, and ServiceNow provide best-of-breed features to run certain functions of your business. To provide business insights to your users, you might have to combine data from multiple SaaS applications, for example opportunities from Salesforce (*https://www.salesforce.com*) and actual sales from SAP. These SaaS applications provide APIs or extractors to extract data from the applications at a transactional level or an application level.

Amazon AppFlow is a fully managed integration service that helps you securely transfer data between SaaS applications such as Salesforce, SAP, Google Analytics, Facebook Ads, and ServiceNow and AWS services such as Amazon S3 and Amazon Redshift in just a few clicks.

With Amazon AppFlow (Figure 3-11), you can perform transformations and enrich the data through filters and validations. It supports data connectivity to 50 connectors, and you can move data bidirectionally to AWS services like Amazon S3 and Amazon Redshift. You can also create your own custom connector that can read from any API source to stream data into Amazon Redshift. To transfer data to Amazon Redshift from any source application, create an Amazon AppFlow flow (*https://oreil.ly/AQs8T*), and choose Amazon Redshift as the data destination. For detailed steps to connect Amazon Appflow to your Amazon Redshift data warehouse, refer to this documentation (*https://oreil.ly/ythnj*).

Figure 3-11. ETL integration using Amazon AppFlow

Before you begin your data ingestion, it is important to plan and prepare your data flow. This includes identifying the source and target apps and services, the data you want to transfer, and any specific requirements or constraints that need to be considered. You should also test your data flow in a nonproduction environment to ensure that everything is working as expected.

Once you have planned and prepared for your data flow, you can create a new flow in AppFlow. To do this, you will need to specify the source app and service, the target app and service, and the data you want to transfer. AppFlow supports many popular apps and services, including Salesforce, ServiceNow, Slack, and many more.

Next, you will need to configure the settings for your flow. This includes specifying the schedule for the flow, such as how often the data should be transferred and any specific options or settings for the source and target apps and services.

After you have configured the settings for your flow, you can create the flow. When you create a flow, AppFlow will create all the necessary resources, such as connectors and triggers, to move the data between the source and target apps and services.

When the flow is created, AppFlow will automatically begin transferring data from the source app and service to the target. You can monitor the progress of the flow using the AppFlow console or the AWS CLI.

When the data is transferred, it will be ingested into your Amazon Redshift data warehouse, where it can be queried and analyzed using standard SQL. You can then use your existing BI tools to create reports and visualizations based on the data.

Amazon AppFlow provides a simple and easy way to ingest data into Amazon Redshift. By following the steps outlined in this chapter, you can plan, prepare, and perform your data ingestion with confidence, knowing that your data will be transferred quickly and securely to your data warehouse. AppFlow enables you to automate the data flow process between different apps and services and make it more efficient. For a real use case using Amazon AppFlow to pull data from Salesforce into Amazon Redshift, refer to this blog (*https://oreil.ly/Zhrpk*).

Streaming Ingestion

Streaming ingestion is the process of continuously loading data into a data warehouse or BI system in real time or near real time. This allows for real time analysis and reporting of the data, which is critical for time-sensitive applications such as financial trading, transportation, and logistics. Streaming ingestion typically uses a streaming data platform, such as Apache Kafka or Amazon Kinesis, to collect and manage the data streams. The data streams are then processed and loaded into the target data warehouse or BI systems.

There are several benefits to using streaming ingestion, including the ability to handle high-velocity and high-volume data, perform real-time analytics and reporting, and detect and respond to events in real time. However, streaming ingestion also poses some challenges, such as the need for efficient data processing and storage capabilities, robust data integration and management tools, and specialized skills and expertise.

Use cases for Amazon Redshift streaming ingestion center around working with data that is generated continually (streamed) and needs to be processed within a short period (latency) of its generation. Sources of data can vary, from IoT devices to system telemetry, utility service usage, geolocation of devices, and more. There can be multiple use cases for streaming ingestion,including the following:

Monitoring equipment in real time for alerts

Consider a fleet of vehicles equipped with sensors that collect data on various metrics such as speed, temperature, and fuel consumption. The sensor data needs to be analyzed in real time to provide alerts on any outliers to be able to proactively address issues.

Real-time ad placements on websites

Analyzing social media data from multiple platforms, such as Twitter and Facebook, for real-time ad placements or preventing misinformation or obscenity.

Improve the gaming experience

You can focus on in-game conversions, player retention, and optimizing the gaming experience by analyzing real-time data from gamers.

Real-time retail analytics on streaming POS data

You can access and visualize all your global point of sale (POS) retail sales transaction data for real-time analytics, reporting, and visualization.

Amazon Redshift supports loading real-time data using streaming services. You can use either Amazon Kinesis Data Firehose or Kinesis Data Streams independently or use the native integration with Amazon Redshift:

- The first option is to use Kinesis Firehose or Kinesis Data Streams. This involves connecting the stream to Amazon Kinesis Data Firehose and waiting for Kinesis Data Firehose to stage the data in Amazon S3, using various-sized batches at varying-length buffer intervals. After this, Kinesis Data Firehose initiates a COPY command to load the data from Amazon S3. Previously, this usually involved latency in the order of minutes and needed data pipelines on top of the data loaded from the stream. Now, you can ingest data directly from the data stream.

- The second option is native integration with Amazon Kinesis Data Streams or Amazon Managed Streaming for Apache Kafka (MSK) data streams. Natively integrating with Amazon streaming engines, Amazon Redshift streaming ingestion ingests hundreds of MB of data per second so you can query data in near real time. With Amazon Redshift streaming ingestion, you can connect to multiple Amazon Kinesis Data Streams or Amazon MSK data streams and pull data directly to Amazon Redshift without staging data in Amazon S3. Define a scheme or choose to ingest semistructured data with SUPER data type; you can also set up and manage ELT pipelines with SQL.

The native Amazon Redshift streaming ingestion capability allows you to connect to Kinesis Data Streams directly, without the latency and complexity associated with staging the data in Amazon S3 and loading it into the data warehouse. You can now connect to and access the data from the stream using SQL and simplify your data pipelines by creating materialized views directly on top of the stream. The materialized views can also include SQL transforms as part of your ELT pipeline.

After you define the materialized views, you can refresh them to query the most recent stream data. This means that you can perform downstream processing and transformations of streaming data using SQL at no additional cost and use your existing BI and analytics tools for real-time analytics.

Amazon Redshift streaming ingestion works by acting as a stream consumer. A materialized view is the landing area for data that is consumed from the stream. When the materialized view is refreshed, Amazon Redshift compute nodes allocate each data shard to a compute slice. Each slice consumes data from the allocated shards until the materialized view attains parity with the stream. The very first refresh of the materialized view fetches data from the TRIM_HORIZON of the stream. Subsequent refreshes read data from the last SEQUENCE_NUMBER of the previous refresh until it reaches parity with the stream data. Figure 3-12 illustrates this workflow.

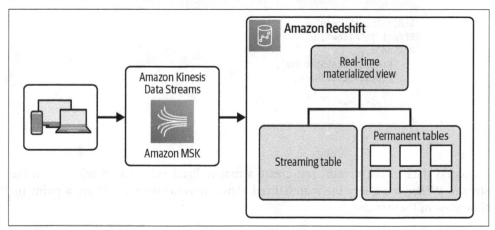

Figure 3-12. Streaming ingestion workflow

Steps to get started with streaming ingestion

The first step is to set up a Kinesis Data Stream as the source for the streaming ingestion pipeline. You can use Kinesis Streams data generator to set up test data as discussed in the blog "Testing Your Streaming Data Solution with the New Amazon Kinesis Data Generator" (*https://oreil.ly/Iz7xC*).

After setting up the data stream, you define a schema in Amazon Redshift with CREATE EXTERNAL SCHEMA to reference a Kinesis Data Streams resource.

```
CREATE EXTERNAL SCHEMA kds
FROM KINESIS
IAM_ROLE { default | 'iam-role-arn' };
```

Create an IAM role as in Example 3-15 with a trust policy that allows your Amazon Redshift data warehouse to assume the role.

Example 3-15. IAM policy that grants access to your stream

```
{
    "Version": "2012-10-17",
    "Statement": [
        {
            "Sid": "ReadStream",
            "Effect": "Allow",
            "Action": [
                "kinesis:DescribeStreamSummary",
                "kinesis:GetShardIterator",
                "kinesis:GetRecords",
                "kinesis:DescribeStream"
            ],
            "Resource": "arn:aws:kinesis:*:0123456789:stream/*"
        },
        {
            "Sid": "ListStream",
            "Effect": "Allow",
            "Action": [
                "kinesis:ListStreams",
                "kinesis:ListShards"
            ],
            "Resource": "*"
        }
    ]
}
```

To access data in the stream, you create a materialized view with a select from the stream. When you query the materialized view, the returned records are a point-in-time view of the stream:

```
CREATE MATERIALIZED VIEW my_view AS
SELECT approximate_arrival_timestamp,
JSON_PARSE(kinesis_data) AS Data
FROM schema_one.my_stream_name
WHERE CAN_JSON_PARSE(kinesis_data)
AUTO REFRESH YES;
```

Next, you refresh the view to do an initial load of data from streams to the materialized view:

```
REFRESH MATERIALIZED VIEW my_view;
```

Now you can query the data from the materialized view using standard SQL statements:

```
SELECT * FROM my_view;
```

 You can store stream records in the semistructured SUPER format or define a schema that results in data converted to Amazon Redshift data types.

For detailed steps to set up a streaming ingestion from Amazon Kinesis Data Streams, refer to "Getting Started with Streaming Ingestion from Amazon Kinesis Data Streams." (*https://oreil.ly/2rhbT*)

Important considerations and best practices

The following are important considerations and best practices for performance and billing as you set up your streaming ingestion environment.

Auto refresh queries for a materialized view or views are treated as any other user workload. Auto refresh loads data from the stream as it arrives.

Auto refresh can be turned on explicitly for a materialized view created for streaming ingestion. To do this, specify AUTO REFRESH in the materialized view definition. Manual refresh is the default. To specify auto refresh for an existing materialized view for streaming ingestion, you can run ALTER MATERIALIZED VIEW to turn it on. For more information, see CREATE MATERIALIZED VIEW (*https://oreil.ly/syJfX*) or ALTER MATERIALIZED VIEW (*https://oreil.ly/UBWgM*).

For Amazon Redshift serverless, the setup and configuration instructions are the same as setting up streaming ingestion on a provisioned cluster. It is important to size Amazon Redshift serverless with the necessary level of RPUs to support streaming ingestion with auto refresh and other workloads.

When you configure streaming ingestion, Amazon Redshift attempts to connect to an Amazon MSK cluster in the same Availability Zone (AZ), if rack awareness is enabled for Amazon MSK. If all of your nodes are in different AZs from your Amazon Redshift data warehouse, you can incur cross-AZ data-transfer cost. To avoid this, keep at least one Amazon MSK broker cluster node in the same AZ as your Amazon Redshift data warehouse.

After creating a materialized view, its initial refresh starts from the TRIM_HORIZON of a Kinesis stream, or from offset 0 of an Amazon MSK topic.

Supported data formats are limited to those that can be converted from VARBYTE. For more information, see VARBYTE type (*https://oreil.ly/MyZiJ*) and VARBYTE operators (*https://oreil.ly/XPn3v*).

It is possible to ingest a stream and land the data into multiple materialized views. For instance, a use case where you ingest a stream containing sports data, but you organize data for each sport into separate materialized views. However, when you ingest data into and refresh multiple materialized views, there can be higher egress costs, as well as bandwidth, throughput, and performance limitations for your streaming provider. Additionally, consider how higher resource use for reading into more than one materialized view can impact other workloads. For these reasons, we recommend you land the data for each stream in a single materialized view. For more information about pricing for data streams, see Kinesis Data Streams Pricing (*https://oreil.ly/wUws2*) and Amazon MSK Pricing (*https://oreil.ly/Lt7KM*).

Optimize Your Data Structures

Traditionally, databases have been built on Symmetric Multiprocessing (SMP) architecture where multiple CPUs access shared memory and disks. This tightly coupled multiprocessor system is unable to scale linearly to meet data growth and keep up with query execution throughput requirements.

These challenges are overcome by MPP architecture. MPP architectures are of two types:

- Shared-disk architectures: here CPU and memory are parallel processing, but the disk is shared.
- Shared-nothing architecture: here CPU, memory as well as disk, all are processing in parallel.

As mentioned earlier in this book, Amazon Redshift is an MPP shared-nothing architecture that achieves linear scalability by processing data on each node using the memory and CPU attached to the node. This architecture achieves massive scale as there is no single executor bottleneck to slow down the system, and adding or removing nodes provides linear scalability. The physical storage of data of a single object or table on individual nodes means MPP systems have distributed or replicated tables and the distribution style plays a crucial role in query performance. Michael Stonebraker, from the University of California, Berkeley, covers The Case for Shared Nothing (*https://oreil.ly/eMiar*) in his paper.

When you create your database objects, certain key table design decisions influence overall query performance. These design choices also have a significant effect on storage requirements, which in turn could affect query performance. The key goal is to reduce the number of I/O operations and minimize the memory required to process queries.

Amazon Redshift automates many of these decisions for you through a combination of "Automatic Table Optimization and Autonomics", however there may be times when you want to fine-tune your environment and set your own "Distribution Style", "Sort Key", or "Compression Encoding".

Automatic Table Optimization and Autonomics

Amazon Redshift uses automatic table optimization (ATO) to choose the right distribution style, sort keys, and encoding when you create a table with AUTO options. Hence it is a good practice to take advantage of the auto feature and create tables with DISTSTYLE AUTO, SORTKEY AUTO, and ENCODING AUTO. When tables are created with AUTO options, Amazon Redshift initially creates tables with optimal keys for the best first-time query performance possible using information such as the primary key and data types. In addition, Amazon Redshift analyzes the data volume and query usage patterns to evolve the distribution strategy and sort keys to optimize performance over time. Finally, Amazon Redshift will perform table maintenance activities on your tables that reduce fragmentation and ensure statistics are up-to-date. We discuss more on the topic of ATO in Chapter 5, "Scaling and Performance Optimizations".

Distribution Style

Since Amazon Redshift is an MPP data warehouse based on compute nodes, the way you distribute the data is important to ensure you utilize the resources optimally for a given workload. When you execute a query, the query optimizer may need to redistribute the rows to the compute nodes to perform any joins. The goal in selecting a table distribution style is to minimize the impact of the redistribution step by locating the data where it needs to be before the query is run to join two or more tables. There are four data distribution strategies: AUTO, EVEN, ALL, and KEY (see Figure 3-13).

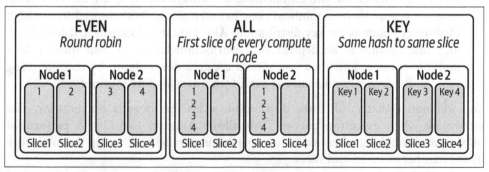

Figure 3-13. Data distribution between compute nodes slices

AUTO *distribution*

As mentioned earlier, using the AUTO keyword means Amazon Redshift uses its built-in AI and ML capabilities, and based on the data volume and query patterns, it performs the best data distribution automatically. This is the preferred distribution for many personas, especially those who might not be well versed with architecture but still need to analyze datasets to obtain business insights.

EVEN *distribution*

In this distribution strategy, the data is stored in round-robin fashion to each slice of your Amazon Redshift data warehouse, so the data is evenly distributed with very minimal skew or imbalance between data volume across slices and nodes. EVEN distribution is best suited for large fact tables, which do not typically participate in joins with other dimension tables. Another good candidate is materialized views, where all the joins have already been executed and results have been captured, and queries mostly only filter rows.

ALL *distribution*

In this distribution strategy, a full copy of the entire table is stored on the first slice of each compute node of your Amazon Redshift data warehouse. It is best suited for dimension tables to facilitate joins with fact tables without requiring data movement across nodes. As you can see, this facilitates faster query execution at the expense of increased storage costs.

KEY *distribution*

In this distribution strategy, the fact table is distributed based off of hash generated on the designated column value, such that all values that result in the same hash are stored on the same slice of your Amazon Redshift data warehouse. This strategy is applied when joining two tables on the same key distributed column. The two tables can be two fact tables, a fact and a dimension table, or a staging and a target table.

KEY distribution allows for co-located join execution as the fact table and corresponding rows of the dimension table are always available on the very same slice. To ensure there is minimal skew between slices, it is required to use high cardinality columns for key distribution. Also note that Amazon Redshift allows only one column to be defined as a distribution key, so if your queries do a multiple column, join then you should create a new column by concatenating those individual column values as part of your data loading routines.

You will notice that in all three distribution styles the focus is on reducing data movement when executing queries. This allows Amazon Redshift to perform at maximum throughput where each slice operates in parallel by dividing the total work by the number of nodes and slices.

Let's take a scenario where you have a sales data warehouse, the `fact_sales` is the largest fact with billions of rows, which is joined very frequently with `dim_customer`, which has tens or hundreds of millions of rows. You then have `dim_calendar`, `dim_product`, and `dim_region`, which have comparatively lower number of records. You also have materialized views for `sales_annual_mv`, `sales_qtrly_mv`, and `sales_monthly_mv` where various measures from the sales fact are preaggregated for dashboards and reports. After analyzing the data in this data warehouse, here are some recommendations for distribution:

- `fact_sales` and `dim_customer` are good candidates for `KEY` distribution on `customer_key` but not on `calendar_key` or `product_key`.
- Other dimensions are good candidates for `ALL` distribution.
- The materialized views are good candidate for `EVEN` distribution.

 Since with Amazon Redshift you can choose only one column as your distribution key, if you import data from a source that has a multicolumn primary/foreign key, you may see that tables are being joined on more than one column. In this scenario, consider creating a new column in your tables with a concatenation of the join columns and use that new column as the distribution key.

Sort Key

Along with how data is distributed among compute node slices, the next aspect is how the data is physically sorted on disk. Amazon Redshift does not have indexes, but sort keys—along with zone maps—provide a similar functionality. Data is stored on disk in sorted order according to the sort key and the query optimizer uses sort order when it determines optimal query plans. Queries will be efficient with fewer I/O operations because they can skip entire blocks that fall outside the time range. The columns that are used as predicates to filter data are good candidates for defining as sort key columns.

Zone maps are the high and low values for each 1 MB block of storage for each column in the table. If the column is already sorted on, then you get nonoverlapping zone maps. These zone maps further reduce I/O by allowing Amazon Redshift to target only those blocks that a query needs to access. Refer to table attributes of the `Create Table` command (*https://oreil.ly/t2Pp8*) for setting up sort keys.

Figure 3-14 illustrates how the blocks of a sales table may be stored in your Amazon Redshift data warehouse. It also shows the zone map for the first 1 MB block of the sales_dt column where the minimum value is 20010523 and the maximum value is 20010527. This header record is scanned first by the query processor to determine if the data in the predicate clause or filter could exist in the block. If the predicate value is outside of the range in the zone map, then Amazon Redshift will skip the entire block and move to the next block. This minimizes the I/O and improves performance of the query.

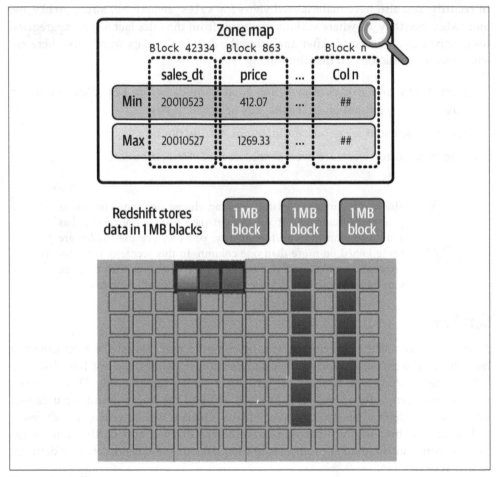

Figure 3-14. Zone maps

In another example, consider a query on the course_outcomes_fact table. You may filter this table on a particular date, say, Jun-09-2012:

```
SELECT count(*)
FROM course_outcomes_fact
WHERE date_registered = '06-09-2017';
```

The query processor is able to skip blocks as shown in Figure 3-15 irrespective of whether the table is sorted or unsorted. On the unsorted table, the processor skips one block and has to scan three out of four blocks based on the MIN/MAX value in the zone map. However, for the sorted table, the processor has to scan only one out of four blocks.

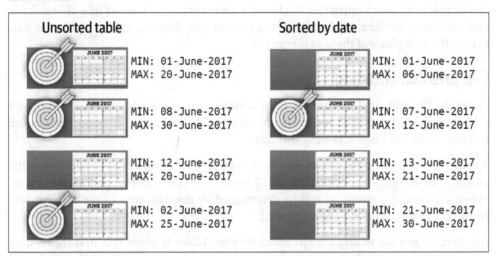

Figure 3-15. Sort key and zone maps

As mentioned previously, we recommend that you create your tables with SORTKEY AUTO to let Amazon Redshift ATO choose the best sort key. In the case of SORTKEY AUTO, Amazon Redshift will analyze the query pattern for your table and apply a sort key, which is used most often in query predicates. By using automation to tune the design of your tables, you can get started more easily and get the fastest performance quickly without needing to invest time to manually tune and implement table optimizations.

When choosing your own sort key, refer to this query (*https://oreil.ly/DIkwX*) as a way to identify predicate columns. It is recommended to have no more than five columns in your sort key. Also, it is recommended to not apply any compression to the first column of the sort key to be able to effectively filter data blocks quickly as it reduces decompression overhead. The compound sort keys are highly effective in filtering data when leading columns are used instead of filtering only on the trailing columns. If you see that a different leading sort key column is equally popular in user queries, then leverage Amazon Redshift materialized views (MV). MVs provide automatic query rewrite, and the query optimizer will pick the appropriate MV instead of a base table.

If you perform frequent range filtering or equality filtering on one column, specify that column as the sort key. In analytics use cases, it is common that data is queried based on components of date and time, and it's a good idea to create the table with a date or timestamp column as the leading column for the sort key.

If you frequently join a table and you don't typically filter on either of the join tables, you can specify the join column as both the sort key and the distribution key. Doing this enables the query optimizer to choose a sort merge join instead of a slower hash join. Because the data is already sorted on the join key, the query optimizer can bypass the sort phase of the sort merge join.

Compression Encoding

Amazon Redshift applies column level compression, also known as encoding, to achieve three to four times compression compared to raw data. This also reduces the I/O requirements when accessing the data.

As mentioned earlier, the easiest way to manage encoding on your Amazon Redshift tables is to leverage the `ENCODING AUTO` option in your `create table` statement. When enabled, the encoding will be determined by the data type of the column and by the heuristics of the data being loaded.

Another option for setting the encoding on your tables is when you first ingest data using a `COPY` command into an empty table. By default, Amazon Redshift will choose the appropriate compression type by either sampling the incoming data or by using the data type of the column. This can be controlled in the `COPY` command using the `COMPUPDATE` parameter. With the `PRESET` option, the compression type will be determined based on data type, `ON` option will sample the dataset, and `OFF` option will not change the compression type. If you reload the same table over and over, you don't have to analyze compression every time. `PRESET` is fast and works well in most scenarios. These options give you control over when and how the compression is determined and can ensure the properties of the table do not change if you are happy with the performance.

In cases where your data profile has changed, it is a good idea to analyze if the compression settings in the table are optimal. You can do this using the `ANALYZE COMPRESSION` command (see Example 3-16). Note that the command can be executed on the entire table or a specific set of columns in the table.

Example 3-16. ANALYZE COMPRESSION command

```
ANALYZE COMPRESSION
[ [ table_name ]
[ ( column_name [, ...] ) ] ]
[COMPROWS numrows]
[Script, SQL]
```

There are several best practices, if implemented, that ensure the most compression:

- If not using AUTO, use the appropriate encodings for your data types. For example, use run-length encoding (RLE) for columns with a high degree of repetition and delta encoding for columns with a high degree of similarity between rows.
- Use the COPY command to load data as it automatically applies encoding parameters.
- Use the VACUUM command to increase compression by reducing fragmentation.
- Monitor the size of your tables and the amount of disk space they are using for opportunities to apply additional compression.
- Avoid encoding small dimension tables because a 1 MB block (per column) can hold a large quantity of data, and in those cases compression will not yield an I/O benefit.
- Use compression for frequently accessed columns.

Summary

This chapter discussed key differences between a Data Lake first approach and a Data Warehouse first approach and scenarios where you can consider either approach. In addition, you created the sample data model and various types of transformation tools and strategies.

The next chapter dives deeper into in-database transformation (ELT) and external transformations (ETL) for data in Amazon Redshift as well as how to query and transform all your data even when the data is not loaded in your data warehouse. We will also discuss strategies for orchestrating your data loads.

CHAPTER 4

Data Transformation Strategies

A recent report published by Forbes (*https://oreil.ly/q-xZU*) describes how some stockbrokers and trading firms were able to access and analyze data faster than their competitors. This allowed them to "execute trades at the best price, microseconds ahead of the crowd. The win was ever so slight in terms of time, but massive in terms of the competitive advantage gained by speed to insight."

When considering an analytics solution, speed to insights is important and the quicker an organization can respond to a shift in their data, the more competitive they will be. In many cases, to get the insights you need, the data needs to be transformed. As briefly discussed in Chapter 3, "Setting Up Your Data Models and Ingesting Data", you can use an ETL approach, which reads the source data, processes the transformations in an external application, and loads the results, or you can use an ELT approach, which uses the data you just loaded and transforms the data in-place using the power of the Amazon Redshift compute.

In this chapter, we'll start by "Comparing ELT and ETL Strategies" to help you decide which data loading strategy to use when building your data warehouse. We'll also dive deep into some of the unique features of Redshift that were built for analytics use cases and that empower "In-Database Transformation" as well as how you can leverage in-built "Scheduling and Orchestration" capabilities to run your pipelines. Then we'll cover how Amazon Redshift takes the ELT strategy even further, by allowing you to "Access All Your Data" even if it was not loaded into Redshift. Finally, we'll cover when it may make sense to use an "External Transformation" strategy and how to use AWS Glue Studio to build your ETL pipelines.

Comparing ELT and ETL Strategies

Regardless of an ELT or ETL strategy, each can support the common goals of your data management platform, which typically involve cleansing, transforming, and aggregating the data for loading into your reporting data model. These are all resource-intensive operations, and the primary difference between the two strategies is where the processing happens: in the compute of your ETL server(s) or in the compute of your data warehouse platform. ETL processes involve reading data from multiple sources and transforming the data using the functions and capabilities of the ETL engine. In contrast, ELT processes also involve extracting data from various sources but first loading it into the data warehouse. The transformation step is performed after the data has been loaded using familiar SQL semantics. Some things to consider when choosing between the two include:

Performance and scalability

ETL processes are dependent on the resources of the ETL server(s) and require platform owners to correctly manage and size the environment. Compute platforms like Spark can be used to parallelize the data transformations and AWS Glue is provided as a serverless option for managing ETL pipelines. ELT processing is performed using the compute resources of the data warehouse. In the case of Amazon Redshift, the power of the MPP architecture is used to perform the transformations. Historically, transforming the data externally was preferred because the processing is offloaded to independent compute. However, modern data warehouse platforms, including Amazon Redshift, scale dynamically and can support mixed workloads, making an ELT strategy more attractive. In addition, since data warehouse platforms are designed to process and transform massive quantities of data using native database functions, ELT jobs tend to perform better. Finally, ELT strategies are free from network bottlenecks, which are required with ETL to move data in and out for processing.

Flexibility

While any transformation code in your data platform should follow a development lifecycle, with an ETL strategy, the code is typically managed by a team with specialized skill in an external application. In contrast, with an ELT strategy, all of your raw data is available to query and transform in the data management platform. Analysts can write code using familiar SQL functions leveraging the skills they already have. Empowering analysts shortens the development lifecycle because they can prototype the code and validate the business logic. The data platform owners would be responsible for optimizing and scheduling the code.

Metadata management and orchestration

One important consideration for your data strategy is how to manage job metadata and orchestration. Leveraging an ELT strategy means that the data platform owner needs to keep track of the jobs, their dependencies, and load schedules.

ETL tools typically have capabilities that capture and organize metadata about sources, targets, and job characteristics as well as data lineage. They also can orchestrate jobs and build dependencies across multiple data platforms.

Ultimately, the choice between ETL and ELT will depend on the specific needs of the analytics workload. Both strategies have strengths and weaknesses, and the decision of which you use depends on the characteristics of the data sources, the transformation requirements, and the performance and scalability needs of the project. To mitigate the challenges with each, many users take a hybrid approach. You can take advantage of the metadata management and orchestration capabilities of ETL tools as well as the performance and scalability of ELT processing by building jobs that translate the ETL code to SQL statements. In "External Transformation" on page 146, we will discuss in more detail how this is possible.

In-Database Transformation

With the variety and velocity of data present today, the challenge of designing a data platform is to make it both scalable and flexible. Amazon Redshift continues to innovate and provide functionality to process all your data in one place with its in-database transformation (ELT) capabilities. Being an ANSI SQL compatible relational database, Amazon Redshift supports SQL commands (*https://oreil.ly/d6v8t*), making it a familiar development environment for most database developers. Amazon Redshift also supports advanced functions present in modern data platforms such as Window Functions (*https://oreil.ly/5I6s6*), HyperLogLog Functions (*https://oreil.ly/cIqsB*), and Recursive CTE (common table expressions) (*https://oreil.ly/rRPCc*), to name a few. In addition to those functions you may be familiar with, Amazon Redshift supports unique capabilities for analytical processing. For example, Amazon Redshift supports in-place querying for "Semistructured Data", providing analysts a way to access this data in a performant way and without waiting for it to be loaded into tables and columns. In addition, if you need to extend the capabilities of Amazon Redshift, you can leverage "User-Defined Functions" that can run inside the database or call external services. Finally, "Stored Procedures" allow you to package your transformation logic. They can return a result set given input parameters or even perform data loading and managed operations like loading a fact, dimension, or aggregate table.

Semistructured Data

Semistructured data falls under the category of data that doesn't conform to a rigid schema expected in relational databases. Semistructured formats are common and often preferred in web logs, sensor data, or API messages because these applications often have to send data with nested relationships, and rather than making multiple round-trips, it is more efficient to send the data once. Semistructured data contains complex values such as arrays and nested structures that are associated with serialization formats, such as JSON. While there are third-party tools you can use to transform your data outside the database, it would require engineering resources to build and maintain that code and may not be as performant. Whether you are accessing "External Amazon S3 Data" or locally loaded data, Amazon Redshift leverages the PartiQL (*https://oreil.ly/9kqbr*) syntax for analyzing and transforming semistructured data. A special data type, SUPER (*https://oreil.ly/oyUbd*), was launched to store this data in its native form. However, when accessed from Amazon S3, it will be cataloged with a data type of struct or array.

In the following example, we're referencing a file that has landed in an Amazon S3 environment. You can catalog this file and make it accessible in Amazon Redshift by creating an external schema and mapping any file that exists in this Amazon S3 prefix to this table definition.

The first query (Example 4-1) finds the total sales revenue per event.

Example 4-1. Create external table from JSON data

```
CREATE external SCHEMA IF NOT EXISTS nested_json
FROM data catalog DATABASE 'nested_json'
IAM_ROLE default
CREATE EXTERNAL DATABASE IF NOT EXISTS;

DROP TABLE IF EXISTS nested_json.nested_json;
CREATE EXTERNAL TABLE nested_json.nested_json (
    c_name varchar,
    c_address varchar,
    c_nationkey int,
    c_phone varchar,
    c_acctbal float,
    c_mktsegment varchar,
    c_comment varchar,
    orders struct<"order":array<struct<
      o_orderstatus:varchar,
      o_totalprice:float,
      o_orderdate:varchar,
      o_order_priority:varchar,
      o_clerk:varchar,
      o_ship_priority:int,
      o_comment:varchar
      >>> )
row format serde 'org.openx.data.jsonserde.JsonSerDe'
with serdeproperties ('paths'='c_name,c_address,c_nationkey,c_phone,
  c_acctbal,c_mktsegment,c_comment,Orders')
stored as inputformat 'org.apache.hadoop.mapred.TextInputFormat'
outputformat 'org.apache.hadoop.hive.ql.io.HiveIgnoreKeyTextOutputFormat'
location 's3://redshift-immersionday-labs/data/nested-json/';
```

This data file is located in the us-west-2 region, and this example will work only if your Amazon Redshift data warehouse is also in that region. Also, we've referenced the `default` IAM role. Be sure to modify the role to allow read access to this Amazon S3 location as well as to have access to manage the AWS Glue Data Catalog.

Now that the table is available, it can be queried and you can access top-level attributes without any special processing (Example 4-2).

Example 4-2. Top-level attributes

```
SELECT cust.c_name,
  cust.c_nationkey,
  cust.c_address
FROM nested_json.nested_json cust
WHERE cust.c_nationkey = '-2015'
  AND cust.c_address like '%E12';
```

Using the PartiQL syntax, you can access the nested `struct` data. In Example 4-3, we are un-nesting the data in the `orders` field and showing the multiple orders associated to the customer record.

Example 4-3. Un-nested attributes (external)

```
SELECT cust.c_name,
    cust_order.o_orderstatus,
    cust_order.o_totalprice,
    cust_order.o_orderdate::date,
    cust_order.o_order_priority,
    cust_order.o_clerk,
    cust_order.o_ship_priority,
    cust_order.o_comment
FROM nested_json.nested_json cust,
    cust.orders.order cust_order
WHERE cust.c_nationkey = '-2015'
  AND cust.c_address like '%E12';
```

In addition to accessing data in S3, this semistructured data can be loaded into your Amazon Redshift table using the SUPER data type. In Example 4-4, this same file is loaded into a physical table. One notable difference when loading into Amazon Redshift is that no information about the schema of the `orders` column mapped to the SUPER data type is required. This simplifies the loading and metadata management process as well as provides flexibility in case of metadata changes.

Example 4-4. Create local table from JSON data

```
DROP TABLE IF EXISTS nested_json_local;
CREATE TABLE nested_json_local (
    c_name varchar,
    c_address varchar,
    c_nationkey int,
    c_phone varchar,
    c_acctbal float,
    c_mktsegment varchar,
    c_comment varchar,
    orders SUPER);

COPY nested_json_local
from 's3://redshift-immersionday-labs/data/nested-json/'
IAM_ROLE default REGION 'us-west-2'
JSON 'auto ignorecase';
```

 We've referenced the `default` IAM role. Be sure to modify the role to grant access to read from this Amazon S3 location.

Now that the table is available, it can be queried. Using the same PartiQL syntax, you can access the order details (Example 4-5).

Example 4-5. Unnested attributes (local)

```
SET enable_case_sensitive_identifier TO true;
SELECT cust.c_name,
    cust_order.o_orderstatus,
    cust_order.o_totalprice,
    cust_order.o_orderdate::date,
    cust_order.o_order_priority,
    cust_order.o_clerk,
    cust_order.o_ship_priority,
    cust_order.o_comment
FROM nested_json_local cust,
    cust.orders."Order" cust_order
WHERE cust.c_nationkey = '-2015'
  AND cust.c_address like '%E12';
```

 The `enable_case_sensitive_identifier` is an important parameter when querying SUPER data if your input has mixed case identifiers. For more information, see the online documentation (*https://oreil.ly/Ou8HU*).

For more details and examples on querying semistructured data, see the online documentation (*https://oreil.ly/YjliK*).

User-Defined Functions

If a built-in function is not available for your specific transformation needs, Amazon Redshift has a few options for extending the functionality of the platform. Amazon Redshift allows you to create *scalar user-defined functions* (UDFs) in three flavors: SQL, Python, and Lambda. For detailed documentation on creating each of these types of functions, see the online documentation (*https://oreil.ly/VO8gm*).

> A scalar function will return exactly one value per invocation. In most cases, you can think of this as returning one value per row.

An SQL UDF leverages existing SQL syntax. It can be used to ensure consistent logic is applied and to simplify the amount of code each user would have to write individually. In Example 4-6, from the Amazon Redshift UDFs GitHub Repo (*https://oreil.ly/Rd33u*), you'll see an SQL function that takes two input parameters; the first varchar field is the data to be masked, and the second field is the classification of the data. The result is a different masking strategy based on the data classification.

Example 4-6. SQL UDF definition

```
CREATE OR REPLACE function f_mask_varchar (varchar, varchar)
  returns varchar
immutable
AS $$
  SELECT case $2
    WHEN 'ssn' then
      substring($1, 1, 7)||'xxxx'
    WHEN 'email' then
      substring(SPLIT_PART($1, '@', 1), 1, 3) + 'xxxx@' + SPLIT_PART($1, '@', 2)
    ELSE substring($1, 1, 3)||'xxxxx' end
$$ language sql;
```

Users can reference an SQL UDF within a SELECT statement. In this scenario, you might write the SELECT statement as shown in Example 4-7.

Example 4-7. SQL UDF access

```
SELECT
  f_mask_varchar (name, NULL) mask_name, name,
  f_mask_varchar (email, 'email') mask_email, email,
  f_mask_varchar (ssn, 'ssn') mask_ssn, ssn
FROM Customer;
```

The SELECT statement in Example 4-7 results in the following output:

mask_name	name	mask_email	email	mask_ssn	ssn
Janxxxxx	Jane Doe	jdoxxxx@org.com	jdoe@org.com	123-45-xxxx	123-45-6789

A Python UDF allows users to leverage Python code to transform their data. In addition to core Python libraries, users can import their own libraries to extend the functionality available in Amazon Redshift. In Example 4-8, from the Amazon Redshift UDFs GitHub Repo (*https://oreil.ly/d_ief*), you'll see a Python function that leverages an external library, ua_parser, which can parse a user-agent string into a JSON object and return the client OS family.

Example 4-8. Python UDF definition

```
CREATE OR REPLACE FUNCTION f_ua_parser_family (ua VARCHAR)
RETURNS VARCHAR IMMUTABLE AS $$
  FROM ua_parser import user_agent_parser
  RETURN user_agent_parser.ParseUserAgent(ua)['family']
$$ LANGUAGE plpythonu;
```

Similar to SQL UDFs, users can reference a Python UDF within a SELECT statement. In this example, you might write the SELECT statement shown in Example 4-9.

Example 4-9. Python UDF access

```
SELECT f_ua_parser_family (agent) family, agent FROM weblog;
```

The SELECT statement in Example 4-9 results in the following output:

family	agent
Chrome	Mozilla/5.0 (Macintosh; Intel Mac OS X 10_9_4) AppleWebKit/537.36 (KHTML, like Gecko) Chrome/41.0.2272.104 Safari/537.36

Lastly, the Lambda UDF allows users to interact and integrate with external components outside of Amazon Redshift. You can write Lambda UDFs in any supported programming language, such as Java, Go PowerShell, Node.js, C#, Python, Ruby, or a custom runtime. This functionality enables new Amazon Redshift use cases, including data enrichment from external data stores (e.g., Amazon DynamoDB, Amazon ElastiCache, etc.), data enrichment from external APIs (e.g., Melissa Global Address Web API, etc.), data masking and tokenization from external providers (e.g., Protegrity), and conversion of legacy UDFs written in other languages such as C, C++, and Java. In Example 4-10, from the Amazon Redshift UDFs GitHub Repo (*https://oreil.ly/pll2W*), you'll see a Lambda function that leverages the AWS Key Management Service (KMS) and takes an incoming string to return the encrypted value. The first code block establishes a Lambda function, f-kms-encrypt, which expects a nested array of arguments passed to the function. In this example, the user would supply the kmskeyid and the columnValue as input parameters; argument[0] and argument[1]. The function will use the boto3 library to call the kms service to return the encrypted response.

Example 4-10. Lambda function definition

```
import json, boto3, os, base64
kms = boto3.client('kms')
def handler(event, context):
  ret = dict()
  res = []
  for argument in event['arguments']:
    try:
      kmskeyid = argument[0]
      columnValue = argument[1]
      if (columnValue == None):
          response = None
      else:
          ciphertext = kms.encrypt(KeyId=kmskeyid, Plaintext=columnValue)
          cipherblob = ciphertext["CiphertextBlob"]
          response = base64.b64encode(cipherblob).decode('utf-8')
      res.append(response)
    except Exception as e:
      print (str(e))
      res.append(None)
  ret['success'] = True
  ret['results'] = res
  return json.dumps(ret)
```

The next code block establishes the Amazon Redshift UDF, which references the Lambda function (Example 4-11).

Example 4-11. Lambda UDF definition

```
CREATE OR REPLACE EXTERNAL FUNCTION f_kms_encrypt (key varchar, value varchar)
RETURNS varchar(max) STABLE
LAMBDA 'f-kms-encrypt'
IAM_ROLE default;
```

We've referenced the `default` IAM role. Be sure to modify the role to grant access to execute the Lambda function created previously.

Just like the SQL and Python UDFs, users can reference a Lambda UDF within a `SELECT` statement. In this scenario, you might write the `SELECT` statement show in Example 4-12.

Example 4-12. Lambda UDF access

```
SELECT f_kms_encrypt (email) email_encrypt, email FROM customer;
```

The `SELECT` statement in Example 4-12 results in the following output:

email_encrypt	email
AQICAHiQbIJ478Gbu8DZyl0frUxOrbgDIP+CyfuWCuF0kHJyWg …	jdoe@org.com

For more details on Python UDFs, see the "Introduction to Python UDFs in Amazon Redshift" blog post (*https://oreil.ly/aX77w*), and for more details on Lambda UDFs, see the "Accessing External Components Using Amazon Redshift Lambda UDFs" blog post (*https://oreil.ly/cEeQH*).

Stored Procedures

An Amazon Redshift stored procedure is a user-created object to perform a set of SQL queries and logical operations. The procedure is stored in the database and is available to users who have privileges to execute it. Unlike a scalar UDF function, which can operate on only one row of data in a table, a *stored procedure* can incorporate data definition language (DDL) and data manipulation language (DML) in addition to `SELECT` queries. Also, a stored procedure doesn't have to return a value and can contain looping and conditional expressions.

Stored procedures are commonly used to encapsulate logic for data transformation, data validation, and business-specific operations as an alternative to shell scripting, or complex ETL and orchestration tools. Stored procedures allow the ETL/ELT logical steps to be fully enclosed in a procedure. You may write the procedure to commit data incrementally or so that it either succeeds completely (processes all rows) or fails completely (processes no rows). Because all the processing occurs on the data warehouse, there is no overhead to move data across the network and you can take advantage of Amazon Redshift's ability to perform bulk operations on large quantities of data quickly because of its MPP architecture.

In addition, because stored procedures are implemented in the PL/pgSQL programming language, you may not need to learn a new programming language to use them. In fact, you may have existing stored procedures in your legacy data platform that can be migrated to Amazon Redshift with minimal code changes. Re-creating the logic of your existing processes using an external programming language or a new ETL platform could be a large project. AWS also provides the AWS Schema Conversion Tool (SCT) (*https://oreil.ly/h0Tn-*), a migration assistant that can help by converting existing code in other database programming languages to Amazon Redshift native PL/pgSQL code.

In Example 4-13, you can see a simple procedure that will load data into a staging table from Amazon S3 and load new records into the `lineitem` table, while ensuring that duplicates are deleted. This procedure takes advantage of the `MERGE` operator and can accomplish the task using one statement. In this example, there are constant variables for the `l_orderyear` and `l_ordermonth`. However, this can be easily made dynamic using the `date_part` function and `current_date` variable to determine the current year and month to load or by passing in a `year` and `month` parameter to the procedure.

Example 4-13. Stored procedure definition

```
CREATE OR REPLACE PROCEDURE lineitem_incremental()
AS $$
DECLARE
  yr CONSTANT INTEGER := 1998; --date_part('year',current_date);
  mon CONSTANT INTEGER := 8; --date_part('month', current_date);
  query VARCHAR;
BEGIN
  TRUNCATE stage_lineitem;
  query := 'COPY stage_lineitem ' ||
        'FROM ''s3://redshift-immersionday-labs/data/lineitem-part/' ||
          'l_orderyear=' || yr || '/l_ordermonth=' || mon || '/''' ||
    ' IAM_ROLE default REGION ''us-west-2'' gzip delimiter ''|''';
  EXECUTE query;

  MERGE INTO lineitem
  USING stage_lineitem s ON s.l_orderkey=lineitem.l_orderkey
  AND s.l_linenumber = lineitem.l_linenumber
  WHEN MATCHED THEN DELETE
  WHEN NOT MATCHED THEN INSERT
    VALUES ( s.L_ORDERKEY, s.L_PARTKEY, s.L_SUPPKEY, s.L_LINENUMBER,
      s.L_QUANTITY, s.L_EXTENDEDPRICE, s.L_DISCOUNT, s.L_TAX,
      s.L_RETURNFLAG, s.L_LINESTATUS, s.L_SHIPDATE, s.L_COMMITDATE,
      s.L_RECEIPTDATE, s.L_SHIPINSTRUCT, s.L_SHIPMODE, s.L_COMMENT);

END;
$$ LANGUAGE plpgsql;
```

We've referenced the default IAM role. Be sure to modify the role to grant access to read from this Amazon S3 location.

You can execute a stored procedure by using the call keyword (Example 4-14).

Example 4-14. Stored procedure access

```
CALL lineitem_incremental();
```

For more details on Amazon Redshift stored procedures, see the "Bringing Your Stored Procedures to Amazon Redshift" (*https://oreil.ly/z3RUq*) blog post.

Scheduling and Orchestration

When you start to think about orchestrating your data pipeline, you want to consider the complexity of the workflow and the dependencies on external processes. Some users have to manage multiple systems with complex dependencies. You may have advanced notification requirements if a job fails or misses an SLA. If so, you may consider a third-party scheduling tool. Popular third-party enterprise job scheduling tools include Tivoli (*https://oreil.ly/c0QVz*), Control-M (*https://oreil.ly/eEY_P*), and AutoSys (*https://oreil.ly/fVA8y*), which each have integrations with Amazon Redshift allowing you to initiate a connection and execute one or multiple SQL statements. AWS also offers the Amazon Managed Workflow orchestration for Apache Airflow (MWAA) (*https://oreil.ly/eRpJA*) service, which is based on the open source Apache Airflow (*https://airflow.apache.org*) project. This can be useful if you are already running an Apache Airflow workflow and would like to migrate it to the cloud.

However, if you can trigger your loads based on time-based triggers, you can leverage the query scheduler. When you're using the query scheduler, the UI will leverage the foundational services of the Amazon Redshift Data API and EventBridge.

To use the query scheduler to trigger simple time-based queries, navigate to the Query Editor V2 (*https://oreil.ly/OfaXg*), prepare your query, and click the Schedule button (Figure 4-1). For this example, we will use a COPY statement to load the stage_lineitem table.

Set the connection (Figure 4-2) as well as the IAM role the scheduler will assume to execute the query. In the subsequent dialog, select the applicable Amazon Redshift data warehouse from the list and the corresponding account and region. In our case, we will use "Temporary credentials" to connect. See Chapter 2, "Getting Started with Amazon Redshift" for more details on other connection strategies.

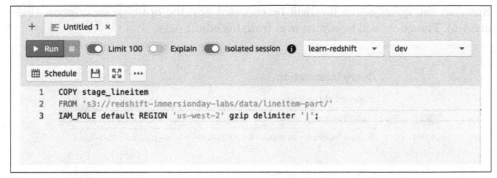

Figure 4-1. Schedule button

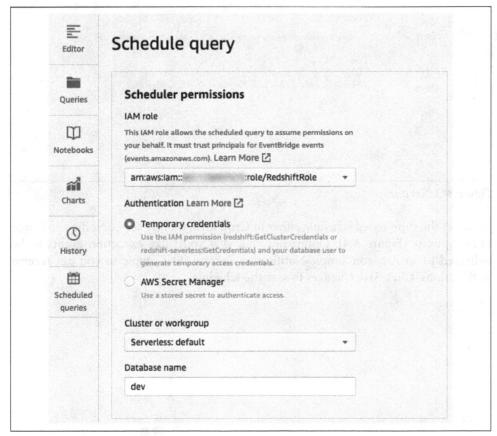

Figure 4-2. Choose connection

Next, set the query name that will be executed and the optional description (Figure 4-3). The query will be copied over from the editor page.

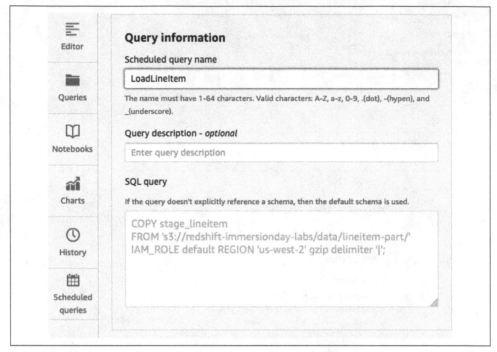

Figure 4-3. Set query

Next, set the time-based schedule either in Cron format or by selecting the applicable radio options (Figure 4-4). Optionally, choose if you'd like execution events to be delivered to an Amazon Simple Notification Service (SNS) topic so you can receive notifications. Click Save Changes to save the schedule.

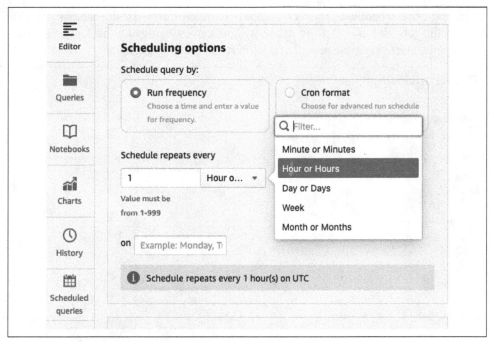

Figure 4-4. Set schedule

To see the list of scheduled queries, navigate to the Scheduled queries page (*https://oreil.ly/jvCFh*) of the Query Editor V2 (Figure 4-5).

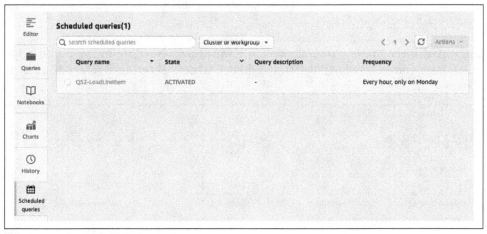

Figure 4-5. List scheduled queries

To manage the scheduled job, click on the scheduled query. In this screen you can modify the job, deactivate it, or delete it. You can also inspect the history, which contains the start/stop time as well as the job status (see Figure 4-6).

QS2-LoadLineItem

General information

Cluster or workgroup	default	SNS topic	-	IAM role	RedshiftRole [↗]	
Database name	dev	State	ACTIVATED	Authentication	temporary credentials	
Query description						

Schedule history

🔍 Search scheduled history

ID	Start time	End time	Query status

No query run history
Your query run history appear here after you execute a query.

Query statement

```
1   COPY stage_lineitem
2   FROM 's3://redshift-immersionday-labs/data/lineitem-part/'
3   IAM_ROLE default REGION 'us-west-2' gzip delimiter '|';
```

Figure 4-6. See schedule history

You can also see the resources created in EventBridge. Navigate to the EventBridge Rules page (*https://oreil.ly/Phb4H*) and notice a new Scheduled rule was created (Figure 4-7).

Amazon EventBridge > Rules > QS2-LoadLineItem

QS2-LoadLineItem

[Edit] [Disable] [Delete] [CloudFormation Template ▼]

Rule details Info

Rule name	Status	Event bus name	Type
QS2-LoadLineItem	⊘ Enabled	default	Scheduled Standard
Description	Rule ARN	Event bus ARN	
	🗂 arn:aws:events:us-east-2:048474	🗂 arn:aws:events:us-east-2:048474	
	525513:rule/QS2-LoadLineItem	525513:event-bus/default	

Figure 4-7. Scheduled rule

Inspecting the rule target (Figure 4-8), you will see `Redshift cluster` target type along with the parameter needed to execute the query.

Figure 4-8. Scheduled rule target

Access All Your Data

To complete the ELT story, Amazon Redshift supports access to data even if it was not loaded. The Amazon Redshift compute will process your data using all the transformation capabilities already mentioned without the need of a separate server for processing. Whether it is "External Amazon S3 Data", "External Operational Data", or even "External Amazon Redshift Data", queries are submitted in your Amazon Redshift data warehouse using familiar ANSI SQL syntax; only the applicable data is processed by the Amazon Redshift compute. It can be joined to local data and used to populate tables local to your Amazon Redshift data warehouse.

External Amazon S3 Data

Amazon Redshift enables you to read and write external data that is stored in Amazon S3 using simple SQL queries. Accessing data on Amazon S3 enhances the interoperability of your data because you can access the same Amazon S3 data from multiple compute platforms beyond Amazon Redshift. Such platforms include Amazon Athena, Amazon EMR, Presto, and any other compute platform that can access Amazon S3. Using this feature Amazon Redshift can join external Amazon S3 tables with tables that reside on the local disk of your Amazon Redshift data warehouse. When using a provisioned cluster, Amazon Redshift will leverage a fleet of nodes called Amazon Redshift Spectrum, which further isolates the Amazon S3 processing and applies optimizations like predicate pushdown and aggregation to the Amazon Redshift Spectrum compute layer, improving query performance. Types of predicate operators you can push to Amazon Redshift Spectrum include: =, `LIKE`, `IS NULL`, and `CASE WHEN`. In addition, you can employ transformation logic where many aggregation and string functions are pushed to the Amazon Redshift Spectrum layer. Types of aggregate functions include: COUNT, SUM, AVG, MIN, and MAX.

Amazon Redshift Spectrum processes Amazon S3 data using compute up to 10 times the number of slices in your provisioned cluster. It also comes with a cost of $5/TB scanned. In contrast, when you query Amazon S3 data using Amazon Redshift serverless, the processing occurs on your Amazon Redshift compute and the cost is part of RPU pricing.

Querying external Amazon S3 data works by leveraging an external metadata catalog that organizes datasets into databases and tables. You then map a database to an Amazon Redshift schema and provide credentials via an IAM ROLE, which determines what level of access you have. In Example 4-15, your metadata catalog is the AWS Glue data catalog, which contains a database called externaldb. If that database doesn't exist, this command will create it. We've mapped that database to a new schema, externalschema, using the default IAM role attached to the data warehouse. In addition to the AWS Glue data catalog, users may map to a hive metastore if your data is located in an EMR cluster or in a self-managed Apache Hadoop environment. For more details on options when creating external schema, see the online documentation (*https://oreil.ly/FtiZ-*).

Example 4-15. Create external S3 schema

```
CREATE EXTERNAL SCHEMA IF NOT EXISTS externalschema
FROM data catalog DATABASE 'externaldb'
IAM_ROLE default
CREATE EXTERNAL DATABASE IF NOT EXISTS;
```

We've referenced the default IAM role. Be sure to modify the role to have access to manage the AWS Glue Data Catalog.

Once the external schema is created, you can easily query the data similar to a table that was loaded into Amazon Redshift. In Example 4-16, you can query data from your external table joined with data that is stored locally.

Example 4-16. External S3 table access

```
SELECT
 t.returnflag,
 t.linestatus,
 c.zip,
 sum(t.quantity) AS sum_qty,
 sum(t.extendedprice*(1-t.discount)*(1+t.tax)) AS sum_charge
FROM externalschema.transactions t
JOIN public.customers c on c.id = t.customer_id
WHERE t.year = 2022 AND t.month = 1
GROUP BY t.returnflag, t.linestatus, c.zip;
```

This query has a filter that restricts the data from the external table to January 2022 and a simple aggregation. When using a provisioned cluster, this filter and partial aggregation will be processed at the Amazon Redshift Spectrum layer, reducing the amount of data sent to your compute nodes and improving the query performance.

Because you'll get the best performance when querying data that is stored locally in Amazon Redshift, it is a best practice to have your most recent data loaded in Amazon Redshift and query less frequently accessed data from external sources. By following this strategy, you can ensure the hottest data is stored closest to the compute and in a format that is optimized for analytical processing. In Example 4-17, you may have a load process that populates the transaction table with the latest month of data but have all of your data in Amazon S3. When exposed to your users, they will see a consolidated view of the data, but when they access the hottest data, Amazon Redshift will retrieve it from local storage.

Example 4-17. Union S3 and local data

```
CREATE VIEW public.transactions_all AS
  SELECT … FROM public.transactions
  UNION ALL
  SELECT … FROM externalschema.transactions
  WHERE year != date_part(YEAR, current_date)
    AND month != date_part(MONTH, current_date);
WITH NO SCHEMA BINDING;
```

The clause `NO SCHEMA BINDING` must be used for external tables to ensure that data can be loaded in Amazon S3 without any impact or dependency on Amazon Redshift.

For more details on Amazon Redshift Spectrum optimization techniques, see the Amazon Redshift Spectrum best practices blog (*https://oreil.ly/A1_Xz*).

External Operational Data

Amazon Redshift federated query enables you to directly query data stored in transactional databases for real-time data integration and simplified ETL processing. Using federated query, you can provide real-time insights to your users. A typical use case is when you have a batch ingestion to your data warehouse, but you have a requirement for real-time analytics. You can provide a combined view of the data loaded in batch from Amazon Redshift, and the current real-time data in transactional database. Federated query also exposes the metadata from these source databases as external tables, allowing BI tools like Tableau and Amazon QuickSight to query federated sources. This enables new data warehouse use cases where you can seamlessly query operational data, simplify ETL pipelines, and build data into a late-binding view combining operational data with Amazon Redshift local data. As of 2022, the transactional databases supported include Amazon Aurora PostgreSQL/MySQL and Amazon RDS for PostgreSQL/MySQL.

Amazon Redshift federated query works by making a TCP/IP connection to your operational data store and mapping that to an external schema. You provide the database type and connection information as well as the connection credentials via an AWS Secrets Manager secret. In Example 4-18, the database type is POSTGRES with the connection information specifying the DATABASE, SCHEMA, and URI of the DB. For more details on options when creating external schema using federated query, see the online documentation (*https://oreil.ly/zhWJR*).

Example 4-18. Create external schema

```
CREATE EXTERNAL SCHEMA IF NOT EXISTS federatedschema
FROM POSTGRES DATABASE 'db1' SCHEMA 'pgschema'
URI '<rdsname>.<hashkey>.<region>.rds.amazonaws.com'
SECRET_ARN 'arn:aws:secretsmanager:us-east-1:123456789012:secret:pgsecret'
IAM_ROLE default;
```

 We've referenced the default IAM role. Be sure to modify the role to grant access to use Secrets Manager to retrieve a secret named pgsecret.

Once the external schema is created, you can query the tables as you would query a local Amazon Redshift table. In Example 4-19, you can query data from your external table joined with data that is stored locally, similar to the query executed when querying external Amazon S3 data. The query also has a filter that restricts the data from the federated table to January 2022. Amazon Redshift federated query intelligently pushes down predicates to restrict the amount of data scanned from the federated source, greatly improving query performance.

Example 4-19. External table access

```
SELECT
  t.returnflag,
  t.linestatus,
  c.zip,
  sum(t.quantity) AS sum_qty,
  sum(t.extendedprice*(1-t.discount)*(1+t.tax)) AS sum_charge
FROM federatedschema.transactions t
JOIN public.customers c ON c.id = t.customer_id
WHERE t.year = 2022 AND t.month = 1
GROUP by t.returnflag, t.linestatus, c.zip;
```

 Since federated query executes queries on the transactional system, be careful to limit the data queried. A good practice is to use data in Amazon Redshift local tables for historical data and access only the latest data in the federated database.

In addition to querying live data, federated query opens up opportunities to simplify ETL processes. A common ETL pattern many organizations use when building their data warehouse is `upsert`. An `upsert` is when data engineers are tasked with scanning the source of your data warehouse table and determining if it should have new records inserted or existing records updated/deleted. In the past, that was accomplished in multiple steps:

1. Creating a full extract of your source table, or if your source has change tracking, extracting those records since the last time the load was processed.

2. Moving that extract to a location local to your data warehouse. In the case of Amazon Redshift, that would be Amazon S3.

3. Using a bulk loader to load that data into a staging table. In the case of Amazon Redshift, that would be the `COPY` command.

4. Executing `MERGE` (`UPSERT`—`UPDATE` and `INSERT`) commands against your target table based on the data that was staged.

With federated query, you can bypass the need for incremental extracts in Amazon S3 and the subsequent load via `COPY` by querying the data in place within its source database. In Example 4-20, we've shown how the customer table can be synced from the operational source by using a single `MERGE` statement.

Example 4-20. Incremental update with MERGE

```
MERGE INTO customer
USING federatedschema.customer p ON p.customer_id = customer.customer_id
  AND p.updatets > current_date-1 and p.updatets < current_date
WHEN MATCHED THEN UPDATE SET customer_id = p.customer_id,
  name = p.name, address = p.address,
  nationkey = p.nationkey, mktsegment = p.mktsegment
WHEN NOT MATCHED THEN INSERT (custkey, name, address, nationkey, mktsegment)
  VALUES ( p.customer_id, p.name, p.address, p.nationkey, p.mktsegment )
```

For more details on federated query optimization techniques, see the blog post "Best Practices for Amazon Redshift Federated Query" (*https://oreil.ly/fhtqi*), and for more details on other ways you can simplify your ETL strategy, see the blog post "Build a Simplified ETL and Live Data Query Solution Using Amazon Redshift Federated Query" (*https://oreil.ly/wYhtm*).

External Amazon Redshift Data

Amazon Redshift data sharing enables you to directly query live data stored in the Amazon RMS of another Amazon Redshift data warehouse, whether it is a provisioned cluster using the RA3 node type or a serverless data warehouse. This functionality enables data produced in one Amazon Redshift data warehouse to be accessible in another Amazon Redshift data warehouse. Similar to other external data sources, the data sharing functionality also exposes the metadata from the producer Amazon Redshift data warehouse as external tables, allowing the consumer to query that data without having to make local copies. This enables new data warehouse use cases such as distributing the ownership of the data and isolating the execution of different workloads. In Chapter 7, "Collaboration with Data Sharing", we'll go into more detail on these use cases. In the following example, you'll learn how to configure a datashare using SQL statement and how it can be used in your ETL/ELT processes. For more details on how you can enable and configure data sharing from the Redshift console, see the online documentation (*https://oreil.ly/3DCQT*).

The first step in data sharing is to understand the namespace of your producer and consumer data warehouses. Execute the following on each data warehouse to retrieve the corresponding values (Example 4-21).

Example 4-21. Current namespace

```
SELECT current_namespace;
```

Next, create a datashare object and add database objects such as a `schema` and `table` in the producer data warehouse (Example 4-22).

Example 4-22. Create datashare

```
CREATE DATASHARE transactions_datashare;
ALTER DATASHARE transactions_datashare
  ADD SCHEMA transactions_schema;
ALTER DATASHARE transactions_datashare
  ADD ALL TABLES IN SCHEMA transactions_schema;
```

You can now grant the datashare access from the producer to the consumer by referencing its `namespace` (Example 4-23).

Example 4-23. Grant datashare usage

```
GRANT USAGE ON DATASHARE transactions_datashare
TO NAMESPACE '1m137c4-1187-4bf3-8ce2-CONSUMER-NAMESPACE';
```

Lastly, you create a database on the consumer, referencing the datashare name as well as the `namespace` of the producer (Example 4-24).

Example 4-24. Create datashare database

```
CREATE DATABASE transactions_database from DATASHARE transactions_datashare
OF NAMESPACE '45b137c4-1287-4vf3-8cw2-PRODUCER-NAMESPACE';
```

 Datashares can also be granted across accounts. In this scenario, an additional step is required by the administrator associated with the datashare. See the online documentation (*https://oreil.ly/072-D*) for more information.

Once the external database is created, you can easily query the data as you would a table that was local to your Amazon Redshift data warehouse. In Example 4-25, you're querying data from your external table joined with data that is stored locally, similar to the query executed when using external Amazon S3 and operational data. Similarly, the query has a filter that restricts the data from the external table to January 2022.

Example 4-25. Datashare access

```
SELECT
 t.returnflag,
 t.linestatus,
 c.zip,
```

```
 sum(t.quantity) as sum_qty,
 sum(t.extendedprice*(1-t.discount)*(1+t.tax)) as sum_charge
FROM transactions_database.transcations_schema.transactions t
JOIN public.customers c on c.id = t.customer_id
WHERE t.year = 2022 AND t.month = 1
GROUP by t.returnflag, t.linestatus, c.zip;
```

You can imagine a setup where one department may be responsible for managing sales transactions and another department is responsible for customer relations. The customer relations department is interested in determining their best and worst customers to send targeted marketing to. Instead of needing to maintain a single data warehouse and share resources, each department can leverage their own Amazon Redshift data warehouse and be responsible for their own data. Instead of duplicating the transaction data, the customer relations group can query it directly. They can build and maintain an aggregate of that data and join it with data they have on previous marketing initiatives as well as customer sentiment data to construct their marketing campaign.

Read more about data sharing in "Sharing Amazon Redshift Data Securely Across Amazon Redshift Clusters for Workload Isolation" (*https://oreil.ly/UOfaa*) and "Amazon Redshift Data Sharing Best Practices and Considerations" (*https://oreil.ly/jf1Mu*).

External Transformation

In scenarios where you want to use an external tool for your data transformations, Amazon Redshift can connect to an ETL platform of your choice using JDBC and ODBC drivers either packaged with those applications or which can be downloaded. Popular ETL platforms that integrate with Amazon Redshift include third-party tools like Informatica (*https://www.informatica.com*), Matillion (*https://www.matillion.com*), and dbt (*https://www.getdbt.com*) as well as AWS-native tools like "AWS Glue". ETL tools are a valuable way to manage all the components of your data pipeline. They provide a job repository to organize and maintain metadata, making it easier for organizations to manage their code instead of storing that logic in SQL scripts and stored procedures. They also have scheduling capabilities to facilitate job orchestration, which can be useful if you are not using the "Scheduling and Orchestration" available natively in AWS.

Some ETL tools also have the ability to "push down" the transformation logic. In the case where you may be reading and writing from your Amazon Redshift data warehouse, you can design your job using the visual capabilities of the ETL tool, but instead of actually extracting the data to the compute of the ETL server(s), the code is converted into SQL statements that run on Amazon Redshift. This strategy can be very performant when transforming high quantities of data, but can also consume a lot of resources that your end users may need for analyzing data. When you are not using the push-down capabilities of your ETL tool, either because your job is not reading and writing to Amazon Redshift or because you've decided you want to offload the transformation logic, it's important to ensure that your ETL tool is reading and writing data from Amazon Redshift in a performant way.

As discussed in Chapter 3, "Setting Up Your Data Models and Ingesting Data", the most performant way to load data is to use the COPY statement. Because of the partnership between AWS and ETL vendors like Informatica and Matillion, AWS has ensured that vendors have built connectors with this strategy in mind. For example, in the Informatica Amazon Redshift architecture in Figure 4-9, you can see that if you have specified an Amazon Redshift target and a staging area in Amazon S3, instead of directly loading the target via an insert, the tool will instead write to Amazon S3 and then use the Amazon Redshift COPY statement to load into the target table. This same strategy also works for update and delete statements, except instead of directly loading the target table, Informatica will write to a staging table and perform postload update and delete statements. This optimization is possible because AWS partners with multiple software vendors to ensure that users easily leverage the tool and ensure their data pipelines are performant. See the following guides, which have been published for more details on best practices when using some of the popular third-party ETL tools:

- Informatica—Amazon Redshift Connector Best Practices (*https://oreil.ly/CX57A*)
- Matillion—Amazon Redshift Best Practices for ETL Processing (*https://oreil.ly/0jRs2*)
- dbt—Best Practices for Leveraging Amazon Redshift and dbt (*https://oreil.ly/mRYaI*)

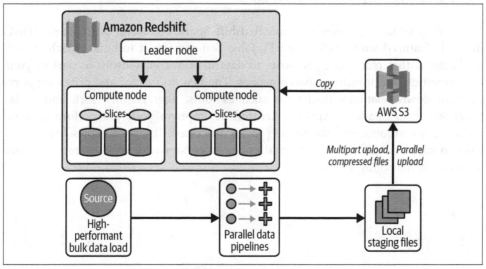

Figure 4-9. Informatica Amazon Redshift architecture

AWS Glue

AWS Glue is one of the native serverless data integration services commonly used to transform data using Python or Scala language and run on a data processing engine. With AWS Glue (Figure 4-10), you can read Amazon S3 data, apply transformations, and ingest data into Amazon Redshift data warehouses as well other data platforms. AWS Glue makes it easier to discover, prepare, move, and integrate data from multiple sources for analytics, ML, and application development. It offers multiple data integration engines, which include AWS Glue for Apache Spark, AWS Glue for Ray, and AWS Glue for Python Shell. You can use the appropriate engine for your workload, based on the characteristics of your workload and the preferences of your developers and analysts.

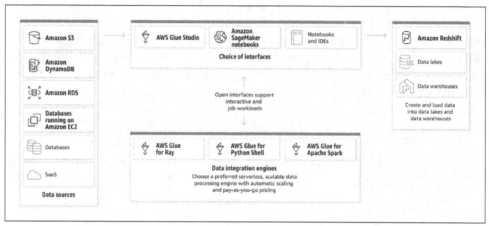

Figure 4-10. ETL integration using AWS Glue

Since AWS Glue V4, a new Amazon Redshift Spark connector with a new JDBC driver is featured with AWS Glue ETL jobs. You can use it to build Apache Spark applications that read from and write to data in Amazon Redshift as part of your data ingestion and transformation pipelines. The new connector and driver supports pushing down relational operations such as joins, aggregations, sort, and scalar functions from Spark to Amazon Redshift to improve your job performance by reducing the amount of data needing to be processed. It also supports IAM-based roles to enable single sign-on capabilities and integrates with AWS Secrets Manager for securely managing keys.

To manage your AWS Glue jobs, AWS provides a visual authoring tool, AWS Glue Studio (*https://oreil.ly/vvdyo*). This service follows many of the same best practices as the third-party ETL tools already mentioned; however, because of the integration, it requires fewer steps to build and manage your data pipelines.

In Example 4-26, we will build a job that loads incremental transaction data from Amazon S3 and merge it into a lineitem table using the key (l_orderkey, l_line number) in your Amazon Redshift data warehouse.

Example 4-26. Create lineitem table

```
CREATE TABLE lineitem (
  L_ORDERKEY varchar(20) NOT NULL,
  L_PARTKEY varchar(20),
  L_SUPPKEY varchar(20),
  L_LINENUMBER integer NOT NULL,
  L_QUANTITY varchar(20),
  L_EXTENDEDPRICE varchar(20),
  L_DISCOUNT varchar(20),
  L_TAX varchar(20),
  L_RETURNFLAG varchar(1),
  L_LINESTATUS varchar(1),
  L_SHIPDATE date,
  L_COMMITDATE date,
  L_RECEIPTDATE date,
  L_SHIPINSTRUCT varchar(25),
  L_SHIPMODE varchar(10),
  L_COMMENT varchar(44));
```

To build a Glue job, we will follow the instructions in the next two sections.

Register Amazon Redshift target connection

Navigate to "Create connection" (*https://oreil.ly/Jlypu*) to create a new AWS Glue connection. Name the connection and choose the connection type of Amazon Redshift (see Figure 4-11).

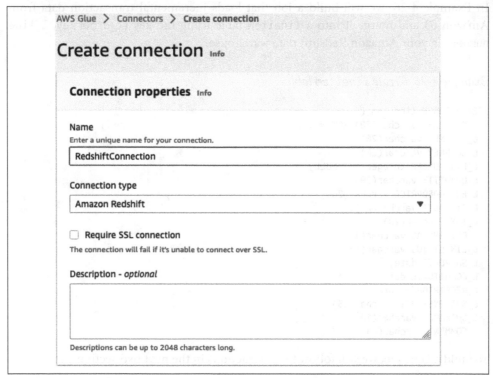

Figure 4-11. Amazon Redshift connection name

Next, select the database instance from the list of autodiscovered Amazon Redshift data warehouses found in your AWS account and region. Set the database name and access credentials. You have an option of either setting a username and password or using AWS Secrets Manager. Finally, click "Create connection" (see Figure 4-12).

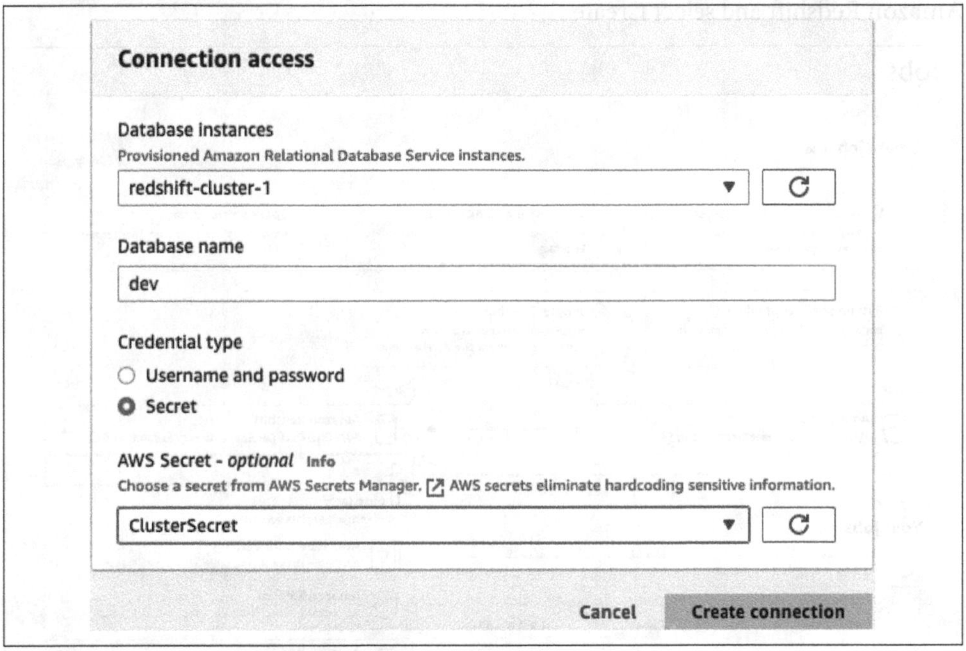

Connection access

Database instances
Provisioned Amazon Relational Database Service instances.

| redshift-cluster-1 | ▼ | C |

Database name

| dev |

Credential type

○ Username and password
◉ Secret

AWS Secret - *optional* Info
Choose a secret from AWS Secrets Manager. [↗] AWS secrets eliminate hardcoding sensitive information.

| ClusterSecret | ▼ | C |

Cancel   **Create connection**

Figure 4-12. Amazon Redshift connection instance

Build and run your AWS Glue job

To build an AWS Glue job, navigate to the AWS Glue Studio jobs page (*https://oreil.ly/ G873X*). You will see a dialog prompting you with options for your job (Figure 4-13). In this example, we will select "Visual with a source and target." Modify the target to Amazon Redshift and select Create.

Figure 4-13. AWS Glue Create job

Next, you will be presented with a visual representation of your job. The first step will be to select the data source node and set the S3 source type (Figure 4-14). For our use case we'll use an S3 location and enter the location of our data: s3:// redshift-immersionday-labs/data/lineitem-part/. Choose the parsing details such as the data format, delimiter, escape character, etc. For our use case, the files will have a CSV format, are pipe (|) delimited, and do not have column headers. Finally, click the "Infer schema" button.

Figure 4-14. AWS Glue set Amazon S3 bucket

 If you have established a data lake that you are using for querying with other AWS services like Amazon Athena, Amazon EMR, or even Amazon Redshift as an external table, you can alternatively use the "Data Catalog table" option.

Next, we can transform our data (Figure 4-15). The job is built with a simple Apply-Mapping node, but you have many options for transforming your data such as joining, splitting, and aggregating data. See "Editing AWS Glue Managed Data Transform Nodes" AWS documentation (*https://oreil.ly/JwlWy*) for additional transform nodes. Select the Transform node and set the target key that matches the source key. In our case, the source data did not have column headers and were registered with generic columns (col#). Map them to the corresponding columns in your `lineitem` table.

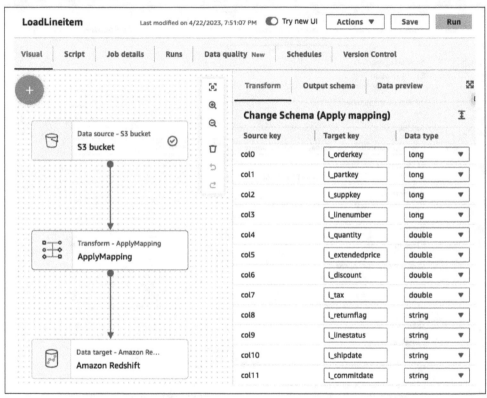

Figure 4-15. AWS Glue apply mapping

Now you can set the Amazon Redshift details (Figure 4-16). Choose "Direct data connection" and select the applicable schema (public) and table (lineitem). You can also set how the job will handle new records; you can either just insert every record or set a key so the job can update data that needs to be reprocessed. For our use case, we'll choose MERGE and set the key l_orderkey and l_linenumber. By doing so, when the job runs, the data will first be loaded into a staging table, then a MERGE statement will be run based on any data that already exists in the target before the new data is loaded with an INSERT statement.

Figure 4-16. AWS Glue set Amazon Redshift target

Before you can save and run the job, you must set some additional job details like the IAM role, which will be used to run the job, and the script filename (Figure 4-17). The role should have permissions to access the files in your Amazon S3 location and should also be able to be assumed by the AWS Glue service. Once you have created and set the IAM role, click Save and Run to execute your job.

Figure 4-17. AWS Glue set job details

You can inspect the job run by navigating to the Runs tab. You will see details about the job ID and the run statistics (Figure 4-18).

Figure 4-18. AWS Glue job run details

For AWS Glue to access Amazon S3, you will need to create a VPC endpoint if you have not created one already. See the online documentation (*https://oreil.ly/440WX*) for more details.

Once the job is completed, you can navigate to the Amazon Redshift console (*https://oreil.ly/aPeIg*) to inspect the queries and loads (Figure 4-19). You'll see the queries required to create the temporary table, load the Amazon S3 files, and execute the merge statement that deletes old data and inserts new data.

	Start time	Query	Status	Duration	SQL
	Apr 23rd, 2023 01:40:07 PM a few seconds ago	401634	⊘ Completed	8 sec	MERGE INTO public.lineitem USING public.lineitem_t emp_88ef9f ON lineitem.l_orderkey = lineitem_tem ...
	Apr 23rd, 2023 01:39:57 PM a minute ago	401632	⊘ Completed	11 sec	/* MERGE REWRITTEN */ UPDATE "public"."lineitem" SET "l_orderkey" = "public"."lineitem_temp_88ef9f"." ...
	Apr 23rd, 2023 01:39:56 PM a minute ago	401630	⊘ Completed	606 ms	padb_fetch_sample: select l_linenumber, l_shipdate, l_commitdate, l_receiptdate from merge_tt_5fa06e4 ...
	Apr 23rd, 2023 01:39:56 PM a minute ago	401629	⊘ Completed	218 ms	padb_fetch_sample: select l_orderkey, l_partkey, l_s uppkey, l_quantity, l_extendedprice, l_discount, l_ta ...
	Apr 23rd, 2023 01:39:46 PM a minute ago	401626	⊘ Completed	10 sec	/* MERGE REWRITTEN */ CREATE TEMP TABLE merg e_tt_5fa06e40f2112 AS (SELECT "public"."lineitem_t ...
	Apr 23rd, 2023 01:39:45 PM a minute ago	401622	⊘ Completed	628 ms	padb_fetch_sample: select l_linenumber, l_shipdate, l_commitdate, l_receiptdate from $lineitem_temp_8 ...
	Apr 23rd, 2023 01:39:45 PM a minute ago	401621	⊘ Completed	420 ms	padb_fetch_sample: select l_orderkey, l_partkey, l_s uppkey, l_quantity, l_extendedprice, l_discount, l_ta ...
	Apr 23rd, 2023 01:39:39 PM a minute ago	401620	⊘ Completed	6 sec	COPY public.lineitem_temp_88ef9f FROM 's3://aws-glue-assets-794378725807-us-west-2/temporary/8 ...

Figure 4-19. Amazon Redshift query history

Summary

This chapter described the various ways you can transform data using Amazon Redshift. With Amazon Redshift's ability to access all your data whether it has been loaded or not, you can transform data in your data lake, operational sources, or other Amazon Redshift data warehouses quickly and easily. In addition, we showed that you can implement time-based schedules using the Amazon Redshift query scheduler to orchestrate these jobs. Lastly, we covered how Amazon Redshift partners with third-party ETL and orchestration vendors to provide optimal execution performance and integrate with tools you may already have in your organization.

In the next chapter, we'll talk about how Amazon Redshift scales when you make changes to your workload. We'll also cover how an Amazon Redshift serverless data warehouse will automatically scale and how you have control over how to scale your provisioned data warehouse. We'll also talk about how you can get the best price performance with Amazon Redshift by implementing best practices.

CHAPTER 5

Scaling and Performance Optimizations

If we told you that the only constant is change, then most likely we would be "preaching to the choir." The challenge today is how fast your data warehouse can adapt to the change. With traditional data warehousing systems, this change is often difficult because of lead time to provision resources. With Amazon Redshift, adapting to change is easy, be it changes in storage needs or changes in compute needs. There are no expensive wrong decisions as you can quickly scale with the increase or decrease in demand.

The objective of scaling is to meet changes in your workload to maintain current performance levels and associated SLA. If you add new workloads to your warehouse, then existing workload SLAs can get impacted; this is where scaling comes in. Scaling could also be required if you are analyzing more data than before, which has caused a visible impact to your workload SLAs. To achieve your scaling goals using Amazon Redshift, there are two strategies to consider: ensuring your data warehouse is sized correctly and ensuring that your workloads are tuned for performance.

With Amazon Redshift, you can size your data warehouse by scaling the compute vertically as well as horizontally (see Figure 5-1). *Vertical scaling* is when you scale "up" by having additional compute that is operating on a single query. Scaling up results in the total number of vCPUs or memory increasing. If you need to retain the SLAs of existing workloads and still take on additional workloads, then you typically will scale "up" your data warehouse. Scaling up is typically used when your workload changes are predictable and allows you to run larger queries that are pulling lots of rows, handling more connections, and managing longer transactions. *Horizontal scaling* is when you scale "out" by adding more replicas to handle additional work-load. When you scale out, each query may be served by isolated compute reading from the shared data. Scaling out is typically used when your workload changes are unpredictable as each individual query receives the same compute, but the system can handle more concurrent workload.

In this chapter, we'll show you how Amazon Redshift will automatically "Scale Storage" if you're using servlerless or an RA3 provisioned data warehouse. In addition, we'll see how for a serverless data warehouse, Amazon Redshift will "Autoscale Your Serverless Data Warehouse" in either direction based on the workload and for a provisioned data warehouse, how you can choose when and in which direction to "Scale Your Provisioned Data Warehouse".

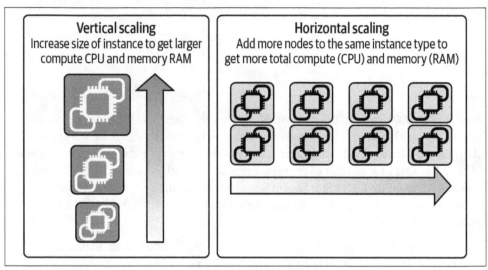

Figure 5-1. Vertical versus horizontal scaling

While ensuring your Amazon Redshift data warehouse is sized correctly is very important, equally important is ensuring your workloads are tuned for performance. The combination of activities will ensure you are making the best use of your resources and you are getting the best price performance. To tune your workload for performance, there are many features in Amazon Redshift that apply to both serverless and provisioned data warehouses. In this chapter, we'll cover some of the best practices. We will describe "WLM, Queues, and QMR", which is a feature specific to provisioned data warehouses. We will show you how "Materialized Views" can support different access patterns, how "Autonomics" will ensure your tables are well maintained, and how "Workload Isolation" can ensure mixed workloads have the compute they need. We will then provide a detailed look at how queries are executed and how you should think about "Query Tuning". Finally, we'll describe a few "Additional Optimizations for Achieving the Best Price and Performance".

Scale Storage

In Chapter 2, "Getting Started with Amazon Redshift" we described how Amazon Redshift is backed by RMS when using serverless or an RA3 provisioned data warehouse. The benefit of RMS is storage elasticity, meaning you don't need to resize your compute simply to accommodate additional historical data. Consider that your data warehouse is typically executing analytical workloads on the last 12 months of data. New data is being added every day, but your compute needs are limited to analyzing the last 12 months. In this scenario, your compute costs will stay the same irrespective of whether your warehouse contains two years of data or five years of data. Since your storage demand has increased, you shall only be paying for additional storage. This is a more common scenario where a data warehouse ends up being a long-term repository of all data, but for analytics only the recent data is queried.

Let's assume that you store 100 GB of data in managed storage with RA3 node types for the first 15 days in April, and 100 TB of data for the final 15 days in April.

Let's calculate the usage in GB-hours for April.

For the first 15 days, you will have the following usage: 100 GB × 15 days × 24 hours/day = 36,000 GB-Hours.

For the last 15 days, you will have the following usage: 100 TB × 1024 GB/TB × 15 days × 24 hours/day = 36,864,000 GB-hours.

At the end of April, total usage in GB-hours is: 36,000 GB-Hours + 36,864,000 GB-hours = 36,900,000 GB-hours

Convert this to GB-months: 36,900,000 GB-hours / 720 hours/month in April = 51,250 GB-months.

Consider us-east-1 region, where managed storage will be charged at $0.024/GB-Month. Monthly storage charges for 51,250 GB-month will be: 51,250 GB-month × $0.024 per GB-month = $1,230.

Total RMS fee for April = $1,230

We haven't shown compute costs here, but they will remain the same irrespective of your data growth. If you have paused your cluster and no queries are executing, then only RMS cost will apply. Note that you will be billed for storage until you delete your cluster, even if no queries are executing.

Autoscale Your Serverless Data Warehouse

Amazon Redshift serverless automatically scales your data warehouse capacity whether you need to scale *up* or scale *out*. Compute resources automatically shut down behind the scenes when there is no activity and resume when you are loading data or there are queries coming in. With Amazon Redshift serverless, you do not need to predict your workload demands or size your compute as it adjusts the compute to meet your workload changes. In many cases, the overall compute needed to execute your workload may decrease using serverless. With serverless, Amazon Redshift will size the compute to meet your workload needs. Queries that were previously paging to disk because the compute was undersized will complete faster, and queries that were queued will no longer wait.

Compute capacity is measured in RPUs, and you pay for the workloads in RPU-hours with per-second billing. To control your costs, you can specify usage limits and define actions that Amazon Redshift automatically takes if those limits are reached. You can specify usage limits in RPU-hours and associate the limit to be checked either daily, weekly, or monthly. Setting higher usage limits can improve the overall throughput of the system, especially for workloads that need to handle high concurrency while maintaining consistently high performance. See Chapter 2, "Getting Started with Amazon Redshift", for Amazon Redshift serverless pricing examples.

Scale Your Provisioned Data Warehouse

When you provision your Amazon Redshift cluster, you choose a particular node type and a number of nodes. The power of when to scale up by adding more nodes or changing the node type and when to scale out by adding parallel compute is put in your hands. Typically you will scale up when you have "Evolving Compute Demand" or "Predictable workload changes", and you will also scale up when you have "Unpredictable Workload Changes".

Evolving Compute Demand

To understand the scenario of evolving compute, let's consider your data warehouse project has been immensely successful and you are adding new analytical workloads to it, but the data in your warehouse is still the same as you are rolling off older data to your data lake. So here your compute needs are growing as you have more users querying the data warehouse to get business insights. To maintain the same user experience and SLAs to your business users, you can scale your cluster up by adding more nodes or migrating to a larger node type.

> When scaling up your cluster, your storage cost stays the same as there is no change in your data volume.

Scaling up by adding nodes or changing the node type of your cluster is a quick process and can be done via the AWS console, CLI, or API. For example, if you change from a 2-node ra3.4xl cluster to a 2-node ra3.16xl cluster, you have scaled up the node four times, from 24 vCPUs to 96 vCPUs, and you get four times the compute and memory. Similarly, if you expand your cluster from a 2-node ra3.4xl to an 8-node ra3.4xl, you get 96 vCPUs. Scaling up by changing your node type can be beneficial if you've reached the limits for the current node type. For example, imagine you are running a 64-node ra3.4xl cluster. Scaling up to a 16-node ra3.16xl cluster will give you the same total compute resources but with a larger leader node.

> Changing node type requires physical data movement from one type of compute to another. You have to plan for downtime, coordinate across teams, and communicate schedules to limit impact to systems, applications, and your users.

To illustrate how scaling would impact pricing, let's say that you started with 2-node ra3.4xlarge cluster and added new projects that needed you to resize to 5-node cluster on the 15th of the month.

For the first 15 days, you will have the following usage: $3.26 per node-hour × 2 nodes × 5 hours/day × 15 days = $489

For the last 15 days, you will have the following usage: $3.26 per node-hour × 5 nodes × 10 hours/day × 15 days = $2,445

Total compute fee for April = $2,934

The following (see Example 5-1) AWS CLI commands show how to scale up by either adding more nodes or choosing a larger node type.

Example 5-1. Scaling provisioned cluster using the CLI

```
# scale up to 4 nodes
aws redshift modify-cluster
  --cluster-identifier mycluster01
  --node-type ra3.4xlarge
  --number-of-nodes 4

# scale up to ra3.16xl cluster
aws redshift modify-cluster
  --cluster-identifier mycluster01
  --node-type ra3.16xlarge
  --number-of-nodes 2
```

Predictable workload changes

Predictable workload changes are when you expect the change, have some idea of timelines, and can come up with a plan to adopt. The predictable change could be one-time as explained in the previous examples, or be recurring periodically. Let's say that your steady state workload is processing daily incremental files. But on the first of every month you are additionally required to process a reconciliation file for the previous month. Now you have optimally sized your Amazon Redshift data warehouse for daily files processing, but you need additional compute on the first of the month to continue the timely processing of daily incremental files and additionally be able to process the reconciliation file.

To handle such a scenario, you can either incorporate the resize as part of the monthly processing job workflow or you can schedule a resize to upsize (up to 4x) on the first of the month and on the third of the month you downsize back to the original node count. Once scheduled, Amazon Redshift will scale up/down per your established schedule.

Amazon Redshift cron expression format for scheduler is:

```
minute hour dayOfMonth month dayOfWeek year
0 0 1 * ? * # upsize on 1st of every month at midnight
0 0 2 * ? * # downsize on 3rd of every month at midnight
```

You can also use the built-in scheduler to schedule the resize as shown in Figure 5-2.

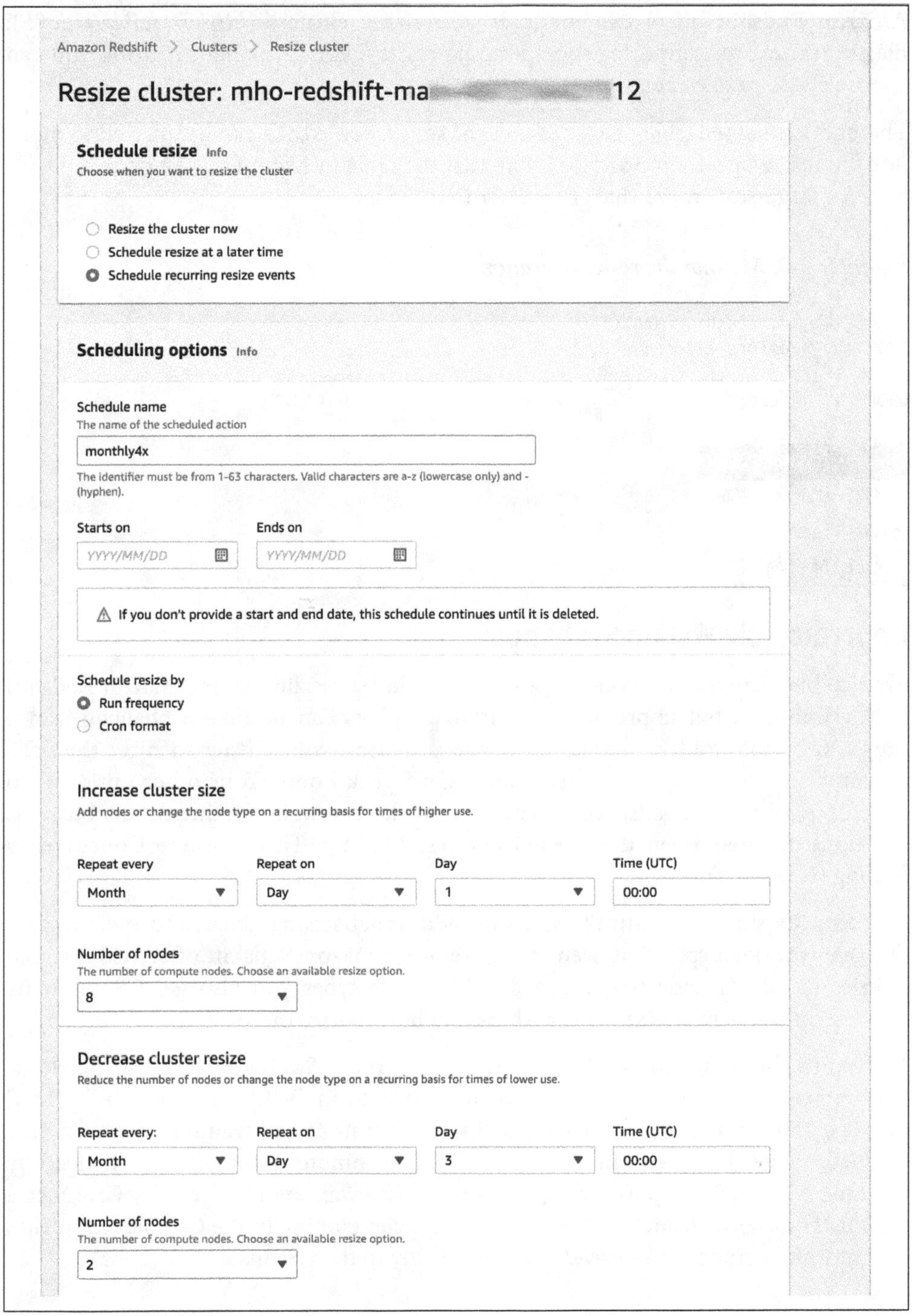

Resize cluster: mho-redshift-ma███████████12

Schedule resize Info
Choose when you want to resize the cluster

○ Resize the cluster now
○ Schedule resize at a later time
◉ Schedule recurring resize events

Scheduling options Info

Schedule name
The name of the scheduled action

```
monthly4x
```

The identifier must be from 1-63 characters. Valid characters are a-z (lowercase only) and - (hyphen).

Starts on   **Ends on**

```
YYYY/MM/DD      ⊞        YYYY/MM/DD      ⊞
```

⚠ If you don't provide a start and end date, this schedule continues until it is deleted.

Schedule resize by
◉ Run frequency
○ Cron format

Increase cluster size
Add nodes or change the node type on a recurring basis for times of higher use.

Repeat every	Repeat on	Day	Time (UTC)
Month ▼	Day ▼	1 ▼	00:00

Number of nodes
The number of compute nodes. Choose an available resize option.

```
8                 ▼
```

Decrease cluster resize
Reduce the number of nodes or change the node type on a recurring basis for times of lower use.

Repeat every:	Repeat on	Day	Time (UTC)
Month ▼	Day ▼	3 ▼	00:00

Number of nodes
The number of compute nodes. Choose an available resize option.

```
2                 ▼
```

Figure 5-2. Schedule resize

Amazon Redshift offers two methods of resizing clusters (*https://oreil.ly/UEo9E*). Elastic resize is preferred for such periodic resizes. For permanent resizing you can choose classic resize or elastic resize.

The undocumented table stv_xrestore_alter_queue_state can be queried to monitor the resize operation progress. Note that the table in Example 5-2 captures details only for large-scale resize that are greater than 5 TBs.

Example 5-2. Monitor the resize operation

```
SELECT db_id, status, count(*)
FROM stv_xrestore_alter_queue_state
GROUP BY 1, 2
ORDER BY 3 desc;
```

db_id	status	count
654321	Waiting	456
654321	Finished	23
654321	Applying	1

Unpredictable Workload Changes

Predictable changes to workload can be handled by resizing your Amazon Redshift data warehouse, but unpredictable workload spikes can become a challenge since they can be intermittent by nature. If you provision your cluster to meet the peak demand, then this wastes resources during off-peak hours. Your other option is to size for typical workloads, which could mean longer waits for important business decisions at times when unexpected queries show up. This is where Concurrency Scaling (CS) steps in.

Amazon Redshift automatically spins off additional scaling clusters to meet unpredictable workload spikes, as seen in Figure 5-3. Amazon Redshift offers CS for read queries on all its node types, and for RA3 node types you also get CS for write queries. Subsequent sections cover where and how to turn on this feature.

You get to choose which queries leverage Concurrency Scaling by configuring workload management (WLM) queues, which is covered in "WLM, Queues, and QMR" on page 169. CS is triggered when the total wait time for all waiting queries in CS–enabled queues is more than a minute. This one-minute setting can be changed by working with AWS Support for instances when you want more aggressive CS. Once a CS cluster has been launched, then any new queries coming in the CS enabled queues do not wait anymore and instead are sent directly to the CS cluster.

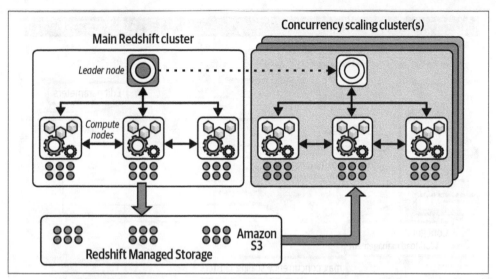

Figure 5-3. Amazon Redshift Concurrency Scaling

Concurrency Scaling is controlled by navigating to the "Workload management" section of the Amazon Redshift console, as shown in Figure 5-4. While you cannot edit the default.redshift-1.0 parameter group, you can create a new parameter group and modify the max_concurrency_scaling_clusters parameter to control the number of CS clusters that can be spun up. Note that the maximum is 10, although you can request an increase if your workloads need more. We will cover parameter groups in depth in "Parameter Group" on page 183.

The Concurrency Scaling cluster operates independently to execute the queries that were assigned for execution. Each query to be executed needs to be compiled first, and note that the compile cache on the main cluster and the CS cluster is independent. During query processing, Amazon Redshift generates query segments and checks if the query segments are available in the cluster's local cache. If they are not available, then it checks if the query segments are available in the external code compilation cache, i.e., the global cache. If they are available, then the compiled object gets downloaded from the global cache to the local cache; otherwise, the query segments are sent to the external compilation farm to be compiled with massive parallelism and then stored in the external code compilation cache and respective local compilation cache. So even though the CS cluster does not have the query segments when it is spun up, it still can leverage the global cache if available, or else it will need to recompile the query from scratch.

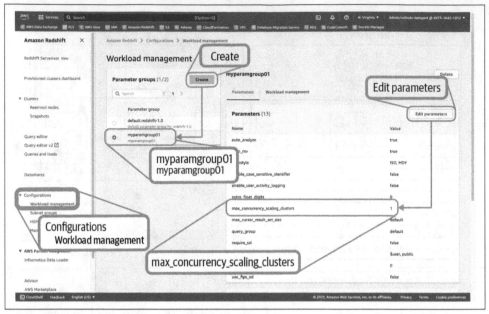

Figure 5-4. Max Concurrency Scaling clusters

With Concurrency Scaling, the user queries run against the most current data irrespective of whether it runs on the main or CS cluster. Amazon Redshift keeps refreshing the CS cluster with the latest data as long as it is servicing queries. Note that there is a cost associated with CS but Amazon Redshift provides one hour of free CS credits for every 24 hours of your main cluster uptime.

Concurrency Scaling clusters are stood up in minutes, are billed on a per second usage, and billed only for the time they are actively running queries, not while they are being provisioned or released. Once CS clusters are released, they go back to the Amazon EC2 pool, where these EC2 virtual machines are fully cleansed and reset before being brought back into the CS fleet for subsequent usage. This ensures no residual objects are accidentally left behind across CS usage from one to another.

 Concurrency Scaling usage is billed at on-demand rates, and Amazon Redshift provides discounts with Reserved Instances (RI) pricing. So if you see high Concurrency Scaling usage then you should evaluate if you are better off by adding nodes to your RI cluster instead.

Concurrency Scaling cost controls can be set up right in the Amazon Redshift console. Once your defined limits have been reached then Amazon Redshift can write log records into the system table or completely turn the Concurrency Scaling feature off. Any query that was executing when the usage limit is reached will be executed to completion in the Concurrency Scaling cluster, but subsequent queries will stay on the main cluster and be queued until executed.

 The Concurrency Scaling limits can be changed dynamically without needing a cluster reboot. As of this writing, the Concurrency Scaling feature is available in commercial regions only, and is not available in AWS GovCloud regions.

WLM, Queues, and QMR

A typical organization would have various type of users with different performance expectations. The *workload management* (WLM) feature of Amazon Redshift provisioned clusters offers capability to run workloads based on business priorities (see Figure 5-5). WLM provides you the necessary controls to maximize the warehouse throughput, i.e., the number of queries processed in a given time duration. You can define up to eight queues to logically segregate the queries being executed. Each queue has a unique service class identifier. Identifiers 1 through 4 are reserved for system use, 5 is for the superuser queue, and 15 for housekeeping activities by Amazon Redshift. Refer to the WLM system tables and views (*https://oreil.ly/7nZea*) for more details.

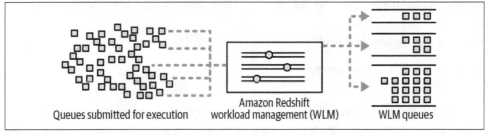

Queues submitted for execution   Amazon Redshift workload management (WLM)   WLM queues

Figure 5-5. Amazon Redshift WLM queues

In Figure 5-5, you can see three queues have been defined, and WLM allocates the queries coming from the left to specific WLM queues on the right based on queue assignment rules.

Queue Assignment

Amazon Redshift default configuration comes with one queue, the default queue, and all queries will execute in it unless the query is routed to another queue based off of assignment rules.

WLM assigns a query to a queue based on matching logic as follows:

1. If a user with superuser privilege submits a query and query group has been set to superuser, then assign to superuser queue.

2. If regular user submits a query and user group is matched, then assign to the matching queue.

3. If regular user submits a query and query group is matched, then assign to the matching queue.

4. If no matches are found, then assign to default queue.

Refer to the WLM queue assignment rules (*https://oreil.ly/nnBdx*) for a flowchart and examples for queue assignment.

 If a query matches multiple queues, then it gets allocated to the first queue that it is matched to.

Each query gets allocated a single slot for execution. A slot is a portion of your cluster's memory or RAM. Superuser queue always has concurrency of one irrespective of manual WLM or auto WLM. And you must manually set the query group as superuser to run your query in the superuser queue (see Example 5-3).

Example 5-3. Superuser queue

```
SET query_group TO 'superuser';
RESET query_group;
```

Each queue can map to either user group or query group. User group is nothing but a logical grouping of users, for example, a user group `etl_group` in which all individual applications etl users, `app_1_etl_usr`,`app_2_etl_usr`, are put together. Query group is a text label that is set at runtime (see Example 5-4). This is typically used by a BI tool that uses a single database user ID but wants to prioritize a certain dashboard query over other queries.

Example 5-4. Set query group

```
SET query_group TO 'c_level_dashboard';
```

By default each query gets allocated a single slot, and if the query is able to complete its execution within the allocated memory then you will see faster performance compared to when the query spills to disk.

Use the Example 5-5 query to check on disk spill queries.

Example 5-5. Check disk spill

```
WITH q_spill AS
(
 SELECT
    starttime,
    q.query,
    round(nvl(query_temp_blocks_to_disk,0)::decimal/1000,2) spill
 FROM stl_query q
 LEFT JOIN svl_query_metrics_summary m
 USING (query)
 WHERE q.userid >= 100
 )
SELECT
    date_trunc('d',starttime) AS day,
    count(query) AS queries,
    sum(CASE WHEN spill = 0
      THEN 1 ELSE 0 END) AS no_spill,
    sum(CASE WHEN spill > 0 AND
      spill < 5 THEN 1 ELSE 0 END) AS "<5GB",
    sum(CASE WHEN spill
      BETWEEN 5 AND 200 THEN 1 ELSE 0 END) AS "5-200GB",
    sum(CASE WHEN spill
      BETWEEN 201 AND 500 THEN 1 ELSE 0 END) AS "201-500GB",
    sum(CASE WHEN spill
      BETWEEN 501 AND 1000 THEN 1 ELSE 0 END) AS "501GB-1TB",
    sum(CASE WHEN spill > 1000
      THEN 1 ELSE 0 END) AS ">1TB",
    round(max(spill),2) AS max_spill_gb
FROM
    q_spill
GROUP BY 1
ORDER BY 1;
```

The number of slots and amount of memory allocated per slot are crucial for query execution performance.

 You can use the wlm_query_slot_count parameter to allocate more slots to speed up large queries, like VACUUM. This temporarily reduces the concurrency on your cluster until you reset the query slot count. This works in manual WLM as well as auto WLM mode.

You can choose to set up these slots yourself in manual WLM or let Amazon Redshift manage them with auto WLM.

Short Query Acceleration

There also is a special queue for queries that are short-running, called the *short query acceleration (SQA) queue*. Amazon Redshift estimates the execution time for each query and if eligible sends to SQA. If the actual query runtime exceeds SQA time, then the query gets moved out to one of the matching WLM queues. Only read-only queries are eligible for SQA. The service class identifier for SQA is 14.

With manual WLM you can specify the maximum runtime (in seconds) to qualify a query for SQA, but in auto WLM this is automatically determined by Amazon Redshift based on your query patterns.

If you are using manual WLM, then you can use SQL Example 5-6 to analyze your workload queues and choose between 70th to 90th percentile to set an SQA threshold.

Example 5-6. SQA threshold

```
SELECT
  service_class AS QUEUE,
  count(1) AS queries,
  avg(total_queue_time)/1000000 AS avg_q_sec,
  min(total_queue_time)/1000000 AS min_q_sec,
  max(total_queue_time)/1000000 AS max_q_sec,
  round(percentile_cont(0.7)
    WITHIN group
      (ORDER BY total_queue_time)/1000000,0) AS p70_sec,
  round(percentile_cont(0.9)
    WITHIN group
      (ORDER BY total_queue_time)/1000000,0) AS p90_sec
FROM
  stl_wlm_query
WHERE
  userid >= 100
GROUP BY
  service_class
ORDER BY
  service_class;
```

queue	queries	avg_q_sec	min_q_sec	max_q_sec	p70_sec	p90_sec
5	20103	23	0	95	15	19
6	3421	42	15	32	18	23
7	42	178	109	466	176	261
8	196	398	99	1399	108	206

In the previous example, setting SQA between 15 and 18 will allow most queries to take advantage of SQA.

Query Monitoring Rules

In both WLM modes Amazon Redshift provides *query monitoring rules* (QMR) to control the cluster behavior based on certain rules for query execution. You have 16 system-defined metrics available to define QMR conditions, and Amazon Redshift also provides 5 system-defined templates for you to get started with QMR quickly. Once an executing query breaches the defined boundary, the defined action is triggered. The actions can be to abort, log, change query priority (auto WLM only), or hop (manual WLM only) the query to another matching queue. You can define up to 25 QMR across all queues, and each QMR can evaluate up to 3 conditions. When all of a rule's conditions are met, WLM writes a row to the STL_WLM_RULE_ACTION system table. This row contains details for the query that triggered the rule and the resulting action.

Amazon Redshift serverless does not have WLM, but it does have Query Limits (*https://oreil.ly/jywZ-*), which follow the same rule logic as QMR. Use these to ensure that users don't issue runaway queries.

The QMR metrics are evaluated every 10 seconds, so you might see some rules take time to fire.

You can set up QMR to get notified of bad queries and proactively take action instead of reactively handling it when your user complains after experiencing slowness. With QMR you can also identify areas of learning for your user community and help them grow their technical skills by logging poorly written queries and having follow-up discussions and workshops for educating your warehouse users.

Leverage system tables and views to determine threshold values for defining QMR. The table STV_QUERY_METRICS displays the metrics for *currently running* queries, table STL_QUERY_METRICS records the metrics for *completed* queries, view SVL_QUERY_METRICS shows the metrics for *completed* queries, and view SVL_QUERY_METRICS_SUMMARY shows the *maximum values* of metrics for completed queries.

For a typical BI queue you should set up QMR for a nested loop join, which often results in a large Cartesian product due to a missing joins predicate. Use a low row count to find a potentially runaway query early. If you dedicate a queue to simple, short-running queries, then include a rule that finds queries returning an abnormally high row count. Use the `unload` option instead of returning billions of rows.

For a typical `Analyst queue` you should set up QMR for joins with a high number of rows, which might indicate a need for more restrictive filters. Or high disk usage when writing intermediate result that can be the result of a rogue query, which usually is also the query that uses the most disk space.

For severe violation cases, for example, a `Dashboard queue` where queries finish under 10 seconds, set up QMR on query execution time greater than 20 seconds, which can indicate an erroneous query, with the action of `abort`.

For a typical `Data scientist queue` where long-running queries are expected, set up QMR for query queue time to limit the number of queries being submitted and sitting in the queue.

To get you started with QMR, Amazon Redshift provides ready templates where you just need to customize the threshold value for each QMR. See query monitoring rules templates (*https://oreil.ly/qjn8u*) for additional details.

 Initially, you start with the `log` action for various rules. Have a weekly cadence with your user community to review the queries that have been logged and provide means for tuning the queries. If things do not improve, then you can change the action to `abort` after giving your users a warning.

Use the following SQL Example 5-7 to reveal the last seven days' usage pattern of you data warehouse, which can help you determine the optimal WLM configuration setting. The query will provide a breakdown by workload queues (referred to as service class) and display data by hour-of-day for `Select`, `UPDATE`, `INSERT`, `DELETE`, `CURSOR`, `CACHED`, `COPY`, `UNLOAD`, `VACUUM`, and `SYSTEM` queries executing on your data warehouse.

Example 5-7. Workload queues breakdown

```
SELECT
  service_class,
  query_hour,
  TO_CHAR(
    MAX(CASE WHEN query_type = 'SELECT' THEN qry_cnt ELSE NULL END),
      '999,999') AS "select_query_count",
  TO_CHAR(
    MAX(CASE WHEN query_type = 'SELECT' THEN exec_s ELSE NULL END),
      '999,999') AS "select_exec_seconds",
  TO_CHAR(
    MAX(CASE WHEN query_type = 'SELECT' THEN queue_s ELSE NULL END),
```

```
     '999,999') AS "select_queue_seconds",
TO_CHAR(
  MAX(CASE WHEN query_type = 'INSERT' THEN qry_cnt ELSE NULL END),
    '999,999') AS "insert_count",
TO_CHAR(
  MAX(CASE WHEN query_type = 'INSERT' THEN exec_s ELSE NULL END),
    '999,999') AS "insert_exec_seconds",
TO_CHAR(
  MAX(CASE WHEN query_type = 'INSERT' THEN queue_s ELSE NULL END),
    '999,999') AS "insert_queue_seconds",
TO_CHAR(
  MAX(CASE WHEN query_type = 'UPDATE' THEN qry_cnt ELSE NULL END),
    '999,999') AS "update_count",
TO_CHAR(
  MAX(CASE WHEN query_type = 'UPDATE' THEN exec_s ELSE NULL END),
    '999,999') AS "update_exec_seconds",
TO_CHAR(
  MAX(CASE WHEN query_type = 'UPDATE' THEN queue_s ELSE NULL END),
    '999,999') AS "update_queue_seconds",
TO_CHAR(
  MAX(CASE WHEN query_type = 'DELETE' THEN qry_cnt ELSE NULL END),
    '999,999') AS "delete_count",
TO_CHAR(
  MAX(CASE WHEN query_type = 'DELETE' THEN exec_s ELSE NULL END),
    '999,999') AS "delete_exec_seconds",
TO_CHAR(
  MAX(CASE WHEN query_type = 'DELETE' THEN queue_s ELSE NULL END),
    '999,999') AS "delete_queue_seconds",
TO_CHAR(
  MAX(CASE WHEN query_type = 'CURSOR' THEN qry_cnt ELSE NULL END),
    '999,999') AS "cursor_count",
TO_CHAR(
  MAX(CASE WHEN query_type = 'CURSOR' THEN exec_s ELSE NULL END),
    '999,999') AS "cursor_exec_seconds",
TO_CHAR(
  MAX(CASE WHEN query_type = 'CURSOR' THEN queue_s ELSE NULL END),
    '999,999') AS "cursor_queue_seconds",
TO_CHAR(
  MAX(CASE WHEN query_type = 'CACHED' THEN qry_cnt ELSE NULL END),
    '999,999') AS "cached_query_count",
TO_CHAR(
  MAX(CASE WHEN query_type = 'COPY' THEN qry_cnt ELSE NULL END),
    '999,999') AS "copy_count",
TO_CHAR(
  MAX(CASE WHEN query_type = 'COPY' THEN exec_s ELSE NULL END),
    '999,999') AS "copy_exec_seconds",
TO_CHAR(
  MAX(CASE WHEN query_type = 'COPY' THEN queue_s ELSE NULL END),
    '999,999') AS "copy_queue_seconds",
TO_CHAR(
  MAX(CASE WHEN query_type = 'UNLOAD' THEN qry_cnt ELSE NULL END),
    '999,999') AS "unload_count",
```

```
    TO_CHAR(
      MAX(CASE WHEN query_type = 'UNLOAD' THEN exec_s ELSE NULL END),
        '999,999') AS "unload_exec_seconds",
    TO_CHAR(
      MAX(CASE WHEN query_type = 'UNLOAD' THEN queue_s ELSE NULL END),
        '999,999') AS "unload_queue_seconds",
    TO_CHAR(
      MAX(CASE WHEN query_type = 'VACUUM' THEN qry_cnt ELSE NULL END),
        '999,999') AS "vacuum_count",
    TO_CHAR(
      MAX(CASE WHEN query_type = 'VACUUM' THEN exec_s ELSE NULL END),
        '999,999') AS "vacuum_exec_seconds",
    TO_CHAR(
      MAX(CASE WHEN query_type = 'VACUUM' THEN queue_s ELSE NULL END),
        '999,999') AS "vacuum_queue_seconds",
    TO_CHAR(
      MAX(CASE WHEN query_type = 'OTHER' THEN qry_cnt ELSE NULL END),
        '999,999') AS "system_query_count",
    TO_CHAR(
      MAX(CASE WHEN query_type = 'OTHER' THEN exec_s ELSE NULL END),
        '999,999') AS "system_exec_seconds",
    TO_CHAR(
      MAX(CASE WHEN query_type = 'OTHER' THEN queue_s ELSE NULL END),
        '999,999') AS "system_queue_seconds"
FROM
    (SELECT
      NVL(w.service_class,14) service_class,
      CASE
        WHEN w.query IS NULL
            THEN 'CACHED'
        WHEN q.userid = 1
            THEN 'OTHER'
        WHEN REGEXP_INSTR("querytxt", '(padb_|pg_internal)')
            THEN 'OTHER'
        WHEN REGEXP_INSTR("querytxt", '[uU][nN][dD][oO][iI][nN][gG]')
            THEN 'OTHER'
        WHEN REGEXP_INSTR("querytxt", '[uU][nN][lL][oO][aA][dD] ')
            THEN 'UNLOAD'
        WHEN REGEXP_INSTR("querytxt", '[cC][uU][rR][sS][oO][rR] ')
            THEN 'CURSOR'
        WHEN REGEXP_INSTR("querytxt", '[fF][eE][tT][cC][hH] ')
            THEN 'CURSOR'
        WHEN REGEXP_INSTR("querytxt", '[dD][eE][lL][eE][tT][eE] ')
            THEN 'DELETE'
        WHEN REGEXP_INSTR("querytxt", '[cC][oO][pP][yY] ')
            THEN 'COPY'
        WHEN REGEXP_INSTR("querytxt", '[uU][pP][dD][aA][tT][eE] ')
            THEN 'UPDATE'
        WHEN REGEXP_INSTR("querytxt", '[iI][nN][sS][eE][rR][tT] ')
            THEN 'INSERT'
        WHEN REGEXP_INSTR("querytxt", '[vV][aA][cC][uU][uU][mM][ :]')
            THEN 'VACUUM'
```

```
          WHEN REGEXP_INSTR("querytxt", '[sS][eE][lL][eE][cC][tT] ')
              THEN 'SELECT'
          ELSE 'OTHER'
        END AS query_type,
        DATEPART(hour, q.starttime) AS query_hour,
        COUNT(1) AS qry_cnt,
        ROUND(SUM(w.total_exec_time)::NUMERIC/1000000,0) AS exec_s,
        ROUND(SUM(w.total_queue_time)::NUMERIC/1000000,0) AS queue_s
      FROM
          stl_query       q
      LEFT
      JOIN stl_wlm_query w
        ON q.userid = w.userid
       AND q.query = w.query
      WHERE
        q.endtime >= DATEADD(day, -7, CURRENT_DATE)
      AND q.userid > 1
      AND NVL(w.service_class,14) > 4
      GROUP BY
        service_class,
        query_type,
        query_hour
   )
GROUP BY
  service_class,
  query_hour
ORDER BY
  service_class,
  query_hour;
```

Automatic WLM

Auto WLM is the default mode that is enabled when you launch Amazon Redshift. With auto WLM, you let Amazon Redshift dynamically allocate the total number of slots and memory to each slot automatically. You can create up to eight queues with the service class identifiers 100 to 107. You associate each queue with a priority from lowest to highest, and if there are queries contending for resources across multiple queues, then your higher priority queries will take precedence over the lower priority queries to ensure that the most important queries are not starved resources by lesser importance queries. During times when resource-heavy queries are executing, you want lower concurrency and more memory per query, and conversely, when lighter queries are executing, you want higher concurrency to execute more queries. This key purpose of auto WLM is to accommodate and execute as many queries as it can at any point in time.

Although not shown in the AWS console, serverless data warehouses use auto WLM to ensure each query is allocated resources that are appropriate for the query needs.

Auto WLM respects the priority you have associated with the queue and accordingly prioritizes higher priority queries. So you have to ensure you associate the business priority to the queue priority. For example, say the business priority is getting the most up-to-date data, then you can define the ETL queue with higher priority than the reporting queue. Amazon Redshift will throttle the cluster concurrency as needed depending on the relative size of the queries being executed. If heavy ETL queries are being executed, Amazon Redshift will detect the high resource needs per query and fewer queries will run concurrently. In contrast, when lighter dashboard queries are executing, Amazon Redshift will detect the low resource needs per query and more queries will run concurrently. You can also enable Concurrency Scaling for each queue and achieve higher throughput by scaling out your clusters. If your cluster is executing, all higher priority queries and new queries come in then; without Concurrency Scaling, those new queries will have to wait for the current queries to finish.

There are six priorities offered by Amazon Redshift, as listed here:

1. Lowest
2. Low
3. Normal
4. High
5. Highest
6. Critical

You can associate any of the first five to WLM queues. The critical priority can be applied only by a superuser, at query or session level. Only one query can execute at Critical priority.

Auto WLM by default defines five heavy slots and five light slots to begin with. The heavy slots are allocated 95% of cluster memory, and the light slots get the remaining 5% memory. These slots get utilized as the workload queries come in, and if required, more slots are created. Fewer slots implies increasing the memory per slot, which is good for heavy queries, and more slots implies reducing memory per slot, which is for light queries. The five light slots are reserved for short-running queries, and heavy queries cannot utilize those slots. But the five heavy slots, if unoccupied, can be used by light queries.

You can query the undocumented view `stl_wlm_auto_concurrency` to gain insights about your auto WLM concurrency.

Example 5-8. Check auto WLM concurrency

```
select
  now,
  heavy_slots AS hs,
  heavy_queries_finished AS hqf,
  heavy_queries_exec_time AS hqe,
  heavy_queries_queued AS hqq,
  light_slots AS ls,
  light_queries_finished AS lqf,
  light_queries_exec_time_sec AS lqe,
  light_queries_queued AS lqq
FROM
  stl_wlm_auto_concurrency
WHERE
  NOW BETWEEN '2023-01-16 21:08:00' AND '2023-01-16 21:33:00'
ORDER BY 1;
```

now	hs	hqf	hqe	hqq	ls	lqf	lqe	lqq
1/16/23 9:09:53 PM	5	17	1.78	0	5	4	0.03	0
1/16/23 9:11:54 PM	20	411	683.69	12	5	96	14.73	10
1/16/23 9:13:55 PM	20	375	562.20	23	5	113	15.60	16
1/16/23 9:15:58 PM	17	418	552.47	11	5	152	21.61	18
1/16/23 9:19:00 PM	20	352	720.27	63	5	90	15.30	10
1/16/23 9:22:02 PM	20	445	757.10	44	5	119	17.91	38
1/16/23 9:24:03 PM	20	414	719.95	25	5	87	13.24	12
1/16/23 9:26:05 PM	20	356	335.15	13	5	98	6.45	9
1/16/23 9:28:06 PM	13	482	355.50	9	5	130	9.05	9
1/16/23 9:30:07 PM	10	217	183.45	1	5	91	6.33	0
1/16/23 9:31:08 PM	7	131	79.04	0	5	44	3.83	0
1/16/23 9:32:06 PM	5	27	33.81	0	5	8	1.43	0

> Auto WLM has the potential to kill a lower priority query that has not yet started returning data, if a higher priority query needs resources and none are available.

It is recommended to use auto WLM when your workloads are dynamic and you want to drive your workloads based off of the business priority of various users or workloads. Auto WLM maximizes the cluster resources and pushes through as many queries as can be executed concurrently. It is highly recommended to set up QMR, which is covered in "Query Monitoring Rules" on page 173, when using auto WLM as you do not want a rogue query to consume all your resources.

Manual WLM

With *manual WLM*, you get more control over the concurrency and memory allocation for each query. If you have a workload that requires dedicated resources 24-7, then you can use manual WLM. An example would be when you have a consistent ETL ingestion pipeline, where you ingest data throughout the day; you can set up a queue with a percentage of memory allocated. Similar to auto WLM, you can create a maximum of eight queues with manual WLM. The key difference is that you can manually control the number of slots and the percentage of memory allocated to each queue. You can create up to eight queues with the service class identifiers 6 to 13. The recommended total slots is 15 across all your manual WLM queues.

 Manual WLM is available only for provisioned data warehouses. Serverless data warehouses use auto WLM.

If your warehouse has 300 GiB memory and you have set 40% memory to ETL queue with 3 slots, then each query will get 300 x 0.40 / 3 = 40 GiB of memory allocated. If the query needs more than 40 GiB, then queries will spill to disk and take longer to execute. In manual WLM mode the memory is reserved for each queue slot, and if more queries than the slots defined come in, then they are queued up for execution. To scale beyond the allocated memory for each queue, you can enable Concurrency Scaling. Concurrency Scaling is enabled for each queue, and only if that particular queue is filled, queries will be routed to the scaling clusters.

 With manual WLM, once all slots of a queue are occupied, subsequent queries have to wait even if another queue has free slots available.

It is recommended to use manual WLM when you are very familiar with your workloads and you want the most control over your cluster resources. But it has the potential of leaving resources underutilized. Instances with very consistent and repeatable workloads are candidates for manual WLM, but every time a new workload gets introduced you should reevaluate the manual slot and memory allocation if the workload has any defined SLAs. If the new workload does not have strict SLAs, then it can go to the default queue and will get completed as it gets its turn for execution.

You should consider manual WLM when you notice (using the Example 5-5 query) that auto WLM is spilling a lot to disk or, not spilling but instead queuing a lot and your system can use more slots. Note that while it will take more effort to manage manual WLM it could give better cost optimization. In the spilling-a-lot scenario, a costlier but easier to manage option would be to scale up your cluster. In the never-spilling-but-queuing scenario, one option would be to use more Concurrency Scaling, but that can turn expensive, so instead manual WLM can give you better cost optimization.

If you define manual WLM and do not allocate 100% of total memory, then Amazon Redshift will allocate the unallocated portion to any queue that needs more memory. This can be considered as a hybrid WLM mode where you are starting off with a minimum memory allocation per queue and letting Amazon Redshift do some automatic memory allocation on top of your manual setup.

Table 5-1 summarizes the features of auto WLM and manual WLM.

Table 5-1. Auto WLM versus manual WLM

Characteristic	Auto WLM	Manual WLM	Additional info
Define queue priority	Yes	No	Queue priority is available only in auto WLM.
Define queue concurrency	No	Yes	Number of slots in queue is available only in manual WLM.
Define queue memory allocation	No	Yes	Amount of memory for the queue in available only in manual WLM.
Over-allocate memory per query	No	Yes	If you define too few slots in manual WLM.
Under-allocate memory per query	No	Yes	If you define too many slots in manual WLM.
Maximum number of queries executing concurrently	Dynamic	Fixed	In manual WLM the total slots defined across all queues is the maximum number of queries that will execute.
Define query priority by queue	Yes	No	In manual WLM more slots on a queue implies lower priority, and fewer slots implies higher priority.
Query spilled to disk	Lower	Higher	Auto WLM throttles the concurrency to allow fewer queries so more memory gets allocated per query. In manual WLM you must allocate more slots per query basis.
Define short query time	Auto	Yes	You can choose between 1 and 20 seconds in manual WLM.
QMR action: Hop	No	Yes	WLM attempts to route the query to the next matching queue based on the WLM queue assignment rules. However, the query is canceled if no other queue definition is matched; it is not assigned to the default queue.
Concurrency Scaling (CS)	CS cluster uses auto WLM	CS cluster capped at 5 slots	If multiple CS clusters are enabled, then additional clusters can be created for the main cluster.

The objective of WLM is to manage resources for the queries executing on your warehouse. You can query Amazon Redshift system tables to analyze your workloads and set up the WLM configuration accordingly.

Use query Example 5-9 to see hourly query execution statistics.

Example 5-9. Hourly query execution statistics

```
SELECT DATE_TRUNC('hour',starttime) AS start_hour
     , MIN(starttime)              AS first_query_start_time
     , MAX(starttime)              AS last_query_start_time
     , COUNT(*)                    AS query_count
FROM stl_query
WHERE userid > 1
GROUP BY start_hour
ORDER BY start_hour DESC
;
```

Use query Example 5-10 to understand the peak memory per queue or service class. Note you can also filter by column `service_class_start_time` for a particular date–time range as required.

Example 5-10. Peak memory estimate

```
SELECT
    w.service_class,
    COUNT(*) query_count,
    ROUND(PERCENTILE_CONT(0.25)
      WITHIN GROUP
        (ORDER BY est_peak_mem)/1024^2,0)::INT AS prcntl25_mb,
    ROUND(PERCENTILE_CONT(0.50)
      WITHIN GROUP
        (ORDER BY est_peak_mem)/1024^2,0)::INT AS prcntl50_mb,
    ROUND(PERCENTILE_CONT(0.75)
      WITHIN GROUP
        (ORDER BY est_peak_mem)/1024^2,0)::INT AS prcntl75_mb,
    ROUND(PERCENTILE_CONT(0.90)
      WITHIN GROUP
        (ORDER BY est_peak_mem)/1024^2,0)::INT AS prcntl90_mb,
    ROUND(PERCENTILE_CONT(0.95)
      WITHIN GROUP
        (ORDER BY est_peak_mem)/1024^2,0)::INT AS prcntl95_mb,
    ROUND(PERCENTILE_CONT(0.99)
      WITHIN GROUP
        (ORDER BY est_peak_mem)/1024^2,0)::INT AS prcntl99_mb,
    ROUND(MAX(est_peak_mem)/1024^2,0)::INT AS p100_mb
FROM stl_wlm_query w
WHERE w.userid > 1
GROUP BY w.service_class
```

```
ORDER BY w.service_class
;
```

If you need to ensure that multiple workloads are executing at the same time, and you cannot set different priorities for these workload queues, then you have two choices. One option is to use manual WLM, and the second is to create two separate clusters, thus isolating the two workloads, and use data sharing with auto WLM on each of these clusters. With the second approach you get to maximize the throughput for each workload on their own isolated cluster and still ensure there is full utilization of resources. Chapter 7 covers this at length.

Parameter Group

A *parameter* is a value of a setting, for example auto_mv, which can be true or false. And a *parameter group* is a collection of such parameters (refer back to Figure 5-4). Parameter groups are only applicable to provisioned data warehouses. A parameter group applies to all of the databases on the cluster that the parameter group is associated with. Amazon Redshift comes with a default parameter group that cannot be edited, but you can create a new parameter group and customize your database settings.

You can create multiple parameter groups, each one having different values for various database parameter settings. You can associate a parameter group to one or more clusters. By modifying a parameter group, you can change the configuration of all clusters that use the same parameter group. Some WLM properties are static, which requires a reboot, while other properties are dynamic and take effect immediately.

In Example 5-11 you can see how to use the the modify-cluster CLI command to change the parameter group.

Example 5-11. AWS CLI command to modify-cluster

```
aws redshift modify-cluster
  --cluster-identifier mycluster01
  --cluster-parameter-group-name pg_bi
```

 You can set up a parameter group for write-heavy ETL workloads and another parameter group for read-heavy BI workloads. If you carefully choose only the dynamic properties in these two parameter groups, then you can effectively switch the cluster from one configuration to the other without needing a reboot. This strategy is applied to configure your cluster in a workload-specific configuration based on ETL/BI time windows, although auto WLM does this dynamically for you.

WLM Dynamic Memory Allocation

In each queue, WLM creates as many slots as the concurrency limit set for the queue. The memory allocated to the queue is then divided equally per slot. If you change the memory allocation or concurrency, Amazon Redshift dynamically manages the transition to the new WLM configuration. Active queries continue toward completion using the memory that has already been allocated.

The workload manager performs the transition in following steps:

1. Calculate the new memory allocation for each slot.

2. Unoccupied slot releases the memory it was previously allocated.

3. Active slots execute until query finishes and the associated memory is subsequently released.

4. New slots are added as soon as enough memory becomes available.

5. Once all previously running queries have finished, the transition to the new WLM configuration is complete and the slot count equals the new concurrency level.

In effect, queries that are running when the change takes place continue to use the original memory allocation. Queries that are queued when the change takes place are routed to new slots as they become available. Because of the dynamic nature of memory allocation by Amazon Redshift, you can change the memory allocation percentage for the WLM queue in the parameter group without needing a reboot.

Materialized Views

Materialized views (MV) are a powerful tool to speed up resource-intensive join queries that are repetitive and predictable. Typical use cases are dashboard queries with expensive joins and aggregations. The materialized view stores the results from the base query. This is different from a normal database view, where only the query definition is stored and the view query is executed every time the view is accessed.

The Amazon Redshift query optimizer automatically recognizes when an existing materialized view can be used to satisfy a request. It then transparently rewrites the request to use the materialized view. Queries go directly to the materialized view and not to the underlying detail tables. This automatic query rewrite feature means your application queries once written do not need to be changed to take advantage of newly created MVs.

MVs can be built on top of other MVs, thus allowing you to create different MVs for different levels of aggregation so any flavor of aggregation, from an end-user query can be satisfied faster using one or the other MV. Note that refreshing an MV is not a cascading process, so you should start with refreshing the deepest MV first, and keep refreshing MVs working upward.

The MV holds point-in-time data as of its last refresh timestamp. Amazon Redshift supports fast incremental refresh where it tracks changes to base tables and only pulls in impacted records. If an MV is not incremental refresh eligible, then it will be recomputed fully when it is refreshed. You can refresh the MV right after the base tables have been loaded so you know the MVs will always have the most up-to-date results and can always be used to provide query results with the automatic query rewrite feature.

The following tables provide crucial information about MVs:

STV_MV_INFO *table*
    Contains a row for every MV, whether the data is stale, and its state information

STL_MV_STATE *view*
    Contains a row for every state transition of a materialized view

SVL_MV_REFRESH_STATUS *view*
    Contains a row for the refresh activity of materialized views

When querying external tables from your data lake, performing large table joins can be an expensive operation. One optimization technique is to create materialized views in Amazon Redshift with aggregated data from external tables. If row-level data is required for deeper analysis, then the individual files can always be accessed via an external table query.

Autonomics

Amazon Redshift's auto-tuning capabilities are empowered by machine learning. Amazon Redshift is establishing smart defaults for many of its architectural settings based on best practices, and it is auto-tuning the physical data layout based on heuristics. These are covered under the umbrella of autonomics in this section.

Table SVL_AUTO_WORKER_ACTION records all the automatic optimization activities done by Amazon Redshift.

Auto Table Optimizer and Smart Defaults

Automatic table optimization is a self-tuning capability that automatically optimizes the design of tables by applying sort and distribution keys without the need for administrator intervention. Auto Table Optimizer (ATO) automatically picks the best distribution style and sort key for your tables defined with AUTO for distribution style and sort key.

By using automation to tune the design of tables, you can get started more easily and get the fastest performance quickly without needing to invest time to manually tune and implement table optimizations. Primary key (PK) defined on tables is generally a good high cardinality column with no duplicates. Thus the primary key is a good candidate to be used as distribution key and the Smart Defaults algorithms will apply it as the Auto Distribution Key for the table.

Also, Amazon Redshift Advisor will apply heuristics by using the primary key to make the recommendation even if the PK has not yet participated in joins. This will ensure that recommendations are made sooner rather than later. Once more workload data is available, Advisor can make a better recommendation. Tables with composite primary keys, typically the fact table, will not be made a recommendation based on heuristic, since foreign keys for fact tables typically reference primary keys of dimension tables, and when there are multiple dimension tables it is better to make a recommendation based on the actual joins applied in the workloads. Once this workload pattern can be analyzed, the ATO worker may choose a distribution key that is used most often in joins.

Another optimization the ATO worker will implement, if Auto DK is chosen, is to migrate from a PK-based distribution to an ALL-type distribution for small tables. This is an effective optimization because typically dimension tables, which are used in many joins, have lesser rows when compared to fact tables. Modifying the distribution style for small tables ensures join co-location and better performance, for example, calendar dimension with ALL distribution style.

Auto Vacuum

The auto vacuum worker background process performs two tasks. First is auto vacuum delete, to reclaim disk space occupied by rows that were marked for deletion by previous Update and Delete operations. Second is auto vacuum sort, to sort the physical data blocks by the sort key columns defined for the table. If more than 95% of a table is already sorted, then the auto vacuum worker will skip sorting this table.

The Example 5-12 query provides unsortedness of sample tables.

Example 5-12. Table sort benefit

```
SELECT
  "table",
  unsorted,
  vacuum_sort_benefit,
  tbl_rows,
  estimated_visible_rows
FROM
  svv_table_info
ORDER BY 1;

 table | unsorted | vacuum_sort_benefit | tbl_rows | estimated_visible_rows
-------+----------+---------------------+----------+-----------------------
 sales |    85.71 |                   5 | 17686548 | 17601203
 event |    35.24 |                  67 | 27586582 | 27486080
(2 rows)
```

The sales table is heavily unsorted (86%), but there is very little benefit (5%) from vacuum sort. The event table is relatively lesser unsorted (35%), but sorting rows can benefit a lot (67%) for queries.

Amazon Redshift continues to look for opportunity to perform vacuum every hour, and the auto vacuum worker threshold is based on the number of WLM slots occupied by user queries. As long as more than half the WLM slots are available, the auto vacuum worker will allocate itself 100 MB of memory, load 100 blocks of a table, and begin its operation. After each iteration it will assess the WLM state and go for another batch. If user queries arrive and more than 50% of WLM slots get occupied by user queries, then the auto vacuum worker will terminate. Any partial work done gets discarded, and the auto vacuum worker will reallocate 100 MB next time, but previously completed work is saved. In contrast, if a user issues a VACUUM command, then the same vacuum worker will begin its work but this time there is no check for 50% WLM slots, and instead it will take the vacuum job to completion.

The vacuum recluster option sorts the portions of the table that are unsorted. Portions of the table that are already sorted by automatic vacuum sort are left intact. This option does not merge the newly sorted data with the sorted region, nor reclaim

---

all space that is marked for deletion. If you have frequent data ingestion and your queries access only the most recent data, then use the `recluster` option.

User queries can access the tables while they are being vacuumed by the auto or manual vacuum process. You can perform both `select` and `insert` operations while a table is being vacuumed, but if you run `update` or `delete` while a VACUUM is running, both the VACUUM and the `update` or `delete` operations might take longer.

 If you need to prioritize vacuum for a particular table and you have free compute resources, then use the BOOST option, which allocates multiple slots to the vacuum operation so that it completes sooner.

If a large table is heavily unsorted, then a deep copy can be a faster operation than a vacuum, as the deep copy operates on an entire table in one go compared to vacuum, which operates on chunks. This also means that your storage is doubled for the duration of the deep copy operation.

Sample deep copy for table `my_tbl` is provided in Example 5-13.

Example 5-13. Deep copy

```
CREATE TABLE new_tbl (LIKE my_tbl);
INSERT INTO new_tbl (SELECT * FROM my_tbl);
DROP TABLE my_tbl;
ALTER TABLE new_tbl rename TO my_tbl;
```

Any data changes to `my_tbl` during the `insert` step are not visible to the deep copy operation. So during deep copy operations, you will need to track changes and apply them yourself. A better option is to perform this operation during minimal to no activity, like your scheduled maintenance window.

Auto Vacuum Sort

The auto vacuum sort keeps the table data in sorted order by the defined sort key columns for the table. It also checks for 50% of WLM slots free, and when available it borrows 3 GB memory from WLM. It then performs physical sorting of data in the data blocks and works in tandem with auto vacuum worker. It prioritizes which blocks of the table to sort by analyzing query patterns using machine learning. Amazon Redshift Advisor will provide a recommendation if there is a benefit to explicitly run vacuum sort on a given table. Refer back to Example 5-12 for the vacuum sort benefit.

Auto Analyze

The auto analyze worker generates or updates the table statistics metadata that is used to choose the optimal query execution plan for better query performance. It runs when your data warehouse is idle with over 10 minutes of inactivity. Auto analyze works incrementally, and a user-issued analyze command will automatically skip tables which have up-to-date statistics.

Typical data warehouse tables have many columns that are used predominantly in the SELECT clause, and relatively fewer columns used for JOIN and FILTER. Use the analyze command option PREDICATE COLUMNS to analyze only those columns that have been used as predicates in queries, like dist key column, sort key columns, and columns used in JOIN, FILTER, or GROUP BY clauses. This option provides the most benefit by gathering statistics of the column that will have the most impact on query performance. If no columns are marked as predicate columns, for example because the table has not yet been queried, then all of the columns are analyzed, so this is a very safe option to use by default.

Amazon Redshift automatically runs analyze on tables that you create with CREATE [TEMP] TABLE AS or SELECT INTO commands. The default analyze threshold is 10% of rows changed. But you can choose to set a different analyze threshold at session level to fine-tune this behavior.

You may want to explicitly analyze tables as part of ETL when subsequent steps could benefit from latest statistics, or when Amazon Redshift doesn't auto analyze because your data warehouse is heavily utilized and there are no periods of inactivity for Amazon Redshift to run auto analyze background tasks.

Auto Materialized Views (AutoMV)

We covered use cases for materialized views in "Materialized Views" on page 184, and the AutoMV feature now builds, refreshes, and drops MVs on your behalf based on it's built-in ML algorithms identifying query patterns that will benefit from new materialized views. Your end-user queries do not need to change as Amazon Redshift seamlessly fetches results from MV to provide faster query response times.

Amazon Redshift uses a technique called predicate elevation to create generalized AutoMVs by moving the filtered columns from user queries into the GROUP BY clause for AutoMV. Thus Amazon Redshift stores the full range of data in the materialized view, which allows similar queries to use the same materialized view. This approach is driven by dashboard-like workloads that often issue identical queries with different filter predicates.

Amazon Redshift applies AI to calculate which candidate materialized view provides the best performance benefit and system-wide performance optimization. In addition, it calculates a cost for system resources required to create and maintain the candidate MV. Existing manual materialized views are also considered, and an AutoMV will not be created if a manual materialized view already exists that covers the same scope. Manual materialized views have higher auto refresh priority over AutoMVs. Also AutoMVs related to queries on a higher priority queue are created before AutoMVs related to queries on a lower priority queue. The created AutoMVs are then monitored by a background process that checks their activity, such as how often they have been queried and refreshed. If Amazon Redshift determines that an AutoMV is not being used or refreshed, for example due to changes in the base table structure or change in query pattern, then the AutoMV is automatically dropped.

The refresh of AutoMVs is handled in the background automatically. If for some reason Amazon Redshift is unable to refresh an AutoMV, then it is marked as stale and it is not used to provide query results. Later on, when it is refreshed, then the AutoMV is again used for queries.

Amazon Redshift Advisor

Amazon Redshift Advisor is like having a 24-7 DBA who is monitoring your workloads and offers you specific recommendations related to operations and data warehouse settings to improve the throughput of your warehouse and save on operating costs. It also prioritizes the recommendations and ranks them in order of performance impact to your workloads.

Amazon Redshift Advisor recommendations are based on observations regarding performance statistics and operational data for your specific workloads. It develops recommendations by running tests on your data warehouse to determine if a suspect value is within a specified range. If the test result is outside of that range, Advisor generates recommendations for your data warehouse. At the same time, Advisor provides actionable steps for how to bring the deviated value back into the best-practice range. Advisor only displays recommendations that would have a significant impact on performance. It also removes recommendation from your recommendations list once you have addressed it.

See Amazon Redshift Advisor (*https://oreil.ly/YfSA_*) best practices on working with recommendations from Amazon Redshift Advisor.

Currently it covers the following topics:

- Compress Amazon S3 file objects loaded by COPY
- Isolate multiple active databases
- Reallocate workload management (WLM) memory
- Skip compression analysis during COPY
- Split Amazon S3 objects loaded by COPY

- Update table statistics
- Enable short query acceleration
- Alter distribution keys on tables
- Alter sort keys on tables
- Alter compression encodings on columns
- Data type recommendations

Each recommendation is provided with the analysis performed, time range of data that was analyzed, and either a query to implement the recommendation or a query to list impacted objects.

If you don't see a recommendation, that doesn't necessarily mean that your current table setup is the most appropriate. Advisor doesn't provide recommendations when there isn't enough data or the expected benefit of making changes is small.

The time when Advisor runs is not under user control. It kicks in when your data warehouse isn't busy and Amazon Redshift can use some empty cycles and resources to perform its analysis. This is similar to when your warehouse is very busy and auto-tuning activities like auto vacuum, auto table optimization (ATO), and auto analyze may not run.

As of 2022, Amazon Redshift Advisor needs at least 100 queries to be executed on a table to be able to make a recommendation. This requirement will relax going into the future, and you will see recommendations even sooner.

Workload Isolation

A *workload* is a set of queries run by a team, department, or group. And to be able to support multiple workloads on a single Amazon Redshift cluster, you need to design for workload isolation. *Workload isolation* is how to make sure that one workload does not consume resources in a way that it impacts other workload execution. You have seen earlier how WLM queues and associated QMR provide controls and a method for workload isolation. In these cases the resources of one cluster are being shared for multiple user workloads. Such a design can lead to conflicts, especially if each workload is owned by a different team and these teams are forced to share the resources of that single cluster. You can define only eight queues, and for complex multiuser workloads eight queues might not be enough for segregation.

With the Data Sharing feature you can achieve even more workload isolation and tighter control over resource allocation by segregating workloads into their own Amazon Redshift data warehouses. Each warehouse can then implement its own WLM queues and further allocate compute resources. You can even mix and match provisioned and serverless data warehouses based on workload duration and have multiple consumers for the same data shared by producer. Refer to Chapter 7 to learn more about how to use data sharing for workload isolation.

Additional Optimizations for Achieving the Best Price and Performance

Today's analytics environments are very demanding, and workloads are continuously evolving with data volumes only increasing over time. "Autonomics" on page 185 discussed how Amazon Redshift is making it easier by automating more and more tasks. Here are some considerations where you can optimize for achieving the best balance between price and performance of your warehouse.

Database Versus Data Warehouse

Consider your data volume and evaluate Amazon Aurora, specially for data volumes in GBs, even for analytics workloads. Amazon Redshift is good for processing large volumes of data, and it comes at a higher cost for smaller workloads. For workloads with relaxed query response time requirements, you can even consider offloading the final transposed analytical data to the Amazon S3 data lake in open formats like Parquet and leverage Amazon Athena query capabilities.

Amazon Redshift Serverless

If you're not already using Amazon Redshift serverless, it is a good choice when it is difficult to predict compute needs because you have variable workloads, periodic workloads with intermittent idle time, or spikes in between steady-state workloads. Amazon Redshift serverless scales automatically as your query pattern changes with more concurrent users and new workloads. And you are billed for compute only when user query is executed on user data; queries that execute on metadata or system tables are not billable.

If you are starting out with analyzing a dataset, then Amazon Redshift serverless provides you with a fast and easy way to get started without having to size or choose an appropriate cluster configuration. With serverless, your set compute is measured in Redshift Processing Units (RPUs), which equate to a certain processor and memory configuration. Serverless sets a default RPU, and you can change the default based on your workload requirement. Serverless takes care of automatically scaling RPUs based on the incoming workloads. The effort to maintain an appropriately sized provisioned cluster tuned to performance could be outweighed by the benefits of autoscaling RPUs.

Multi-Warehouse Environment

Instead of trying to manage one huge cluster, it might be beneficial to break down your data warehouse environment into many smaller data warehouses. Along with workload isolation, you can also get granularity for budgets, accounting, and ownership. Each team, department, and organizational unit can independently size and pay for compute as they see fit for their use case and still leverage data sharing to democratize their data.

Amazon Redshift supports setting up multi-warehouse environments with provisioned as well as serverless data warehouses using the data-sharing feature. The producer as well as the consumer can either be provisioned or serverless. This flexibility coupled with AWS Lake Formation integration for all data catalogs, data access, and data governance will enable your organization to easily and quickly build a data mesh architecture across the organization; refer to the AWS blog (*https://oreil.ly/VhBwX*) for details.

AWS Data Exchange

AWS Data Exchange makes it easy to get the data you need with unified billing. You can search through the catalog of all listed products and filter by industry, vendor, or delivery method. AWS Data Exchange (ADX) offers free as well as paid subscription options for you to first try out the data before committing to a subscription. It also offers public pricing and private pricing agreements so you can negotiate the terms and conditions for the product before purchase. ADX will automatically revoke access once subscription lapses so data provider and data consumer can both be assured that only authorized data products are accessible. You can also monetize your Amazon Redshift data by creating an ADX Data Share and listing it as a product on AWS Marketplace.

If your workload needs third-party data, then you should leverage ADX to simplify the data procurement process. You can get data in Amazon S3 files, Amazon Redshift datashares, or live data via APIs. Refer to AWS Data Exchange (*https://oreil.ly/fsRC_*) for details.

Table Design

If you are coming from other databases to Amazon Redshift, then take particular note of the technical differences between these two technologies.

When choosing key distribution style, you are limited to a single column. If your tables are being joined on multiple columns, you can fabricate a new column with concatenated data from all original join columns and use that as distribution key. If the base columns contain variable length string fields, then you hash the concatenated result to get a fixed-length column as distribution key. This will ensure co-located joins, minimize internode data movement, and thus provide best performance.

Amazon Redshift has automated most aspects of data architecture, and you need not worry too much about table design. But this is based off of machine learning and it needs data to draw inferences, so there is a lag before Amazon Redshift tunes the tables for you. Follow the table design best practices (*https://oreil.ly/tjjaO*) so you can get good performance from the very beginning of your data warehouse journey.

Indexes Versus Zone Maps

Amazon Redshift does not offer indexes or table partitions. It uses Zone Maps, which are min and max column values for each data block, to locate the data for you. Zone maps are most effective when data is sorted. For small tables, you can skip defining a sort key. For larger tables with even distribution style, choose most frequently filtered upon column for the sort key. If using key distribution, then you can specify the join column as both the sort key and the distribution key, which enables the faster sort merge join.

Drivers

Always use the latest drivers (*https://oreil.ly/QWgZW*) from Amazon Redshift so you can keep up with the latest features provided. If your third-party software provides its own driver for Amazon Redshift, then use that. You should use a previous version of the Amazon Redshift driver only if your tool requires a specific version of the driver.

Simplify ETL

Leverage features like Amazon Redshift federated query (*https://oreil.ly/zuJIB*) to simplify ETL by tapping into operational data directly or replicating it to your warehouse and implementing the ELT approach. To reduce data movement over the network and improve performance, Amazon Redshift distributes part of the computation for federated queries directly into the remote operational databases.

Amazon Redshift integration for Apache Spark (*https://oreil.ly/kO62y*) makes it easy to build and run Spark applications on Amazon Redshift. Your Spark applications can read from and write to your Amazon Redshift data warehouse without compromising on transactional consistency of the data or performance by leveraging the Amazon Redshift push-down optimizations.

The feature for Amazon Aurora zero-ETL integration with Amazon Redshift (*https://oreil.ly/-9Yal*) can be leveraged if you are loading entire transactional data from Amazon Aurora into Amazon Redshift for running analytics. This zero-ETL is a storage-level replication mechanism and is more efficient than exporting or copying rows from source to target.

Query Editor V2

Amazon Redshift Query Editor V2 is a fully managed SQL editor in your browser. It will automatically scale as your user community grows. There is no desktop software to install, and it reduces the number of steps required to be able to run your first query. As a additional team scalability feature, it improves collaboration with saved queries and the ability to share results and analyses between users.

In this chapter, you have learned how to scale your Amazon Redshift data warehouse, how to set up workload management, and optimize for best price and performance of your workloads.

Query Tuning

Amazon Redshift uses queries based on structured query language (SQL) to interact with data and objects in the system. *Data manipulation language* (DML) is the subset of SQL that you use to view, add, change, and delete data. *Data definition language* (DDL) is the subset of SQL that you use to add, change, and delete database objects such as tables and views. Before we dive into query writing best practices and performance tuning your queries, let's first understand how Amazon Redshift processes queries.

Query Processing

All queries submitted to Amazon Redshift are first parsed and then the optimizer develops a query execution plan (see Figure 5-6).

The three steps for each query are:

1. Query planning
2. Query compilation
3. Query execution

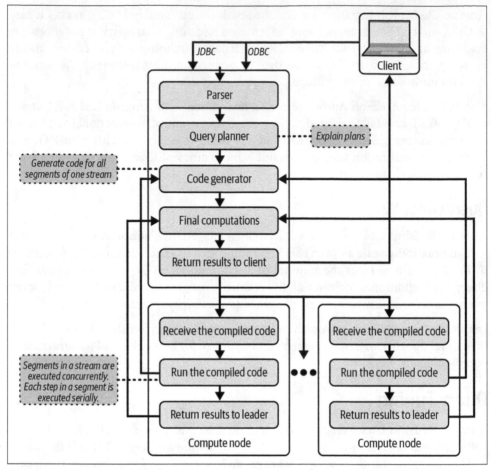

Figure 5-6. Amazon Redshift query processing

Query planning and execution workflow

The Amazon Redshift leader node receives the query and parses the SQL query. Any syntax errors are reported, and if parsing succeeds then the parser produces a logical representation of the original query. This initial query tree is sent to the query optimizer.

The query optimizer evaluates the query, analyzes table statistics to determine join order and predicate selectivity, and rewrites the query to maximize its efficiency. The query optimizer generates a query plan that describes execution order and network operations to be performed, and examples join types, join order, aggregation options, and data distribution requirements. The optimized query plan is then submitted as input to the execution engine.

The execution engine first checks the compile cache for a query-plan match. If none is found, then the execution engine translates the query plan into steps, segments, and streams. The execution engine generates compiled C++ code based on steps, segments, and streams as shown in Figure 5-7. This compiled code is added to the cache and then broadcast to the compute nodes.

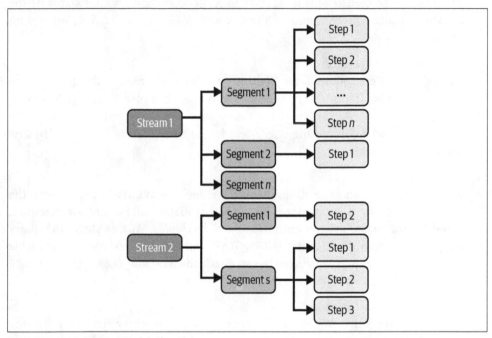

Figure 5-7. Amazon Redshift query steps

The compute node slices execute the query segments in parallel. When compute nodes are done with the execution, they return the query results to the leader node for final processing. The leader node merges the results from the compute nodes into a single result set and addresses any needed sorting or aggregation before returning the results to the query submitter.

Query stages and system tables

Now we will take a look at the details for each stage and the associated system tables that will capture the particulars.

Stage 1: Parsing and validation

During query planning the SQL query is first parsed and syntax is validated. If the query is valid, then a query tree is generated. At this point an entry is made in the STV_RECENTS (*https://oreil.ly/XRDLI*) system table. Also, at this stage, if Redshift identifies that the query can be cached, the cache will be checked for any existing entry and if found, the results are fetched from the Redshift cache and sent to the client by the leader node without the query going through the following stages. The information on query caching can be found in the SVL_QLOG (*https://oreil.ly/rZeZq*) system table.

Stage 2: Query requests locks

The query tree then is sent to acquire locks. The current locking status of the Redshift cluster can be found in the STV_LOCKS (*https://oreil.ly/bRo5n*) system table.

Stage 3: Planner and optimizer

After the locks are acquired, the Redshift optimizer will rewrite the query to the optimal form for Redshift. The output of this stage is a plan tree, which is PostgreSQL compliant. At this stage the query plan will be logged in STL_EXPLAIN (*https://oreil.ly/YPo9j*) and the query text in the STL_QUERYTEXT (*https://oreil.ly/mb1Ln*) system tables.

Stage 4: WLM scheduler

After successful plan generation, the query enters the WLMscheduler. Here, the query will wait for a queue slot, which when available will be sent for execution based on the queue assignment (*https://oreil.ly/kMvtF*). At this stage, the query makes an entry in the STV_WLM_QUERY_STATE (*https://oreil.ly/sFzSz*) system table for details on the query queue state and check the STV_WLM_QUERY_QUEUE_STATE (*https://oreil.ly/CdFQu*) system table.

Stage 5: Code generator/compiler

After acquiring the WLM slot for execution, an entry is made in the STV_INFLIGHT (*https://oreil.ly/KWfG0*) system table. Now, the Redshift execution planner will make the generated plan tree compliant with the Redshift distributive architecture, i.e. the query is now divided into streams, segments, and steps. After this, the segments are sent for compilation; here we can check the SVL_COMPILE (*https://oreil.ly/FZoD1*) system table for the compile time records and location of each query segment.

Stage 6: Distribution

The leader node distributes the code to the compute node. All segments of a stream are sent for execution through all slices since the data is distributed across the slices. Once the segments of the first stream complete execution through all slices, the second stream's segments will be executed.

Stage 7: Query execution

The compute node performs computations and processes the query. The information about query execution at this stage can be found in STV_EXEC_STATE (*https://oreil.ly/mxgBz*) (when in Running state) and post execution, in

SVL_QUERY_REPORT (*https://oreil.ly/mhu-U*) and SVL_QUERY_SUMMARY (*https://oreil.ly/igWRB*) system tables.

Stage 8: Final computation/aggregation

At this stage, the compute node sends results to the leader node. The leader node performs the final computation and sends results back to the client. After this stage you can find the query information in the STL_QUERY (*https://oreil.ly/A_Iox*) and STL_WLM_QUERY (*https://oreil.ly/56idm*) system tables.

Stage 9: Commit queue (if needed)

The query enters commit queue. For queries that require commit operation (for example, DDL commands), the query undergoes this additional stage before returning the results to the client. This information is logged in STL_COM MIT_STATS (*https://oreil.ly/gDAM9*). After the commit operation is performed on all CNs, the LN sends the results to the client.

To get an overview of the query execution runtime, please use the SYS_QUERY_HIS TORY (*https://oreil.ly/76IZa*) system table.

 Cached compile code is shared across sessions, so subsequent executions of the same query will be faster, even with different parameters. Query plan compilation and execution of compiled code happen only once for each stream.

Understanding the query plan

You can run the explain command to view the query execution plan as shown in Example 5-14. It gives you the information for the operations the execution engine performs. Reading the plan is from bottom to top, innermost step to outer. You will see which tables and columns are used in each operation and how much data, in terms of row count and row width in bytes, is processed in each operation. You also see the cost of each operation. It is important to note that this cost does not provide any precise information about actual execution times or memory consumption. The query optimizer compares cost across various execution plans and picks the best one for execution. The cost for each step gives you an indication of which particular operation within a given query is estimated to consume the most resources.

Example 5-14. Query execution plan

```
EXPLAIN
  SELECT AVG(DATEDIFF(day, listtime, saletime)) AS avgwait
  FROM sales, listing
  WHERE sales.listid = listing.listid
;

QUERY PLAN
-------------------------------------------------------------
XN Aggregate (cost=6350.30..6350.31 rows=1 width=16)
-> XN Hash Join DS_DIST_NONE (cost=47.08..6340.89 rows=3766 width=16)
   Hash Cond: ("outer".listid = "inner".listid)
 -> XN Seq Scan on listing (cost=0.00..1924.97 rows=192497 width=12)
 -> XN Hash (cost=37.66..37.66 rows=3766 width=12)
   -> XN Seq Scan on sales (cost=0.00..37.66 rows=3766 width=12)
```

The XN Seq Scan indicates a sequential scan operator on the particular table. Seq Scan scans each selected column in the table sequentially from beginning to end and evaluates any query predicates specified in the WHERE clause, for every row scanned.

The cost is provided as (cost=0.00..37.66 rows=3766 width=12); here the cost is shown for fetching the first row and for fetching the last row; the estimated row count and the row width is also displayed.

The XN Hash operator creates the hash table for the inner table in the join. The XN Hash Join operator is used for inner joins and left and right outer joins. The hash join operator reads the outer table, hashes the joining column, and finds matches in the inner hash table.

The cost is provided as XN Hash Join DS_DIST_NONE (cost=47.08..6340.89 rows=3766 width=16); here rows=3766 represents the estimated rows resulting from the join operation.

 Review the plan to see if the rows from the join operation are in the anticipated range. Too high a number here can indicate missing statistics or missing primary-key or foreign-key constraints. These can aid the query planner in producing better row estimates.

Amazon Redshift also has the nested loop join, which is used mainly for cross-joins (Cartesian products) and some inequality joins.

The nested loop join is the least optimal join in Amazon Redshift.

Amazon Redshift also has the merge join, which is used for inner joins and outer joins but not used for full joins. Merge is typically the fastest join operator, used when joining tables where the join columns are both distribution keys and sort keys, and when less than 20% of the joining tables are unsorted.

The XN `Aggregate` operator is for queries that involve aggregate functions and GROUP BY operations. You can view the query execution plan for the aggregate functions as in Example 5-15.

Example 5-15. Query execution plan for aggregate operator

```
explain
SELECT eventname, sum(pricepaid) FROM sales, event
WHERE sales.eventid = event.eventid
GROUP BY eventname
ORDER BY 2 DESC;

QUERY PLAN
-----------------------------------------------------------------
XN Merge (cost=1002815366604.92..1002815366606.36 rows=576 width=27)
Merge Key: sum(sales.pricepaid)
-> XN Network (cost=1002815366604.92..1002815366606.36 rows=576 width=27)
 Send to leader
 -> XN Sort (cost=1002815366604.92..1002815366606.36 rows=576 width=27)
  Sort Key: sum(sales.pricepaid)
  -> XN HashAggregate (cost=2815366577.07..2815366578.51 rows=576 width=27)
   -> XN Hash Join DS_BCAST_INNER (cost=109.98..2815365714.80 rows=172456 width=27)
    Hash Cond: ("outer".eventid = "inner".eventid)
    -> XN Seq Scan on sales (cost=0.00..1724.56 rows=172456 width=14)
    -> XN Hash (cost=87.98..87.98 rows=8798 width=21)
     -> XN Seq Scan on event (cost=0.00..87.98 rows=8798 width=21)
```

Figure 5-8 shows the preceding query and associated query plan. It displays how the query operations involved map to steps that Amazon Redshift uses to generate compiled code for the compute node slices. Each query plan operation maps to multiple steps within the segments, and sometimes to multiple segments within the streams.

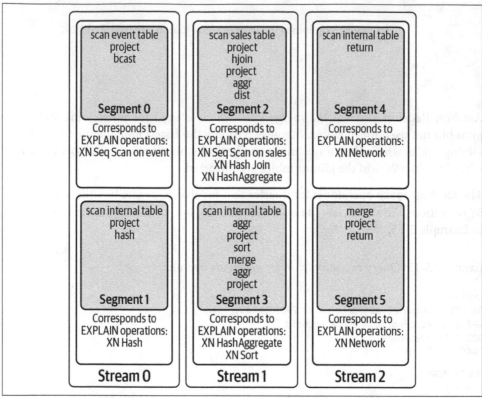

Figure 5-8. Amazon Redshift query streams

The query optimizer runs the query plan as follows:

1. In Stream 0, the query runs Segment 0 with a sequential scan operation to scan the events table. The query continues to Segment 1 with a hash operation to create the hash table for the inner table in the join.

2. In Stream 1, the query runs Segment 2 with a sequential scan operation to scan the sales table. It continues with Segment 2 with a hash join to join tables where the join columns are not both distribution keys and sort keys. It again continues with Segment 2 with a hash aggregate to aggregate results. Then the query runs Segment 3 with a hash aggregate operation to perform unsorted grouped aggregate functions, and a sort operation to evaluate the ORDER BY clause and other sort operations.

3. In Stream 2, the query runs a network operation in Segment 4 and Segment 5 to send intermediate results to the leader node for further processing.

The last segment of a query returns the data. If the return set is aggregated or sorted, the compute nodes each send their piece of the intermediate result to the leader node. The leader node then merges the data and provides the final result back to the query submitter.

Factors affecting query performance

The following aspects of your data warehouse and overall database operations determine how quickly your queries execute:

Number of nodes
> More nodes means more processors and more slices, which enables your queries to process faster by running portions of the query concurrently across the slices, but you need to find a good balance between performance and cost.

Node types
> Amazon Redshift provisioned cluster offers different node type, each with different sizes and limits to help you scale your cluster appropriately. These node types determine the storage capacity, memory, CPU, and price of each node in the cluster.

Data distribution
> When you run a query, the query optimizer redistributes the data to the compute nodes as needed to perform any joins and aggregations. Choosing the right distribution style for a table helps minimize the impact of the redistribution step by locating the data where it needs to be before the joins are performed.

Sort order
> The query optimizer and the query processor use the information about where the data is located to reduce the number of blocks that need to be scanned and thereby improve query speed.

Dataset volume
> Queries on large data volume can impact query performance, because more rows need to be scanned and redistributed. Running regular vacuums, archiving of infrequently queried data, and restricting the query dataset by using predicates can improve performance.

WLM setup
> Each query operation takes one or more slots in an available query queue and uses the memory associated with those slots. If other operations are running, enough query queue slots might not be available. In this case, the query has to wait for slots to open before it can begin processing.

Code compilation

> Amazon Redshift generates and compiles code for each query execution plan, and caches this information for subsequent invocations. You will have some overhead cost the first time code is generated and compiled. The compiled code segments are cached locally on the cluster and in a virtually unlimited cache. This cache persists after cluster reboots. Subsequent executions of the same query run faster because they can skip the compilation phase.

Analyzing Queries

If a query is taking longer than expected, you need to identify and correct issues that might be negatively affecting the query's performance. Sometimes a query that should run quickly is forced to wait until another, longer-running query finishes. In such a case you can improve overall system performance by creating and using query queues for different types of queries.

Reviewing query alerts

Use the STL_ALERT_EVENT_LOG (*https://oreil.ly/o5wOu*) system table to identify and correct potential performance issues with your query. This table captures the potential issue for the query, and also provides recommended solutions to resolve the alert.

Analyzing the query plan

Use the explain command and analyze the query plan. Concentrate on optimizing the steps with the highest cost. Look at the joins being executed, merge being the best; hash are fairly common and OK for inner tables, whereas nested loop are to be avoided except for a small number of rows or loops.

> Amazon Redshift chooses the smaller table for the inner join and the larger table for the outer join. If you see otherwise, then likely your table statistics are not updated.

During join steps, a slice may need to work with data not stored locally, and network transmission is by far the most expensive operation for a query.

Table 5-2. Distribution joins

Join type	Description
DS_DIST_NONE	This is the ideal situation that indicates that the data for the join is co-located on the same slice. This is the most efficient option as no network transfer will occur.
DS_DIST_ALL_NONE	Indicates that the join is occurring with a table that has DISTSTYLE ALL and also does not incur network transfer.

Join type	Description
DS_DIST_ALL_INNER	Indicates that the *inner* join table is being sent to a single node because the join table uses `DISTSTYLE ALL`. This join is executed on a single node and will likely be slow.
DS_DIST_INNER, DS_DIST_OUTER	Indicates which table is being redistributed when using an outer join (inner or outer table); if one of the tables is much smaller or infrequently updated, consider changing it to `DISTSTYLE ALL`.
DS_BCAST_INNER	Indicates that the *inner* join table is being broadcast to all nodes.
DS_BCAST_BOTH	Indicates that both tables in the join are being broadcast to all nodes. This is the worst possible option.

Identifying Queries for Performance Tuning

The first three joins from Table 5-2 are where you will see minimal performance deterioration, so if you see queries that are frequently run or have a business SLA falling under the bottom three, then these queries are good candidates for performance tuning.

Lets take the example of a trading company's data warehouse that has two main fact tables, `fact_executions` for all the trade executions, and `fact_allocation` for all the trade allocations, as in Figure 5-9. The thicker lines represent a co-located join because of matching distribution keys for these tables.

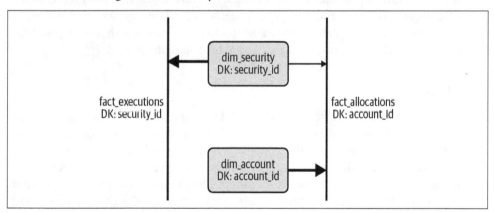

Figure 5-9. Multifact schema

Consider that most of the time you analyze the executions by the security dimension, and you analyze the allocations by the account dimension. Note that the security dimension still joins to the allocations fact since every allocation is for a particular traded security.

Based on this design most of your execution reports will perform well since you join mostly with security dimension. Most of your allocations reports will also perform well since you mostly join with account dimension. But you will see redistribution of security dimension data if you need to perform some analysis on allocations by security, since this is not a co-located join. If this analysis is not done often, then it is less business critical and a slower query response should be tolerable. But if this analysis is deemed business critical and has strict SLAs defined, then you might need to change the security dimension to distribution style of ALL so the analysis, allocations by security, and executions by security, becomes a co-located join. In this case, to be able to meet the performance needs, you can be paying more for storage.

 Not all queries need to be or can be tuned for performance. Based on the business priority of the query, you need to weigh the trade-offs for time spent on tuning and the cost to achieve the performance.

Additionally, refer to top candidates for tuning (*https://oreil.ly/dYmc0*) to identify priority queries amongst all your queries, tables with data skew or unsorted rows (*https://oreil.ly/IJd66*) to identify candidate tables for considering a different distribution strategy and manual vacuum needs, queries with nested loops (*https://oreil.ly/csbQS*) to identify possibly ill-written queries and candidates for implementing query monitoring rules on specific queues, queue wait times for queries (*https://oreil.ly/eY_GK*) to identify opportunities for changing WLM setup and leverage Concurrency Scaling to reduce queue waits, query alerts (*https://oreil.ly/hmGvH*) to identify table alerts and recommendations for fixing queries, and tables with missing statistics (*https://oreil.ly/cRTmL*) to identify tables for manual statistics gathering.

Summary

In this chapter, we covered scaling for predictable demand as well as dealing with unpredictable spiky workloads, went through how to set up workload management and query monitoring rules to minimize the blast radius of bad queries and protecting your Amazon Redshift data warehouse. We also covered how to leverage the materialized views, various automations offered by Amazon Redshift, and how to implement workload isolation using the data sharing feature. The chapter ended with a discussion of the optimizations for balancing price-performance and performance tuning techniques for queries and how to identify and tune queries.

In the next chapter, we'll cover machine learning. We will describe the different problem sets that data scientists have to solve and the types of algorithms they apply to solve these problems. Finally, we'll show how Amazon Redshift demystifies predictive analytics by enabling data scientists, data engineers, and even data analysts with tools to build, train, and run predictions using Amazon Redshift. We'll show how users can run the entire machine learning lifecycle directly using SQL commands and how advanced users can integrate Amazon Redshift with Amazon SageMaker.

CHAPTER 6

Amazon Redshift Machine Learning

Machine learning and artificial intelligence have come from being concepts of science fiction to everyday companions, be it on your mobile device or empowering businesses with the ability to disrupt and enhance existing processes in every segment of decision making.

According to research by GlobalNewsWire (*https://oreil.ly/6keHq*), the AI/ML market is projected to grow to a $1.4 trillion industry by 2029. The PwC 2022 AI Business Survey (*https://oreil.ly/jACdB*) shows 86% of respondents said AI technology is a mainstream part of their company, and 52% of respondents are accelerating adoption for AI/ML.

Here's an example of how a company using Redshift's AI/ML capabilities improved their business. Jobcase, a leading online job-search platform for job seekers, needs to perform job matching for more than 110 million registered members across the United States by identifying strong matches to suggest quality jobs for its members. It also helps employers hire qualified workers. Its recommendation system generates specific job listing recommendations, as well as search suggestions and company recommendations. Using AI/ML, Jobcase was able to achieve 5% improvement in member engagement metrics, which translates to an improved member experience, higher member retention, and a corresponding increase in revenue. They were also able to reduce testing time from 1 to 2 months to under a week, eliminated the need to move data to a separate ML environment, improved scalability, and were able to make billions of predictions in around 15 minutes instead of 4 to 5 hours. See the case study "Jobcase Scales ML Workflows to Support Billions of Daily Predictions Using Amazon Redshift ML" (*https://oreil.ly/v12dX*) for additional details.

Here's another example: Magellan Rx Management, a division of Magellan Health, Inc., develops and delivers predictive analytics to forecast future drugs costs, identify drugs that will drive future trends, and proactively identify patients at risk for becoming nonadherent to their medications, via their MRx Predict solution built on top of Amazon Redshift ML. Prior to Amazon Redshift ML, they had data analysts and clinicians manually categorize any new drugs into the appropriate therapeutic conditions. With Amazon Redshift ML, they now make the predictions using standard SQL programming to predict appropriate drug therapeutic conditions, which improves their operational efficiency while maintaining a high level of clinical accuracy. See the blog post "How Magellan Rx Management Used Amazon Redshift ML to Predict Drug Therapeutic Conditions" (*https://oreil.ly/x6mXd*) for additional details.

In this chapter, we will cover the end-to-end "Machine Learning Cycle" and how "Amazon Redshift ML" enables multiple personas in your organization with the tools to start leveraging "Machine Learning Techniques" to drive innovation. We will also dive deep in the different "Machine Learning Algorithms" and show you through an example how you can use "Integration with Amazon SageMaker Autopilot" to predict outcomes of a fictitious street race between humans and machines. We will also continue with our student information system dataset and explain "Using Amazon Redshift ML to Predict Student Outcomes". We'll also describe how certain ML problems can't be solved with Amazon SageMaker Autopilot. In those cases you can use "Amazon SageMaker Integration with Amazon Redshift" to access Amazon Redshift data with the Amazon SageMaker canvas tool to build your model. With your model in place, you can leverage "Integration with Amazon SageMaker—Bring Your Own Model (BYOM)" to run inferences in Amazon Redshift. Lastly, we'll cover the "Amazon Redshift ML Costs".

Machine Learning Cycle

The typical steps involved in machine learning (Figure 6-1) include the following: data gathering, data preparation and cleansing, ML model and algorithm selection, setting up the training environment, training the ML model, evaluating and tuning the ML model, deploying the ML model for production usage with scaling, and finally, making predictions to drive business decisions.

The quality of your ML model is directly influenced by the quality of the data you use. Incorrect or outdated data will result in wrong outcomes or predictions that are not relevant. Thus preparing your data for building ML models involves cleansing data to remove unwanted data, missing values, duplicate values, and even converting data types for certain attributes. You might even need to restructure the dataset and transpose the rows and columns or index of rows and columns. You also need to split the dataset into training dataset and testing dataset used to check the accuracy of your model after training. A good training dataset is relevant, contains minimal missing and repeated values, and provides a good representation of the various subcategories/classes present. With Amazon Redshift ML you can leverage your data warehouse data that is already cleansed and validated as source data for building ML models.

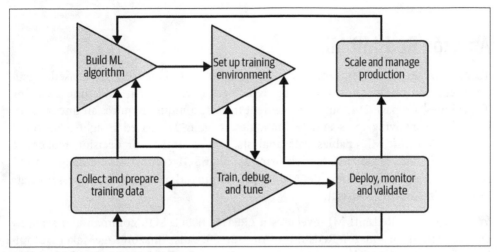

Figure 6-1. Typical ML lifecycle

Once you have your dataset for ML, you need to choose a model for training. The ML model determines the output you get after running an ML algorithm on the collected data. It is important to choose a model that is relevant to your task at hand. Scientists and engineers have developed various ML models, like linear regression, decision tree, nearest neighbor, and random forest, to name a few. These are suited for different tasks like speech recognition, image recognition, prediction, and numerous various use cases. Apart from model type, you also need to choose your model algorithm based on whether it is suited for numerical or categorical data and choose one accordingly.

Once you have decided on the model type, you now need to set up the model training environment. You have to configure the infrastructure components that build up your ML training environment and decide on storage for your data, code, and models. Identify what compute is best suited for the type of ML model you are trying to build. Install necessary software, integrated development environments (IDE), frameworks, and algorithms to begin your ML journey.

You train, debug, and tune your ML model iteratively in your training environment. When ready, you need to deploy to your production environment, validate the predictions, and monitor the performance of your ML model execution. This step often involves scaling your infrastructure to achieve the performance expectations and business SLAs for model execution.

We have covered the ML process at only a high level, but you can see that it is a very intensive and iterative process until you get the perfectly tuned model fitting your specific use case.

Amazon Redshift ML

To solve business problems, organizations use ML techniques like supervised, unsupervised, and reinforcement learning, which we cover later in "Machine Learning Techniques" on page 214. But to implement these techniques requires an understanding of ever-evolving tools and technologies to gain ML-based insights. However, Amazon Redshift ML enables data analysts, data scientists, or decision makers to create, train, and deploy ML models using familiar SQL commands. To create an ML model, users need to write a CREATE MODEL command and pass the necessary data available in Amazon Redshift.

When Amazon Redshift ML executes a CREATE MODEL SQL command, it securely exports data from Amazon Redshift to Amazon S3, calls Amazon SageMaker Autopilot to prepare data and train the ML model, and finally Amazon SageMaker Neo to make the ML model available as an SQL function in Amazon Redshift (see Figure 6-2).

In other words, Amazon Redshift ML communicates with various cloud-based services like Amazon S3, Amazon SageMaker, and Amazon Redshift under the hood to simplify model development with SQL queries.

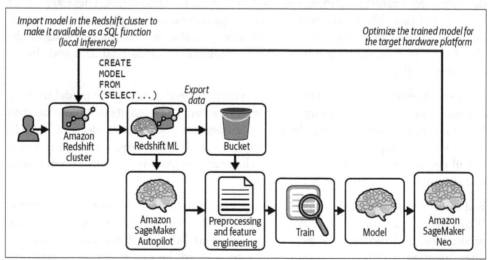

Figure 6-2. Amazon Redshift ML Architecture

Amazon Redshift ML uses Amazon SageMaker to build and train ML models. Amazon SageMaker (*https://aws.amazon.com/sagemaker*) is a fully managed service for preparing data and building, training, and deploying ML models and running predictions with fully managed infrastructure, tools, and workflows.

Amazon SageMaker Autopilot preprocesses the training data, such as substituting missing data with a different value, to retain most of the data/information of the dataset. It recognizes the characteristics of categorical columns like country/state/zip code, and properly formats them for training. It chooses the best preprocessors and identifies the most fitting algorithm and algorithm hyperparameters that will deliver the model with the most accurate predictions.

When the model has been trained, Amazon Redshift ML uses Amazon SageMaker Neo (*https://aws.amazon.com/sagemaker/neo*), which optimizes the ML model for deployment and makes it available as an SQL function within Amazon Redshift. You can use the SQL function to apply the ML model to your data in queries, reports, and dashboards. All this is happening automatically by executing the CREATE MODEL command, covered in "Create Model" on page 218.

Amazon Redshift ML Flexibility

Amazon Redshift ML provides the CREATE MODEL command with the default option of AUTO ON. When you use AUTO ON with Amazon Redshift ML and run the SQL command to create the model, Amazon Redshift ML exports the specified data from Amazon Redshift to Amazon S3 and calls SageMaker Autopilot to automatically prepare the data, select the appropriate prebuilt algorithm, and apply the algorithm for model training. Amazon Redshift ML handles all the interactions between Amazon Redshift, Amazon S3, and SageMaker, abstracting the steps involved in training and compilation. After the model is trained, Amazon Redshift ML makes it available as a SQL function in your Amazon Redshift data warehouse.

The AUTO OFF option is for advanced users who know the model type and hyperparameters to use for training. This will turn off the create model automatic discovery of preprocessors and hyperparameters and can reduce the time taken to create models compared to the AUTO ON option. With the AUTO OFF option, you can have finer control on training of Amazon Redshift models.

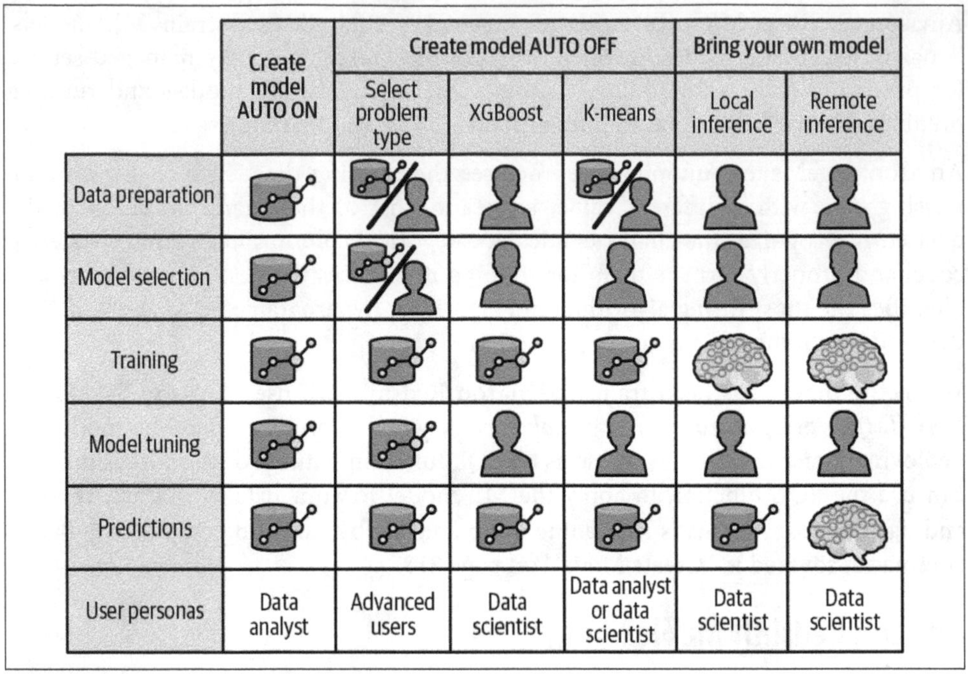

	Create model AUTO ON	Create model AUTO OFF			Bring your own model	
		Select problem type	XGBoost	K-means	Local inference	Remote inference
Data preparation						
Model selection						
Training						
Model tuning						
Predictions						
User personas	Data analyst	Advanced users	Data scientist	Data analyst or data scientist	Data scientist	Data scientist

Figure 6-3. Amazon Redshift ML flexibility

In Figure 6-3, you can see that Amazon Redshift ML provides channels for varying levels of ML knowledge. Any data analyst who is familiar with SQL language can use the auto option to get started with Amazon Redshift ML. There is no requirement to know the details of the ML algorithms or ML programming languages like Python (*https://www.python.org/about*) or R (*https://www.r-project.org/about.html*). Amazon Redshift ML is also useful for data scientists who have a good handle on the ML algorithms and want to tune the model for specific properties. Amazon Redshift ML also supports a Bring Your Own Model (BYOM) approach, which we cover in "Integration with Amazon SageMaker—Bring Your Own Model (BYOM)" on page 229, where you leverage a SageMaker environment to choose the particular runtimes and compute types to build, train, and tune the model. You can then import the model and run inferences in Amazon Redshift or draw remote inferences directly from SageMaker using your data from Amazon Redshift.

Getting Started with Amazon Redshift ML

Amazon Redshift needs explicit permissions granted to interact with Amazon Sage-Maker for its machine learning capabilities. Set this up by configuring your IAM role (*https://oreil.ly/M6Wvn*) for Amazon Redshift ML.

As a best practice, you should segregate permissions for creating a model versus permissions for using the model for prediction functions. The queries in Example 6-1 showcase two groups, `model_create_grp` with permissions to create models, and `model_user_grp` with permissions to use your ML model for inference.

Example 6-1. Grants for Amazon Redshift ML

```
GRANT CREATE MODEL TO GROUP model_create_grp;
GRANT EXECUTE ON MODEL demo_ml.ml_model TO GROUP model_user_grp;
```

Amazon Redshift supports different languages along with default `sql` language. You can query table `SVV_LANGUAGE_PRIVILEGES` to see all the languages and the privileges granted to the user, role, or group. Amazon Redshift ML is also another language in Amazon Redshift and will show up as `mlfunc` in this table.

Amazon Redshift grants privileges to the ML language when you execute the grant statement to allow creating models (see Example 6-2).

Example 6-2. Language privileges

```
SELECT
    language_name,
    privilege_type,
    identity_type,
    identity_name,
    identity_id,
    admin_option
FROM
    svv_language_privileges;
```

language_name	privilege	identity_type	identity_name	identity_id	admin_option
c	USAGE	public	public	0	false
internal	USAGE	public	public	0	false
mlfunc	USAGE	group	model_create_grp	834679	false
plpgsql	USAGE	public	public	0	false
sql	USAGE	public	public	0	false
plpythonu	USAGE	public	public	0	false

Machine Learning Techniques

Machine learning models find patterns in your data and then apply these patterns to generate predictions on new data. There are many varieties of ML techniques, but here are three general approaches:

Supervised machine learning
> The algorithm analyzes labeled data and learns how to map input data to an output label. It is often used for classification and prediction.

Unsupervised machine learning
> Unlike supervised, this algorithm is not used for predicting an outcome, so it is considered unlabeled. This algorithm finds patterns by clustering data and identifying similarities in clustered data. Popular uses include recommendation systems and targeted advertising.

Reinforcement learning
> This technique is where the ML model learns in a fashion similar to how a human learns, through trial and error. Reinforcement learning is geared toward a digital agent who is put in a specific environment to learn problem solving. Similar to how we learn new things, the agent faces a game-like situation and must make a series of decisions to try to achieve the correct outcome. Through trial and error, the agent will learn what to do and what not to do, and is rewarded or punished accordingly. Every time it receives a reward, it reinforces the behavior and signals the agent to use the same tactic again next time. Through such training, machine learning models can be taught to follow instructions, conduct tests, and operate equipment, for example.

Amazon Redshift ML supports the supervised and unsupervised learning approaches. Due to the complex nature of reinforcement learning, while it is supported in Amazon SageMaker, it is not a technique supported by Amazon Redshift ML.

Supervised Learning Techniques

Supervised learning is the most common ML approach, where you begin with a training dataset that has input data columns and output data columns. These input data attributes to your ML model are referred to as "features," and the output data attributes are referred as "labels." This training dataset is designed to train the ML algorithm into classifying data or predicting output label accurately.

There are two types of supervised-learning ML problems that Amazon Redshift ML supports: classification and regression. Your particular use case will fall in only one of these distinct problem types:

- Classification problems are for assigning data into specific categories. There are two types of classifications:

  — Binary classification refers to the problem of predicting one of *two* outcomes, such as classifying spam in your inbox or predicting whether a customer churns or not.

  — Multiclass classification refers to the problem of predicting one of *many* outcomes, such as predicting which particular credit card from your broad array for credit cards a particular customer might be most interested in pursuing.

- A regression problem is the task of approximating a mapping function from input variables to a continuous output variable. It uses an algorithm to understand the relationship between dependent and independent variables (features), and defines the mapping function to predict the output variable (label). A continuous output variable is a real-value, an integer or floating point value, often quantities like amounts and sizes, such as sales revenue projections for a given business or the total spending of customers.

A specific regression problem where input variables are ordered by time is called a time series forecasting problem. This problem is solved by a forecast model.

Amazon Forecast (*https://aws.amazon.com/forecast*) is a fully managed service that uses statistical and machine learning algorithms to deliver time-series forecasts. Amazon Redshift ML supports building forecasting models using Amazon Forecast. This lets you use historical data over a time period to make predictions about future events. Common use cases of Amazon Forecast include using retail product data to decide how to price inventory, historical orders to predict market demand, historical manufacturing and sales data to predict how much of one item to order, and web traffic data to forecast how much traffic a web server might receive.

Quota limits from Amazon Forecast are enforced in Amazon Redshift forecast models; for example, the maximum number of forecasts is 100, although this can be changed via a support request.

Dropping a forecast model doesn't automatically delete the associated resources in Amazon Forecast.

Unsupervised Learning Techniques

Unsupervised learning uses ML algorithms to analyze datasets to discover hidden patterns in data without the need for human intervention, and hence falls under the unsupervised learning category. Unlike supervised learning, where you have defined input attributes and defined output attributes, unsupervised learning is about identifying anomalies or outliers in your data.

There are three types of unsupervised ML problem types that Amazon Redshift ML supports via Amazon SageMaker: clustering, association, and dimensionality reduction. Your particular use case can fall in more than one of these problem types at the same time.

Clustering is a technique for grouping unlabeled data based on their similarities or differences and then identifying the outliers; for example, *k*-means clustering algorithms assign similar data points into groups, where the *k* value represents the size of the grouping and granularity. It attempts to find discrete groupings within data, whereby members of a group are as similar as possible to one another and as different as possible from members of other groups. This clustering technique is helpful for segmentation, where you want to minimize the variance within each cluster or segment; for example, a credit card company can segment its loyalty card customers into different groups based on their buying behavior and launch targeted campaigns or promotional products.

Association uses different rules to find relationships between variables in a given dataset, along the lines of recommendations such as "customers who bought this item also bought" type of problems.

Dimensionality reduction is used when the number of features (or dimensions or input columns) in a given dataset is too high. It reduces the number of data inputs to a manageable size while also preserving the data integrity, such as when encoders remove noise from visual data to improve picture quality.

Machine Learning Algorithms

We've covered problem types, and now we'll discuss algorithms that can be used to solve these problem types. For a deeper understanding of the specific problem types and the particular algorithm that can be used to solve that particular problem type, see the documentation on Amazon SageMaker's built-in algorithms (*https://oreil.ly/ LaxlD*).

For supervised learning, Amazon Redshift ML supports Extreme Gradient Boosting (XGBoost), multilayer perceptron (MLP), and linear learner algorithms.

The XGBoost algorithm is an optimized open source implementation of the gradient boosted trees algorithm. XGBoost is designed from the ground up to handle many data science problems in a efficient, flexible, portable, and accurate way. XGBoost can be used for regression, binary classification, multiclass classification, and ranking problems. Ranking problem types are for finding artifacts in relevance order. They associate a numeric score for each input in the query to the final artifact. Once you have the relevance score of each artifact, you can rank the artifacts according to those scores and predict the top N best match values. For details on XGBoost and SageMaker, see the blog post "Introducing the Open-Source Amazon SageMaker XGBoost Algorithm Container" (*https://oreil.ly/NmfuI*).

An MLP is a supervised deep-learning method that deals with training multilayer artificial neural networks, also called deep neural networks. MLP learns the relationship between linear and nonlinear data. It is a feed-forward artificial neural network that generates a set of outputs from a set of inputs. An MLP is characterized by several layers of input nodes connected as a directed graph between the input and output layers. Typical applications for MLP algorithms are for image classification, speech recognition, and machine translation.

Linear models are supervised learning algorithms used for solving either classification or regression problems. You give the linear learner model labeled data and the algorithm learns a linear function, or, for classification problems, a linear threshold function. Use linear learner algorithms for use cases such as predicting sales of a product, determining marketing effectiveness, or to predict customers' willingness to purchase a product or service. You can read more about the SageMaker linear learner (*https://oreil.ly/vtXU7*) algorithm, which explores different training objectives or accuracy metrics, and chooses the best solution from a validation set.

For unsupervised learning, Amazon Redshift ML supports Amazon SageMaker Random Cut Forest (RCF) and *k*-means algorithms. These have to be built in Amazon SageMaker and imported to Amazon Redshift as Bring Your Own Models. We will cover BYOM in "Integration with Amazon SageMaker—Bring Your Own Model (BYOM)" on page 229.

RCF is a clustering technique that detects anomalous data points within a dataset that diverges from otherwise well-structured or patterned data. With each data point, RCF associates an anomaly score. Low score values indicate that the data point is considered "normal." High values indicate the presence of an anomaly in the data. The definitions of "low" and "high" depend on the application, but common practice suggests that scores beyond three standard deviations from the mean score are considered anomalous.

If you're using *k*-means, you define the attributes that you want the algorithm to use to determine *similarity*. It identifies discrete groups within your data, such that members of a group are as similar as possible to each another, and as different as possible from members of other groups. The number k decides the number of groups this algorithm will generate. *k*-means is suitable for when you want to make groups of similar things from a randomly distributed collection of things.

Integration with Amazon SageMaker Autopilot

Amazon SageMaker (*https://aws.amazon.com/sagemaker*) is a fully managed machine learning service for data scientists and developers to build, train, and directly deploy models into a production-ready hosted environment.

Amazon Redshift ML leverages the Amazon SageMaker Autopilot (*https://oreil.ly/VrhVT*) feature that trains and tunes multiple machine learning models based on your data and keeps the model with the highest accuracy. Amazon SageMaker Autopilot provides automatic data cleaning, automatic data preprocessing, automatic algorithm selection for linear regression, binary classification, and multiclass classification. It also supports automatic hyperparameter tuning optimization (HPO) (*https://oreil.ly/kkrib*), distributed training, automatic instance, and cluster size selection.

Amazon SageMaker Autopilot makes it easy to build models in Amazon Redshift without knowing much theory about machine learning itself.

Create Model

Let's dive into some practice creating a model. Let's pretend you want to predict the results of a futuristic street race between humans and machines. You have historical data for previous races, the city where the race took place, the weather during the race, the condition of the road, the distance to be covered and the speed at which the human and the machine is running, and the actual result—did the human win the race. Yes, we are rooting for the humans!

All you need is the table to be used for training the model and an Amazon S3 bucket to hold the training artifacts. The code in Example 6-3 will prepare the tables for you. You have a training table to train the ML model and an inference table to draw ML inferences on. Later (see Example 6-4), you'll see the create model syntax.

Example 6-3. Prepare race schema

```
CREATE SCHEMA race;

CREATE TABLE race.speed_training(
    city                varchar(10),
    machine_distance    decimal,
    human_distance      decimal,
    weather             varchar(5),
    road_condition      varchar(5),
    machine_speed       decimal,
```

```
    human_speed       decimal,
    human_win_y_n     boolean);

COPY race.speed_training
FROM 's3://redshift-demos/ANT402/training.csv'
region 'us-east-1'
iam_role default
csv delimiter ',';

CREATE TABLE race.speed_inference(
    city              varchar(10),
    machine_distance  decimal,
    human_distance    decimal,
    weather           varchar(5),
    road_condition    varchar(5),
    machine_speed     decimal,
    human_speed       decimal,
    human_win_y_n     boolean);

COPY race.speed_inference
FROM 's3://redshift-demos/ANT402/inference.csv'
region 'us-east-1'
iam_role default
csv delimiter ',';
```

In Example 6-4, Amazon SageMaker Autopilot is doing all the heavy lifting for you and will figure out the best ML model to predict if the human will win. Tell the model to use the label human_win_y_n, which can be True or False, on training data. Since the desired target human_win_y_n is binary, Autopilot will determine that this is a binary classification problem and will choose the most accurate algorithm.

Example 6-4. Create model

```
CREATE MODEL race.human_vs_machine
FROM race.speed_training
TARGET human_win_y_n
FUNCTION fnc_will_human_win
IAM_ROLE default
SETTINGS (
  S3_BUCKET 'my_ml_bucket',
  MAX_RUNTIME 10800);
```

> We have set MAX_RUNTIME higher than default 5400 (1.5 hours) for this example to ensure the model explainability report in Table 6-3 is generated successfully.

Use the `show model` command in Example 6-5 to review the ML model status. Inspect the `Model State` to determine if the model is ready. When you first create your model, you will see the a status of `TRAINING`.

Example 6-5. Show model

```
SHOW MODEL race.human_vs_machine;
```

Table 6-1. Show model—TRAINING

Key	Value
Model Name	human_vs_machine
Schema Name	race
Owner	model_create_user
Creation Time	Tue, 12.12.2023 05:10:15
Model State	TRAINING
...	

When your model has a state of `READY`, the process is complete and you can begin using your model. You can check the `objective` and corresponding `validation` score to determine the model accuracy. As shown in Table 6-2, the objective is `f1` and the score is 0.93432, i.e., 93.43% accuracy score. The estimated cost is the estimated SageMaker processing hours (*https://oreil.ly/S-aSp*) needed to derive the model. A model with a higher accuracy score will generate more accurate model predictions, but that higher accuracy can come at a higher cost. We will cover costs in "Amazon Redshift ML Costs" on page 230.

Table 6-2. Show model—READY

Key	Value
Model Name	human_vs_machine
Schema Name	race
Owner	model_create_user
Creation Time	Tue, 12.12.2023 05:10:15
Model State	READY
Training Job Status	MaxAutoMLJobRuntimeReached
validation:f1_binary	0.93432
Estimated Cost	20.805736
TRAINING DATA:	
Table	race.speed_training
Target Column	HUMAN_WIN_Y_N

Key	Value
PARAMETERS:	
Model Type	xgboost
Problem Type	BinaryClassification
Objective	F1
AutoML Job Name	redshiftml-20230114201510598817
Function Name	fnc_will_human_win
	fnc_will_human_win_prob
Function Parameters	city machine_distance human_distance
	weather road_condition machine_speed
	human_speed
Function Parameter Types	varchar numeric numeric
	varchar varchar numeric
	numeric
IAM Role	default-aws-iam-role
S3 Bucket	my_ml_bucket
Max Runtime	3800

An accuracy score above 80% is considered a good score, but based on your specific use case you can choose to tune further to go higher.

To run inferences, simply use the function fnc_will_human_win in your SQL queries. You need to grant execute privilege on your model to identities that will be running inferences, as shown in Example 6-6.

Example 6-6. Run inference using model

```
SELECT
    city,
    machine_distance,
    human_distance,
    weather,
    road_condition,
    machine_speed,
    race.fnc_will_human_win
      (city,
        machine_distance,
        human_distance,
        weather,
        road_condition,
        machine_speed,
```

```
        human_speed) AS predicted
FROM
    race.speed_inference;
```

 It is good practice to have a set of *untrained* data to validate the F1 score. Run an inference query and compare the ML model predicted value to the actual value from the *untrained* data.

In the preceding example, we showed how you can use Amazon SageMaker Autopilot to create your model by only providing the table with training data and the target column in the table you are trying to predict. Amazon Redshift ML also provides options to create models with user guidance parameters where you can specify options like model type, problem type, objective, and preprocessors in the CREATE MODEL command, as shown in Example 6-7. If you know the problem type and/or model type and/or objective, then specifying these values in the CREATE MODEL command will reduce the model create time and the associated cost. In some cases, you need a custom algorithm or preprocessor. In those situations, you will need to specify these parameters.

See the create model documentation (*https://oreil.ly/KbxLq*) to review details for all the options shown in Example 6-7.

Example 6-7. Full create model

```
CREATE MODEL model_name
    FROM { table_name | ( select_statement ) }
    TARGET column_name
    FUNCTION function_name
    IAM_ROLE { default }
    [ MODEL_TYPE { XGBOOST | MLP | LINEAR_LEARNER} ]
    [ PROBLEM_TYPE (
      REGRESSION | BINARY_CLASSIFICATION |
      MULTICLASS_CLASSIFICATION ) ]
    [ OBJECTIVE ( 'MSE' | 'Accuracy' | 'F1' | 'F1Macro' | 'AUC') ]
    [ PREPROCESSORS ( TRANSFORMERS ) ]
    SETTINGS (
      S3_BUCKET 'bucket',
      S3_GARBAGE_COLLECT { ON | OFF },
      KMS_KEY_ID 'kms_key_id',
      MAX_CELLS integer,
      MAX_RUNTIME integer (, ...)
    );
```

The setting S3_GARBAGE_COLLECT is used to automatically clear the Amazon S3 bucket used to hold the training artifacts after the model is ready. However, if disabled, you can use the files created in Amazon S3 a few different ways using the BYOM strategy (see "Integration with Amazon SageMaker—Bring Your Own Model (BYOM)" on page 229). If you delete your Amazon Redshift data warehouse, you can use the files to re-create your inference function. You can also use the files to implement model versioning; for example, before re-training your model, you can create an *old* version of the model using the files. Lastly, you can create your model on one Amazon Redshift data warehouse, but expose the model on another Amazon Redshift data warehouse without going through the process of training it.

Label Probability

A label is the value or outcome you are predicting. For the human_vs_machine model, you are predicting whether the human will win, which has two possible outcomes or labels: true for when the human wins, and false for when the human does not win. The label probability metrics assign a probability value to each label to indicate the likelihood of its occurrence. You can access the label probability metrics assigned to each label by using the fnc_will_human_win_prob inference function, which will output a percentage likelihood of its occurrence. The probability metrics are available when creating AUTO ON models with a problem type of either binary classification or multiclass classification.

The label probabilities are computed for each row, and without actually running the ML model. You can run this on your inference dataset to get an indication of expected outcome.

The probability function fnc_will_human_win_prob is automatically created by Amazon Redshift ML using the function name fnc_will_human_win you provided for the ML model and adding the _prob suffix.

Example 6-8. Label probabilities

```
SELECT
  race.fnc_will_human_win_prob
    (city,
    machine_distance,
    human_distance,
    weather,
    road_condition,
    machine_speed,
```

```
    human_speed)
FROM
    race.speed_inference
LIMIT 5;
```

fnc_will_human_win_prob
{"probabilities":[0.98792028,0.01207972],"labels":["f","t"]}
{"probabilities":[0.99937975,0.00062025],"labels":["f","t"]}
{"probabilities":[0.91194165,0.08805832],"labels":["t","f"]}
{"probabilities":[0.95782197,0.04217804],"labels":["t","f"]}
{"probabilities":[0.93414819,0.06585180],"labels":["t","f"]}

Here you can see that probability for a human to win the race is lower on the input data for the first two rows, and higher on the next three.

Explain Model

In machine learning, each independent variable used as input to the model is called a feature. In Amazon Redshift ML, the columns that you used to build the model are the features for that model.

The explain_model command (Example 6-9) provides the ML models explainability report, which contains information about the Shapley value (*https://oreil.ly/HwYfZ*) for all model features. These Shapley values help you understand the contribution that each feature made to model predictions. Shapley value is the mean marginal contribution of each feature value across all possible values in the feature space. A higher Shapley value for a feature implies this particular feature has higher influence on the prediction result.

Example 6-9. Explain model command

```
SELECT explain_model('race.fnc_will_human_win_prob');
```

You see in Table 6-3 that city and human_speed influence much less compared to road_condition with 1.04 and weather with 1.46. You may be able to infer from this data that either humans or machines are better at adapting to weather and road conditions.

Table 6-3. Explain model results

explain_model
{"explanations":{"kernel_shap":{"label0":{ "expected_value":-0.5694439538988466, "global_shap_values": { "city":0.2865426473431818, "human_distance":0.8485933955733828, "human_speed":0.4954490773124456, "machine_distance":0.8925393014624781, "machine_speed":0.7125560417928333, "road_condition":1.0487996886952989, "weather":1.460974788708901} }}},"version":"1.0"}

The `explain_model` command leverages Amazon SageMaker Clarify, which provides tools to help explain how ML models make predictions. See Amazon SageMaker Clarify Model Explainability (*https://oreil.ly/-V9BF*) for additional details.

The model explainability report is automatically generated after the ML model has been trained. You might see an error returned for `explain_model` if the model training was interrupted due to a `MAX_RUNTIME` parameter. In such cases you can increase the `MAX_RUNTIME` value and rerun the training.

Using Amazon Redshift ML to Predict Student Outcomes

In Chapter 3, we discussed "Student Information Learning Analytics Dataset" on page 88. Let's use what we learned about Amazon Redshift ML and use the student learning dataset to build a model that predicts a student's performance result: pass, fail, withdraw, or distinction. You will also determine the most important factors influencing the student's performance.

You will first create the training dataset as a table from the historical data. This table will contain student demographic information, the data gathered from learning management system (LMS), and scores from student assessments. You will use these inputs as features for building your ML model to predict a student's performance result, the `final_result` column.

Table `tbl_student_lmsactivities_and_score` in Example 6-10 is created by joining the `student_info`, the aggregate of clicks from `student_lms`, and the aggregate of scores from `student_assessment`. This is an important aspect of *feature engineering*, i.e., the pivoting of data so that all inputs can go into the training/inference process.

Example 6-10. Openlearn ML model features

```
CREATE TABLE tbl_student_lmsactivities_and_score AS
SELECT
  st.school_id, st.id_student, st.code_module,
  st.code_presentation, st.gender, st.region,
  st.highest_education, st.imd_band, st.age_band,
  st.num_of_prev_atteempts, st.studied_credits,
  st.disability, st.final_result,
  st_lms_clicks.sum_of_clicks, scores.total_score,
  scores.mean_score
FROM
  openlearnm.student_info st
  LEFT JOIN
    (SELECT school_id, code_module,
      code_presentation, id_student,
```

```
      sum(sum_click) AS sum_of_clicks
    FROM
      OPENLEARNM.student_lms
    GROUP BY 1,2,3,4) st_lms_clicks
 ON st.school_id = st_lms_clicks.school_id
 AND st.code_module = st_lms_clicks.code_module
 AND st.code_presentation = st_lms_clicks.code_presentation
 AND st.id_student = st_lms_clicks.id_student
 LEFT JOIN
   (SELECT
      school_id, id_student,
      sum(score) AS total_score,
      avg(score) AS mean_score
    FROM
      openlearnm.student_assessment
    GROUP BY 1,2) scores
 ON st.school_id = scores.school_id
 AND st.id_student = scores.id_student
 ;
```

Now, run the CREATE MODEL command on the tbl_student_lmsactivi
ties_and_score table to invoke Amazon SageMaker Autopilot.

Example 6-11. Openlearn create model

```
CREATE MODEL student_result
FROM tbl_student_lmsactivities_and_score
TARGET final_result
FUNCTION fnc_final_result
IAM_ROLE default
SETTINGS (
  S3_BUCKET 'my_ml_bucket',
  MAX_RUNTIME 10800
  )
;
```

 Similar to the previous example, we have set MAX_RUNTIME higher
than default 5400 (1.5 hours) for this example to ensure the model
explainability report in Table 6-3 is generated successfully.

Now, you can execute the show model command to see details of the model Amazon
SageMaker Autopilot chose. You will see in Table 6-4 that it was able to choose a
model with 87% accuracy, and since you are determining one of several possible
labels (Withdrawn, Pass, Distinction, and Fail), it has determined that the problem
type is a multiclass classification.

Example 6-12. Show model

```
show model student_result;
```

Table 6-4. Show model output

Key	Value
Model Name	student_result
Schema Name	public
Owner	model_create_user
Creation Time	Sun, 05.03.2024 18:54:11
Model State	READY
validation:accuracy	0.870610
Estimated Cost	29.814964
TRAINING DATA:	
Table	tbl_student_lmsactivities_and_score
Target Column	FINAL_RESULT
PARAMETERS:	
Model Type	xgboost
Problem Type	MulticlassClassification
Objective	Accuracy
AutoML Job Name	redshiftml-20230305185411524819
Function Name	fnc_final_result
	fnc_final_result_prob
Function Parameters	id_student code_module code_presentation
	gender region highest_education imd_band
	age_band num_of_prev_atteempts
	studied_credits disability sum_of_clicks
	total_score mean_score
Function Parameter Types	int4 varchar varchar
	bpchar varchar varchar varchar
	varchar int2
	int2 bpchar int8
	int8 int8
IAM Role	default-aws-iam-role
S3 Bucket	my_ml_bucket
Max Runtime	10800

Lastly, you can execute the explain_model command to see the Shapley values. You see in Example 6-13 that gender, region, previous attempts, and disability influence much less compared to age band with 0.51, highest education with 0.59, and studied credits with 0.66. Number of clicks with a value of 0.99 seems to be the most important factor in determining student performance. Number of clicks represents interactions with virtual learning environments. Based on this ML model, you can expect that increasing engagement with virtual learning environments should lead to improvement in students results—for example, adding a pop quiz between virtual course content.

Example 6-13. Explain model student_result

```
SELECT
  t.r.explanations.kernel_shap.label0.global_shap_values
FROM (SELECT
        explain_model('student_result') AS r
      ) AS t
;
```

global_shap_values
"age_band":0.510843481387332466, "code_module":0.1775745286500845, "code_presentation":0.09353407379714834, "disability":0.051944180058839748, "gender":0.05065581722765354, "highest_education":0.592895528627924518, "id_student":0.00000483678127755, "imd_band":0.033637420953443259, "mean_score":0.2120711173613374, "num_of_prev_attempts":0.05241636943859941, "region":0.13375708054846678, "studied_credits":0.6551317963150247, "sum_of_clicks":0.9983975396249064, "total_score":0.25218934352064467

Amazon SageMaker Integration with Amazon Redshift

So far, we've described how users can create models and run inferences using SQL. For data scientist users who build and train models in Amazon SageMaker, the Amazon SageMaker Studio is an IDE that provides a single web-based visual interface where you can access tools to perform all machine learning. SageMaker notebooks is a popular interface running the Jupyter Notebook app to prepare and process data, write code to train models, deploy models to SageMaker hosting, and test or validate your models. The Amazon Redshift Data API discussed in "Amazon Redshift Data API" on page 66 simplifies the connectivity management, and Jupyter Notebook is preloaded with libraries needed to access Amazon Redshift Data API. This makes it easy to use data from Amazon Redshift for advanced ML training in Amazon SageMaker.

Amazon SageMaker Canvas allows business analysts to build ML models without writing code or requiring ML expertise. Once you grant users permissions for Amazon Redshift (*https://oreil.ly/WSKwt*), then you can import Amazon Redshift data by using SQL queries and joins that are pushed down to Amazon Redshift to leverage native features.

Integration with Amazon SageMaker—Bring Your Own Model (BYOM)

For advanced ML models created outside of Amazon Redshift, if it meets the requirements for Redshift ML, you can bring it into Amazon Redshift for running ML inferences. You can import these pretrained models and use them for either local inferences or remote inferences. The models could have been created and trained using Amazon Redshift data, as described in "Amazon SageMaker Integration with Amazon Redshift" on page 228, or they could have been created and trained with other data sources.

To bring your own SageMaker model to Amazon Redshift, the following criteria must be met:

- The model must accept inputs in the format of CSV through a content type of text or CSV in SageMaker.
- The endpoint must be hosted by the same AWS account that owns the Amazon Redshift data warehouse.
- The outputs of models must be a single value of the type specified on creating the function.
- The models must accept nulls as empty strings.
- The Amazon SageMaker endpoint must have enough resources to accommodate inference calls from Amazon Redshift or the SageMaker endpoint can be automatically scaled (*https://oreil.ly/gvDJk*).

BYOM Local

Example 6-14 is query syntax for BYOM local inferences. You can specify either a SageMaker job name or the Amazon S3 location of the `.tar.gz` model artifact file that was generated by a SageMaker job. The ML model gets stored as a locally compiled Amazon Redshift function.

Example 6-14. BYOM local

```
CREATE MODEL public.predict_customer_churn
FROM 'job_customer_churn-xxxxxxxxxx'
FUNCTION fn_customer_churn(int)
RETURNS decimal(8,7)
iam_role 'arn:aws:iam::123456789012:role/myRSMLrole';
```

When running inferences on a local BYOM ML model, the Amazon Redshift SQL function is invoked locally within Amazon Redshift and predictions are drawn, thus there is no SageMaker involved.

BYOM Remote

You can also draw remote inferences in Amazon Redshift referencing the SageMaker model endpoint. Example 6-15 is query syntax for BYOM remote inferences. The `sagemaker` keyword tells Amazon Redshift ML that this particular ML model is a SageMaker model for remote inferences.

When running inference queries in Amazon Redshift on a remote BYOM model, the SageMaker ML model is invoked and predictions are drawn directly from SageMaker.

Example 6-15. BYOM remote

```
CREATE MODEL public.remote_random_cut_forest
FUNCTION fn_remote_rcf(int)
RETURNS decimal(10,6)
sagemaker 'randomcurforest-xxxxxxxxxx'
iam_role 'arn:aws:iam::123456789012:role/myRSMLrole';
```

To see additional use cases for creating models, see create model use cases (*https:// oreil.ly/aYm_k*).

Amazon Redshift ML Costs

Amazon Redshift ML uses Amazon SageMaker for training your model, so there always is a cost associated with training your ML model. There are no additional charges for enabling the Amazon Redshift ML features. Also, there are no Amazon SageMaker costs for predictions that happen locally in Amazon Redshift, but remote predictions do incur Amazon SageMaker costs additionally.

The `create model` statement provides you with `MAX_RUNTIME` and `MAX_CELLS` options to control the costs, time, and potential model accuracy when training an ML model in Amazon Redshift:

MAX_RUNTIME
> The default value is 5400 seconds or 90 minutes. This is the maximum amount of time for Amazon SageMaker training. Lowering this value limits the amount of time and computation spend in Amazon SageMaker, and thus reduces cost for training the model.

MAX_CELLS

The default value is 1,000,000 cells, where a cell is a single data point in your dataset. So if your training data table has 12 columns and 20,000 rows, then it has 240,000 cells for training the ML model. Using lower value for max cells results in Amazon Redshift ML selecting a reduced dataset for training, and this reduces cost and time to train the model.

 After the training is completed, Amazon Redshift takes some time to compile and install the models locally, so you might see that your create model statement execution is taking longer than the max_runtime you specified.

If the actual cells in the training dataset are more than the MAX_CELLS value, then Amazon Redshift will randomly choose fewer records from the training dataset. This randomization helps to prevent bias in the reduced training dataset while still providing good ML predictions.

 Setting too low values for MAX_CELLS and MAX_RUNTIME can lead to Amazon Redshift ML being unable to determine a ML model for you or even ending up selecting a model with reduced accuracy.

The majority of ML use cases fall under the one million cells default, which keeps the training cost under $20 for most use cases. However, if your training data is more than one million cells, then pricing increases as demonstrated in the following example.

The first 10 million cells are priced at $20 per million cells. The next 90 million cells are priced at $15 per million cells. Over 100 million cells are priced at $7 per million cells.

Here's a pricing example for 125 million cells:

```
First 10 million = 10 x $20 =  $200
 Next 90 million = 90 x $15 = $1350
Over 100 million = 25 x $07 =  $175
-----------------------        ------
TOTAL 125 million cells        $1825
-----------------------        ------
```

Additionally, there are Amazon S3 charges incurred based upon Amazon S3 usage to store the training data and model-related artifacts while the training is ongoing. The default garbage collection mode is to automatically remove this temporary Amazon S3 data once the model has been created, thus the Amazon S3 costs are minimized.

Summary

This chapter covered some of the machine learning use cases you can solve with Amazon Redshift ML. We discussed how classification and regression problems can be solved with supervised learning techniques that can be initiated directly in Amazon Redshift using the `CREATE MODEL` command. We also detailed how clustering, association, and dimensionality problems can be solved with unsupervised learning techniques in Amazon SageMaker, how you can import the data needed to train those models from Amazon Redshift through built-in connectors, and how those models can then be used back in Amazon Redshift for inference through the Bring Your Own Model strategy.

Throughout this book we've talked about data sharing and how it enables a modern data strategy because of the ability to isolate and scale workloads independently while enabling users with a unified data platform. In the next chapter, we'll describe different use cases for data sharing and how to set up data-shares whether they are in the same account and region or not as well as how you can use Amazon DataZone to manage data-share access.

CHAPTER 7

Collaboration with Data Sharing

Data sharing is a business necessity to accelerate digital transformation.
—Gartner (*https://oreil.ly/wmkIV*)

Data sharing is the ability to provide access to information for internal and external stakeholders that they can't access in their own data systems. Data sharing allows stakeholders to access data produced or collected and stored in the producer's domain and collaborate on shared business goals and priorities. Data organizations are moving away from being a single large monolithic department, which usually causes slow-moving data platforms to small distributed teams to create modular fast-moving data products. This Modern Data Community (*https://oreil.ly/b30m_*) is an organizational and cultural shift from monolithic data organizations to decoupled, agile, smaller teams.

By building a robust data sharing architecture, data and analytics leaders will have access to the right data at the right time to deliver meaningful business outcomes. Organizations like National Institutes of Health (NIH) have implemented data management and sharing policies (*https://oreil.ly/KWuJI*) to establish that data sharing is a fundamental component of the research process to maximize public access to research results.

Data sharing encourages making use of the information and resources available to us in the present moment wherever it resides and taking action based on that information. The sooner a company starts sharing data and using it to inform their decision making, the more time they will have to deliver business outcomes.

The phrase *data is the new oil* was originally coined by Clive Humby, a British mathematician and data science entrepreneur, and this has proven to be true over the last two decades. Data drives business decisions, informs research, and powers technology. Organizations are collecting and storing more data than ever before.

But with the abundance of data comes the challenge of how to effectively share and collaborate on that data.

In this chapter, you'll learn how to use Amazon Redshift to share and collaborate on large amounts of data. We'll start by providing an "Amazon Redshift Data Sharing Overview" and describe different "Data Sharing Use Cases". Next, we'll dive deeper into the "Key Concepts of Data Sharing" with Amazon Redshift and walk through "How to Use Data Sharing". We'll explore options for "Sharing Data Across Accounts Using Cross-Account Data Sharing" and show different options for using Amazon Redshift data sharing in an "Analytics as a Service Use Case with Multi-Tenant Storage Patterns". Next, we'll talk about how you can enable "External Data Sharing with AWS ADX Integration" to monetize your data and provide your customers with instant access to data using their Amazon Redshift compute. We'll also briefly cover how you can "Query from the Data Lake and Unload to the Data Lake" as your mechanism for data sharing. Lastly, we'll cover how to catalog and govern access to your data-shares by using "Amazon DataZone to Discover and Share Data".

Amazon Redshift Data Sharing Overview

Amazon Redshift data sharing enables instant, granular, and live data access across data warehouses without the need to copy or move data. This enables you to create a multiwarehouse architecture and scale each data warehouse for various types of workloads. Amazon Redshift data sharing is included with your serverless or RA3 provisioned data warehouse and provides the following capabilities:

- Live and transactionally consistent views of data across all consumers
- Secure and governed collaboration within and across organizations
- Sharing data with external parties to monetize your data

The live access and transactionally consistent views of data ensures users always see the most up-to-date and consistent information as it is updated in the data warehouse. You can securely share data with Amazon Redshift data warehouses in the same account or different AWS accounts within the same region or across regions. When building a scalable architecture for analytics, you'll need to consider performance of the query and ingestion workloads, elasticity, and price for performance to meet the requirements of dynamic workloads. The Amazon Redshift data sharing feature provides another mechanism to scale and meet demands of various types of workloads.

Amazon Redshift RA3 architecture enables the data sharing feature. In the RA3 architecture, data stored in Amazon RMS is committed to Amazon S3 but is also available in a solid-state drive (SSD) local cache to the compute nodes for faster processing of recently used data. The queries from the consumer data warehouse read data directly from the Amazon RMS layer. Hence there is no impact in performance of the producer data warehouse, and workloads accessing shared data are isolated from each other. This architecture is shown in Figure 7-1, and it enables you to set up a multiwarehouse architecture with separate consumer data warehouses for different types of workloads. You can provision flexible compute resources that meet workload-specific price performance requirements and be scaled independently as needed in a self-service fashion.

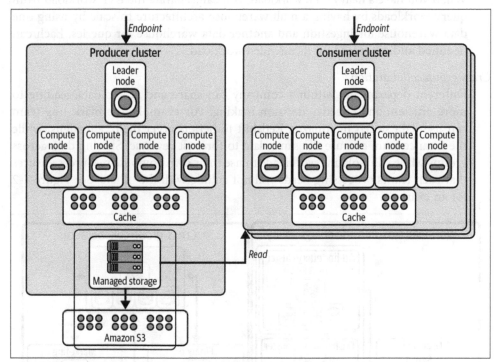

Figure 7-1. Amazon Redshift data sharing architecture

 Amazon Redshift data sharing is not available on the DC2 node type because DC2 nodes do not take advantage of Redshift Managed Storage (RMS). See the Upgrading to RA3 Node Types documentation (*https://oreil.ly/rc-ms*) or the Migrating to Amazon Redshift Serverless documentation (*https://oreil.ly/9eZSf*) for details on how to take advantage of data sharing.

Data Sharing Use Cases

According to Gartner (*https://oreil.ly/1WsD6*), "Data and analytics leaders who share data externally generate three times more measurable economic benefit than those who do not." Data sharing has proven to have measurable economic benefits, and organizations who have a data sharing strategy outperform their peers. Use cases for data sharing range from helping you enhance scalability by separation of workloads, increase collaboration, build Analytics as a Service (AaaS) solutions, and improve operational efficiency, data quality, and generally improve access to data. Let's take a closer look at these use cases:

Separation of workloads

When you have a heavy ETL workload, you can separate the ETL workload from query workloads by having a multiwarehouse architecture to scale by using one data warehouse for ingestion and another data warehouse for queries. Each can be tuned and optimized for its intended workload.

Cross-group collaboration

Different departments within a company can share and access data, leading to more efficient and effective decision making. For example, the marketing team can use data stored in Amazon Redshift to better target their campaigns, while the finance team can use the same data to forecast revenue. Sharing data across groups while still isolating workloads to use their own compute resources ensures that each team's processing needs will not collide with the others. See Figure 7-2 for an example.

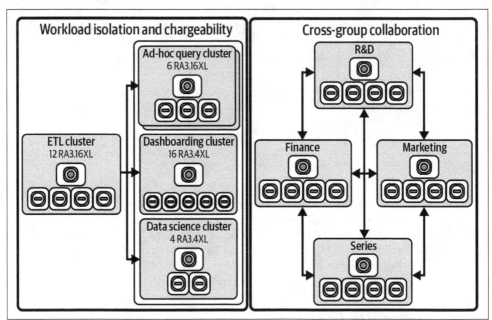

Figure 7-2. Data sharing use cases separation of workload and collaboration

Analytics as a Service

AaaS providers can collect and aggregate data from various sources such as social media, web analytics, and ERP systems into the data warehouse and add business insight transformations before sharing with subscribers. For example, using the student data model defined in Chapter 3, "Setting Up Your Data Models and Ingesting Data", an educational technology AaaS provider can collect data about student attendance and grades, and derive insights on how to improve student outcomes. They can then share these insights using a subscription model using AWS Data Exchange (ADX) integration (*https://oreil.ly/_FDWr*) with the educational institutions and monetize the data that they already collected through their transactional systems. Producers of data can also use AWS Clean Rooms (*https://aws.amazon.com/clean-rooms*) to collaborate with partners or other AWS users without sharing raw data.

Improved agility for software development life cycle (SDLC)

During the development lifecycle of applications, most organizations struggle with not having good data for testing in development or quality systems in the DevOps landscape. With data sharing, you can share data from your production to development systems to improve your quality of testing by validating all test cases, and accelerate delivery of applications. If you have specific security policies around sharing production data in other environments, you can also use the dynamic data masking (DDM) (*https://oreil.ly/h9mGq*) capability of Amazon Redshift to mask certain Personally Identifiable Information (PII) data. See Figure 7-3 for an example.

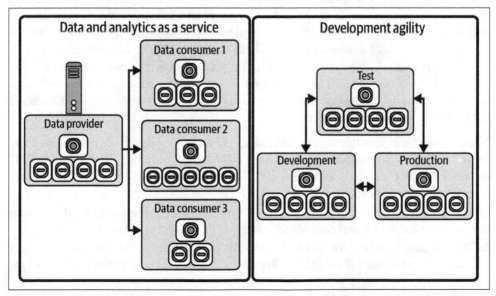

Figure 7-3. Data sharing use cases analytics as a service and development agility

Key Concepts of Data Sharing

A *datashare* is the unit of sharing data in Amazon Redshift (see Figure 7-5). A data owner can add database objects to the datashare to share with subscribers. A datashare acts as a container to hold references to other database objects. A data owner who produces and shares data is called a *producer*, and a subscriber is called a *consumer*. Amazon Redshift allows you to set up access controls and permissions, ensuring that sensitive data is shared only with authorized personnel. This is especially important when sharing data with external partners or other AWS users who have stringent data governance and security requirements. Each datashare is associated to a specific database in your Amazon Redshift data warehouse.

Data producers are Amazon Redshift data warehouses that own the data and from where the data is being shared from. Producer data warehouse administrators and database owners can create datashares using the `CREATE DATASHARE` command. You can add database objects such as schemas, tables, views, and SQL UDFs to a datashare in the producer to share with consumers. Amazon Redshift data warehouses that share data can be in the same or different AWS account or different AWS regions, so you can share data across organizations and collaborate with other parties.

Data consumers are Amazon Redshift data warehouses that receive datashares from producer data warehouses. When producers grant datashare access to a consumer, consumer data warehouse administrators can create a database referencing the data-share to the consumer-shared data. Note that this database is a reference to the data-share and not a physical persistent storage on the consumer side. The administrator then assigns permissions for the database to users and groups in the consumer data warehouse. After permissions are granted, users and groups can query the datashare objects using a three-part notation `database.schema.object`. Authorized users can also list the shared objects using standard metadata queries, and track usage. For cross-account datasharing, it is an additional step on the producer side to authorize the datashare, and on the consumer side to associate one or more Amazon Redshift data warehouses to the datashare.

Namespaces are identifiers that identify an Amazon Redshift provisioned or serverless data warehouse. A namespace Globally Unique Identifier (GUID) is automatically created and assigned to your Amazon Redshift data warehouse. A namespace Amazon Resource Name (ARN) is in the `arn:{partition}:redshift:{region}:{account-id}:namespace:{namespace-guid}` format for provisioned and `arn:{partition}:redshift-serverless:{region}:{account-id}:namespace:{namespace-guid}` for serverless. You can see the namespace details of a data warehouse in the Amazon Redshift console general information page (see Figure 7-4).

Figure 7-4. Data sharing namespace

In the data sharing workflow, the namespace GUID value and the namespace ARN are used to share data with other Amazon Redshift data warehouses in the AWS account. You can also find the namespace for the current data warehouse by using the current_namespace function. For cross-account data sharing, AWS accounts can be consumers for datashares and are each represented by a 12-digit AWS account ID. Consumer accounts can then associate one or more Amazon Redshift data warehouses to the datashare to read that data.

With Amazon Redshift, you can share data through the database objects at different levels, and you can create multiple datashares for a given database. A datashare can contain objects from multiple schemas in the database on which sharing is created. However, you can share only the datashare object and not individual objects to consumers. By having this flexibility in sharing data, you get fine-grained access control. You can tailor this control for different users and businesses that need access to Amazon Redshift data. For example, you may want to share only the student details from a particular school with a school administrator. In businesses, you may want to control sharing the sales details with a vendor for the corresponding items they supply (Figure 7-5).

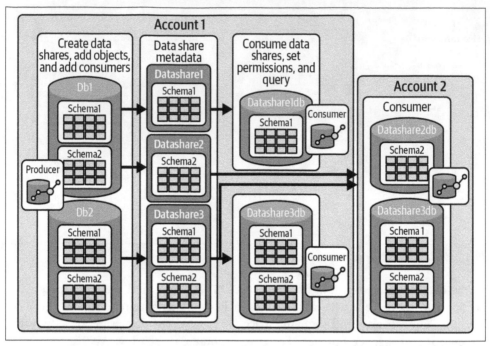

Figure 7-5. Key concepts of data sharing and how it works

How to Use Data Sharing

To use data sharing, first identify the data you want to share and identify the respective schema, tables, and views that have the relevant data. To share data, create a DATASHARE metadata object and add database objects including schemas, tables, and views to this datashare. Then, grant access to other namespaces within the same account or to another AWS account. Let's look at a specific example and walk through the whole process.

Sharing Data Within the Same Account

Let's use the student learning dataset from Example 3-1 to understand how you can share data. This section shows you how to share a student learning dataset within the same account with the consumers within the organization. You can use the console or SQL scripts to create and share a datashare. The following scripts in Examples 7-1 and 7-2 provide you with the steps.

Example 7-1. Creating a datashare

```
-- Creating a datashare (producer)
CREATE DATASHARE learnshare SET PUBLICACCESSIBLE TRUE;
```

In the previous statement, `learnshare` is the name of the datashare. The datashare name must be unique in the namespace. `SET PUBLICACCESSIBLE` is a clause that specifies whether the datashare can be shared to data warehouses that are publicly accessible. The default value for `SET PUBLICACCESSIBLE` is `FALSE`.

Example 7-2. Adding objects to datashare

```
-- Add schema to datashare
ALTER DATASHARE learnshare
  ADD SCHEMA openlearn;

-- Add openlearn materialized view to datshares.
ALTER DATASHARE learnshare
  ADD TABLE openlearnm.mv_student_lmsactivities_and_score;

-- View shared objects
SHOW DATASHARES;
SELECT * FROM SVV_DATASHARE_OBJECTS;
```

share_name	share_owner	source_database	consumer_database	share_type	createdate
learnshare_adx	100	dev	null	OUTBOUND	2023-03-18 19:51:28
learnshare	100	dev	null	OUTBOUND	2023-02-24 18:32:28

is_publicaccessible	share_acl	producer_account	producer_namespace
true	null	<awsaccount>	xxxxc8ee-f6a5-xxxx-xxxx-yyyy66d7zzzz
true	null	<awsaccount>	xxxxc7ee-xxxx-468f-xxxx-yyyy77d7zzzz

> To add all tables in a schema, use the following syntax:
>
> ```
> ALTER DATASHARE learnshare ADD ALL TABLES IN SCHEMA openlearn;
> ```

To get the namespace of the consumer, you can log in to the consumer Amazon Redshift data warehouse and run the SQL in Example 7-3 to select the `current_name space`, or you may get it from the console.

Example 7-3. Viewing current user and namespace

```
SELECT user, current_namespace;
```

Now, with the namespace `<<consumer namespace>>` of your data warehouse, you can grant usage on the datashare from the producer to the consumer using the `GRANT` command as shown in Example 7-4.

Example 7-4. Granting access to datashare

```
GRANT USAGE ON DATASHARE learnshare TO NAMESPACE '<<consumer namespace>>';
```

On the consumer side, create a database referencing the datashare on the producer or serverless data warehouse. Note that this database is just a pointer to the datashare and does not hold any data on its own. Once you create the database, you can query the data live as shown in Example 7-5 using a three-part notation of db_name.schema.view.

Example 7-5. Creating local database from remote datashare

```
CREATE DATABASE openlearn_db
FROM DATASHARE learnshare
OF NAMESPACE '<producer_namespace>';

SELECT school_id, code_module, code_presentation,
  final_result, sum(sum_of_clicks)
FROM  openlearn_db.openlearnm.mv_student_lmsactivities_and_score
GROUP BY 1,2,3,4
ORDER BY 1,2,3,4;
```

Optionally, you can create an external schema in the consumer data warehouse pointing to the schema in the database of the producer data warehouse. Creating a local external schema in the consumer data warehouse allows schema-level access controls within the consumer data warehouse and allows you to use a two-part notation when referencing shared data objects (localschema.table versus external_db.producer schema.table), as shown in Example 7-6.

Example 7-6. Creating external schema from local database

```
CREATE EXTERNAL SCHEMA openlearn_schema
FROM REDSHIFT DATABASE 'openlearn_db' SCHEMA 'openlearn';

SELECT school_id, code_module, code_presentation,
  final_result, sum(sum_of_clicks)
FROM  openlearn_schema.mv_student_lmsactivities_and_score
GROUP BY 1,2,3,4
ORDER BY 1,2,3,4;
```

Sharing Data Across Accounts Using Cross-Account Data Sharing

In addition to internal data sharing to break down data silos within an organization, you can also share your data securely to external organizations using the cross-account data sharing feature. Here are some common use cases:

- A subsidiary organization reporting back financial statements to its parent organization
- A business organization or government agency sharing data with another organization or related agency
- An AaaS provider sharing data with their subscribers
- A healthcare organization sharing data with a government agency

When you share data across accounts, you will create a `datashare` object and add the database object you want to share, similar to sharing within an account. But here you will grant access to a consumer AWS account to access that datashare, as shown in Example 7-7. On the consumer side, an administrator can associate one or more data warehouses to be able to read the datashare.

Amazon Redshift supports data sharing for data warehouses with homogeneous encryption configuration. In other words, you can share data among two or more encrypted Amazon Redshift data warehouses. Or you can share data among two or more unencrypted Amazon Redshift data warehouses for data warehouses that are within the same AWS account. When sharing data between encrypted data warehouses, you can use different encryption keys for each data warehouse. For cross-account and cross-region data sharing, both the producer and consumer data warehouse must be encrypted.

Example 7-7. Granting access to AWS account on datashare

```
-- Granting access to consumer AWS Account
GRANT USAGE ON DATASHARE learnshare TO ACCOUNT <AWS_Account>;
```

For cross-account sharing, there is an additional step to authorize the datashare before it becomes visible for a consumer account. This process allows for a manager or a data owner to approve the datashare, as shown in Figure 7-6. Once authorized, the datashare will be available for the consumer account.

Figure 7-6. Authorize step for cross-account data sharing

Users can manage multiple datashares across multiple Amazon Redshift data warehouses in different accounts and regions. To centrally manage all datashares across all accounts, with designated owners or administrators to authorize or associate datashare, you may build a custom web interface. To automate the process of authorization and association, you can also use the CLI commands `authorize-data-share` (*https://oreil.ly/pduVL*) and `associate-data-share-consumer` (*https://oreil.ly/TDvF8*).

On the consumer side, you can associate one or more Amazon Redshift data warehouses to the datashare. Note that the datashare will show up in the "From other accounts" tab when you choose the datashares menu option. You can choose the datashare and click the Associate button to associate the consumer to the datashare, as shown in Figure 7-7.

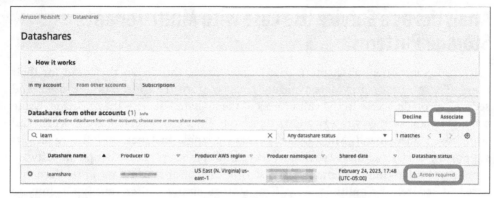

Figure 7-7. Associate consumer data warehouse to producer datashare

Once you associate the consumer data warehouse to the datashare, you can log in to the consumer data warehouse that you associated and query the data from the objects in the datashare with just a couple of steps. First, create a database reference to the datashare, then use a three-part notation with `db_name.schema.table` as shown in Example 7-8's SQL scripts.

Example 7-8. Creating local database from remote datashare

```
CREATE DATABASE openlearn_db
FROM DATASHARE learnshare
OF ACCOUNT '<<producer_account>>' NAMESPACE '<<producer_namespace>>';

SELECT * FROM learn_db.learnshare. mv_student_lmsactivities_and_score;
```

When this query is passed to the producer from this consumer, the `current_name space` variable will have the namespace of this consumer. Hence the materialized view will filter the records just from this consumer based on the join condition from the school table. As discussed earlier, you can create an external schema to use a two-part notation when referencing shared data objects (e.g. `external_schema.table`) versus a three-part notation (`external_db.producer_schema.table`).

For detailed steps on setting up cross-account data sharing, refer to the documentation on sharing data across AWS accounts (*https://oreil.ly/Uk_sp*).

Analytics as a Service Use Case with Multi-Tenant Storage Patterns

AaaS providers offer subscription-based analytics capabilities in the cloud for their users. These service providers typically have to store data for multiple users and securely provide access to the subscribers of the analytics service they provide. Using a multi-tenant storage strategy allows them to build a cost-effective architecture and scale based on demand. Multi-tenancy means a single instance of software and its supporting infrastructure is shared to serve multiple users. For example, a software service provider could generate data that is housed in a single data warehouse, but accessed securely by multiple users. This storage strategy offers an opportunity to centralize management of data, simplify ETL processes, and optimize costs. Without data sharing, it is challenging for service providers to manage a multi-tenant environment because they have to balance between cost and providing a better user experience.

Scaling Your Multi-tenant Architecture Using Data Sharing

AaaS providers implementing multi-tenant architectures were previously limited to resources of a single data warehouse to meet the compute and concurrency requirements of users across all the tenants. As the number of tenants increased, you could either turn on Concurrency Scaling or create additional data warehouses. However, the addition of new data warehouses means additional ingestion pipelines and increased operational overhead.

With data sharing in Amazon Redshift (*https://oreil.ly/5SXnv*), you can scale and meet both objectives of managing costs by simplifying storage and ETL pipelines while still providing consistent performance. You can ingest data into a data warehouse designated as a producer and share this live data with one or more consumers. Data ingested into the producer is shared with one or more consumers, which allows total separation of ETL and BI workloads. Clusters accessing this shared data are isolated from each other, therefore performance of a producer isn't impacted by workloads on consumers. This enables consumers to get consistent performance based on their individual compute capacity.

Several consumers can read data from the managed storage of a producer. This enables instant, granular, and high-performance access to data without copies or movement. Workloads accessing shared data are isolated from each other and the producer. You can distribute workloads across multiple data warehouses while simplifying and consolidating the ETL ingestion pipeline into one main producer data warehouse, providing optimal price for performance.

Consumer data warehouses can in turn be producers for the datasets they own. You can optimize costs even further by co-locating multiple tenants on the same consumer. For instance, you can group low volume tier 3 tenants into a single consumer to provider a lower cost offering, while high volume tier 1 tenants get their own isolated compute data warehouses. Consumer data warehouses can be created in the same account as the producer or in a different AWS account. With this you can have separate billing (*https://oreil.ly/kY718*) for the consumers, where you can charge-back to the business group that uses the consumer or even allow your users to use their own Amazon Redshift data warehouse in their account, so they pay for usage of the consumer data warehouse. Figure 7-8 shows the difference in ETL and consumer access patterns in a multi-tenant architecture using data sharing versus a single data warehouse approach without data sharing.

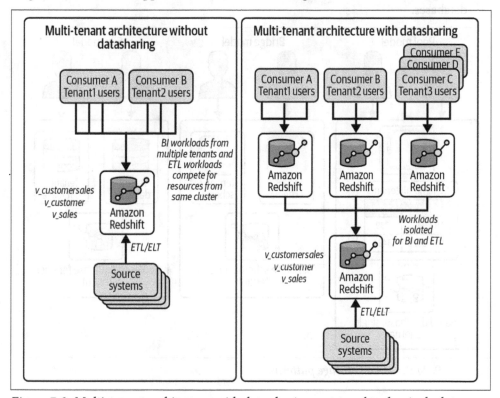

Figure 7-8. Multi-tenant architecture with data sharing compared to the single data warehouse approach

Multi-tenant Storage Patterns Using Data Sharing

In a *multi-tenant* strategy, data is stored in a shared location for all tenants, enabling simplification of the ETL ingestion pipeline and data management. There are a few storage strategies to support this kind of multi-tenant access pattern, as shown in Figure 7-9.

Pool model

Data is stored in a single database schema for all tenants, and a new column (tenant_id) is used to scope and control access to individual tenant data. Access to the multi-tenant data is controlled using views built on the tables.

Bridge model

Storage and access to data for each tenant is maintained in separate schemas in the same database.

Silo model

Storage and access control to data for each tenant is maintained in separate databases.

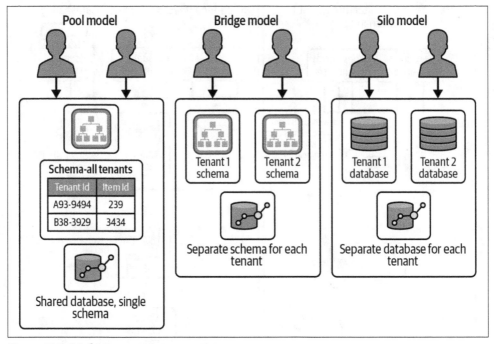

Figure 7-9. Multi-tenant storage patterns

We will use the student analytics data model to demonstrate multiple strategies that leverage data sharing to implement a scalable multi-tenant architecture. We will cover detailed steps involved for each strategy using the data model we created in Chapter 3, "Setting Up Your Data Models and Ingesting Data". In this use case, the producer is an AaaS provider and is responsible for loading and processing the data in one Amazon Redshift data warehouse. The consumers (tenants) are schools who have subscribed to the student insights dataset in one or many other Amazon Redshift data warehouses.

The high-level steps involved in enabling data sharing across data warehouses are as follows:

1. Create a datashare in the producer and assign database objects to the datashare.
2. From the producer, grant usage on the datashare to the consumer, identified by namespace or AWS account.
3. From the consumer, create an external database using the datashare from the producer.
4. Query the tables in the datashare through the external shared database in the consumer. Grant access to other users to access this shared database and objects.

In the following examples, we will use the school table to identify our consumers (tenants). Since all the tables have the `school_id` column, you can use this column to differentiate and securely share only the authorized data to the respective consumers.

Before we get started, get the namespaces of the producer and consumer data warehouses. You can do this by using the AWS console, or you can log into each of the data warehouses and execute the SELECT CURRENT_NAMESPACE statement.

> In the following code samples, replace the `producer_namespace` and `consumer_namespace` placeholders with the corresponding namespaces from your environment.

To demonstrate the multi-tenant architecture patterns, we will use a modified version of the Open University Learning Analytics dataset and include `school_id` to all tables to store data for multiple schools. The multi-tenant version of the dataset with `school_id` added is available in Amazon S3 (*https://oreil.ly/aQaBC*). You can use this dataset to ingest into Amazon Redshift after you create the tables using the scripts in Example 7-9. Note that there is a new table school, to store the details of individual schools, and the `school_id` column is added to each of the tables. The sample data consists of data for two different schools, which we will use to demonstrate how you can build a multi-tenant storage strategy using the Amazon Redshift data sharing feature.

Example 7-9. Creating schema and tables for student information data

```
/* We will use a modified version of the Open University Learning Analytics */
/* dataset to demonstrate multi-tenant architecture by storing data */
/* for multiple schools https://analyse.kmi.open.ac.uk/open_dataset */
/* https://analyse.kmi.open.ac.uk/open_dataset#rights */
/* Kuzilek J., Hlosta M., Zdrahal Z. Open University Learning Analytics dataset */
/* Sci. Data 4:170171 doi: 10.1038/sdata.2017.171 (2017). */

CREATE SCHEMA openlearnm;

CREATE TABLE "openlearnm"."school"(
school_id       integer,
school_name     varchar(50),
address         varchar(100),
city            varchar(80),
website_url     varchar(100),
consumer_namespace varchar(100))
DISTSTYLE AUTO
SORTKEY AUTO
ENCODE AUTO;

CREATE TABLE "openlearnm"."assessments"
(
    school_id integer,
    code_module varchar(5),
    code_presentation varchar(5),
    id_assessment integer,
    assessment_type varchar(5),
    assessment_date bigint,
    weight decimal(10,2)
    )
diststyle AUTO
SORTKEY AUTO
ENCODE AUTO;

CREATE TABLE "openlearnm"."courses"
(
    school_id   integer,
    code_module             varchar(5),
    code_presentation       varchar(5),
    module_presentation_length integer
    )
DISTSTYLE AUTO
SORTKEY AUTO
ENCODE AUTO;

CREATE TABLE "openlearnm"."student_assessment"
(
    school_id     integer,
    id_assessment integer,
    id_student    integer,
```

```
    date_submitted bigint,
    is_banked       smallint,
    score           smallint
    )
DISTSTYLE AUTO
SORTKEY AUTO
ENCODE AUTO;

CREATE TABLE "openlearnm"."student_info"
(
    school_id   integer,
    code_module             varchar(5),
    code_presentation       varchar(5),
    id_student              integer,
    gender                  CHAR(1),
    region                  varchar(50),
    highest_education       varchar(50),
    imd_band                varchar(10),
    age_band                varchar(10),
    num_of_prev_atteempts   smallint,
    studied_credits         smallint,
    disability              char(1),
    final_result            varchar(20)
    )
DISTSTYLE AUTO
SORTKEY AUTO
ENCODE AUTO;

CREATE TABLE "openlearnm"."student_registration"
(
    school_id   integer,
    code_module             varchar(5),
    code_presendation       varchar(5),
    id_student              integer,
    date_registration       bigint ,
    date_unregistration     bigint
    )
DISTSTYLE AUTO
SORTKEY AUTO
ENCODE AUTO;

CREATE TABLE "openlearnm"."student_lms"
(
    school_id   integer,
    code_module             varchar(5),
    code_presentation varchar(5),
    id_student              integer,
    id_site                 integer,
    date                    bigint,
    sum_click               integer
    )
DISTSTYLE AUTO
```

```
SORTKEY AUTO
ENCODE AUTO;

CREATE TABLE "openlearnm"."lms"
(
    school_id    integer,
    id_site            integer,
    code_module        varchar(5),
    code_presentation varchar(5),
    activity_type     varchar(20),
    week_from          smallint,
    week_to            smallint
    )
DISTSTYLE AUTO
SORTKEY AUTO
ENCODE AUTO;
```

To ingest the multi-tenant version of the sample student information dataset, use the commands as shown in Example 7-10.

Example 7-10. Create schema and tables for student information data

```
COPY "openlearnm"."assessments"
FROM 's3://openlearnm-redshift/assessments'
iam_role default
delimiter ',' region 'us-east-1'
REMOVEQUOTES IGNOREHEADER 1;

COPY "openlearnm"."courses"
FROM 's3://openlearnm-redshift/courses'
iam_role default
delimiter ',' region 'us-east-1'
REMOVEQUOTES IGNOREHEADER 1;

COPY "openlearnm"."student_assessment"
FROM 's3://openlearnm-redshift/studentAssessment'
iam_role default
delimiter ',' region 'us-east-1'
REMOVEQUOTES IGNOREHEADER 1;

COPY "openlearnm"."student_info"
FROM 's3://openlearnm-redshift/studentInfo'
iam_role default
delimiter ',' region 'us-east-1'
REMOVEQUOTES IGNOREHEADER 1;

COPY "openlearnm"."student_registration"
FROM 's3://openlearnm-redshift/studentRegistration'
iam_role default
delimiter ',' region 'us-east-1'
REMOVEQUOTES IGNOREHEADER 1;
```

```
COPY "openlearnm"."student_lms"
FROM 's3://openlearnm-redshift/studentlms'
iam_role default
delimiter ',' region 'us-east-1'
REMOVEQUOTES IGNOREHEADER 1;

COPY "openlearnm"."lms"
FROM 's3://openlearnm-redshift/lms'
iam_role default
delimiter ',' region 'us-east-1'
REMOVEQUOTES IGNOREHEADER 1;
```

Pool model

The *pool model* represents an all-in, multi-tenant model where all tenants share the same storage constructs, and it provides the most benefit in simplifying the AaaS solution. With this model, data storage is centralized in one database, and data for all tenants is stored in the same data models. Data security to prevent cross-tenant access is one of the main aspects to address with the pool model. You can implement row-level filtering and provide secure access to the data using database views and apply dynamic filtering based on the tenant querying the data through the use of the current_namespace variable. To scope and control access to tenant data, add a column (consumer_namespace) that serves as a unique identifier for each tenant.

Let's continue working through the use case and add the consumer_namespace to the school table to control access for subscribers from various schools through their Amazon Redshift data warehouse. When you run the query in Example 7-11, you can see the consumer_namespace has unique values for each of the schools.

Example 7-11. School mapping to consumer_namespace

```
SELECT * FROM openlearnm.school;
```

school_id	school_name	address	city	website_url	consumer_namespace
101	New York Public School	null	New York	www.nyps.edu	xxxxc8ee-f6a5-xxxx-xxxx-yyyy66d7zzzz
102	California Public School	null	Sacramento	www.caps.edu	xxxxc7ee-xxxx-468f-xxxx-yyyy77d7zzzz

Figure 7-10 illustrates the pool model architecture.

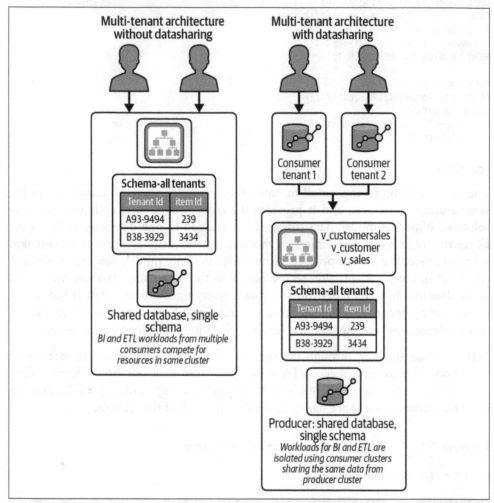

Figure 7-10. Pool model multi-tenant architecture with data sharing compared to the single data warehouse approach

Creating database views in the producer. For the multi-tenant architecture, you can create a materialized view as we did earlier in "Building a Star Schema" on page 95. But here you include the school table and use `school_id` in the where clause to manage row-level security. You can use the script in Example 7-12 to create the materialized view for the multi-tenant pool model. Note that we are using a different schema `openlearnm` to store database objects related to the multi-tenant model.

Example 7-12. Student activities: `total_score` and `mean_score`

```
CREATE materialized view openlearnm.mv_student_lmsactivites_and_score AS
SELECT st.school_id, st.id_student, st.code_module,st.code_presentation, st.gender,
  st.region, st.highest_education, st.imd_band,st.age_band,st.num_of_prev_attempts,
  st.studied_credits, st.disability, st.final_result, st_lms_clicks.sum_of_clicks,
  scores.total_score, scores.mean_score
FROM openlearnm.student_info st
  LEFT JOIN
    (SELECT school_id, code_module, code_presentation,
      id_student, sum(sum_click) AS sum_of_clicks
    FROM openlearnm.student_lms
    GROUP BY school_id, code_module,code_presentation,id_student) st_lms_clicks
  ON st.school_id = st_lms_clicks.school_id
  AND st.code_module = st_lms_clicks.code_module
  AND st.code_presentation = st_lms_clicks.code_presentation
  AND st.id_student = st_lms_clicks.id_student
  LEFT JOIN
    (SELECT school_id, id_student, sum(score) AS total_score,
      avg(score) AS mean_score
      FROM openlearnm.STUDENT_ASSESSMENT
      GROUP BY school_id, id_student)  scores
      ON st.school_id = scores.school_id
      AND st.id_student = scores.id_student;
```

To control and restrict row-level access to allow access to only the students of the school from which the consumer is accessing the data, you can create a view `v_student_lmsactivites_and_score` and filter the records based on the consumer namespace that is querying the data. The view in Example 7-13 is a join between *mv_student_lmsactivities_and_score* and the table *school* with a where condition to filter values based on `current_namespace` (*https://oreil.ly/OfJWE*). This system variable `current_namespace` contains the value of the namespace of the consumer data warehouse from which the query is initiated.

Example 7-13. Creating view for calculating student scores

```
/* create view to calculate student activities total_score mean_score  */
/* use current_namespace system variable to use the consumer namespace */
/* from where the query is run to filter the selected records for the school */

CREATE VIEW openlearnm.v_student_lmsactivites_and_score AS
SELECT mvs.school_id, mvs.id_student, mvs.code_module,
  mvs.code_presentation, mvs.gender, mvs.region, mvs.highest_education,
  mvs.imd_band, mvs.age_band, mvs.num_of_prev_atteempts,
  mvs.studied_credits, mvs.disability,mvs.final_result,
  mvs.sum_of_clicks, mvs.total_score, mvs.mean_score
FROM openlearnm.mv_student_lmsactivites_and_score mvs
  LEFT JOIN openlearnm.school s
    ON mvs.school_id = s.school_id
WHERE s.consumer_namespace = current_namespace;
```

Creating datashares in producer and granting usage to the consumer.   Now you are ready to create a datashare and share the view with the consumers. Connect to your producer data warehouse and create the datashare learnsharem, add the openlearn schema, and add the view you created to be shared with the consumers as in Example 7-14. In the GRANT USAGE statement, replace the *consumer namespace* with the namespace of your data warehouse.

Example 7-14. Setting up producer datashare

```
CREATE DATASHARE learnsharem;

ALTER DATASHARE learnsharem
  ADD SCHEMA openlearnm;

ALTER DATASHARE learnsharem
  ADD TABLE openlearnm.v_student_lmsactivities_and_score;

Grant USAGE ON DATASHARE learnsharem
  TO NAMESPACE '<<consumer namespace>>'
```

Note the name of the datashare ends with *m*, indicating schema for for multi-tenant as a naming convention to differentiate from the earlier datashare learnshare you created.

Now connect to your consumer to create a database referencing the datashare on the producer, as in Example 7-15. Note again that this database is just a pointer to the datashare and does not hold any data on its own.

Example 7-15. Creating local database from remote datashare

```
CREATE DATABASE openlearnm_db
FROM DATASHARE learnsharem
OF NAMESPACE '<producer_namespace>';
```

Once you create the database, you can query the data live using a three-part notation of db_name.schema.view as in Example 7-16. When you query from the consumer, note that even without the where clause to filter out certain records, data returned will be for only the students that correspond to the consumer cluster from which the query is being triggered. This is controlled at the view level, where the data is restricted based on the consumer namespace, which is joined to the school table.

Example 7-16. Querying the view

```
SELECT *
FROM openlearnm_db.learnsharem.v_student_lmsactivities_and_score;
```

When you select from the view v_student_lmsactivities_and_score, you will see only the data associated with the consumer namespace you are using to query the data. When this query is passed to the producer from this consumer, the current_namespace variable will have the namespace of this consumer. Hence, the materialized view will filter the records just from this consumer based on the join condition from the school table.

For a detailed description of how you can set up and test multiple consumers, you can refer to the blog "Implementing Multi-tenant Patterns in Amazon Redshift Using Data Sharing" (*https://oreil.ly/YXYbF*).

Using Role-Level Security. Instead of using database views defined on the producer, you can use *row-level security* (RLS), which is built on the foundation of role-based access control (RBAC) (*https://oreil.ly/dNIsy*) to restrict rows for each consumer. RLS allows you to control which users or roles can access specific records of data within tables based on security policies that are defined at the database object level. This RLS capability in Amazon Redshift enables you to dynamically filter existing rows of data in a table.

Using the previous example, assume the school table still has the consumer_name space field but all tables are shared with all consumers. The following RLS policy in Example 7-17 can be defined and will force a join to the school table to ensure that only schools where the consumer_namespace = current_namespace are returned.

Example 7-17. Creating row-level security policy

```
CREATE RLS POLICY consumer
WITH (school_id int)
USING (school_id = (
  SELECT school_id
  FROM school
  WHERE consumer_namespace = current_namespace));

GRANT SELECT ON
  student,
  course_outcome,
  course_registration,
  degree_plan
TO RLS POLICY consumer;
```

Next, you can attach this policy, as shown in Example 7-18, to any table containing the school_id field and any user who is associated to the database role school will have this policy applied and see only their data.

Example 7-18. Associating policy on object to role

```
ATTACH RLS POLICY consumer ON student TO ROLE school;
ATTACH RLS POLICY consumer ON course_outcome TO ROLE school;
ATTACH RLS POLICY consumer ON course_registration TO ROLE school;
ATTACH RLS POLICY consumer ON degree_plan TO ROLE school;
```

Bridge model

In the *bridge model,* you store data for each tenant in its own schema in a database with a similar set of tables. You create datashares for each schema and share them with the corresponding consumer so the query workloads on each schema can be routed to consumers. This is an appealing balance between the silo and pool model, providing both data isolation and reuse of ETL code across different schemas. Using a bridge model without data sharing, queries from all users are directed to a single data warehouse. With Amazon Redshift, you can create up to 9,900 schemas, so if your use case requires more than this limit, you can consider creating more databases. For more information, see Quotas and Limits in Amazon Redshift (*https://oreil.ly/_qd3j*). Figure 7-11 illustrates the bridge model.

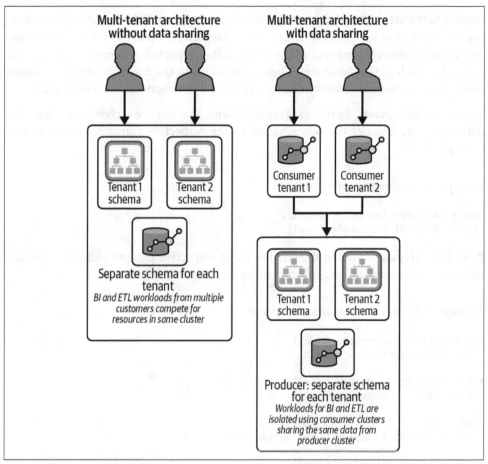

Figure 7-11. Bridge model multi-tenant architecture with data sharing compared to the single data warehouse approach

Creating database schemas and tables in the producer. Let's continue using the previous use case. As you did in the pool model, the first step is to create the database schema and tables. Log in to the producer and create separate schemas for each tenant. For example, you can create two schemas, learnschema_school1 and learn schema_school2, to store student data from two different schools, and the same tables you created in Example 3-1 under each schema. To maximize ETL code reuse, ensure the data models are the same across all schemas.

Creating datashares in the producer and granting usage to the consumer. To create data-shares in a bridge model, create two datashares, `learnshare-school1` and `learnshare-school2`, and add all the tables in the respective schema for school1 and school2 to each of the datashares. Then grant access to the corresponding consumers in the same account or a different account for the consumers to access the data.

Create two datashares, `learnshare-school1` and `learnshare-school2`, to share the database objects under the two schemas to the respective consumers as shown in Example 7-19.

Example 7-19. Creating datashares

```
CREATE DATASHARE learnshare-school1;
CREATE DATASHARE learnshare-school2;
```

Alter the datashare and add the schema(s) for respective tenants and the respective tables to be shared with the consumer using the scripts in Example 7-20.

Example 7-20. Adding objects to datashares

```
ALTER DATASHARE learnshare-school1
  ADD SCHEMA learnschema_school1;

ALTER DATASHARE learnshare-school2
  ADD SCHEMA learnschema_school2;

ALTER DATASHARE learnshare-school1
  ADD ALL TABLES IN SCHEMA learnschema_school1;

ALTER DATASHARE learnshare-school2
  ADD ALL TABLES IN SCHEMA learnschema_school2;
```

Now grant usage on the datashare for the first school `learnshare-school1` to the namespace of the consumer data warehouse for school1, as in Example 7-21.

Example 7-21. Allowing access to datashare

```
GRANT USAGE ON DATASHARE learnshare-school1
  TO NAMESPACE '<consumer1_namespace>';
```

To access consumer data of school1, log into the data warehouse for the first school and create a database referencing the datashare using script in Example 7-22. You can also view the datashares from the `SVV_DATASHARES` system view, or the command `SHOW DATASHARES`. If you want to view the list of objects in each datashare, you can view the details by querying the `SVV_DATASHARE_OBJECTS` system view.

Example 7-22. Creating local database from remote datashare

```
CREATE DATABASE learndb_school1
  FROM DATASHARE learnshare-school1
  OF NAMESPACE '<producer_namespace>';

SELECT *
  FROM learndb_school1.learnschema_school1.v_student_lmsactivities_and_score;

SHOW DATASHARES;

SELECT * FROM SVV_DATASHARES;

SELECT * FROM SVV_DATASHARE_OBJECTS;
```

In the bridge model, since the database objects for the respective schools are organized under each schema, and the datashare contains only the respective schema for the school, a consumer can access only the database objects relevant for that school. In this example, school1 will be restricted to querying data from learn schema_school1.

Silo model

The third option is to store data for each tenant in separate databases within a data warehouse if you want to have distinct data models and separate monitoring, management, and security footprints—the *silo model*. Amazon Redshift supports cross-database queries across databases, which allows you to simplify data organization. You can store common or granular datasets used across all tenants in a centralized database and use the cross-database query capability to join relevant data for each tenant.

The steps to create a datashare in a silo model are similar to the bridge model; however, unlike the bridge model (where datashare is for each schema), the silo model has a datashare created for each database. Figure 7-12 illustrates the architecture of the silo model.

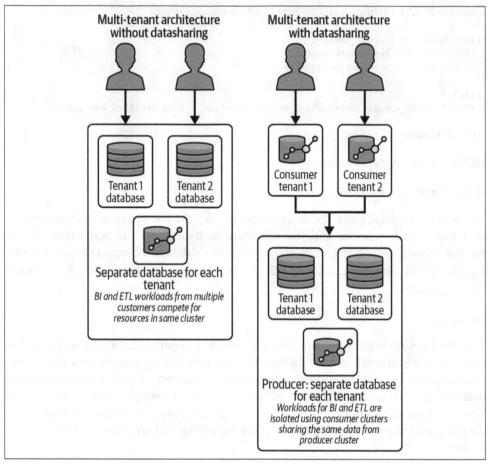

Figure 7-12. Silo model multi-tenant architecture with data sharing compared to the single data warehouse approach

Creating databases and datashares in the producer. Again, let's continue using the previous use case. To create datashares for the silo model in the producer, complete the following steps:

Log in to the producer as an admin user and create separate databases for each tenant, as in Example 7-23.

Example 7-23. Creating databases

```
CREATE DATABASE learndb_school1;
CREATE DATABASE learndb_school2;
```

Log in again to the producer database learndb_school1 with the user ID for the first school and create the schema learnschema, as in Example 7-24. Similarly, you can log in to the producer database learndb_school2 with the user ID for the second school and create the schema learnschema.

Example 7-24. Creating schema

```
CREATE SCHEMA learnschema;
```

Then, using the scripts in Example 3-1, create the tables for the student information data model in each database, storing the student data for each respective school. One benefit of this strategy is that because the schema and table names are identical, the ETL process can be reused with only the connection parameter of the database name being changed.

Creating datashares in the producer and granting usage to the consumer. Next, create the datashares like you did in the "Bridge model" on page 258, this time connecting to each database separately. For the first school, you could execute the script in Example 7-25.

Example 7-25. Setting up datashare for the first school

```
CREATE DATASHARE learnshare-school1;
ALTER DATASHARE learnshare-school1 ADD SCHEMA learnschema;
ALTER DATASHARE learnshare-school1 ADD ALL TABLES IN SCHEMA learnschema;
GRANT USAGE ON DATASHARE learnshare-school1 TO NAMESPACE '<consumer1_namespace>';
```

For the second school, you could execute this script in Example 7-26.

Example 7-26. Setting up datashare for the second school

```
CREATE DATASHARE learnshare-school2;
ALTER DATASHARE learnshare-school2 ADD SCHEMA learnschema;
ALTER DATASHARE learnshare-school2 ADD ALL TABLES IN SCHEMA learnschema;
GRANT USAGE ON DATASHARE learnshare-school2 TO NAMESPACE '<consumer2_namespace>';
```

External Data Sharing with AWS ADX Integration

For some users, sharing data within an account or between accounts is sufficient for intra-organization collaboration, but for inter-organization collaboration and monetization use cases, you can use ADX. With ADX, you can share data from Amazon S3 or directly query data from Amazon Redshift data warehouses through a datashare.

AWS Data Exchange (ADX) is a data marketplace where data providers can host their data products for subscribers to access on a subscription basis. ADX hosts data products from over three hundred providers and provides subscription-based access for data as files, APIs, or Amazon Redshift datashares. Subscribers can access the data directly through data lakes, applications, analytics, and machine learning models that use the data. As an AWS service, ADX is secure and compliant, integrated with AWS and third-party tools and services, and offers consolidated billing and subscription management.

With its integration for Amazon Redshift, you can license access to your Amazon Redshift data through ADX. When you subscribe to a product with ADX datashares, ADX automatically adds you as a data consumer on all of its datashares included with the product. You can automatically generate invoices and collect payments centrally and automatically disburse through AWS Marketplace Entitlement Service.

Providers can license data in Amazon Redshift at a granular level, such as schemas, tables, views, and UDFs. You can use the same ADX datashare across multiple ADX products. Any objects added to the ADX datashare are available to consumers. Producers can view all AWS Data Exchange datashares managed by ADX on their behalf using Amazon Redshift API operations, SQL commands, and the Amazon Redshift console. Consumers who subscribe to a product of ADX datashares have read-only access to the objects in the datashares.

An *AWS Data Exchange datashare* is a unit of licensing for sharing your data through ADX. AWS manages billing and payments associated with subscriptions to ADX and use of Amazon Redshift data sharing. Approved data providers can add ADX datashares to ADX products. When you subscribe to a product with ADX datashares, you get access to the datashares in the product. We will cover more details on how ADX integration with Amazon Redshift works in "External Data Sharing with AWS ADX Integration" on page 264. Data producers who are approved providers for ADX datashares can add ADX datashares and license data as a product through ADX.

When you subscribe to a product with AWS Data Exchange datashares, ADX automatically adds you as a data consumer on all ADX datashares included with the product. ADX also removes you from ADX datashares when your subscription ends. ADX integrates with AWS billing to provide unified billing, invoicing, payment collection, and payment distribution for paid products with ADX datashares. To register as an ADX data provider, see Getting Started as a Provider (*https://oreil.ly/iokOZ*).

If you are a consumer with an active ADX subscription (also known as subscribers on ADX), you can find, subscribe to, and query granular, up-to-date data in Amazon Redshift without the need to extract, transform, and load the data.

If you want to consume third-party producer data, you can browse the AWS Data Exchange catalog to discover and subscribe to datasets in Amazon Redshift. After your ADX subscription is active, you can create a database from the datashare in their data warehouse and query the data in Amazon Redshift.

As a subscriber, you can directly use data from providers without any further processing, without need for an ETL process. Because you don't have to do any processing, the data is always current and can be used directly in your Amazon Redshift queries. ADX for Amazon Redshift takes care of managing all entitlements and payments for you, with all charges billed to your AWS account.

Publishing a Data Product

To publish a data product in Amazon Redshift using ADX, you can create ADX datashares that connect to your Amazon Redshift data warehouses. To add ADX datashares to products on ADX, you must be a registered ADX provider.

Once you are registered as a provider, you can create AWS Data Exchange datashares for Amazon Redshift to publish as a data product in data exchange. When you subscribe to a product containing datashares, you are granted read-only access to the tables, views, schemas, and user-defined functions that a data provider adds to the datashare.

Let's walk through how you can share the student materialized view as a data product through data exchange. The first step is to create a data exchange datashare, and you can create this datashare either using the console as shown in Figure 7-13 or using scripts.

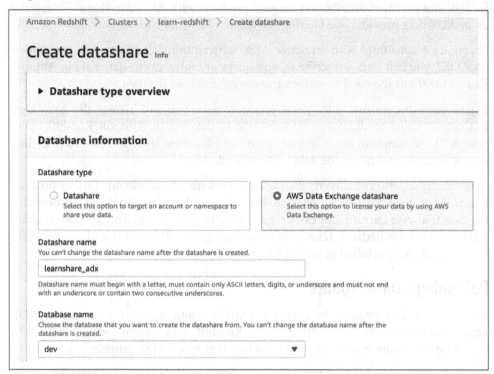

Figure 7-13. Create a data exchange datashare

Then you add the database objects for the datashare; in this case, choose mv_stu dent_lmsactivities_and_score (see Figure 7-14).

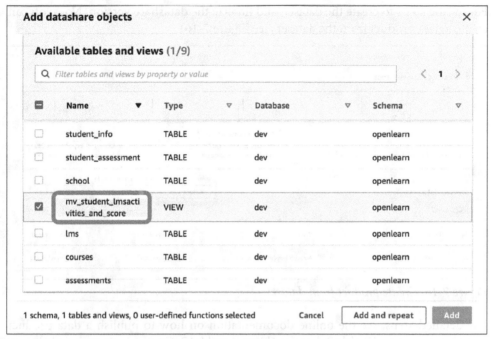

Figure 7-14. Add data exchange datashare objects

Once you create the datashare and add the database objects to it, you can select the datashare `learnshare_adx` and create a dataset on AWS Data Exchange (see Figure 7-15). This datashare will then be listed in AWS Data Exchange for consumers to subscribe to the dataset.

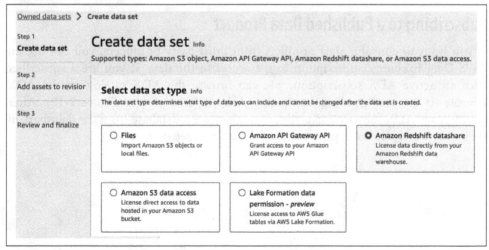

Figure 7-15. Creating ADX Dataset from Redshift Datashare

Follow the steps to create the dataset, and finalize the datashare version. Now you can create a data product from the dataset (see Figure 7-16).

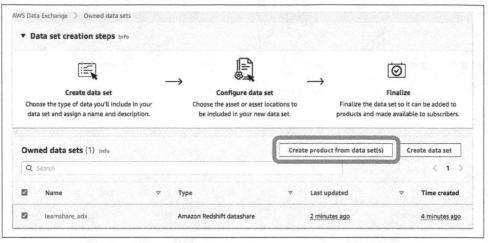

Figure 7-16. Create product from dataset

For detailed steps, see the online documentation on how to publish a data product containing Amazon Redshift datasets (*https://oreil.ly/QyO4p*).

 Note that you need to register as a marketplace seller to publish data products. If you would like to provide paid products and are eligible to do so, you must submit your tax and banking information.

Subscribing to a Published Data Product

If you want to consume data products from third-party producers, you can use an AWS Data Exchange subscription to get access to the data. If you are a subscriber with an active ADX subscription, you can browse the ADX catalog on the ADX console to discover products containing ADX datashares (see Figure 7-17). After getting your ADX subscription active, you can create a database from the datashare in their data warehouse and query the data in Amazon Redshift.

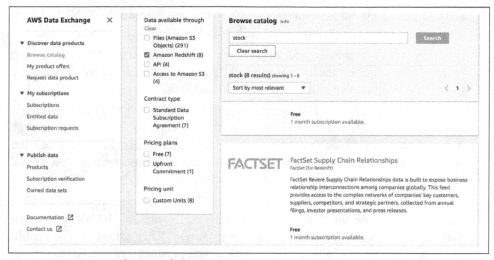

Figure 7-17. Browse data products on ADX

After you subscribe to a product that contains AWS Data Exchange datashares, create a database from the datashare within your data warehouse. You can then query the data in Amazon Redshift directly without extracting, transforming, and loading the data. With ADX datashares added to an ADX product, consumers automatically have access to a product's datashares when their subscription starts and retain their access as long as their subscription is active.

For more information, see the online documentation on working with AWS Data Exchange datashares as a consumer (*https://oreil.ly/-Gtit*).

Considerations When Using AWS Data Exchange for Amazon Redshift

When using AWS Data Exchange for Amazon Redshift, consider the following:

- Both producers and consumers must use the RA3 node type to use Amazon Redshift datashares. Producers must use the RA3 node types or serverless with both the producer and consumer data warehouses encrypted.

- You must be registered as an ADX provider to list products on ADX, including products that contain ADX datashares. For more information, see Getting Started as a Provider (*https://oreil.ly/vFwMO*).

- You don't need to be a registered ADX provider to find, subscribe to, and query Amazon Redshift data through ADX.

- To control access to your data through ADX datashares, you have to have the Publicly Accessible setting turned on. This doesn't mean that your datashare is public or even that the consumer's data warehouse is public, but it means they are allowed to make it public. To alter an ADX datashare, turn off the Publicly Accessible setting using `ALTER DATASHARE SET PUBLICACCESSIBLE FALSE` command.

- Producers can't manually add or remove consumers from ADX datashares because access to the datashares is granted based on having an active subscription to an ADX product that contains the ADX datashares.

- Producers can't view the SQL queries that consumers run. They can only view metadata, such as the number of queries or the objects consumers query, through Amazon Redshift tables that only the producer can access. Producers can use this information to understand how their subscribers are using their product and inform their decisions based on data usage patterns.

- We recommend that you don't delete an ADX datashare shared to other AWS accounts using the `DROP DATASHARE` statement. If you do, the AWS accounts that have access to the datashare will lose access. This action is irreversible. Performing this type of alteration can breach data product terms in ADX.

- For cross-region data sharing, you can create ADX datashares to share licensed data.

We recommend that you make your datashares publicly accessible. If you don't, subscribers on AWS Data Exchange with publicly accessible consumer data warehouses won't be able to use your datashare.

Query from the Data Lake and Unload to the Data Lake

You may have use cases where you want to share data that has been curated in the data warehouse with external applications. Because Amazon Redshift is integrated with the data lake, you can take a data warehouse-first approach to store the data in your Data Warehouse first, and offload data to the data lake as required. Since Amazon Redshift supports decoupling of storage and compute, it enables you to store large volumes of data up to 128TB per node within the data warehouse. So, for OLAP workloads, you can store all your data in your data warehouse. When you want to share data in your Amazon Redshift data warehouse with other services like Amazon SageMaker, you can use the `UNLOAD` option to offload the data from your Amazon Redshift local tables to Amazon S3. You can directly convert to a recommended format like Parquet or ORC while unloading to Amazon S3, and share with other services.

For the general syntax of the UNLOAD command, refer to the documentation for the UNLOAD command (*https://oreil.ly/N9z_r*). Using the running example, if you want to share the student learning management engagement with partners or users who use other services to access data, then you can unload the student activities data using the UNLOAD command, as shown in Example 7-27.

Example 7-27. UNLOAD example

```
UNLOAD ('select * from mv_student_lmsactivities_and_score')
TO 's3://openlearn/studentactivities'
IAM_ROLE default
PARQUET
PARTITION BY (school_id);
```

You can also use INSERT INTO SELECT query to load the results into existing external table on external catalogs, as in Example 7-28, for AWS Glue, AWS Lake Formation, or an Apache Hive metastore. Use the same AWS IAM role used for the CREATE EXTERNAL SCHEMA command to interact with external catalogs and Amazon S3. For detailed steps on using the insert into external table command, you can refer to the documentation on inserting results of a SELECT query into an external table (*https://oreil.ly/cGyyl*).

Example 7-28. Writing data to external table

```
INSERT INTO external_schema.table_name
{ select_statement }
```

Amazon DataZone to Discover and Share Data

A data warehouse typically means building a centralized data store by transferring detailed transactional data from multiple sources systems and consolidating data into a single source of truth. The detailed data is transformed by applying business rules and stored in a format that is aggregated and stored for fast query performance. A relatively new architecture has evolved for data management around decentralized data management and governance. This is the data mesh architecture, which you read about in "Data Mesh" on page 26. Data mesh embraces decentralized ownership of data and is intended to enable easy access to data without having to move or copy data in a central data store.

Data producers who are subject matter experts create data assets and define the data catalog, add business definitions for easy consumption, and organize as data domains. They then register data products in a data catalog for consumers to search and access the data relevant to their business needs. As a refresher, the four key concepts of data mesh architecture are:

- Domain-oriented ownership of data
- Federated data governance
- Self-service data infrastructure
- Data as a product thinking

In the next section, you'll see how Amazon DataZone components can enable key capabilities that constitute a data mesh architecture.

Use Cases for a Data Mesh Architecture with Amazon DataZone

There are many use cases for a data mesh architecture, especially in organizations that have multiple lines of business or business units and subsidiaries that require data sharing across business units. Here are a few examples.

As part of the modernization strategy, a large financial organization embarked on a journey to migrate their legacy on-premises workloads to AWS Cloud, including managed services such as Amazon Redshift and Amazon S3. They chose to build a modern data platform on AWS Cloud that serves as the central data store for analytics, research, and data science. In addition, this platform was also built to serve for governance, regulatory, and financial reports. With the initial design to store data for all businesses in a centralized data store and a central AWS account, they ran into limits and complexities in making data accessible.

To address the growing pains and needs of a large data footprint, they decentralized and delegated ownership of the data stores and associated management functions to their respective business units. The data mesh architecture allowed them to keep data of the respective business units in their own accounts, yet enable a seamless access across the business unit accounts in a secure manner. They reorganized the AWS account structure to have separate accounts for each of the business units wherein business data and dependent applications were co-located in their respective AWS accounts in Amazon Redshift and Amazon S3. With this decentralized model, the business units independently managed the responsibility of hydration, curation, and security of their data.

An investment banking organization that had multiple LOBs and corporate functions needed an architecture to freely share data across the enterprise while managing the risk of unauthorized access. They took a two-pronged approach to addressing this requirement. First, by defining data products, which are curated by people who understand the data and its management requirements, permissible uses, and limitations. And second, by implementing a data mesh architecture, which allowed them to align their data technology to those data products.

A healthcare organization can create a data product that provides real-time patient monitoring data, which can be used by various departments such as emergency services, patient care, and research. In a school system, where student data is stored in a student information system, the IT department can be the producer of data and the individual schools would be subscribers of the data relevant to the students in their school. You can build a data mesh architecture to enable teachers, students, and administrators to collaborate and share data securely, embracing a producer–consumer model. A retail company might have separate domains for sales, inventory, customer data, and marketing. Each domain can have its own data team responsible for collecting, storing, and analyzing data specific to that domain. Adopting a data mesh architecture will allow each domain to own and manage its data, enabling them to make data-driven decisions independently.

These are just a few examples of how data mesh architecture can be applied in practice. The main goal is to decentralize data management, empower domain teams, and create a scalable and sustainable data ecosystem within organizations.

Key Capabilities and Use Cases for Amazon DataZone

Amazon DataZone (*https://aws.amazon.com/datazone*) is a data management service that embraces the data mesh architecture and enables data producers to publish data products and make them available to the business data catalog through a web interface. Once data products are published, users have a streamlined way to search for data. With the Amazon DataZone catalog, you can make data visible with business context to find and understand data quickly. You can create business use cases based on groupings of teams, analytics tools, and data assets to simplify access to AWS analytics tools. With the automated publish/subscribe workflow, you can adjust data ownership to protect data between producers and consumers.

You can set up security policies to ensure that the people with the right permissions get access to your data. With Amazon DataZone, you have federated data governance where the data owners and subject matter experts of that dataset can enforce security and access controls on their relevant data assets. You can extend governance controls setup in the AWS Glue Data Catalog, IAM, and Lake Formation. Amazon DataZone supports data access and data sharing across AWS services like Amazon Redshift, Amazon Athena, AWS Glue, AWS Lake Formation, and Amazon QuickSight.

Amazon DataZone Integrations with Amazon Redshift and Other AWS Services

Amazon DataZone by itself does not store any data, and it acts as a metadata hub to enable ease of data access across siloed datasets. For data access, Amazon DataZone has to integrate with existing AWS services that store, access, and control data. At the time of writing this book, it supports three types of integrations with other AWS services:

Producer data sources

> From a producer perspective, Amazon DataZone integrates with data stored in Amazon S3 data lake or Amazon Redshift. You can publish data assets to the Amazon DataZone catalog from the data stored in Amazon S3 and Amazon Redshift tables and views. You can also manually publish objects from AWS Glue Data Catalog to the Amazon DataZone catalog.

Consumer tools

> You can access data assets using Amazon Redshift query editors or Amazon Athena, through external tables in Amazon Redshift.

Access control and fulfillment

> With Amazon DataZone, you can grant access to AWS Lake Formation-managed AWS Glue tables and Amazon Redshift tables and views. Additionally, Amazon DataZone connects standard events related to your actions to Amazon Event-Bridge. You can use these standard events to integrate with other AWS services or third-party solutions for custom integrations.

Components and Capabilities of Amazon DataZone

AWS introduced the concept of `domain` in Amazon DataZone to help organize data assets and resources associated with these assets. Amazon DataZone domains provide you the flexibility to reflect your organization's business areas and entities including data assets, data sources, metadata, business glossaries, and even associated AWS accounts. There are four key components of Amazon DataZone that enables secure data access across business domains using data products published to the central catalog:

- Business data catalog
- Projects
- Governance and access control
- Data portal

We discuss these components next, and they are part of the domain you create, as shown in Figure 7-18.

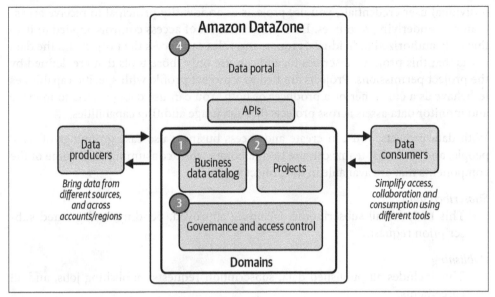

Figure 7-18. Amazon DataZone components

To initially set up Amazon DataZone and its data portal, you will create a domain that will serve as the root domain. Within the data portal, domain administrators can create additional domains. These components work together to provide capabilities to enable you to build and operate a data mesh architecture with decentralized data governance; these are discussed in the next sections.

Business data catalog

The core component of Amazon DataZone is a metadata catalog with business-friendly descriptions. The catalog is built when a data producer publishes the data product and can grow as new products are ready for consumption. This catalog can be from data across disparate data sources. Datasets are published to the catalog, which consumers can access through the Amazon DataZone portal, as shown in Figure 7-24, to search for your desired data.

Amazon DataZone uses ML to automatically suggest business terms while cataloging data assets. This automation reduces the manual work required to add searchable business terms to technical data.

Projects

Amazon DataZone introduces data projects for teams to collaborate and get access to data assets. With projects, a group of users within your organization can collaborate on various business use cases that involve publishing, discovering, subscribing to, and consuming data assets in the Amazon DataZone catalog. Instead of relying on individual user credentials, you use projects as an identity principal to receive access grants to underlying resources. Each project has set of access controls applied to it so that only authorized individuals, groups, and roles can access the project and the data assets that this project subscribes to, and can use only those tools that are defined by the project permissions. Projects are tied to a project profile with specific capabilities to behave as a consumer or a producer or both. You can use data projects to manage and monitor data assets across projects through usage auditing capabilities.

With data projects, you can create and access business use case groupings of data, people, and tools that teams can use to collaborate while consuming data. Some of the components that are available in the project view are:

Subscribed data
This includes all subscriptions including approved, pending, and granted subscription requests.

Publishing
This includes all published data, subscription requests, publishing jobs, and all agreements.

Members
Includes the members of this project and their respective roles.

Settings
Provides details of the project like ID, Account, VPC, and the project capabilities.

Members of the project can collaborate, exchange data, and share artifacts securely, and only those who are explicitly added to the project are able to access the data and analytics tools within it. Projects manage the ownership of data assets produced in accordance with policies applied by data stewards, decentralizing data ownership through federated governance.

Data governance and access control

The automated workflow allows consumers to request access to a data product they find in the business catalog. This request is routed to the data producers or data owners for approval. When a producer approves the request, the consumer gets notified and can access the data without any manual intervention. Data producers can streamline auditing to monitor who is using each dataset, and monitor usage and costs across projects and LOBs. You can find the sample steps to publish and subscribe in the next section.

Data portal

The portal is a personalized homepage outside of the console and provides self-service capability where consumers can search for data in the catalog. The data portal is the primary way users access Amazon DataZone and is a browser-based web application where you can catalog, discover, govern, share, and analyze data. This enables cross-functional collaboration while working with data and analytics tools using existing credentials from your identity provider.

With this portal you can access personalized views for data assets. In Figure 7-19, you see the various state of the subscriptions requested in the workflow. You can analyze data without having to sign in to the AWS Management Console or understand the underlying AWS analytics services.

Figure 7-19. Personalized view of data products in various states of subscriptions

Getting Started with Amazon DataZone

Adopting a data mesh architecture is not just about technology; it requires a mindset change. You have to organize your team and implement processes in your organization to move toward a producer–consumer model. Domains enable an easier transition by providing a mechanism to instill organizational discipline for teams that are producing and cataloging the data in the business data catalog. Any data producer can publish a data asset in the catalog to a particular domain that governs the data and control access of consumers who can access the domain. A domain can have multiple projects associated with each business use case and in which people collaborate and access data.

This section takes you through creating the Amazon DataZone root domain and obtaining the data portal URL. It then takes you through the basic workflows for data producers and data consumers. For detailed steps to set up Amazon DataZone, refer to the "Getting started" documentation (*https://oreil.ly/QzAOG*). This includes the following steps.

Step 1: Create the domain and data portal

To start with Amazon DataZone, the first step is to create a domain. A domain is a collection of Amazon DataZone objects, such as data assets, projects, associated AWS accounts, and data sources. Domains are containers where you and your team can create all related Amazon DataZone entities, including metadata assets. You can publish a data asset to the catalog with a particular domain that governs the data, and control access for associated AWS accounts and resources that can access that domain.

Step 2: Create a producer project

To create and publish a data product as a producer, you need to create a project under which the data product and related assets will be organized. When you create a project, you specify the project profile and the data source connection details. The project profile determines the capabilities of the project and whether the project serves as a producer, consumer, or both; the connection details are for the data source. So, before you create a project, you need to create a project profile and an AWS Glue connection. You can create a project profile by choosing the Catalog Management menu and selecting the Project and Accounts tab.

For a data warehouse producer, you need to enter additional information like the Amazon Redshift cluster name and the AWS Glue connection details. If you do not already have an AWS Glue connection, you can create a Glue connection to the datasource and specify the connection details in the project. You will be publishing data you produce to the catalog from the project, and consumers will access data through the project as well.

To create a project, navigate to the Amazon DataZone data portal using the data portal URL and log in using your single sign-on (SSO) or AWS credentials. Here you can go to the My Projects menu, and click the + sign to create a new project, as shown in Figure 7-20. If you're an Amazon DataZone administrator, you can obtain the data portal URL by accessing the Amazon DataZone console in the AWS account where the Amazon DataZone root domain was created.

Figure 7-20. Create projects with specific data domain

You can also view all the data projects by choosing "Browse all projects." The list of projects will be as shown in Figure 7-21.

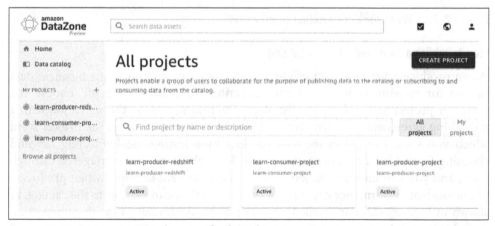

Figure 7-21. List projects under specific data domain

Step 3: Produce data for publishing in Amazon DataZone

Before publishing a data asset to the data catalog, you need to create the data objects and data you want to share with your consumers. From the producer project you created in the previous step, you click on "Query data—Amazon Redshift" under Analytical Tools, as shown in Figure 7-22, and log in to the Amazon Redshift cluster to create the data tables and set up the data. This will take you to Amazon Redshift Query Editor V2, and you log in to the data warehouse using the "Federated user" option. Here you can create the database objects and the data. If you have tables already, you can choose to include those when you publish the data product.

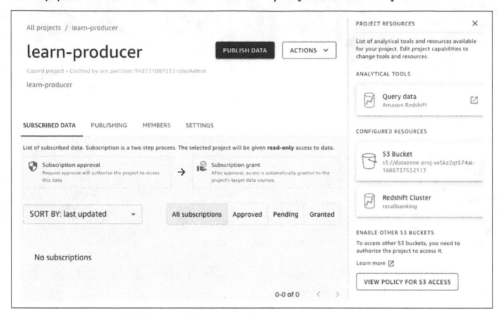

Figure 7-22. Create the data product in producer

Step 4: Publish a data product to the catalog

When producers have the data product ready, they can publish to the business data catalog for consumers to search and subscribe. To publish, you will choose the producer project and choose "Publish data." Publishing is done through a job with a publishing agreement. You can create a publishing agreement from the project from which you want to publish the data product by selecting the Publishing tab and choosing Publishing Agreements under this. The publish process is triggered through a job, and you can monitor the job as well. In our student example, when producers of the Student Performance data product are ready, they can publish to the catalog, as shown in Figure 7-23. For detailed steps to publish data, refer to the documentation on publishing data in Amazon DataZone (*https://oreil.ly/ykTGV*).

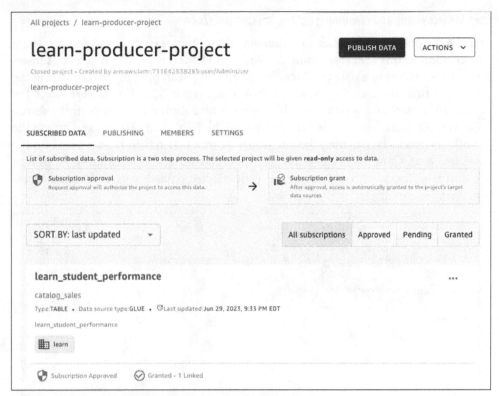

Figure 7-23. Publish Student Performance data product

Step 5: Create a consumer project

For a consumer to subscribe to the underlying data product, again the projects act as an identity principal that receives access grants to underlying resources, without relying on individual user credentials. For a consumer to subscribe to the data produced by a producer, you need to create a consumer project with a consumer profile. For the consumer profile, you will add the capability data warehouse Consumer Capability while creating the consumer profile. When the user identifies a dataset in the catalog using the portal, the user needs to select the consumer project before requesting access for the dataset. Amazon DataZone will validate the request against the set of access controls and authorize only individuals, groups, and roles who can access the project and the data assets.

Step 6: Discovering and consuming data in Amazon DataZone

Once you publish a data asset to a domain, subscribers can discover and request a subscription to this data asset using the Amazon DataZone portal. When consumers wants to subscribe to a data product, they begin with searching for and browsing the catalog to find an asset they want, as shown in Figure 7-24. Consumers select the consumer project and search for a data product by entering key words in the search box. Amazon DataZone will search through all the published catalogs and return the list of data products matching the key words. Search lists return results based on the cataloged data. Consumers can select their desired dataset and learn more about it in the business glossary. After you confirm your selected dataset, you can request access and start your analysis.

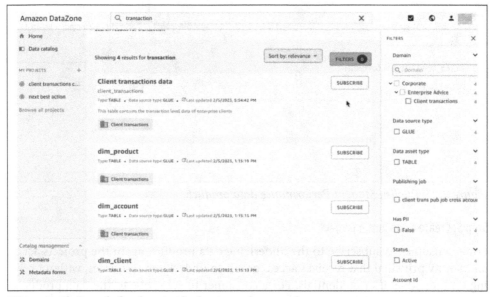

Figure 7-24. Search for data in the business data catalog

You choose to subscribe to the data asset by submitting a subscription request: click the Subscribe button as shown in Figure 7-25 and include justification and the reason for the request. The subscription approver, as defined in the publishing agreement, then reviews the access request. They can either approve or reject the request. For detailed steps, you can refer to the documentation on discovering and consuming data (*https://oreil.ly/7EF48*).

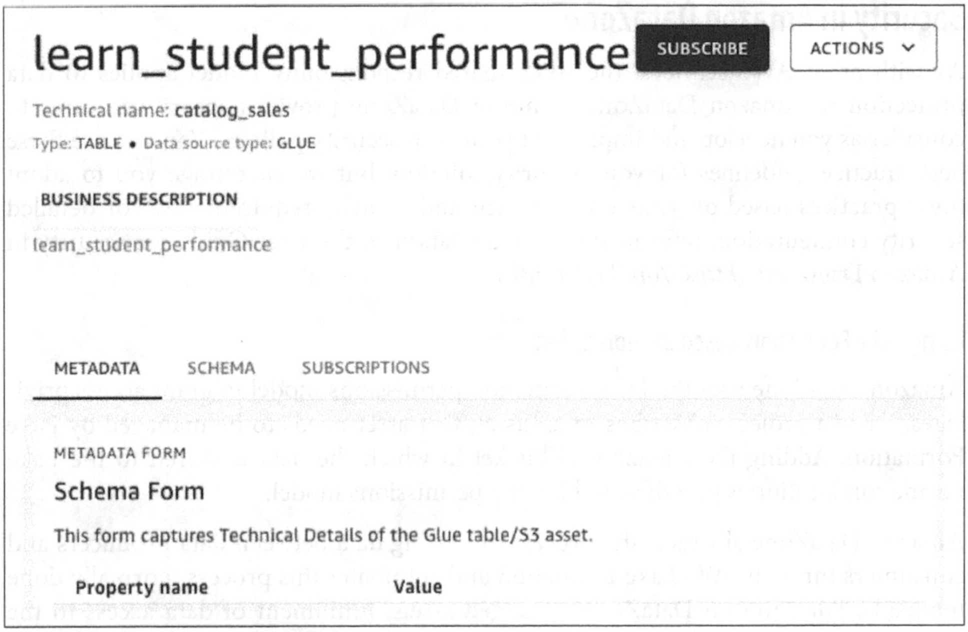

learn_student_performance `SUBSCRIBE`   `ACTIONS ∨`

Technical name: **catalog_sales**

Type: **TABLE** • Data source type: **GLUE**

BUSINESS DESCRIPTION

learn_student_performance

METADATA   SCHEMA   SUBSCRIPTIONS

METADATA FORM

Schema Form

This form captures Technical Details of the Glue table/S3 asset.

Property name	Value

Figure 7-25. Subscribe to the Student Performance data product

Step 7: Approve access to a published data asset as a producer

A producer can approve access to a request by a consumer through the producer project. The producer can view all the subscription requests pending approval by navigating to the producer project and choosing the Subscription Requests tab under the Publishing tab. Here the producer can approve and also specify the reason for approval. This information is recorded for future tracking of who granted approval and details of the approval request.

Step 8: Analyze a published data asset as a consumer

Once approved, a subscriber can view the approval status using the consumer project, and use either Amazon Athena or the Amazon Redshift query editor to view the data, depending on the type of the data source and where the data resides.

Before you begin setting up Amazon DataZone for your data mesh, complete the procedures described in the Setting Up section in the documentation (*https://oreil.ly/4Z4vm*). If you are using a brand-new AWS account, you must configure permissions for the Amazon DataZone management console (*https://oreil.ly/5hOJb*). If you are using an AWS account that has existing AWS Glue Data Catalog objects, you must also configure data lake permissions to Amazon DataZone (*https://oreil.ly/bnllj*).

Security in Amazon DataZone

As with other AWS services, the AWS shared responsibility model applies to data protection in Amazon DataZone. Amazon DataZone provides security features to consider as you develop and implement your own security policies. You can use these best practice guidelines for your security solution, but we encourage you to adopt these practices based on your environment and security requirements. For detailed security configuration, refer to the documentation in the User Guide for security in Amazon DataZone (*https://oreil.ly/rIDBL*).

Using Lake Formation-based authorization

Amazon DataZone uses the Lake Formation permissions model to grant access privileges. Once a project subscribes to an asset, that asset needs to be managed by Lake Formation. Adding the Amazon S3 bucket in which the data is stored to the Lake Formation location is part of switching the permissions model.

Amazon DataZone abstracts the process of sharing data between data producers and consumers through AWS Lake Formation and automates this process, normally done manually. For Amazon DataZone–managed assets, fulfillment of data access to the underlying tables according to the policies applied by data publishers is taken care of without the need for an admin or data movement.

Encryption

Amazon DataZone encrypts service metadata by default with an AWS KMS key that AWS owns and manages for you. You can also encrypt the metadata stored in the Amazon DataZone data catalog using keys that you manage with AWS KMS. Amazon DataZone uses Transport Layer Security (TLS) and client-side encryption for encryption in transit. Communication with Amazon DataZone is always done over HTTPS so your data is always encrypted in transit.

Implement least privilege access

A typical use case for Amazon DataZone will require sharing data across business groups within your organization. Since the basic assumption of a data mesh architecture with Amazon DataZone is a decentralized governance, it is more important to maintain the principle of least privileged access when granting permissions. You analyze who the producer and consumer of data is and what permissions they need to the Amazon DataZone resources and accordingly assign privileges through your administrators. You enable specific actions that you want to allow on those resources. Therefore, you should grant only the permissions that are required to perform a task. Implementing least privilege access is fundamental in reducing security risk and the impact that could result from errors or malicious intent.

Use IAM roles

Communication between producer and consumer in Amazon DataZone is done through IAM roles similar to access between AWS services. Both producer and client applications must have valid credentials, and it is recommended to use an IAM role to manage temporary credentials for your producer and client applications to access Amazon DataZone resources.

 Storing AWS credentials directly in a client application or in an Amazon S3 bucket is not recommended. These are long-term credentials that are not automatically rotated and could have a significant business impact if they are compromised.

For more details on security, you can refer to Data Protection in Amazon DataZone (*https://oreil.ly/tPE-E*).

Summary

This chapter discussed how Amazon Redshift data sharing enables seamless data sharing within and across your organizational boundaries with built-in governance and access controls. You learned how to make data available securely to your business users using data sharing to analyze data with the tool of their choice to make timely decisions. The ability to share data without moving data eliminates potential errors in the ETL process and maintains data integrity of your source data that your users use to make key business decisions.

You learned various use cases of data sharing including workload isolation, cross-departmental collaboration, and Analytics as a Service, and to improve agility of development. You created three types of multi-tenant models with various levels of isolation for the student information dataset. Finally, you learned about Amazon DataZone and how you can use this service to discover and share data with a decentralized data governance model.

In the next chapter, we'll cover how you secure and govern the data in your analytics environment. We will go in detail about the various access controls you can apply to components of Amazon Redshift, giving you both broad and fine-grained control. Finally, we'll cover how to set access controls on external services you may consume in Amazon Redshift such as data in your data lake, operational databases, streaming data, and other AWS services like AWS Lambda and Amazon SageMaker.

CHAPTER 8

Securing and Governing Data

For a typical Fortune 1,000 company, just a 10 percent increase in data accessibility will result in more than $65 million additional net income.

—Richard Joyce, Forrester[1]

In this book, we've already talked about the importance of data and how with Amazon Redshift you can access different types of structured or semistructured data whether it has been loaded locally or queried from an external source. However, equally important to the ability to access and transform data in a cost-performant way is the ability to do it securely, ensuring only the right people have access to the data they should have access to. Many organizations struggle with making all of their data accessible to their users. That balance of accessibility and security is both crucial and hard to achieve in a world where data is ever expanding and where access to data is in such high demand.

In this chapter, we'll discuss the different ways that a user can manage security within Amazon Redshift including "Object-Level Access Controls" and "Database Roles". We'll explore use cases where user communities required fine-grain access controls and how it can be achieved through "Row-Level Security" and "Dynamic Data Masking". Finally, we'll discuss how Amazon Redshift manages security with "External Data Access Control".

Object-Level Access Controls

Amazon Redshift is organized in a hierarchy of objects where each object is governed by a set of permissions. As discussed in Chapter 3, "Setting Up Your Data Models and Ingesting Data", Amazon Redshift can contain multiple databases, each database

---

1 "The Future of Digital Media Buying" (*https://oreil.ly/8cj7p*), Forrester Research, December 2, 2014, p. 10.

can contain multiple schemas, and each schema can hold multiple objects like tables, views, functions, and procedures. In addition to these objects, Amazon Redshift contains administrative objects such as users, groups, and roles that are applicable across all databases.

The user is the individual principal who is logged into the database. A database group is a collection of users, and users can be a member of multiple groups. Finally, "Database Roles" are similar to groups but have additional functionality, which we will discuss later in this chapter. A user, database group, or database role is assigned permissions on objects using the GRANT or REVOKE statement. See Table 8-1 for a list of privileges and the objects they apply to. For more detail on executing GRANT statements, see the online documentation (*https://oreil.ly/TUf0G*). Notice that you may apply UPDATE and SELECT privileges to database columns. This authorization strategy can be useful when restricting access to personally identifiable information (PII) data.

Table 8-1. Object privileges

Privilege	Object
INSERT,DELETE,DROP,REFERENCES	TABLE
UPDATE	TABLE,COLUMN
SELECT	TABLE,VIEW,COLUMN
EXECUTE	FUNCTION,PROCEDURE
CREATE	DATABASE,SCHEMA
TEMP	DATABASE
USAGE	LANGUAGE,SCHEMA
CREATE MODEL,EXECUTE	MODEL
ALTER,SHARE	DATASHARE

As a best practice, grant permissions to database groups or database roles instead of granting permissions directly to users. To further scale the management of privileges, consider managing the assignment of users to database groups and roles by passing user, group, and role information from your corporate identity provider using single sign-on. Using SSO will ensure permissions are granted based on group membership, which can be controlled in a central location. Review the section on connecting in Chapter 2, "Getting Started with Amazon Redshift" for more details.

Object Ownership

Aside from the privileges assigned to an object via a GRANT, the owner of the object implicitly gets *all* privileges on the object. In addition to the object privileges, the object owner has administrative privileges on the object; for example, the owner can run an ALTER TABLE or REFRESH MATERIALIZED VIEW statement (Example 8-1). In some cases, you may need to change the owner of an object. To do so, the object owner can execute an ALTER statement.

Example 8-1. Object ownership

```
ALTER TABLE table1 OWNER TO user1;
```

> You cannot DROP a user if that user owns objects. It's a best practice to restrict where users can create objects so it's easy to identify all objects owned by a user. For example, you may grant CREATE permissions to a schema associated to the user, but SELECT permissions to a shared schema.

When creating your Amazon Redshift data warehouse, you are prompted for an admin user which is granted superuser privileges. A superuser will have all permissions similar to the object owner. The user is also not governed by access controls you define at the object level. Furthermore, a superuser can create other superusers or elevate a user's privilege to superuser by either creating or altering a user with the CREATEUSER attribute (Example 8-2).

Example 8-2. Superuser privilege

```
CREATE USER adminuser CREATEUSER PASSWORD '1234Admin';
ALTER USER adminuser CREATEUSER;
```

> As a best practice, do not use a superuser for everyday activities. Assign the appropriate permissions to database groups and/or database roles so it is clear which permissions are being granted to which user communities.

Default Privileges

To make GRANT management easier, you may set any of the default privileges shown in Table 8-2 so that any object created by a user or in a schema will have privileges granted to another user, group, or role. For more details on how to grant or revoke default privileges, see the online documentation (*https://oreil.ly/A159w*).

Table 8-2. Default privileges

Privilege	Object
INSERT,UPDATE,DELETE,DROP,REFERENCES	TABLE
SELECT	TABLE,VIEW
EXECUTE	FUNCTION,PROCEDURE

Public Schema and Search Path

When your Amazon Redshift data warehouse is launched, a public schema is created in every database and every user created in Amazon Redshift will be a member of the PUBLIC group. By default the PUBLIC group will have read/write access to the public schema in each database within your Amazon Redshift data warehouse. This strategy allows users to collaborate in a public space but requires any additional schemas to be explicitly granted privileges. In addition, when a user is created, the default search_path parameter is set to $user,public. This means that when referencing an object without a database or schema qualifier, Amazon Redshift will search first in a schema that matches the user ID and then in the public schema. This strategy allows users to work on datasets local to their schema in order of preference compared to the shared data in the public schema. As discussed in Chapter 3, "Setting Up Your Data Models and Ingesting Data", it is still a best practice to organize your data model into purpose-built schemas that represent a subject area for easier metadata management and also to simplify access grants. These schemas can also be added to a user's search_path to simplify access to shared data.

Access Controls in Action

To illustrate these access controls, let's use the student information system learning dataset from Chapter 3 and follow an access control model that uses the public schema to store the shared data. The public schema will be readable by all users but writable only by an etluser.

To set up these access controls, first disable write access to the public schema from the PUBLIC group, which will ensure no user can accidentally modify the shared tables. The statement in Example 8-3 will remove any existing *write* privileges as well as ensure the default privilege for new objects will also have *write* privileges revoked. Note: this statement does not revoke the SELECT privileges, meaning that the members of the PUBLIC group will still be able to *read* data from the public schema.

Example 8-3. Revoke write on schema to PUBLIC

```
REVOKE INSERT,UPDATE,DELETE,DROP ON ALL TABLES
  IN SCHEMA public FROM GROUP PUBLIC;
REVOKE CREATE ON SCHEMA public FROM GROUP PUBLIC;
```

```
ALTER DEFAULT PRIVILEGES
    IN SCHEMA public REVOKE INSERT,UPDATE,DELETE ON TABLES FROM PUBLIC;
```

Next, grant the `etluser` all privileges on the public schema and also ensure the default privilege for new objects will also have all privileges (Example 8-4).

Example 8-4. Grant write on schema to user

```
GRANT ALL ON ALL TABLES IN SCHEMA public TO etluser;
GRANT ALL ON SCHEMA public TO etluser;
ALTER DEFAULT PRIVILEGES IN SCHEMA public
    GRANT ALL ON TABLES TO USER etluser;
```

Lastly, let's create a user `faculty_bob` who will inherit `SELECT` access to data in the public schema. Let's also create a schema that matches the username, allowing this user to create copies of the data for analysis and manipulation (Example 8-5).

Example 8-5. Create user schema and grant ALL to user

```
CREATE USER faculty_bob PASSWORD '<your password>';
CREATE SCHEMA faculty_bob;
GRANT ALL ON SCHEMA faculty_bob TO USER faculty_bob;
```

With the privileges in place, assume the `etluser` has loaded the public schema. The query in Example 8-6 will return the `student_cnt` by `semester_id` and `lecture_duration` and will read from the public schema without explicitly referring to it whether you are querying as `faculty_bob` or `etluser` because of the `search_path` and because none of these tables exist in the user's schema.

Example 8-6. Select shared table using the `search_path`

```
SELECT
    co.semester_id,
    cs.lecture_duration,
    count(distinct co.student_id) student_cnt,
FROM course_registration cr
JOIN course_outcome co
  ON cr.student_id = co.student_id AND
    cr.course_id = co.course_id AND
    cr.semester_id = co.semester_id
JOIN course_schedule cs
  ON cr.course_id = cs.course_id AND
    cr.semester_id = cs.semester_id
GROUP BY 1,2;
```

Now, imagine `faculty_bob` is tasked with extending the `course_schedule` table to include a new field, `lecture_duration_band`, that groups the different `lecture_dura tion` values. The user `faculty_bob` can create a copy of the table and extend it with the new field. Note that because of the `search_path`, `faculty_bob` still doesn't need to specify the schema name. The new `course_schedule` table will be created in the `faculty_bob` schema, which he has *write* privileges to (Example 8-7).

Example 8-7. Create user table using the `search_path`

```
CREATE TABLE course_schedule AS SELECT * FROM course_schedule;
ALTER TABLE course_schedule ADD column lecture_duration_band varchar(100);
UPDATE TABLE course_schedule SET lecture_duration_band = CASE
  WHEN lecture_duration BETWEEN 0 AND 60 THEN '0-1 Hour'
  WHEN lecture_duration BETWEEN 61 AND 120 THEN '1-2 Hour'
  WHEN lecture_duration > 120 THEN '2+ Hour' END;
```

To test the results, `faculty_bob` can execute the modified query referencing the new field (Example 8-8).

Example 8-8. Select user table using the search_path

```
SELECT
    co.semester_id,
    cs.lecture_duration_band, -- changed from lecture_duration
    count(distinct co.student_id) student_cnt,
FROM course_registration cr
JOIN course_outcome co
  ON cr.student_id = co.student_id AND
     cr.course_id = co.course_id AND
     cr.semester_id = co.semester_id
JOIN course_schedule cs
  ON cr.course_id = cs.course_id AND
     cr.semester_id = cs.semester_id
GROUP BY 1,2;
```

If the results meet the objectives, the user can pass along the transformation rules to `etluser`, which can modify the `public` schema. Note that because of the `search_path`, `etluser` also doesn't need to specify the schema name. The only `course_schedule` table in the `search_path` of `etluser` is in the `public` schema, which `etluser` has *write* privileges to (Example 8-9).

Example 8-9. Modify shared table

```
ALTER TABLE course_schedule ADD column lecture_duration_band varchar(100);
UPDATE TABLE course_schedule SET lecture_duration_band = CASE
  WHEN lecture_duration BETWEEN 0 AND 60 THEN '0-1 Hour'
  WHEN lecture_duration BETWEEN 61 AND 120 THEN '1-2 Hour'
  WHEN lecture_duration > 120 THEN '2+ Hour' END;
```

Lastly, `faculty_bob` can drop his user table and run the modified SQL, which will reference the updated shared table (Example 8-10).

Example 8-10. Drop user table and query modified shared table

```
DROP TABLE course_schedule;

SELECT
    co.semester_id,
    cs.lecture_duration_band, -- changed from lecture_duration
    count(distinct co.student_id) student_cnt,
FROM course_registration cr
JOIN course_outcome co
  ON cr.student_id = co.student_id AND
    cr.course_id = co.course_id AND
    cr.semester_id = co.semester_id
JOIN course_schedule cs
  ON cr.course_id = cs.course_id AND
    cr.semester_id = cs.semester_id
GROUP BY 1,2;
```

Database Roles

Database roles, while similar to database groups, have two additional features that provide flexibility when managing your Amazon Redshift security.

First, database roles allow you to delegate system privileges to run certain commands that were previously given only to an object owner or superuser, such as altering or dropping a table, refreshing a materialized view, or managing a user. For a detailed list of system privileges, see the online documentation (*https://oreil.ly/fxOTI*).

Second, database roles support nesting of roles, and Amazon Redshift propagates privileges with each role authorization. In the example illustrated in Figure 8-1, granting role R1 to role R2 and then granting role R2 to role R3 authorizes role R3 with all the privileges from the three roles. Therefore, by granting role R3 to a user, the user has all the privileges from roles R1, R2, and R3.

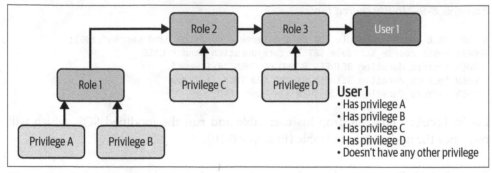

Figure 8-1. Role hierarchy

Amazon Redshift doesn't allow creation of a cyclic role authorization cycle, so role R3 can't be granted to role R1, as that would be cyclic role authorization.

To get started with database roles, Amazon Redshift provides four system-defined roles (Table 8-3), and you can create additional, more granular roles as required. The system-defined roles use the `sys:` prefix, and you can't use this prefix for the roles that you create.

Table 8-3. System-defined roles

Role name	Description of privileges
sys:operator	Can access catalog or system tables, and analyze, vacuum, or cancel queries.
sys:dba	Can create schemas, create tables, drop schemas, drop tables, truncate tables, create or replace stored procedures, drop procedures, create or replace functions, create or replace external functions, create views, and drop views. Additionally, this role inherits all the privileges from the sys:operator role.
sys:superuser	Has the same privileges as the Amazon Redshift superuser.
sys:secadmin	Can create users, alter users, drop users, create roles, drop roles, and grant roles. This role can have access to user tables only when the privilege is explicitly granted to the role.

Database Roles in Action

Using the system-defined roles, you can elevate a user's permissions. Assume you have an `etluser` that is required to manage database objects and monitor load processes but not manage security objects like users, groups, and roles. In Example 8-11, you can see how to grant these privileges to the `etluser`.

Example 8-11. Grant database roles to user

```
GRANT ROLE sys:dba TO etluser;
GRANT ROLE sys:operator TO etluser;
```

Similarly, you can create roles to *limit* access to system privileges. Imagine a scenario where a user needs object management privileges, but should not have user management privileges. In Example 8-12, you can see that etluser was elevated to superuser and that you can use the database role revoke_secadmin, which revokes the user management privileges and is assigned to etluser.

Example 8-12. Drop user table and query modified shared table

```
ALTER USER etluser CREATEUSER;
CREATE ROLE revoke_secadmin;
REVOKE CREATE USER, DROP USER, ALTER USER,
      CREATE ROLE, GRANT ROLE
FROM ROLE revoke_secadmin;
GRANT ROLE revoke_secadmin TO etluser;
```

For more examples of using role-based access control, see the blog post "Simplify Management of Database Privileges in Amazon Redshift Using Role-Based Access Control" (*https://oreil.ly/jZ3kb*).

Row-Level Security

RLS in Amazon Redshift gives you fine-grained access controls that determine if the logged-in user should or should not have access to records within a table and will return only records the user has access to.

The RLS policy is defined by referencing zero or more columns in the table being queried and comparing those values against static values or dynamic values like the current_user or a session configuration variable. See the CREATE RLS POLICY documentation (*https://oreil.ly/U-VbC*) for additional details on how to define an RLS policy and the SET_CONFIG documentation (*https://oreil.ly/TPLMb*) for details on how to set a session configuration variable.

RLS policies are then assigned to a table and must be associated to a user, database role, or the PUBLIC group. See the ATTACH RLS POLICY documentation (*https://oreil.ly/kdU_m*) for details on how to attach an RLS policy.

The blog post "Achieve Fine-Grained Data Security with Row-Level Access Control in Amazon Redshift" (*https://oreil.ly/OW_YI*) illustrates many options when deciding your RLS access control policy.

Row-Level Security in Action

Using the student data model defined in Chapter 3, "Setting Up Your Data Models and Ingesting Data", let's use RLS to ensure that students can only see their own data. To accomplish this task, you need to create a policy that checks the current_user. For this use case, you can assume that the current user will match the student_id column. You can also assume that all students who log into the system will be associated to the student role (Example 8-13).

Example 8-13. Row-level security using current_user

```
CREATE RLS POLICY student
WITH (student_id int)
USING (student_id = current_user);

GRANT SELECT ON
  student,
  course_outcome,
  course_registration,
  degree_plan
TO RLS POLICY student;

ATTACH RLS POLICY student ON student TO ROLE student;
ATTACH RLS POLICY student ON course_outcome TO ROLE student;
ATTACH RLS POLICY student ON course_registration TO ROLE student;
ATTACH RLS POLICY student ON degree_plan TO ROLE student;
```

With this configuration in place, querying any of the tables attached to the policy will return only data relevant to the user. For example, an execution of the statement SELECT * FROM course_outcome; will result in only records associated to the student querying the table.

> RLS in Amazon Redshift supports attaching multiple policies per table. When there are multiple policies defined for a user on a table, either via a direct relationship or the database role, Amazon Redshift applies all the policies with the AND syntax.

In a scenario for a university with thousands of students, you may not be able to create a database user for each student and have an application that uses a shared database login. In this case, let's assume the login is application_user. The previous RLS policy will not work because the student_id will not match the current_user variable. Instead, if the application querying the data knows which student is issuing the request, it can set a session configuration variable. That configuration variable can be used in your RLS policy. You can also assume that the application_user login is associated to the student role (Example 8-14.)

Example 8-14. Row-level security using configuration variable

```
DROP RLS POLICY student CASCADE;
CREATE RLS POLICY student
WITH (student_id int)
USING (student_id = current_setting('app.student_id', FALSE));

GRANT SELECT ON
  student,
  course_outcome,
  course_registration,
  degree_plan
TO RLS POLICY student;

ATTACH RLS POLICY student ON student TO ROLE student;
ATTACH RLS POLICY student ON course_outcome TO ROLE student;
ATTACH RLS POLICY student ON course_registration TO ROLE student;
ATTACH RLS POLICY student ON degree_plan TO ROLE student;
```

Lastly, if the application executes the **set_config** command (*https://oreil.ly/3EFxp*) prior to making any queries to the affected tables, the RLS policy will be applied (Example 8-15).

Example 8-15. Using set_config

```
SELECT set_config('app.student_id', '<VALUE>', FALSE);
```

Let's continue working with the example described in Chapter 7, "Collaboration with Data Sharing" where multiple tenants can access a datashare and apply RLS in the consumer data warehouse. You've already added the field consumer_namespace in the school table. Establishing the RLS policy shown in Example 8-16 on the consumer datashare will ensure only the authorized consumer will be able to query data about the schools it is authorized to access.

Example 8-16. Row-level security using consumer namespace

```
CREATE RLS POLICY consumer
WITH (school_id int)
USING (school_id = (
  SELECT school_id
  FROM school
  WHERE consumer_namespace = current_namespace));

GRANT SELECT ON
  student,
  course_outcome,
  course_registration,
  degree_plan
TO RLS POLICY consumer;
```

```
ATTACH RLS POLICY consumer ON student TO ROLE school;
ATTACH RLS POLICY consumer ON course_outcome TO ROLE school;
ATTACH RLS POLICY consumer ON course_registration TO ROLE school;
ATTACH RLS POLICY consumer ON degree_plan TO ROLE school;
```

Row-Level Security Considerations

With the introduction of RLS, you may wonder how dependent objects like views, materialized views, or objects exposed through data sharing are treated. See Table 8-4 for behaviors and workarounds for these.

Table 8-4. RLS-dependent object behavior

Dependency	Behavior	Workaround
Views	You cannot attach an RLS policy to a view.	Views inherit the policies of the component tables, so attaching an RLS policy to a view is not needed.
Materialized views	You cannot attach an RLS policy to materialized views. In addition, you cannot create an RLS policy on a table referenced by a materialized view.	You can convert the MV code to a stored procedure that manages a physical table and apply the RLS policy on that table.
Datashare	An RLS policy can be attached to a table exposed to a consumer via data sharing; however, the consumer will not be governed by the RLS policy defined on the producer.	The consumer will be able to define its own policy on the datashare object.
Data lake tables	You cannot attach an RLS policy to a table exposed from your data lake as an external table.	You can leverage Lake Formation cell-level filtering (*https://oreil.ly/CKPST*), which can be assigned to the IAM role that is used when creating your external schema.
Federated tables	You cannot attach an RLS policy to a table exposed from a federated source as an external table.	You can leverage a strategy of restricted database views that are granted to the federated user defined in the external schema definition.

For additional considerations when using RLS, see the online documentation (*https://oreil.ly/Kl1Yf*).

Dynamic Data Masking

DDM allows you to mask data and is typically used for regulatory or compliance requirements, or to implement internal privacy standards. DDM allows you to manipulate the display of sensitive data dynamically at query time based on user privilege. DDM is a scalable alternative to obfuscating the data at rest that requires modification to your loading and transformation process. You control access to data through masking policies that attach to a table and column. The policy is applied to a given user, database role, or the PUBLIC group. DDM allows you to respond to evolving privacy requirements without modifying your transformation code, the underlying data, or application SQL queries.

As discussed in "Object-Level Access Controls" on page 287, column-level security (CLS) access controls can be applied via a REVOKE statement. However, when using CLS, user queries will result in an error when attempting to execute a select * statement. In contrast, applying a DDM policy will not result in an error and instead can obfuscate the data or return a NULL value.

The masking policy is defined by referencing the columns you will use to determine how the data will be masked as well as the mechanism you will use to evaluate the column values and determine the masked output value. In most cases, the single column being masked is sufficient to define the masking policy, but in more complex cases, additional columns from the table are required to satisfy the masking requirements.

The mechanisms supported to mask your data include a static value, an inline SQL statement, a scalar SQL UDF or a Python UDF that can reference dynamic values like current_user or session configuration variables. See the online documentation (*https://oreil.ly/ZINmQ*) for additional details on how to define a DDM policy.

DDM policies are then assigned to a table, referencing the input columns used in the masking policy, and must be associated to a user, database role, or the PUBLIC group. See the online documentation (*https://oreil.ly/YjsDj*) for additional details on how to attach a DDM policy.

 In the case where multiple policies are applicable to the same user, because that user belongs to multiple database roles, the PRIORITY qualifier will determine which policy to apply.

Given the flexibility and options of defining a DDM policy, there are many options when deciding your masking strategy. The blog post "How Dynamic Data Masking Support in Amazon Redshift Helps Achieve Data Privacy and Compliance" (*https://oreil.ly/1rvmR*) illustrates many of these options.

Dynamic Data Masking in Action

Let's continue to use the student data model described in Chapter 3, "Setting Up Your Data Models and Ingesting Data" to explore how you can apply a DDM strategy to the data. Assume you are tasked to implement the following masking rules to protect student PII data:

- By default, PII data should be shown as NULL.
- birth_date and email_address are classified as PII.

- Students should see their data unobfuscated.

- Faculty should be able to see the birth month and day but not the year.

- Faculty should be able to see an obfuscated email address.

Let's start by creating some default policies. Because DDM policies must be defined by the column's data type, you can create a generic policy for each data type. In Example 8-17, you can see how to create a policy that returns a null for a varchar field and a policy that returns a null for a date field.

Example 8-17. Define default dynamic data masking policies

```
CREATE MASKING POLICY null_varchar
WITH (i_varchar varchar) USING (NULL);

CREATE MASKING POLICY null_date
WITH (i_date date) USING (NULL);
```

Next, complete requirements 1 and 2 by attaching these policies to the stu dent.email_address field and the student.birth_date field and assigning the policy to the PUBLIC group that all users are a member of. Notice the priority of this policy is set to 99 (Example 8-18). Later, you add policies with a lower priority, and if a user matches one of those policies, it will be used instead of this default policy.

Example 8-18. Attach default dynamic data masking policies

```
ATTACH MASKING POLICY null_varchar
ON student(email_address) TO PUBLIC PRIORITY 99;

ATTACH MASKING POLICY null_date
ON student(birth_date) TO PUBLIC PRIORITY 99;
```

 Optionally, you can omit the phrase TO PUBLIC and if no user or database role is specified, it will default to the PUBLIC group.

Now, let's create policies for users who have full access to the data. In Example 8-19, you can see how to create a policy that assumes two inputs. The first is the column being masked, and the second is any additional data that should be used to define the policy. This policy will check if the student_id matches the current_user variable and if it does, return either the date value or the varchar value. If not, it will return NULL.

Example 8-19. Define passthrough dynamic data masking policies

```
CREATE MASKING POLICY passthrough_varchar_student_id
WITH (i_varchar varchar, student_id int) USING (
  CASE student_id WHEN current_user THEN i_varchar ELSE NULL END
  );

CREATE MASKING POLICY passthrough_date_student_id
WITH (i_date date, student_id int) USING (
  CASE student_id WHEN current_user THEN i_date ELSE NULL END
  );
```

Next, complete requirement 3 by attaching these policies to the stu
dent.email_address field and the student.birth_date field and assigning the policy to the student role. Notice the priority of this policy is set to 25 and when the
user is assigned the student role, this policy will take precedence over the last policy
that was created (Example 8-20).

Example 8-20. Attach passthrough dynamic data masking policies

```
ATTACH MASKING POLICY passthrough_varchar_student_id
ON student(email_address)
USING (email_address, student_id) TO ROLE student PRIORITY 25;

ATTACH MASKING POLICY passthrough_date_student_id
ON student(birth_date)
USING (birth_date, student_id) TO ROLE student PRIORITY 25;
```

Now, let's create a more complex masking policy to satisfy requirement 4 of obfuscating the year. In Example 8-21, we'll use an SQL function to transform the date field
i_date and replace the year with a static value 1900.

Example 8-21. Define date dynamic data masking policies

```
CREATE MASKING POLICY date_noyear
WITH (i_date date) USING (
  (extract('mon' FROM i_date)||'/'||date_part('day', i_date)||'/1900')::date);
```

To satisfy requirement 5 of redacting part of the email, we'll use a Python UDF. The
function replaces the first four characters of a varchar field containing an email
address with a static value. This function has additional logic to ensure the field
has the @ symbol and also to handle situations where the string length before the @
symbol is less than four characters (Example 8-22).

Example 8-22. Define email dynamic data masking policies

```
CREATE OR REPLACE FUNCTION redact_email (i_email TEXT)
RETURNS TEXT IMMUTABLE
AS $$
    md=i_email.find('@')
    ln=len(i_email)
    IF md>0 and ln>0:
      RETURN '####'+i_email[0:md][4:]+i_email[md:]
    ELSE:
      RETURN 'invalid email'
$$ LANGUAGE plpythonu;

CREATE MASKING POLICY email_redact
WITH (i_email varchar) USING (
  redact_email(i_email)
  );
```

Finally, you can complete requirements 4 and 5 by attaching these policies to the `student.email_address` field and the `student.birth_date` field and assigning the policy to the `faculty` role. Notice the priority of this policy is set to 50 and when the user is assigned the `faculty` role, this policy will take precedence over the default policy that was created. However, in the case when the user is a member of the `faculty` and `student` role, the `student` policy will apply because of the lower priority (Example 8-23).

Example 8-23. Attach date and email dynamic data masking policies

```
ATTACH MASKING POLICY date_noyear
ON openlearn.student(birth_date) TO ROLE faculty PRIORITY 50;

ATTACH MASKING POLICY email_redact
ON openlearn.student(email_address) TO ROLE faculty PRIORITY 50;
```

Dynamic Data Masking Considerations

Similar to RLS, with the introduction of DDM, you may wonder how dependent objects like other views, materialized views, and objects exposed through data sharing are treated. See Table 8-5 for behaviors and workarounds for each of these.

Table 8-5. DDM-dependent object behavior

Dependency	Behavior	Workaround
Views	You cannot attach a DDM policy to a view.	Views inherit the policies of the component tables, so attaching a DDM policy to a view is not needed.
Materialized views	You cannot attach a DDM policy to a materialized view. In addition, you cannot create a DDM policy on a table referenced by a materialized view.	You can instead convert the MV code to a stored procedure that manages a physical table, and apply the DDM policy on that table.

Dependency	Behavior	Workaround
Datashare	A DDM policy can be attached to a table exposed to a consumer via data sharing; however, the consumer will not be governed by the DDM policy defined on the producer.	The consumer will be able to define its own policy on the datashare object.
Data lake tables	You cannot attach a DDM policy to a table exposed from your data lake as an external table.	You can obfuscate/tokenize your data lake data at rest and use UDFs on Amazon Redshift to decrypt the data as appropriate.
Federated tables	You cannot attach a DDM policy to a table exposed from a federated source as an external table.	You can obfuscate/tokenize your federated source data at rest and use UDFs on Amazon Redshift to decrypt the data as appropriate.

For additional considerations when using DDM, see the online documentation (*https://oreil.ly/TZF-N*).

External Data Access Control

As discussed in Chapter 1, "AWS for Data", a modern data architecture many times involves allowing users access to data where its produced, even when that is outside of Amazon Redshift. In Chapter 4, "Data Transformation Strategies", we described how users can directly access those external sources when transforming data using Amazon Redshift. To govern access to data stored in these external sources, Amazon Redshift leverages IAM roles. In cases of COPY, UNLOAD, EXTERNAL FUNCTIONS, and CREATE MODEL, the user executing the query will directly reference the IAM role and will require the user to have permissions to assume the IAM role. In cases of operational data, Amazon S3 data, and streaming ingestion, the IAM role is used to create an external schema. For each of these scenarios, let's dive deeper into how you can "Associate IAM Roles" to your Amazon Redshift data warehouse, how you can "Authorize Assume Role Privileges", and how you can use a role to "Establish External Schemas". Finally, we'll look at how you can use "Lake Formation for Fine-Grained Access Control" for fine-grained access control to data in your Amazon S3 data lake.

Associate IAM Roles

Associating IAM roles to your Amazon Redshift can be done when launching your data warehouse, or anytime afterward using the AWS console or by using API commands. However, an IAM role can be attached to your Amazon Redshift data warehouse only if the IAM role has a trust relationship that allows the Amazon Redshift service (redshift.amazonaws.com) or Amazon Redshift serverless service (redshift-serverless.amazonaws.com) to perform the action sts:AssumeRole. In Example 8-24, you can see how to use the AWS command-line client to attach the IAM role myRedshiftRole to a Amazon Redshift data warehouse.

Example 8-24. Cluster add IAM role

```
> aws redshift modify-cluster-iam-roles \
    --cluster-identifier mycluster \
    --add-iam-roles arn:aws:iam::1234567890:role/myRedshiftRole
```

In multiple examples earlier in this book, you interacted with external services like Amazon S3 using the default IAM role, making it easier for users to write their SQL statement and not have to worry about the exact syntax of the IAM role ARN or which IAM role to use. In Example 8-25, you can see how to set the IAM role myRedshiftRole as the default role using the AWS command-line client.

Example 8-25. Cluster set default IAM role

```
> aws redshift modify-cluster-iam-roles \
    --cluster-identifier mycluster \
    --default-iam-role-arn arn:aws:iam::1234567890:role/myRedshiftRole
```

In Example 8-26 (from Chapter 3), you can see how to load data into your Amazon Redshift data warehouse using the default IAM role that has been granted privileges to read from the S3 location s3://openlearn-redshift/assessments.

Example 8-26. Use IAM role for COPY

```
COPY "openlearn"."assessments"
FROM 's3://openlearn-redshift/assessments'
IAM_ROLE default
DELIMITER ',' COMPUPDATE ON REGION 'us-east-1'
REMOVEQUOTES IGNOREHEADER 1;
```

In Example 8-27 (from Chapter 7), you can see how to export data from your Amazon Redshift data warehouse to Amazon S3 if the default IAM role has been granted IAM privileges to write to the S3 location s3://openlearn/studentactivities.

Example 8-27. Use IAM role for UNLOAD

```
UNLOAD ('select * from mv_student_lmsactivities_and_score')
TO 's3://openlearn/studentactivities'
IAM_ROLE default PARQUET PARTITION BY (school_id);
```

In Example 8-28 (from Chapter 4), you can see how to create a scalar UDF in Amazon Redshift that points to a AWS Lambda function. In this case, the IAM role will need to have permissions to execute the lambda function f-kms-encrypt.

Example 8-28. Use IAM role for Lambda UDF

```
CREATE OR REPLACE EXTERNAL FUNCTION
f_kms_encrypt (key varchar, value varchar)
RETURNS varchar(max) STABLE
LAMBDA 'f-kms-encrypt'
IAM_ROLE default;
```

Lastly, in Example 8-29 (from Chapter 6), you can see how to create, train, and start running inference on a machine learning model using the SQL interface. In this case, the IAM role will need to have permissions to use SageMaker, to write to the S3 temporary bucketname.

Example 8-29. Use IAM role for Redshift ML

```
CREATE MODEL demo_ml.customer_churn_model
FROM (SELECT state,
        area_code,
        total_charge/account_length AS average_daily_spend,
        cust_serv_calls/account_length AS average_daily_cases,
        churn
    FROM demo_ml.customer_activity
        WHERE record_date < '2020-01-01')
TARGET churn
FUNCTION predict_customer_churn
IAM_ROLE default
SETTINGS (S3_BUCKET 'bucketname');
```

 To enable access to resources from a different AWS account, you may use a role chaining strategy. This involves establishing a trust relationship between the IAM roles in both accounts. For more information on this strategy, see the online documentation (*https://oreil.ly/oo5-L*).

Authorize Assume Role Privileges

When you associate an IAM role to your Amazon Redshift data warehouse, the default privilege is that anyone who is a member of the PUBLIC group can assume any of the IAM roles. For large deployments with multiple types of users, you may want to further restrict access to which IAM roles a user can assume. To accomplish this, you can execute the REVOKE command shown in Example 8-30, which will remove the default ASSUMEROLE privilege from all users.

Example 8-30. Revoke Assume IAM role

```
REVOKE ASSUMEROLE on ALL from PUBLIC for ALL;
```

Subsequently, you can execute a GRANT statement to ensure the required user, database role, or database group has access to the role(s) they need. By implementing this strategy, you can define specific IAM roles for job functions or resources. For example, you may grant access to the faculty database role to assume the IAM role that has access to call the f_kms_decrypt lambda function (Example 8-31).

Example 8-31. Grant Assume IAM role Lambda

```
GRANT ASSUMEROLE ON 'arn:aws:iam::1234567890:role/myLambdaRole'
TO ROLE faculty FOR EXTERNAL FUNCTION
```

As shown in Example 8-32, you may grant access to the etluser database role to assume the IAM role that has read access to the raw Amazon S3 data used for loading data into your data warehouse.

Example 8-32. Grant Assume IAM role S3

```
GRANT ASSUMEROLE ON 'arn:aws:iam::1234567890:role/myETLRole'
TO ROLE etluser FOR COPY, UNLOAD
```

 You can associate up to 50 roles to your Amazon Redshift data warehouse. Keep this in mind when determining your IAM role strategy.

Establish External Schemas

For real-time querying of external sources like querying open-format files in Amazon S3, operational data stores in MySQL or PostgreSQL databases, or streaming data from Kinesis or managed Kafka, you must first establish an external schema. In the case of each of these external schemas, you may further limit access by managing GRANT USAGE or REVOKE USAGE privileges to the schema. This can ensure that the right users, groups, and roles can query these sources.

In Example 8-33 (from Chapter 4), you can see how to map a schema federated schema in your Amazon Redshift data warehouse to a PostgreSQL operational datastore in Amazon RDS.

Example 8-33. External federated schema using IAM role

```
CREATE EXTERNAL SCHEMA IF NOT EXISTS federatedschema
FROM POSTGRES DATABASE 'db1' SCHEMA 'pgschema'
URI '<rdsname>.<hashkey>.<region>.rds.amazonaws.com'
SECRET_ARN 'arn:aws:secretsmanager:us-east-1:123456789012:secret:pgsecret'
IAM_ROLE default;
```

When accessing an operational datastore using federated query, a network connection is made to the source database and a connection is established using credentials stored in the AWS Secrets Manager. The IAM role you use in the Amazon Redshift external schema definition will need to have read permissions on the AWS Secrets Manager secret. In addition, the credentials received from Secret Manager will need to have database permissions to execute queries on the federated database. Lastly, a TCP/IP network path needs to exist between your Amazon Redshift data warehouse and the federated database. For more details on how to use federated queries, see the online documentation (*https://oreil.ly/P838P*).

In Example 8-34 (from Chapter 3), you can see how to map a schema kds in your Amazon Redshift data warehouse to a Kinesis data stream.

Example 8-34. External streaming schema using IAM role

```
CREATE EXTERNAL SCHEMA kds
FROM KINESIS
IAM_ROLE default;
```

The IAM role associated with the schema will need to have read permissions on the Kinesis stream. You will need to include the appropriate kinesis:Get*, kinesis:List*, and kinesis:Describe* actions in your IAM policy, which can be scoped down and limited to the streams you will access. For more details on streaming ingestion, see the online documentation (*https://oreil.ly/Pp_Fm*).

In Example 8-35 (from Chapter 4), you can see how to map an EXTERNAL SCHEMA in your Amazon Redshift data warehouse to a database in the AWS Glue Data Catalog.

Example 8-35. External S3 schema using IAM role

```
CREATE EXTERNAL SCHEMA IF NOT EXISTS externalschema
FROM data catalog DATABASE 'externaldb'
IAM_ROLE default;
```

In Example 8-35, you'll notice authorization is determined by the `default` IAM role, meaning there is only one identity principal that determines what data can or cannot be accessed. In cases where there are multiple types of users accessing your Amazon Redshift data warehouse, each may require different levels of access control to your S3 data. One option to satisfy this requirement is to establish different external schemas with different IAM roles and grant users access to assume each role using the "Authorize Assume Role Privileges" technique. However, if you are using federated access to your Amazon Redshift data warehouse, you can set it up in such a way that each user group is authenticated to Amazon Redshift with a different IAM role and you can use the keyword `SESSION` in your external schema definition to pass-through the IAM role (Example 8-36). In addition, providing the `CATALOG_ID` parameter that matches your AWS account ID allows for cross-account S3 access. Using this strategy when setting up external schemas eliminates the need for setting up multiple external schemas and for attaching multiple IAM roles to your Amazon Redshift data warehouse. For more details, see the online documentation (*https://oreil.ly/UFyFd*).

Example 8-36. External S3 schema using SESSION authorization

```
CREATE EXTERNAL SCHEMA IF NOT EXISTS externalschema
FROM data catalog DATABASE 'externaldb'
IAM_ROLE 'SESSION'
CATALOG_ID '123456789012';
```

The AWS Glue Data Catalog, in addition to being used by Amazon Redshift, also provides access to Amazon Athena, AWS Glue ETL, and Amazon EMR. The IAM role you use in the Amazon Redshift external schema definition will need to have read permissions on the AWS Glue Data Catalog along with read permission on the objects defined in the AWS Glue Data Catalog. Optionally, you can grant write privileges to the AWS Glue Data Catalog, which will allow Amazon Redshift users to register new external tables with the `CREATE EXTERNAL TABLE` command (*https://oreil.ly/5IHYZ*) without leaving the SQL interface. If Lake Formation has been enabled, the object permissions will be governed by Lake Formation. See the next section for more details.

If Lake Formation is not enabled, the object permissions will be governed by privileges listed in the IAM policy of the IAM role. You will need to include the appropriate `s3:Get*` and `s3:List*` actions, which can be scoped down using resource restrictions to limit access to objects in your Amazon S3 data lake. For more details on how to query Amazon S3 data, see the online documentation (*https://oreil.ly/cHeO2*).

Lake Formation for Fine-Grained Access Control

When managing a large data lake, defining access controls through IAM policies alone can be cumbersome when the user population becomes large and the permissions of different groups start to overlap. In addition, managing permissions through IAM policies is limited to policies you can enforce on the Amazon S3 bucket or Amazon S3 object keys that either give a user access to an entire table, certain partitions of a table, or no access.

There are no changes needed to your external schema definition to start using AWS Lake Formation since Lake Formation shares the same AWS Glue Data Catalog. Migrating from IAM permissions to Lake Formation is a process of maintaining the existing data structures, but first enabling Lake Formation to govern access controls, then removing IAM policy statements from individual IAM roles, migrating them to Lake Formation permissions that are assigned to the IAM roles. See the online documentation (*https://oreil.ly/2kmui*) for more details on the steps involved. When complete, access management is centralized to the AWS Lake Formation console and you may use familiar concepts such as databases, tables, and columns, with more advanced options like row- and cell-level security instead of object-level permissions.

To make the management of permissions to Lake Formation data easier, instead of having to navigate to the Lake Formation interface, you can execute GRANT statements directly in the SQL interface. For example, if you wanted to enforce column-level security on an external transactions table, you might execute the following GRANT statements giving the Finance IAM role access to all the columns, but restricting access to the customer_id from the Analyst IAM role (Example 8-37).

Example 8-37. Grant Lake Formation privileges from Amazon Redshift

```
GRANT SELECT (
  returnflag,linestatus,zip,quantity,extendedprice,
  discount,tax,customer_id,year,month)
ON EXTERNAL TABLE  externalschema.transactions
TO IAM_ROLE 'arn:aws:iam::1234567890:role/myFinanceRole'

GRANT SELECT (returnflag,linestatus,zip,quantity,
  extendedprice,discount,tax,year,month)
ON EXTERNAL TABLE  externalschema.transactions
TO IAM_ROLE 'arn:aws:iam::1234567890:role/myAnalystRole'
```

For additional reading, see the blog post "Centralize Governance for Your Data Lake Using AWS Lake Formation While Enabling a Modern Data Architecture with Amazon Redshift Spectrum" (*https://oreil.ly/h96DT*).

Summary

In this chapter, we illustrated in detail the different access controls for data loaded in Amazon Redshift as well as to data accessible by Amazon Redshift. We covered how you can secure your data while still providing your users with the flexibility they need to analyze data and drive insights.

In the next chapter, we'll go over the considerations and strategies for migrating to Amazon Redshift from your current analytics environment. We'll walk through the different tools and services available, show you an example process for migrating, and cover how you can accelerate your migration with Amazon Redshift.

CHAPTER 9

Migrating to Amazon Redshift

Organizations have been running on-premises data warehouses for years, and these have served them well for the workloads of yesterday. But today's volume, variety, and velocity of data requires customers to modernize their data warehouses to ensure optimal performance. Here are some of the major limitations or shortcomings of the traditional data warehouse:

Slow to obtain
> Procuring your own servers and sizing them takes much longer compared to provisioning infrastructure in the cloud.

Costly to maintain
> They are so rigid in the structure that any modifications means a drastic increase in costs and project timelines.

Resiliency
> Hardware components are bound to fail sooner or later. Designing redundancy around failures and having multiple data centers with standby servers gets expensive really fast.

Inflexible architecture
> The foremost requirement of every business is agility and scalability. The inflexible architecture of the traditional data warehouses makes it next to impossible to bring in changes rapidly.

Technology advances
> Advancements in technology are made every day. The traditional data warehouse you set up for your business was probably done a couple of years back. So, you are already behind.

To address these limitations, one option is to adopt Amazon Redshift for your analytical needs because it is a fully managed, fast, scalable, and cost-effective service that enables you to derive insights from all your data.

However, data warehouse migration projects can be complex and challenging. It's easy to underestimate the complexity of the migration process, resulting in a lack of clarity about what needs to be migrated, how long it will take, and what resources will be required.

This chapter will cover "Migration Considerations", then look at "Migration Strategies" and AWS native "Migration Tools and Services". These topics will assist in clearly outlining the migration complexity and providing you clarity on challenges.

Then we get into details of the actual "Database Migration Process" and finally, discuss how to "Accelerate Your Migration to Amazon Redshift".

Migration Considerations

Data warehouse migration projects can be challenging in terms of project complexity and can expose risk related to resources, time, and cost. Before you begin your data warehouse migration, consider applying the principles covered in "Modern Data Architecture" on page 14 and reevaluate your future state data warehouse architecture. Just because you have all those tables in your current database does not imply that you must move all of them to Amazon Redshift. Evaluate how you can capitalize on this opportunity and modernize your overall data warehouse strategy.

Retire Versus Retain

Migration to any new platform is an opportunity to take stock of your data footprint, and eliminate redundant or unused data and reports. You can start with analyzing the usage of reports and identify if there are any unused ones. Review the reports that might have accumulated over time, and eliminate the ones that are not used anymore. Unless your organization has a periodic recertification process, it is very likely that reports are simply being generated but are not really used.

One of the most common reasons for this is that *business processes evolve over time*, and once that happens, the older report is no longer providing the value it was providing before. The urgency and drive to get a new report that will satisfy the new process takes precedence, and the older report is often left behind.

Another common reason is *report aging*: the report was built as requested and it was very useful, but the data behind it has grown, and now the report runs into too many pages. So a new higher-level or summary report was commissioned and this original report was still used, albeit infrequently, and eventually not at all. If all reports associated to a dataset are determined unnecessary, you may be able to remove that dataset from the ETL processes completely.

Review the data accumulated in your current data warehouse and classify data that needs high performance query execution compared to queries that do not have such strict execution SLA requirements. Consider a modern data architecture, as covered previously in "Reference Architecture for Modern Data Architecture" on page 20.

Clean up any existing backup schemas or tables that are no longer required and if possible, drop those objects. To retain any required backup tables, you can use the unload command as shown in Example 7-27 and offload these tables to your Amazon S3 bucket. Amazon S3 offers a range of storage classes for the objects you store. You choose an S3 storage class depending on your use case scenario and performance access requirements; review the various Amazon S3 storage classes (*https://oreil.ly/ tzKAn*). After the unload, you can apply the S3 lifecycle configuration (*https://oreil.ly/ tuk9u*) policy and move the S3 backup files to less-expensive storage classes. Also review the considerations for transitioning objects to different S3 storage classes (*https://oreil.ly/PGlzY*) to plan out these rules.

You can use the Amazon S3 Glacier Instant Retrieval storage class, which is queryable by Amazon Athena. But to use the objects under S3 Glacier Flexible Retrieval or S3 Glacier Deep Archive storage classes, you need to copy the restored objects back into Amazon S3 to change their storage class.

Once all necessary cleanups are done the next thing is choosing the right migration strategy. This is based on your source data warehouse landscape and the amount of transformation required for the migration to Amazon Redshift. This will reduce the complexity and risk to your data warehouse migration project.

Key factors that can influence your migration strategy decisions are:

- Migration data volume
- Transformations required
- Data volatility and availability
- Migration and ETL tools
- Data movement options
- Usage of Domain Name System

Migration Data Size

The total size of the source data warehouse to be migrated is determined by the number of databases, the number of schemas in those databases, and the number of objects in those schemas that are in scope for the migration. Having a good understanding of the data sources and data domains required for moving to Amazon Redshift will lead to optimal sizing of the migration project.

For example, because you have five schemas on your source data warehouse, it does not imply that you must have five schemas on a single Amazon Redshift data warehouse. Rather, you should try to isolate the schemas and their workloads, evaluate if you could stand up multiple Amazon Redshift data warehouses, and leverage data sharing to provide workload isolation, as we have covered in-depth in "Data Sharing Use Cases" on page 235.

Platform-Specific Transformations Required

Your existing data warehouse might be having some proprietary components specific to your current vendor. Migrating to Amazon Redshift can involve transformation such as data mapping and schema change. The complexity of the data transformation needed to be applied will determine the preprocessing time required for the migration. Also consider if you have your transformation logic coded as Stored Procedures and stored on your schema itself.

Take this opportunity to modernize and have the ETL logic outside your data warehouse. This future-proofs your overall data warehouse design and, if required, enables you to swap out your ETL tool or your data warehouse technology stack independently. Modern ETL tools will take advantage of push-down capabilities to deliver optimal performance based on where it is connecting to. We have previously covered data transformation strategies in Chapter 4 that you can leverage to modernize the transformation process through the use of federation, and we cover "AWS Schema Conversion Tool" on page 319.

Data Volatility and Availability Requirements

Be cognizant of your existing data warehouse's up-time and availability requirements. These requirements may be dictated by ingestion rates, update intervals, and your end user's data consumption patterns. These requirements will influence the options you have for your data warehouse migration project. A source data warehouse with a high data change rate might require a stringent cutover window. If the migration requires an extended period of service downtime, it could lead to higher complexity. You can test migration to ensure you can meet the stringent cutover window.

If you have multiple logical workloads on a single-source data warehouse, you might find that they all have same up-time requirements just because they are sharing the same hardware. Double-check with those individual business stakeholders, discuss workload isolation with multiple target Amazon Redshift data warehouses, and each business stakeholder gets the opportunity to establish their own RTO and RPO objectives (*https://oreil.ly/VqPHN*) individually. We dive deeper into different cutover options in "Migration Strategies" on page 316.

Selection of Migration and ETL Tools

The selection of migration tools to ETL can impact the migration project. When migrating to Amazon Redshift, you can choose to migrate your ETL workflows to a new AWS native service like AWS Glue ETL (*https://oreil.ly/egGZ8*) and leverage AWS Glue Studio visual editor (*https://oreil.ly/Zv8Z5*) or instead just retain your existing ETL tool. You can weight the benefits and plan the ETL migration based on the timeline and budget you have for the project. You can take an iterative approach, where you migrate the Data Warehouse first, retaining the existing ETL workflows in your legacy tool, and eventually migrate the ETL workflows as well. When planning the timelines for the migration project, accounting for additional time required for deployment and setup of these tools can ease the execution cycles. We will cover AWS tools and services in "Migration Tools and Services" on page 318.

Data Movement Considerations

Data warehouse migration involves data transfer between the source data warehouse servers and your AWS infrastructure. Depending on your current network capacity and its existing utilization, you can transfer data over your network connection via Direct Connect as covered in "Private/Public VPC and Secure Access" on page 59, or choose to transfer data offline via services such as the AWS Snow Family (*https://aws.amazon.com/snow*).

Data warehouses ranging under 10 TB can be considered for network transfer, but higher data volumes are typically migrated with the AWS Snowball Edge device. We cover the AWS Snow family of devices, including AWS Snowball Edge, as well as an estimated time to transfer 10 TB data over different network links, in "AWS Snow Family" on page 328.

Domain Name System (DNS)

The consumers of your data warehouse will be using the current data warehouse name or IP address to establish connections to the data warehouse. Migrating to a new data warehouse will require applications to make changes to their connection settings, pointing to the new data warehouse. If you are already using a DNS service, then this migration project will minimize the impact to consumer applications. If not, then this is a good time to introduce a DNS layer in your architecture. This DNS layer can also help during disaster scenarios by transparently failing over to a secondary region; refer the Route 53 failover types (*https://oreil.ly/G_hrv*) for details.

Migration Strategies

Depending on the source data warehouse's data velocity and availability requirements, there are three main migration strategies to choose from:

- One-step migration
- Two-step migration
- Iterative migration

One-Step Migration

One-step migration requires that you freeze your current database and disallow
changes by stopping all ingestion jobs. Then you extract a point-in-time database
snapshot to CSV files, or columnar formats like Parquet. Then, depending on your
connectivity options, you use an existing network or AWS Snow Family services
such as AWS Snowball to deliver datasets to Amazon S3 for loading into Amazon
Redshift. You then test the destination Amazon Redshift data warehouse for data
consistency with the frozen snapshot of your source. After all validations have passed,
you switch over the consumers of your existing database to Amazon Redshift. This is
a good option for databases that don't require continuous availability and you have an
acceptable time window like a weekend or a couple days to perform the migration.

 If your existing data warehouse is predominantly batch-oriented,
then depending on the batch intervals, one-step migration can be a
good fit.

Two-Step Migration

This is commonly used for databases that require continuous operation, such as the
continuous replication. During the migration, the source databases allow ongoing
data changes, and you will need a continuous replication process to keep data
changes in sync between the source data warehouse and Amazon Redshift. The
breakdown of the two-step migration strategy is as follows.

Initial data migration

The initial data is migrated to Amazon Redshift by following the one-step migration
approach previously described. This data snapshot is extracted from the source database during minimal usage periods to minimize the impact to ongoing activity. To
capture changes after the initial snapshot, you can turn on change logs at the same
time you take the snapshot. If you have date-timestamps in all your tables indicating

the update time, you can also use the date-timestamp to capture changes after the initial snapshot. You will conduct testing to ensure data consistency by running validation scripts and/or business users testing reports.

Changed data migration

Data that changed in the source database after the initial data migration is subsequently propagated to the destination before switchover. Your migration tool can facilitate this via ongoing replication jobs, or you can use the date-timestamp as we previously mentioned to identify changed data. This second step synchronizes the source and destination databases. After all the changed data is migrated, you can validate the data in the destination database by running validation scripts and/or business users testing reports. After all validations have passed, the consumers of your existing database are switched over to Amazon Redshift.

Iterative Migration

This migration approach is suitable for large-scale data warehouse migration projects. The principle of iterative migration is to cautiously divide a complex migration project into multiple systematic iterations. This strategy is used to significantly reduce the complexity and the overall risk for the migration project by breaking the total risk into multiple smaller pieces.

You start from a workload that covers a good number of data sources and subject areas, typically with a medium complexity area, then add more data sources and subject areas in each subsequent iteration. The challenge in this approach is to be able to synthetically break down the overall migration project into multiple logical iterations. See the blog "Develop an Application Migration Methodology to Modernize Your Data Warehouse with Amazon Redshift" (*https://oreil.ly/fzDAA*) for more details on how to identify and group data sources and analytics applications to migrate from the source data warehouse to Amazon Redshift using the iterations-based migration approach.

With this strategy, you run both the source data warehouse and Amazon Redshift production environments in parallel for a certain amount of time before you can fully retire the specific workloads that have been successfully migrated in this iteration. Also as you move into the next iteration, if feasible, you can downsize your source system to accommodate the reduction of workload.

Refer to Figure 9-1 to visualize the three migration strategies we discussed.

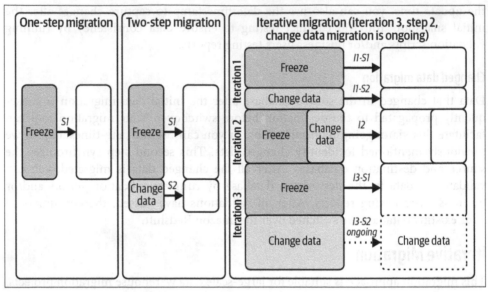

Figure 9-1. Migration strategies

And furthermore, to guide your migration strategy decision, refer to Table 9-1 to map the consideration factors with a preferred migration strategy.

Table 9-1. Migration strategy decision

Migration strategy	One-step migration	Two-step migration	Iterative migration
The number of subject areas in migration scope	Small	Medium to Large	Large
Data transfer volume	Small	Small to Large	Large
Data change rate during migration	None	Minimal	Minimal to Frequent
Data transformation complexity	Small	Medium	Any
Migration change window for switching from source to target	Hours to days	Days	Minutes
Migration project duration	Weeks	Weeks to few months	Multiple months

Migration Tools and Services

Your data warehouse migration to Amazon Redshift will entail migration of schema objects and then migration of data. The objects on your source will include schemas, tables, views, materialized views, and also code objects like functions, stored procedures, and packages. Certain objects that are not supported in Amazon Redshift like sequences, triggers, and indexes will not be migrated.

While you can find hands-on assistance through a combination of Amazon Redshift Partners (*https://oreil.ly/GLUTP*) as well as AWS Professional Services (*https://oreil.ly/xys8u*), this section focuses on AWS native tools and services. These tools and services can be leveraged to migrate from numerous source data warehouse engines to Amazon Redshift, as covered in Table 9-2.

AWS Schema Conversion Tool

AWS SCT (*https://oreil.ly/fluxt*) is a desktop application that provides a project-based UI to automatically convert the database schema of your source database into a format compatible with your target AWS native database. It supports multiple types of source and target databases. Use the AWS SCT to convert your existing database schema from one database engine to another. AWS SCT supports several industry standards, including Federal Information Processing Standards (FIPS), for connections to an Amazon S3 bucket or another AWS resource. AWS SCT is also compliant with the Federal Risk and Authorization Management Program (FedRAMP).

AWS SCT supports the following data warehouse schema conversions, and Table 9-2 provides the specific source privileges needed to be granted, details on how to establish a secure connection, any known limitations for that source, and also how to target Amazon Redshift–specific conversion settings and conversion optimization settings.

Table 9-2. SCT sources supported for Amazon Redshift target

Source data warehouse	Version	Setups required
Amazon Redshift	Any	Amazon Redshift as a source (*https://oreil.ly/8UI5v*)
Azure Synapse	Any	Azure Synapse Analytics as a source (*https://oreil.ly/IPnVK*)
BigQuery	Any	BigQuery as a source (*https://oreil.ly/Pi_Z8*)
Greenplum	4.3 and 6.21	Greenplum as a source (*https://oreil.ly/81HBB*)
MS SQL Server	2008 or later	SQL Server Data Warehouse as a source (*https://oreil.ly/RYHD5*)
Netezza	7.0.3 or later	Netezza as a source (*https://oreil.ly/nbWfU*)
Oracle	10.1 or later	Oracle Data Warehouse as a source (*https://oreil.ly/TL7a2*)
Snowflake	3 or later	Snowflake as a source (*https://oreil.ly/FSfR9*)
Vertica	7.2.2 or later	Vertica as a source (*https://oreil.ly/LcJUG*)
Teradata	13 or later	Teradata as a source (*https://oreil.ly/_65vV*)

Table 9-2 is up-to-date at the time of writing, but refer to the latest data warehouse sources (*https://oreil.ly/wWjxS*).

Additionally, AWS SCT also supports conversions of the following ETL processes to target AWS services; refer to Table 9-3.

Table 9-3. SCT-supported ETL conversions

Source	Target
Microsoft SQL Server Integration Services (SSIS) ETL packages	AWS Glue or AWS Glue Studio
Shell scripts with embedded commands from Teradata Basic Teradata Query (BTEQ)	Amazon Redshift RSQL
Teradata BTEQ ETL scripts	AWS Glue or Amazon Redshift RSQL
Teradata FastExport job scripts	Amazon Redshift RSQL
Teradata FastLoad job scripts	Amazon Redshift RSQL
Teradata MultiLoad job scripts	Amazon Redshift RSQL

SCT overview

AWS SCT performs most of the schema object conversions automatically. But because the source database engines can have many different features and capabilities, AWS SCT attempts to create an equivalent schema in Amazon Redshift wherever possible. AWS SCT allows you to provide source data warehouse statistics so that it can optimize how your data warehouse is converted. You can either collect statistics directly from the database or upload an existing statistics file.

AWS SCT automatically assigns the distribution style and sort keys for Redshift tables based off the primary key and foreign keys from the source tables. Source tables with single-column primary keys are assigned the key distribution style, and the primary key column is set as the distribution key as well as the sort key. Source tables with multi-column primary keys are assigned the key distribution style with the first primary key column being set as the distribution key, and all the source primary key columns added as a composite sort key.

SCT migration assessment report

AWS SCT provides an database migration assessment report (*https://oreil.ly/-1Vky*) with a listing of database objects and their conversion complexity. This report includes an executive summary, license evaluation, cloud readiness (indicating any features in the source database not available on the target), and recommendations for conversion of server objects, backup suggestions, and linked server changes. And most importantly, this report includes estimates of the complexity of effort that it will take to write the equivalent code for your target DB instance that can't be converted automatically.

The report categorizes the estimated time to convert these schema items as:

Simple
> Actions that can be completed in less than two hours.

Medium
> Actions that are more complex and can be completed in two to six hours.

Significant
> Actions that are very complex and take more than six hours to complete.

Using AWS SCT, you can manage target Amazon Redshift sort keys and distribution keys, map data types and objects, and also create manual conversions. If certain objects cannot be automatically converted, then SCT provides a listing of possible actions for you to take manually. AWS SCT creates a local version of the converted schema for you to review. You can either update the source schema and try again, or perform a manual conversion. When you are ready, you can apply the converted schema to the Amazon Redshift target.

SCT data extraction agents

In some migration scenarios, the source and target databases are very different from one another and require additional data transformation. AWS SCT is extensible, so you can address these scenarios using an agent. An agent is an external program that's integrated with AWS SCT, but performs data transformation elsewhere (such as on an Amazon EC2 instance). In addition, an AWS SCT agent can interact with other AWS services on your behalf, such as creating and managing AWS Database Migration Service tasks for you. It also helps you in increasing parallelism of tasks to load into Redshift. Use AWS SCT data extraction agents (*https://oreil.ly/BkWre*) to extract data from your on-premises data warehouse and migrate it to Amazon Redshift. The SCT agent extracts your data and uploads the data to either a Snowball Edge device or over your network directly to Amazon S3. The Snowball Edge device is shipped to AWS, and once received, the data is unloaded to your designated S3. For large-scale migrations, the Snowball Edge device, which we cover in "AWS Snow Family" on page 328, is preferred, as it does not put overhead on your network. You can then use AWS SCT to copy the data to Amazon Redshift, using the SCT copy agent, as shown in Figure 9-2.

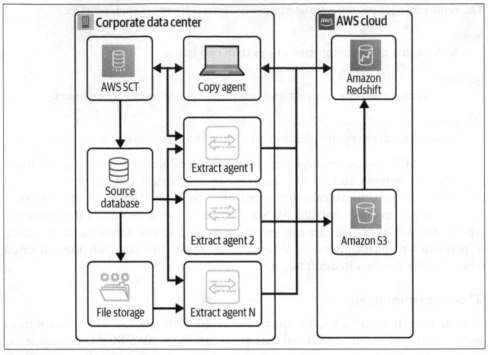

Figure 9-2. AWS SCT agents flow

This configuration can be useful when your source database server supports up to 120 connections and your network has ample storage attached. This methodology is also useful when you have partitioned tables on the source data warehouse and you can extract huge datasets in parallel, especially for the initial load stage of your data warehouse migration.

Install AWS SCT data extractor agents as close as possible to the data source to improve data migration performance and reliability. And to increase the speed of data migration, use several AWS SCT agents in parallel.

Alternatively, you can use AWS DMS, which we cover in "Data Warehouse Migration Service" on page 323, to migrate data to Amazon Redshift. The advantage of AWS DMS is the ability to execute ongoing replication (change data capture) tasks. You can also use an approach where you use a combination of AWS SCT and AWS DMS. Use AWS SCT for initial load and AWS DMS for the ongoing replication tasks.

Migrating BLOBs to Amazon Redshift

Amazon Redshift doesn't support storing binary large objects (BLOBs). However, if you need to migrate one or more BLOBs to Amazon Redshift, AWS SCT can perform the migration. AWS SCT uses an Amazon S3 bucket to store the BLOBs and writes the URL of the objects in Amazon S3 to the table column of the target database.

> We recommend using AWS SCT for very large data warehouse migrations and AWS DMS for small to medium data warehouse migrations. AWS SCT agents migrate data faster than AWS DMS by 15% to 35%, due to data compression, support of parallel migration of table partitions, and different configuration settings.

Data Warehouse Migration Service

AWS DMS is a managed migration and replication service that helps move your database workloads to AWS. AWS DMS supports migration between 20-plus database engines and analytics engines. With AWS DMS, you can discover your source data stores, convert your source schemas, and migrate your data.

Use the DMS Fleet Advisor (*https://oreil.ly/P3tmR*) to discover your source data infrastructure. This service collects data from your on-premises database and analytic servers and builds an inventory of servers, databases, and schemas that you can migrate to the AWS Cloud.

Use DMS Schema Conversion (*https://oreil.ly/wp-O5*) to migrate from your source database engine to AWS database engines. This service automatically assesses and converts your source schemas to a new target engine. Alternatively, you can download the AWS SCT to your local machine to convert your source schemas, as described in "AWS Schema Conversion Tool" on page 319.

After you convert your source schemas and apply the converted code to your Amazon Redshift, you can use AWS DMS to migrate your data. You can perform one-time migrations or replicate ongoing changes to keep sources and targets in sync. Because AWS DMS is a part of the AWS Cloud, you get the cost efficiency, speed to market, security, and flexibility that AWS services offer.

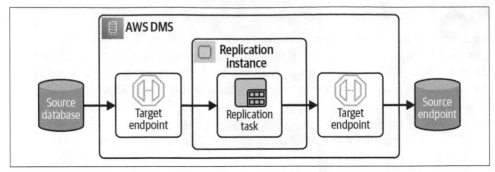

Figure 9-3. AWS DMS replication process

How AWS DMS works

AWS DMS is a server in the AWS Cloud that runs replication software (see Figure 9-3). You create a source and target connection to tell AWS DMS where to extract from and where to load to. Then you schedule a task that runs on this server to move your data. AWS DMS creates the tables and associated primary keys if they don't exist on the target. You can create the target tables yourself if you prefer, or you can use AWS SCT to create some or all of the target database objects.

AWS DMS supports initial load tasks as well as ongoing-replication or change-data-capture (CDC) tasks to migrate new data as it comes in to your source data warehouse. It is worth noting that larger data warehouse migrations can include many terabytes of data. Executing the replication process over your existing network can be cumbersome due to network bandwidth limits. AWS DMS can use AWS Snowball Edge, part of AWS Snow Family (covered in "AWS Snow Family" on page 328), and Amazon S3 to migrate large databases. While AWS DMS allows replication for source tables without a primary or unique key, the CDC latency might be high, resulting in an unacceptable level of performance. So, it is a best practice to always have a primary key defined for every source table.

> If there is no primary key defined on the source table and you do not want to alter the source, then you can use a DMS transformation rule to define a surrogate primary key by concatenating multiple source columns (*https://oreil.ly/CrVOg*) and then telling DMS that it's the primary key for the table. However, this approach requires enhanced logging on the source database where all columns of the table are captured in the logs even if only few columns actually changed.

During ongoing replication, it is critical to identify the network bandwidth between your source database system and your AWS DMS replication instance. Make sure that the network doesn't cause any bottlenecks during ongoing replication. It is also important to identify the rate of change and archive log generation per hour on your source database system. Doing this can help you understand the throughput that you might get during ongoing replication.

AWS DMS uses a pay-as-you-go model. You pay for AWS DMS resources only while you use them, as opposed to traditional licensing models that have up-front purchase costs and ongoing maintenance charges. AWS DMS automatically manages the deployment, management, and monitoring of all hardware and software needed for your migration.

AWS DMS automatically manages all of the infrastructure that supports your migration server, including hardware and software, software patching, and error reporting. AWS DMS provides automatic failover, too; if your primary replication server fails for any reason, a backup replication server can take over with little or no interruption of service.

 Install the AWS SCT and the AWS DMS agent on separate machines. Make sure that the AWS DMS agent is installed on the same machine as the ODBC drivers and the AWS Snowball Edge client for efficient performance, as covered in "AWS Snowball Edge Client" on page 331.

With AWS DMS you create one of three migration tasks:

Migrate existing data (full load only)
Perform a one-time migration from the source endpoint to the target endpoint.

Migrate existing data and replicate ongoing changes (full load and CDC)
Perform a one-time migration from the source to the target, and then continue replicating data changes from the source to the target.

Replicate data changes only (CDC only)
Don't perform a one-time migration, but continue to replicate data changes from the source to the target.

Here are the steps AWS DMS takes to load data into the Amazon Redshift target:

1. AWS DMS writes data from the source to CSV files on the replication server.

2. AWS DMS uses the AWS SDK to upload the CSV files into an S3 bucket you specify from your account.

3. AWS DMS then issues the COPY command in Amazon Redshift to copy data from the CSV files to the target Amazon Redshift table.

4. For ongoing replication, AWS DMS first loads data to a staging table and then runs the DML statements as follows:

a. With enhanced logging

    i. Inserted source rows → Insert on target

    ii. Deleted source rows → Delete on target

    iii. Updated source rows → Delete and Insert to target

b. With partial logging

    i. Inserted source rows → Insert on target

    ii. Deleted source rows → Delete on target

    iii. Updated source rows → Update on target

If you use enhanced VPC routing (*https://oreil.ly/EuQXq*) with your Amazon Redshift target, all COPY traffic between your Amazon Redshift cluster and your data repositories goes through your VPC. If enhanced VPC routing is not enabled, Amazon Redshift routes traffic through the internet, including traffic to other services within the AWS network. If the feature is not enabled, you do not have to configure the network path. However, if the feature is enabled, you must specifically create a network path between your cluster's VPC and your data resources. You can configure either VPC endpoints (*https://oreil.ly/Bv2jc*) or a Network Address Translation (NAT) gateway (*https://oreil.ly/b1Ztm*) in your VPC.

You can also use AWS KMS keys to encrypt data pushed to Amazon S3 and then load to the Amazon Redshift target. You just need the appropriate IAM role with an AWS-managed policy, and KMS key ARN with a permissive key policy, to be specified in AWS DMS settings.

AWS DMS also has resource quotas and constraints, listed at Resource Quotas for AWS Database Migration Service (*https://oreil.ly/baRxg*).

Additionally, you can reference the "Optimizing AWS Database Migration Service Performance with Amazon Redshift as Target" (*https://oreil.ly/PaF-I*) whitepaper.

DMS replication instances

Right sizing the replication server is crucial for performance. Some of the smaller Amazon EC2 instance classes are sufficient for testing the service or for small migrations. But if your migration involves a large number of tables, or if you intend to run multiple concurrent replication tasks, consider using one of the larger EC2 instances with a fair amount of memory and CPU.

The C5 instance classes are designed to deliver the highest level of processor performance for computer-intensive workloads. AWS DMS can be CPU-intensive, especially when performing large-scale migrations to Amazon Redshift.

The R5 instance classes are memory optimized for memory-intensive workloads. The ongoing replication tasks migrations or replications of high-throughput transaction systems using AWS DMS can consume large amounts of CPU and memory. The R5 instances are recommended as they include more memory per vCPU.

Since an AWS DMS server is a compute resource in the AWS Cloud, the performance of your AWS DMS migration tasks will depend on:

- Resource availability on the source
- The available network throughput
- The resource capacity of the replication server
- The ability of the target to ingest changes
- The type and distribution of source data
- The number of objects to be migrated

You can improve performance of full-load and CDC tasks for an Amazon Redshift target endpoint by using multithreaded task settings. They enable you to specify the number of concurrent threads and the number of records to store in a buffer.

Refer to best practices for AWS DMS (*https://oreil.ly/6OXH_*) migrations, which covers a broad range of recommendations.

DMS replication validation

AWS DMS provides support for data validation to ensure that your data was migrated accurately from your source to Amazon Redshift. If enabled, validation begins immediately after a full load is performed for a table. Validation compares the incremental changes for the ongoing replication task as they occur. When validation is enabled for a replication-only task, then all pre-existing data in a table is validated before starting validation of new data.

During the data validation phase, AWS DMS compares each row in the source with its corresponding row at the target, verifies that the rows contain the same data, and reports any mismatches. To accomplish this, AWS DMS issues appropriate queries to retrieve the data.

 DMS validation queries will consume additional resources at the source and the target as well as additional network resources, so be sure to size the DMS instance accordingly.

Data validation requires additional time, beyond the amount required for the migration itself. The extra time required depends on how much data was migrated.

Split up the data validation portion of a migration or replication task into a separate validation-only task. This allows you to control exactly when validation occurs and reduce the load on the main replication instance by having a separate DMS instance for the validation task. Also, having a separate validation-only task allows you to quickly ascertain how many rows don't match at the point in time when you run this task.

 The primary key value from the source is used for tracking ongoing replication changes. Running update and delete operations on source tables that alter or drop the primary key value will need AWS DMS to run a full validation scan. This is an expensive and time-consuming task, unless it is used for small reference data source tables.

Table 9-4 summarizes the AWS migration tools we have discussed so far.

Table 9-4. AWS DMS versus AWS SCT

AWS Database Migration Service	AWS Schema Conversion Tool
Paid service (has a free tier)	Free download software
Servers run on AWS Cloud	Installed on-prem machine
Supports multiple Availability Zones for high availability	One machine at a time
Lesser than 10 TB migrations	More than 10 TB migrations
Either source or target database must be on AWS	Supports on-prem to on-prem conversions
Migrates data from source database tables to target	Converts schema from one database engine to another
Supports change data capture (CDC)	Main use for initial data load
Can work directly with target database	Can work with AWS Snowball Edge
Can read/write from/to encrypted databases	Limited encryption support, Amazon RDS or Amazon Aurora

There are additional data integration partner tools, such as Informatica, Matillion, SnapLogic, Talend, and BryteFlow Ingest, that can be considered, especially if you already have build expertise with them.

AWS Snow Family

The AWS Snow Family (*https://aws.amazon.com/snow*) of devices is used for moving data from your data center to AWS infrastructure without depending on your existing networks that might be in use for your day-to-day activities. AWS Storage Gateway (*https://aws.amazon.com/storagegateway*) and AWS Direct Connect (*https://aws.amazon.com/directconnect*) services are good choices when network bandwidth limitations do not exist. You use AWS Snow Family services for offline data transfer.

Let's look at the estimated time to transfer 10 TB of data over different network links in Table 9-5. The time it takes is expressed in day/hour/min/sec format, and assumes that you are getting the entire bandwidth or rated speed. On a shared line, you typically get anywhere from 1/10 to 1/25 of rated speeds.

Table 9-5. Estimated time to transfer 10 TB

Network type	Rated speed	Estimated time	Shared (1/10)
T3/DS3 line	45 Mbps	20:13:49:38	205:18:16:18
Fast Ethernet	100 Mbps	9:06:13:20	92:14:13:20
T4/DS4 line	275 Mbps	3:08:48:29	33:16:04:51
Gigabit Ethernet	1000 Mbps	0:22:13:20	9:06:13:20
10 Gigabit Ethernet	10 Gbps	0:02:13:20	0:22:13:20

Take this into consideration when choosing between using your existing network for data transfer and AWS Snow devices.

AWS Snow Family key features

Snow Family devices have computing resources to collect and process data at the edge. This provides ability for running transformations like preprocessing data on your site as you write data to the AWS Snow device.

AWS OpsHub (*https://oreil.ly/08UmM*) is a complimentary GUI available to make it easy to set up and manage Snow devices and rapidly deploy edge computing work-loads and migrate data to the cloud. Your on-premise applications can work with Snow Family devices as a Network File System (NFS) mount point. NFS v3 and v4.1 are supported, so you can easily use Snow devices with your existing on-premises servers and file-based applications.

Each Snow device uses an E Ink (*https://oreil.ly/AUIdX*) shipping label for tamper-proof tracking and automatic label updates for return shipping using Amazon Simple Notification Service (SNS), text messages, and via the AWS Console.

All data moved to AWS Snow Family devices is automatically encrypted with 256-bit encryption keys that are managed by the AWS Key Management Service (KMS). Encryption keys are never stored on the AWS Snow device, so your data stays secure during transit.

AWS Snow devices feature a Trusted Platform Module (TPM) that provides a hardware root of trust. Each device is inspected after each use to ensure the integrity of the device and helps preserve the confidentiality of your data.

AWS Snow Family devices

AWS Snowcone is the smallest member of the AWS Snow Family of edge computing and data transfer devices. It offers 22 TB of combined storage, 4 vCPUs, 4 GB memory, and weighs under 5 pounds. You can use Snowcone to collect, process, and move data to AWS, either offline by shipping the device or online with AWS DataSync (*https://aws.amazon.com/datasync*).

AWS Snowball is a suitcase-sized, 50-pound, data migration and edge computing device that comes in two device options—a Compute Optimized device or Storage Optimized device:

Snowball Edge Storage Optimized devices
> Provide 80 TB of hard disk drive (HDD) storage, 1 TB of SSD storage, 40 vCPU, and 80 GB memory for local processing. It is well suited for large local storage for large-scale data transfer.

Snowball Edge Compute Optimized devices
> Provide 28 TB of SSD storage, 104 vCPU, and 416 GB memory for local processing, and an optional GPU for use cases such as advanced machine learning and full-motion video analysis in disconnected environments.

AWS Snowmobile is an exabyte-scale data migration device used to move extremely large amounts of data to AWS. Migrate up to 100 PB in a 45-foot long ruggedized shipping container, pulled by a semi-trailer truck.

When you're using an AWS Snow device, the data migration process can be visualized as shown in Figure 9-4.

1. You use the AWS SCT to extract the data locally and move it to an AWS Snowball Edge device.

2. You ship the Edge device(s) back to AWS.

3. After AWS receives your shipment, the Edge device automatically loads its data into an Amazon S3 bucket.

4. AWS DMS takes the S3 files and applies the data to the target data store.

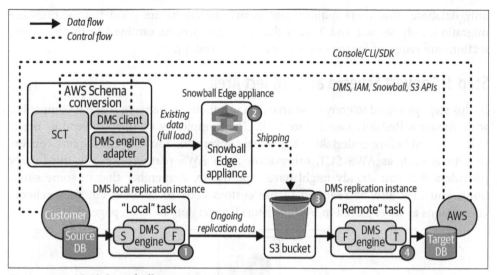

Figure 9-4. AWS Snowball migration process

In AWS DMS, you can specify a particular timestamp or system change number (SCN) to start the CDC. And based off that timestamp or SCN, the CDC files will be generated.

> You can't use an AWS Snowcone device to migrate data with AWS DMS. You can use AWS Snowcone devices only with AWS SCT.

AWS Snowball Edge Client

The Snowball Edge Client is a standalone terminal application that you run on your local server to unlock the AWS Snow device and get credentials, logs, and status information. You can also cluster multiple AWS Snow devices to form a Snowball Edge cluster. You use this Snowball Edge Client for all setups including setting up networking, tags, starting and stopping services, and setting up the cluster. For a full listing on Snowball Edge client commands, including examples of use and sample outputs, refer to Commands for the Snowball Edge Client (*https://oreil.ly/5m33-*).

Database Migration Process

At a high level, the migration process comprises three steps. The two-step migration strategy and iterative migration strategy involve all three migration steps. However, note that the iterative migration strategy runs over a number of iterations, and each iteration has to go through these migration process steps every iteration. Since only databases that don't require continuous operations are good fits for one-step migration, only Steps 1 and 2 from the migration process outlined in the following sections are required for the one-step migration strategy.

Step 1: Convert Schema and Subject Area

In this step, you need to convert source data warehouse schema to make it compatible with Amazon Redshift (see Figure 9-5). The complexity of this conversion needs to be assessed before undertaking the actual conversion. You leverage schema conversion tools such as AWS SCT, other tools from AWS partners, or any third-party providers that you already might have expertise in. Remember that in some situations, you may also be required to use custom code to conduct complex schema conversions as we explored in "AWS Schema Conversion Tool" on page 319.

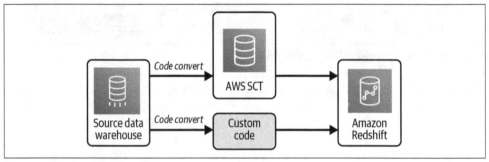

Figure 9-5. AWS SCT schema conversion

Step 2: Initial Data Extraction and Load

In this step, you complete the initial data extraction and load the source data into Amazon Redshift for the first time (see Figure 9-6). You can either create AWS DMS load tasks or use AWS SCT data extractors to extract data from the source data warehouse, as covered in "SCT data extraction agents" on page 321, and load data to Amazon S3 if your data size and data transfer requirements allow you to transfer data over the interconnected network. Alternatively, if there are limitations such as network capacity limit, you can load data to Snowball for transfer to Amazon S3. When the data in the source data warehouse is available on Amazon S3, it is loaded to Amazon Redshift, as covered in "AWS Snow Family" on page 328.

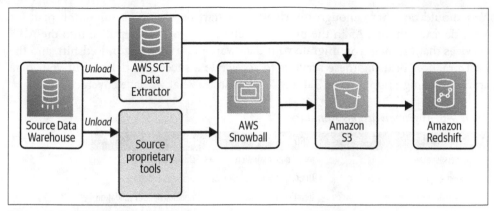

Figure 9-6. AWS SCT initial load

Step 3: Incremental Load Through Data Capture

This is often referred to as the CDC phase, incremental load phase, or ongoing replication phase. CDC is a process that captures changes made in a database and ensures that those changes are replicated to a destination such as a data warehouse. In this step, you use AWS DMS or AWS SCT, and sometimes even source data warehouse native tools to capture and load these incremental changes from sources to Amazon Redshift.

Figure 9-7 shows the AWS services that can be used for the different aspects of your data migration.

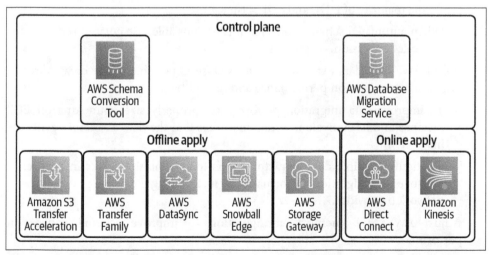

Figure 9-7. AWS data migration services

You should now have enough information to start developing a migration plan for your data warehouse. As in the previous sections, we took a deep dive into the AWS services that can help you migrate your data warehouse to Amazon Redshift, and the best practices of using these services to accelerate a successful delivery of your data warehouse migration project. Table 9-6 summarizes what we have covered so far.

Table 9-6. Migration actions summary

Assess	Migrate	Validate
Retire versus retain	Initial data migration	Schema validation
Migration scope	Ongoing changes replication	Data validation tasks
Data availability	Iterative migration	Ongoing changes validation
ETL tools	Schema conversion	Business validation
Data movement options	Database migration service	Switchover
Migration assessment report	AWS Snow devices	

Amazon Redshift Migration Tools Considerations

To improve and accelerate data warehouse migration to Amazon Redshift, consider the following tips and best practices:

- Use AWS SCT to create a migration assessment report and scope migration effort.

- Automate migration with AWS SCT where possible. AWS SCT can automatically create the majority of DDL and SQL scripts.

  — When automated schema conversion is not possible, use custom scripting for the code conversion.

- Install AWS SCT data extractor agents as close as possible to the data source to improve data migration performance and reliability.

  — To improve data migration performance, properly size your Amazon EC2 instance and its equivalent virtual machines that the data extractor agents are installed on.

  — Configure multiple data extractor agents to run multiple tasks in parallel to improve data migration performance by maximizing the usage of the allocated network bandwidth.

- Adjust AWS SCT memory configuration to improve schema conversion performance.

  — Edit the `JavaOptions` section to set the `minimum` and `maximum` memory available. The following example sets the minimum to 4 GB and the maximum to 40 GB:

```
[JavaOptions]
-Xmx40960M
-Xms4096M
```

- Use Amazon S3 to store large objects such as images, PDFs, and other binary data from your existing data warehouse.

- To migrate large tables, use virtual partitioning and create subtasks to improve data migration performance.

- Understand the use cases of AWS services such as Direct Connect, the AWS Transfer Family, and the AWS Snow Family.

  — Select the right service or tool to meet your data migration requirements.

  — Understand AWS service quotas and make informed migration design decisions.

Accelerate Your Migration to Amazon Redshift

There are several new capabilities to automate your schema conversion, preserve your investment in existing scripts, reports and applications, accelerate query performance, and reduce your overall cost to migrate to Amazon Redshift.

AWS SCT converts proprietary SQL statements including:

- TO_DATE() function

- CURSOR result sets

- IDENTITY columns

- ANY and SOME filters with inequality predicates

- Analytic functions with RESET WHEN

- TD_NORMALIZE_OVERLAP() function

- TD_UNPIVOT() function

- QUANTILE function

- QUALIFY filter

Refer to this automation for proprietary SQL statements blog (*https://oreil.ly/ettSl*) for further details.

In the following sections, we discuss some of the commonly faced migration challenges, including:

Macro conversion
    Macros are a proprietary SQL extension. Essentially, macros are SQL statements that accept parameters and can be called from multiple entry points in your

application code. You can think of macros as a stored procedure that does not return any output values.

Case-insensitive string comparison

ANSI-compliant string comparison is case-sensitive, and Amazon Redshift being ANSI-compliant, an uppercase "A" is different from a lowercase "a". Some databases support case-insensitive string comparison. Here, "A" = "a" is TRUE, as if both operands are converted to lowercase (or uppercase) for the purposes of the comparison. For example, in a Teradata database, case-insensitive collation is the default semantics for sessions running in BEGIN TRANSACTION and END TRANSACTION semantics (BTET mode), which is the default session mode for the Teradata engine.

Recursive common table expressions

Common table expressions (CTEs) are a convenient way to encapsulate query logic in large, complex SQL statements. CTEs are defined using the WITH clause, and the main query uses the CTE by referencing it in a FROM clause.

Proprietary data types

Amazon Redshift does not natively support INTERVAL, PERIOD, or BLOB data types as of this writing. AWS SCT includes automation for INTERVAL and PERIOD data types, automatic type casting, binary data support, and several other data type enhancements.

Macro Conversion

Although Amazon Redshift doesn't natively support macros, AWS SCT can automate this conversion for you. AWS SCT will convert a macro into an Amazon Redshift stored procedure.

Example 9-1 illustrates a macro that gives an employee a raise.

Example 9-1. Example of a Macro

```
CREATE MACRO Give_Emp_Raise (
  EmployeeNo  INTEGER,
  RaisePerc   DECIMAL(4,2)
)
AS
  (
  UPDATE
    Employee
  SET
    NetPay = NetPay * :RaisePerc
  WHERE
    EmployeeNo = :EmployeeNo ;
);
```

This macro will be converted to the stored procedure shown in Example 9-2 and executed in Amazon Redshift data warehouse.

Example 9-2. Macro converted to stored procedure

```
CREATE OR REPLACE PROCEDURE give_emp_raise (
  par_empl_nmbr    INTEGER,
  par_raise_perc   NUMERIC(4,2)
)
AS $BODY$
BEGIN
  UPDATE
    employee
  SET
    netpay = netpay * par_raise_perc
  WHERE
    employeenumber = par_empl_nmbr ;
END;
$BODY$
LANGUAGE plpgsql
```

AWS SCT will also convert any corresponding macro invocations into calls to the corresponding stored procedure, to minimize manual conversions.

Case-Insensitive String Comparison

Case-sensitive comparison is the default semantics in Amazon Redshift. Amazon Redshift uses the normal ANSI-compliant semantics by default. Amazon Redshift now performs case-insensitive comparison natively as a feature of the database engine. With this new feature, you can enable case-insensitive collation when you define a new database, a new column, or use a column in an expression, as shown in Example 9-3.

Example 9-3. Case insensitive sample

```
CREATE DATABASE new_db collate case_insensitive;

CREATE TABLE new_db.test_case_sensitive
( default_col1      varchar(20)
, sensitive_col2    varchar(20) collate case_sensitive
, insensitive_col3  varchar(20) collate case_insensitive
)
;

INSERT INTO new_db.test_case_sensitive
VALUES ('Hello', 'hello', 'HELLO')
;
```

Let's compare the default column and the explicitly declared case-insensitive column with the query in Example 9-4. Because the database default for new_db is CASE_INSENSITIVE, the comparison is case-insensitive and the strings match.

Example 9-4. Case insensitive test

```
SELECT 1 AS tst FROM new_db.test_case_sensitive
WHERE default_col1 = insensitive_col3;

 tst
 ---
  1
(1 row)
```

Similarly, you can override the case sensitivity of a column. In Example 9-5, we override the case-sensitive column to be CASE_INSENSITIVE, and observe that the comparison matches again.

*Example 9-5. Case insensitive **test2***

```
SELECT 1 AS tst2 FROM new_db.test_case_sensitive
WHERE default_col1 = collate(sensitive_col2, 'case_insensitive');

 tst2
 ---
  1
(1 row)
```

Note that Amazon Redshift won't let you directly compare a CASE_SENSITIVE column to a CASE_INSENSITIVE column (as in Example 9-6).

Example 9-6. Case insensitive test3

```
SELECT 1 AS tst3 FROM new_db.test_case_sensitive
WHERE sensitive_col2 = insensitive_col3;

ERROR: Query with different collations is not supported yet.
DETAIL:
-----------------------------------------------
error: Query with different collations is not supported yet.
code: 1020
context:
query: 0
location: parse_expr.c:613
process: padbmaster [pid=17580]
```

To avoid this, make sure you explicitly override the collation of one or both operands appropriately. This is a best practice for your SQL code, and it will be easier to understand when collation is explicitly applied.

Recursive Common Table Expressions

Amazon Redshift supports recursive common table expressions (CTEs). A recursive CTE is useful in querying hierarchical data, such as organization charts that show reporting relationships between employees and managers. Also note that AWS SCT automatically converts queries with recursive CTEs. If you create a view with query johns_org, as shown in Example 9-7, SCT will convert to the equivalent view in Amazon Redshift.

Example 9-7. Recursive CTE example

```
WITH recursive
  john_org (id, name, manager_id, level)
AS
  (
    SELECT id, name, manager_id, 1 AS level
      FROM employee
     WHERE name = 'John'
  UNION ALL
    SELECT e.id, e.name, e.manager_id, level + 1 AS next_level
      FROM employee e, john_org j
     WHERE e.manager_id = j.id
       AND level < 4
  )
SELECT distinct id, name, manager_id
  FROM john_org
ORDER BY manager_id
;
```

Proprietary Data Types

AWS SCT automatically converts INTERVAL data types for you. AWS SCT converts an INTERVAL column into a CHARACTER VARYING column in Amazon Redshift. Then AWS SCT converts your application code that uses the column to emulate the INTERVAL semantics.

Consider the following table, which has a MONTH interval column. This table stores different types of *leaves of absences* and the allowable *duration* for each. Your application code uses the leave_duration column, as shown in Example 9-8. Here, the INTERVAL MONTH field is added to the current date to compute when a leave of absence ends as if it starts today.

Example 9-8. Interval example

```
-- source table with INTERVAL data type
CREATE TABLE src_schema.employee_leaves
(
  leave_type_id INTEGER ,
  leave_name VARCHAR(100) CHARACTER SET LATIN ,
  leave_duration INTERVAL MONTH(2)
)
UNIQUE PRIMARY INDEX ( leave_type_id )
;

-- source view with interval logic implemented
CREATE VIEW src_schema.employee_leaves_projected
AS
SELECT
  leave_type_id,
  leave_name,
  leave_duration,
  current_date AS projected_start_date,
  current_date + leave_duration AS projected_end_date
FROM
  src_schema.employee_leaves
;
```

When AWS SCT converts the table to Amazon Redshift, AWS SCT replaces INTERVAL with a VARCHAR data type, as shown in Example 9-9 for column leave_duration. And now since the data is stored as VARCHAR, AWS SCT adds the proper type CAST into the Amazon Redshift code to interpret the string values as a MONTH interval. It then converts the view arithmetic logic using Amazon Redshift date function for dateadd MONTH.

Example 9-9. Interval converted to date

```
-- target table with VARCHAR data type
CREATE TABLE rs_schema.employee_leaves(
  leave_type_id INTEGER
, leave_name VARCHAR(100)
, leave_duration VARCHAR(64)
)
DISTSTYLE KEY
DISTKEY ( leave_type_id )
SORTKEY ( leave_type_id )
;

-- target view with interval logic implemented
CREATE OR REPLACE VIEW rs_schema.employee_leaves_projected
SELECT
  leave_type_id,
  leave_name,
```

```
  leave_duration,
  current_date AS projected_start_date,
  dateadd
    (MONTH,
     CAST (leave_duration AS INTEGER),
     CURRENT_DATE
     )::DATE AS projected_end_date
FROM
  rs_schema.employee_leaves
;
```

By using a VARCHAR data type for the leave_duration column, AWS SCT has reduced the chances of table conversion failure, thus increasing the probability of data migration success. If some manual rewrite is required, then it will most likely be the SQL code in the view.

AWS SCT automatically converts PERIOD data types into two DATE (or TIME or TIME STAMP) columns as appropriate on Amazon Redshift. Then AWS SCT converts your application code that uses the column to emulate the source engine semantics (see Example 9-10).

Example 9-10. Period example

```
CREATE SET TABLE src_schema.period_table
(
  id INTEGER ,
  period_col PERIOD(timestamp)
)
UNIQUE PRIMARY INDEX (id);

CREATE VIEW src_schema.period_view_begin_end
AS
SELECT
  BEGIN(period_col) AS period_start ,
  END(period_col) AS period_end
FROM
  src_schema.period_table
;
```

AWS SCT converts the PERIOD(TIMESTAMP) column in the CREATE SET TABLE statement in Example 9-10 into two TIMESTAMP columns, as shown in Example 9-11's CREATE TABLE IF NOT EXISTS command. Then, it converts the application code for the view period_view_begin_end` to use the two new TIMESTAMP columns:

Example 9-11. Period converted to timestamp

```
CREATE TABLE IF NOT EXISTS
rs_schema.period_table
(
  id INTEGER ,
  period_col_begin TIMESTAMP ,
  period_col_end TIMESTAMP
)
DISTSTYLE KEY
DISTKEY ( id )
SORTKEY ( id )
;

CREATE OR REPLACE VIEW rs_schema.period_view_begin_end
AS
SELECT
  period_col_begin AS period_start ,
  period_col_end AS period_end
FROM
  rs_schema.period_table
;
```

Summary

Data volume is growing faster than ever. Traditionally only a fraction of this invaluable asset is available for analysis. On-premises data warehouses have rigid architectures that don't scale for modern big data analytics use cases. These traditional data warehouses are expensive to set up and operate, and require large up-front investments both in terms of software and hardware investments.

We covered how Amazon Redshift can help you analyze all your data and achieve performance at any scale with low and predictable cost. To migrate your data warehouse to Amazon Redshift, you need to consider a range of factors, such as the total size of the data warehouse, data change rate, and data transformation complexity, before picking a suitable migration strategy and process to reduce the complexity and cost of your data warehouse migration project.

With AWS services such AWS Schema Conversion Tool (SCT) and AWS Database Migration Service (DMS), and by adopting the tips and best practices of these services, you can automate migration tasks, scale migration, and accelerate the delivery of your data warehouse migration projects.

In the next chapter, we will cover the aspects of monitoring and administration for your Amazon Redshift data warehouse.

CHAPTER 10

Monitoring and Administration

You can't improve what you don't measure.
—Peter Drucker

As a fully managed cloud data warehouse, Amazon Redshift continuously monitors your database and automatically captures and stores data related to the resource utilization and details of workloads you run on your data warehouse. As a user of the data warehouse, you can focus on ingesting and analyzing data and need not continuously monitor or administer. Amazon Redshift makes the operational data available for you to monitor and handle exceptions to ensure optimal performance of the data warehouse.

You can view your Amazon Redshift data warehouse operational metrics on the Amazon Redshift console, use AWS CloudWatch, and directly query Amazon Redshift system tables. In this chapter, we will start with an "Amazon Redshift Monitoring Overview" and dive into various options to monitor Amazon Redshift provisioned cluster and serverless. We'll start with "Monitoring Using Console", and discuss "Monitoring and Administering Serverless" and "Monitoring Provisioned Data Warehouse Using Console". Then we will cover both provisioned cluster and serverless "Monitoring Using Amazon CloudWatch" and "Monitoring Using System Tables and Views". Today, resilience and high availability have becoming important for data warehouse workloads. We will cover how you can set up "High Availability and Disaster Recovery" along with "Snapshots, Backup, and Restore". Since the monitoring details are stored within Redshift in tables and views, you can create your own custom visualizations to monitor the data warehouse. We'll cover "Bring Your Own Visualization Tool to Monitor Amazon Redshift" to help you understand how you can use your tool of choice to create custom visualizations.

Amazon Redshift Monitoring Overview

Amazon Redshift provides performance metrics and data so that you can track the health and performance of your clusters and databases. Amazon CloudWatch (*https://oreil.ly/rkTBj*) is a monitoring service that captures logs and metrics from various services in AWS. Amazon Redshift records performance data every minute and provides performance data from CloudWatch metrics and statistics about query and load data that it stores in system tables. You can monitor your Amazon Redshift workloads and resources using the console, CloudWatch, or the system tables and views. With the Amazon Redshift console, you can view both the CloudWatch metrics and the query/load performance data. In addition, you can use Amazon CloudWatch to view system utilization and performance information by using standard dashboard templates or by creating custom templates.

You can use this information to identify and diagnose workloads that take a long time to process and create bottlenecks that prevent other workloads from executing efficiently. The use cases for monitoring and diagnosing arise from user questions, and they can be categorized as monitoring, troubleshooting, and optimization activities. We address some of the common questions in the following sections.

Monitoring

Monitoring is a proactive activity where you want to actively look for exceptions in your data warehouse to ensure you can put processes in place to avoid downtime due to an event that causes a failure in the system. These questions include:

- How is my data warehouse doing in terms of query performance and resource utilization?
- How is my data warehouse throughput, concurrency, and latency looking?
- Are queries being queued in my cluster?
- Which queries or loads are running now?
- Which queries or loads are taking longer than usual?
- What are my top queries by duration in the last hour or last 24 hours?
- Which queries have failed?
- Is the average query latency for my data warehouse increasing or decreasing over time?
- When will I run out of resources and should consider scaling or workload isolation?

Troubleshooting

When an event has occurred and you are engaged in resolving the issue, you are in reactive mode, and the Redshift console provides you with options:

- A user complained about performance issues at a specific time. How do I identify that SQL and diagnose problems?
- Which other queries were running when my query was slow? Were all queries slow?
- Is my database overloaded with queries from other users? Is my queue depth increasing or decreasing?
- How do I identify queries that a specific user runs?
- The resources of my data warehouse are running very high. How do I find out which queries are running?

Optimization

When you design your data models for your warehouse initially, you go with certain assumptions about how the data will be used. However, the user query patterns could be different from these assumptions. By monitoring, you can identify areas where you can optimize your data warehouse for better performance and utilization:

- How can I optimize the SQL that our end users author?
- Is there any optimization required in my schema design?
- Is there any tuning required for my WLM queues?
- Can I get any benefit if I enable Concurrency Scaling?
- Can I proactively monitor workloads to prevent runaway queries?

Monitoring Using Console

The Amazon Redshift console features a monitoring dashboard and options for you to create and manage Amazon Redshift data warehouses. The console leverages data from Amazon CloudWatch and other system tables to provide you with insights into the overall resource utilization of the database and the performance metrics. The metrics are available for both provisioned and serverless data warehouses, and you can view them in the respective dashboard screens. Both the serverless and provisioned cluster dashboards have a main dashboard that shows metrics across all the namespaces or clusters you have in the account. You can either view the metrics across all namespaces or select a particular namespace or cluster to monitor a specific data warehouse. Using the console helps you simplify management of your data warehouse by having visibility to the health and performance of the data warehouse in one location. The console monitoring metrics are organized in various parts on the console, which we'll discuss in the following sections.

Monitoring and Administering Serverless

This includes a list of namespaces, query metrics, RPU capacity, and any alarms in CloudWatch, as shown in Figure 10-1. The main serverless dashboard shows details of the query and database metrics across all namespaces or workgroups in the account. With this view, you can correlate the query workloads with the RPU capacity used to understand which part of the day your utilization is higher, and if you need to increase the base RPU for serverless. You can also get a view of all failed queries for further analysis on the reasons for failure.

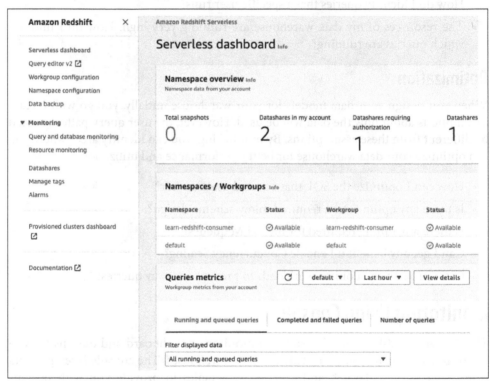

Figure 10-1. Serverless query and database monitoring

The detailed list of metrics available in the serverless dashboard is shown in Table 10-1. For individual serverless instance level metrics, see the next section.

Table 10-1. Monitoring metrics in the main dashboard of serverless

Metric	Details
Query metrics	Running and queued queries
	RPU capacity used
Completed and failed queries	Queries completed or failed across timeline
	RPU capacity used
Number of queries	Count of queries across timeline
	RPU capacity used

Additional monitoring options to monitor query, database, and resources are available, which you can get to by clicking the left menu buttons. Here, under Monitoring, you will see the option for "Query and database monitoring" and "Resource monitoring."

Query and database monitoring serverless

When you have to monitor workloads, most often it will be with respect to a specific namespace or workgroup. To filter the metrics for a specific serverless namespace or a workgroup, you can choose the specific namespace from the main dashboard either by clicking on the link or by filtering the namespace. This will display query and database resource metrics for that specific namespace.

Serverless query and database monitoring. When you select "Query and database monitoring," you can select the serverless workgroup to analyze the query and load workloads. Here you have options to monitor "Query history" or "Database performance," as shown in Figure 10-1. Since serverless will autoscale and add RPU capacity as required up to the maximum RPU value configured, there is no need to monitor or manage the workload or workload concurrency as you saw in provisioned cluster. Under "Query history," you can use the "Query runtime" graph to see which queries are running in the same timeframe, and choose a query to view more query execution details. You can also analyze and view details of a query's completion status, duration, and SQL statement.

You also have the option for additional filters to choose time range, type of queries, and type of SQL commands used or to choose a specific user or database, as shown in Figure 10-2.

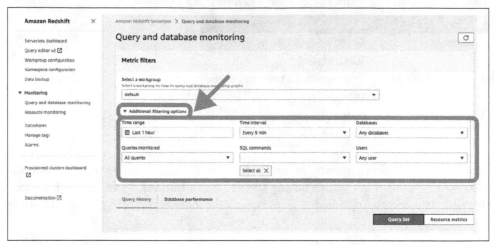

Figure 10-2. Serverless query and database monitoring additional filter

Serverless query monitoring drill-down query. You can further drill down on the Query ID to view the details of the query SQL, query plan, and related metrics, as shown in Figure 10-3. The query plan will be based on the rewritten query, and the related metrics has the RPU capacity used and the active database connections used.

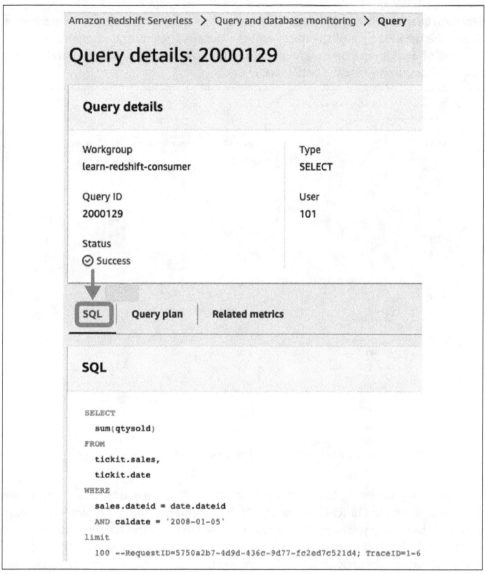

Figure 10-3. Serverless query monitoring drill down

Serverless query monitoring drill-down query plan. The query Plan screen in Figure 10-4 shows the detailed plan of the query and the various streams and segments with the runtime of each stream and segment. In addition, you also see the input and output rows to determine where the bottleneck exists.

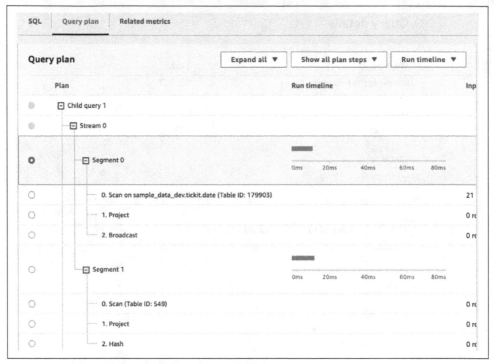

Figure 10-4. Serverless query monitoring drill-down

Serverless query monitoring drill-down related metrics. The related metrics show the overall capacity used in RPUs in the last 10 hours and the number of active database connections to help you correlate the capacity used to the active database connections during that time. For example, in Figure 10-5 you see from 12:00 p.m. to 3:00 p.m. there were active database connections that were not executing any queries except for a brief period around 1:30 p.m. This is why the RPU capacity stays at zero for part of the time between 12:00 p.m. to 3:00 p.m.

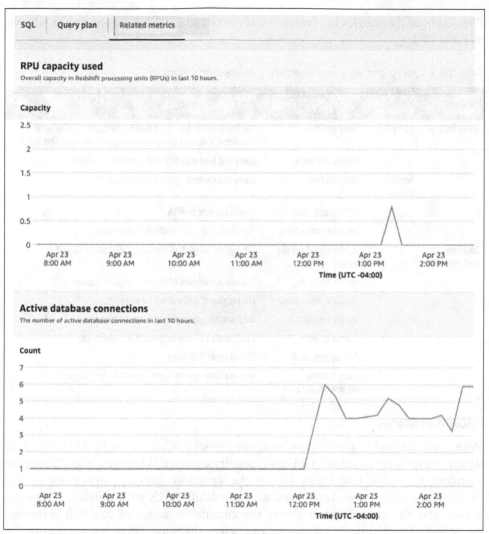

Figure 10-5. Serverless query monitoring drill down

The details of the metrics for the serverless query and database monitoring are shown in Table 10-2.

Table 10-2. Query and database monitoring metrics for serverless

Query/Database	Query/Resource	Metric	Details
Query history	Query list	Query runtime	Use this graph to see which queries are running in the same timeframe. Choose a query to view more query execution details.
		Queries and loads	Query and load statistics with start time, duration
	Resource metrics	Query runtime	Query to view more query execution details
		RPU capacity used	Overall capacity in RPUs
		Database connections	The number of active database connections
Database performance		Queries completed per second	The average number of queries completed per second
		Queries duration	The average amount of time to complete a query
		Database connections	The number of active database connections
		Running queries	Total number of running queries at a given time
		Queued queries	Total number of queries queued at a given time
		RPU capacity used	Overall capacity in RPUs
		Query runtime breakdown	The total time queries spent running by query type

Resource monitoring

With Amazon Redshift serverless, compute capacity is measured in RPU, and each RPU corresponds to a related CPU and memory capacity. When you select "Resource monitoring" as shown in Figure 10-6 in the serverless console, you see two graphs; the first one shows the overall capacity in Redshift RPUs with timeline across the x-axis, and the second graph shows the cumulative usage of Redshift serverless by period. As discussed earlier, you can select the time range by expanding the Additional Filtering options. As you can see, the RPU capacity is provisioned only when workloads need to be processed; capacity drops down to zero after actual compute usage for workloads drop and it trails the compute usage pattern. Similarly, the RPU capacity leads the usage graph, as only when the query workloads start to come in to the serverless endpoint, the RPU capacity automatically scales up. This demonstrates that the RPU capacity scales automatically to meet the incoming workloads. A consistently large cumulative usage can be an indication that you can set a higher initial RPU for your serverless to get the workload executed faster, yet at the same cost.

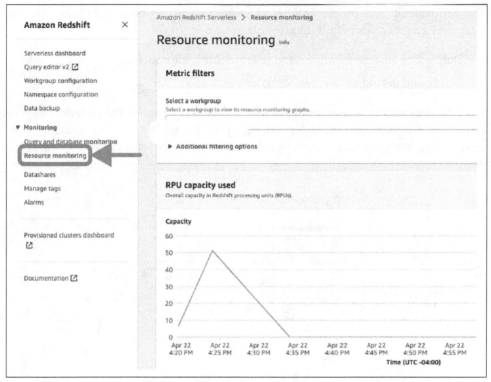

Figure 10-6. Serverless resource monitoring

The details of the metrics for the serverless resource monitoring are shown in Table 10-3.

Table 10-3. Resource monitoring for serverless

Metric	Details
RPU capacity used	Overall capacity in RPUs
Compute usage	The accumulative usage of Redshift Serverless by period for the selected time range

Monitoring Provisioned Data Warehouse Using Console

The main dashboard for Amazon Redshift provisioned data warehouse shows metrics across all clusters, and you have the option to select a specific provisioned data warehouse to monitor. As shown in Figure 10-7, you can switch between the various metrics to view queries, database connections, disk space, and CPU utilization.

The performance data for provisioned clusters that you can view and monitor in the Amazon Redshift console falls into two categories:

- Data warehouse performance and resource utilization metrics
- Query and data ingestion performance metrics

With the data warehouse performance metrics, you can monitor the system resources and analyze if there is a need for scaling up or down. With query and ingestion metrics, you analyze how a certain workload has performed with the given resources.

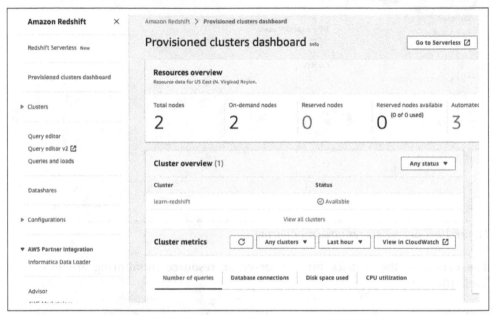

Figure 10-7. Monitor data warehouse performance

These metrics available in the main dashboard can be summarized as shown in Table 10-4.

Table 10-4. Monitoring metrics in main dashboard of provisioned cluster

Metric	Details
Cluster metrics	Number of queries
	Database connections
	Disk space used
	CPU utilization
Query overview	Queries workloads (short, medium, and long) for specific time

Data warehouse performance and resource utilization metrics

Physical aspects of your cluster, such as CPU utilization, latency, and throughput are captured in Amazon CloudWatch. These metrics are displayed directly in the Amazon Redshift console, in context to the data warehouse you are viewing, as shown in Figure 10-8 for provisioned cluster. For monitoring serverless, you can jump to "Monitoring and Administering Serverless" on page 346 for more details on resource monitoring. You can also view the same metrics in the CloudWatch console by creating dashboards and selecting the metrics you want to analyze. The details of these metrics are covered in "Monitoring Using Amazon CloudWatch" on page 374. Alternatively, you can use AWS CLI or one of the AWS SDKs to consume the metrics using a custom web interface.

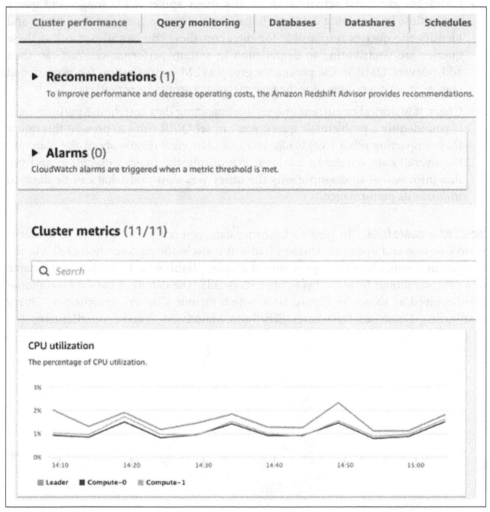

Figure 10-8. Monitor data warehouse performance

When you size your provisioned data warehouse or set a base RPU for your serverless instance, you typically start with an estimate of your current data volume and the percentage of hot data. As your workloads and data volume grow, you can resize your data warehouse or increase the RPU. The data warehouse performance metrics in the Redshift console give you an indication of whether your data warehouse resources are underutilized or overutilized, and this data helps you monitor database activity and performance. The Redshift Advisor also analyzes your workloads and provides you with sizing recommendations.

By using data warehouse metrics in Amazon Redshift, you can do the following common performance tasks:

- Check for abnormal activity such as disk usage spikes, CPU usage, and query queue time by reviewing data warehouse metrics over a specified time range and identify the queries responsible for the anomalies. You can also check if these queries are contributing to degradation in system performance. You can then add relevant QMR in the parameter group WLM configuration for provisioned cluster or set query limits for the serverless workgroup for serverless.

- Check if historical or current queries are impacting data warehouse performance. If you identify a problematic query, you can set QMR rules to prevent this query from impacting other workloads. You can then view details about the plan and the overall data warehouse performance during the query's execution and use this information to diagnose why the query was slow and what can be done to improve its performance.

View Performance Data. To view performance data, you can login to the AWS Management Console and open the Amazon Redshift console (*https://oreil.ly/IxcVd*). On the navigation menu, choose the provisioned clusters dashboard, then choose the name of a data warehouse from the list to open its details. The details of the data warehouse are displayed as shown in Figure 10-9, which include Cluster performance, Query monitoring, Databases, Datashares, Schedules, Maintenance, and Properties tabs.

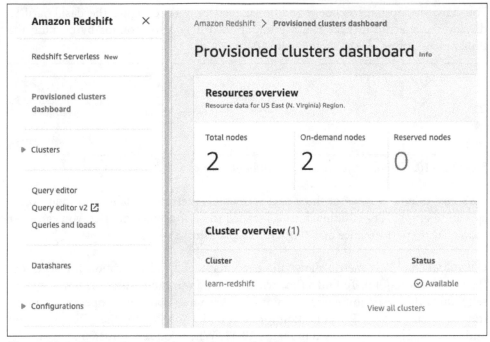

Figure 10-9. Choose the provisioned clusters dashboard

Choose the Cluster performance tab to review the performance information as shown in Table 10-5.

Table 10-5. Cluster performance metrics in dashboard of provisioned cluster

Metrics	Details
Alarms	CloudWatch alarms are triggered when a metric threshold is met.
Events	Events that occur on your cluster.
CPU utilization	The percentage of CPU utilization.
Percentage disk space used	The percent of disk space used.
Auto vacuum space freed	Space reclaimed by auto vacuum in all tables.
Database connections	The number of database connections to a cluster.
Health status	Indicates the health of the cluster.
Query duration	The average amount of time to complete a query.
Query throughput	The average number of queries completed per second.
Query duration per WLM queue	The average length of time to complete a query for a WLM queue.
Query throughput per WLM queue	The average number of queries completed per second for a WLM queue.
Concurrency scaling activity	Concurrency scaling usage limit.
Usage limit for Redshift Spectrum	Redshift Spectrum usage limit.

You have the option to choose additional metrics and configure the dashboard to display the specific metrics that are important for you to monitor by clicking the Preferences button, as shown in Figure 10-10.

Figure 10-10. Choose preferences for additional metrics

Let's take a look at some of these data warehouse metrics available and their corresponding graphs. For additional details related to performance metrics, you can refer to the cluster performance data (*https://oreil.ly/aKtuE*).

CPU utilization. This metric shows the percentage of CPU utilization for all nodes (leader and compute). To find a time when the data warehouse usage is lowest before scheduling data warehouse migration or other resource-consuming operations, monitor this chart to see CPU utilization for each node. You can see the CPU utilization and percentage disk space used in Figure 10-11. When you see consistently high CPU utilization, that is an indication that your workloads could benefit from resizing the cluster. If the CPU utilization is sporadic with intermittent spikes, this could be a good case for cost savings with serverless.

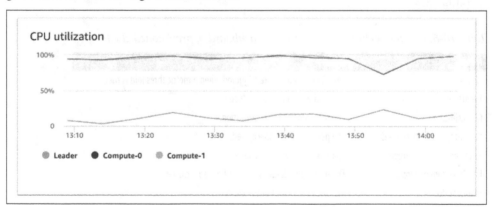

Figure 10-11. Monitor CPU utilization

Percentage disk space used. This metric shows the percentage of disk space usage per each compute node, and not for the data warehouse as a whole, as shown in Figure 10-12. You can explore this chart to monitor the disk utilization and estimate if you need to resize. When you use RA3 nodes, each node of ra3.4xl and ra3.16xl can store up to 128 TB, and ra3.xlplus can store up to 32 TB. So, you can store a large volume of data, but for resizing you should consider your compute requirements as well.

 Maintenance operations like VACUUM and COPY use intermediate temporary storage space for their sort operations, so a spike in disk usage is expected.

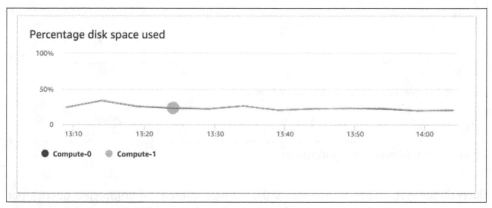

Figure 10-12. Monitor disk space used

Database connections. This shows the number of database connections to a cluster, as shown in Figure 10-13. You can use this chart to see how many connections are established to the database and find a time when the data warehouse usage is lowest. You can also correlate the DB connections with the query metrics like query duration and query throughput, and analyze if the number of database connections have an impact on the query workloads.

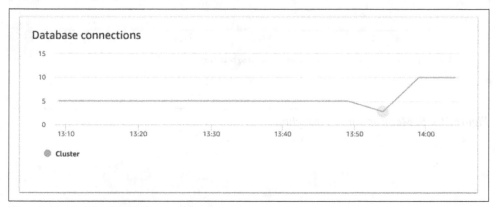

Figure 10-13. Monitor DB connections

Query duration. This metric shows the average amount of time to complete a query in microseconds, as shown in Figure 10-14. You can benchmark the data on this chart to measure I/O performance within the data warehouse and tune its most time-consuming queries if necessary.

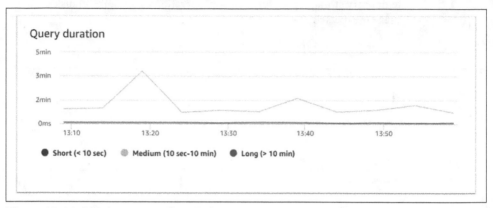

Figure 10-14. Monitor query duration

Query throughput. This metric shows the average number of completed queries per second, as shown in Figure 10-15. You can analyze data on this chart to measure database performance and characterize the ability of the system to support a multiuser workload in a balanced way.

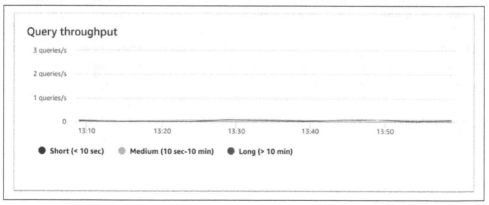

Figure 10-15. Monitor query throughput

Query and data ingestion performance metrics: Query Monitoring tab

The Amazon Redshift console provides information about the performance of queries that run in the data warehouse. When you have users complaining of query performance issues, and you need to be able to identify the reasons for slow performance, you can use the query monitoring dashboard to isolate the query performance problems. You can also compare query runtime metrics and data warehouse performance metrics on the same timeline to identify if there is a correlation between the data warehouse resources and the impact in performance. This helps you identify poorly performing queries, look for bottleneck queries, and determine if you need to resize your data warehouse for your workload.

This data is aggregated in the Amazon Redshift console to help you easily correlate what you see in performance metrics with specific database query and load events, as shown in Figure 10-16. For serverless, you can refer to Figure 10-1 for query and database monitoring.

 Single-AZmance data is displayed only in the Amazon Redshift console, and is not published as CloudWatch metrics.

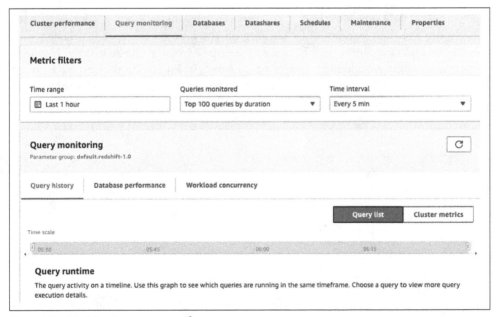

Figure 10-16. Monitor query performance

The details of the query and data ingestion performance metrics are shown in Table 10-6.

Table 10-6. Query monitoring metrics in the data warehouse dashboard of provisioned cluster

Monitoring	Metrics	Details
Query history	Query runtime	The query activity on a timeline. Use this graph to see which queries are running in the same timeframe. Choose a query to view more query execution details.
	Queries and loads	Query execution details.
Database performance	Workload execution breakdown	The time used in query processing stages.
	Queries by duration range	The number of short, medium, and long queries.
	Query throughput	The average number of queries completed per second.
	Query duration	The average amount of time to complete a query.
	Average queue wait time by priority	The total time queries spent waiting in the WLM queue by query priority.
Workload concurrency	Queued versus Running queries on the cluster	The number of queries running (from the main data warehouse and Concurrency Scaling cluster) compared to the number of queries waiting in all WLM queues in the cluster.

Query history at data warehouse level. To display query history for a specific cluster, you choose the data warehouse by clicking on the link for the specific cluster, then choose the Query monitoring tab. You will see three tabs for Query history, Database performance, and Workload concurrency, as shown in Figure 10-17. Here you choose the Query history tab, and you can toggle between query list and cluster metrics using buttons on the window.

When you choose Query List, the tab includes the following graphs:

Query runtime

This shows query activity on a timeline (see Figure 10-17). Use this graph to see which queries are running in the same timeframe. Choose a query to view more query execution details. The x-axis shows the selected period. You can filter the graphed queries by running, completed, loads, and so on. Each horizontal bar represents a query, and the length of the bar represents its runtime from the start of the bar to the end. The queries can include SQL data manipulation statements (such as SELECT, INSERT, DELETE) and loads (such as COPY). By default, the top 100 longest-running queries are shown for the selected time period.

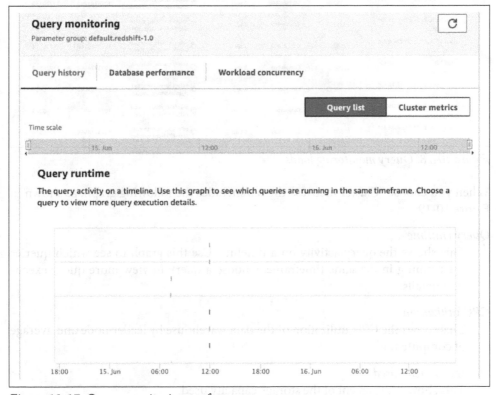

Figure 10-17. Query monitoring performance

Queries and loads

This shows a list of queries and loads that ran on the cluster (see Figure 10-18), where you can also drill down into the Query ID to view the query plan to further analyze the query. You also have an option to terminate a query here.

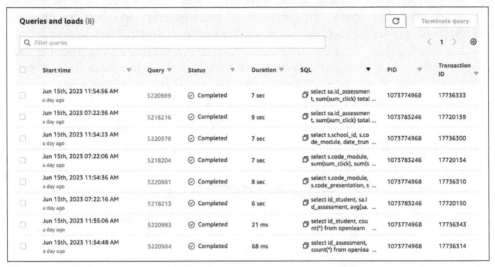

Figure 10-18. Query monitoring loads

When you choose "Cluster metrics," the tab includes the following graph, as shown in Figure 10-19:

Query runtime

This shows the query activity on a timeline. Use this graph to see which queries are running in the same timeframe. Choose a query to view more query execution details.

CPU utilization

This shows the CPU utilization of the data warehouse by leader node and average of compute nodes.

Storage capacity used

This shows the percent of the storage capacity used.

Active database connections

This shows the number of active database connections to the cluster.

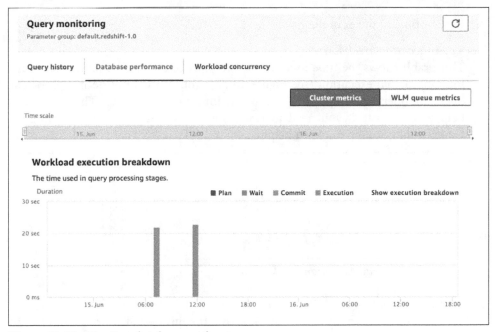

Figure 10-19. Monitor database performance

Database performance for queries. The database performance metrics has details on where the query time is spent either in plan, wait, commit, or execution and the throughput of the database. These metrics are available under two tabs, "Cluster metrics" and "WLM queue metrics," and you can use database performance metrics in Amazon Redshift to do the following:

- Analyze the time spent by queries by processing stages, and look for unusual trends like high query wait time, runtime, or execution time where the amount of time spent in a stage is large.

- Filter based on query status: running, completed, failed, or stopped queries.

- Analyze the number of queries, duration, and throughput of queries by duration ranges (short: < 10 seconds, medium: 10 seconds to 10 minutes, long: > 10 minutes).

- Look for trends in query wait time by query priority (Lowest, Low, Normal, High, Highest, Critical). With workload management (WLM), you can set up multiple queues with different priorities, as we covered in "WLM, Queues, and QMR" on page 169.

- Look for trends in the query duration, throughput, or wait time by WLM queue.

We discuss some of the example graphs next:

Workload execution breakdown

This graph shows the time used in the query processing stages plan, wait, commit, and actual execution (see Figure 10-20). You can determine if a particular query or queries are spending too much time in a wait state. This detail will help you evaluate if you need to resize your cluster. In this case, turning on Concurrency Scaling might be helpful.

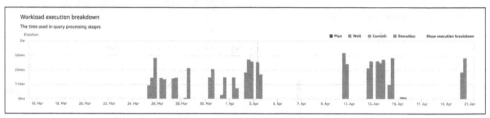

Figure 10-20. Workload execution breakdown

Queries by duration range

This graph, as shown in Figure 10-21, shows the number of short, medium, and long queries.

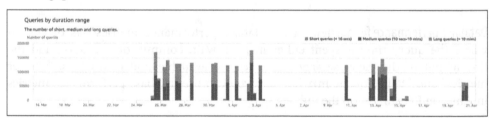

Figure 10-21. Queries by duration range

Query throughput

This graph, as shown in Figure 10-22, shown an average number of queries completed per second.

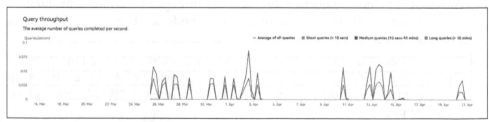

Figure 10-22. Query throughput

Query duration

Figure 10-23 shows the average amount of time to complete a query.

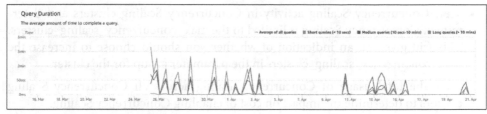

Figure 10-23. Query duration

Average queue wait time by priority

The graph in Figure 10-24 shows the total time queries spent waiting in the WLM queue by query priority.

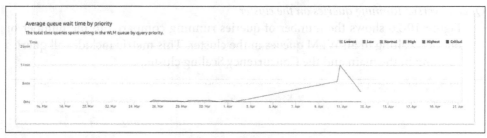

Figure 10-24. Average queue wait time by priority

Query throughput by queue

This graph, as shown in Figure 10-25, shows the query runtime and throughput for each of the WLM queues.

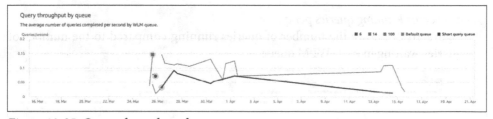

Figure 10-25. Query throughput by queue

Workload concurrency

You learned in Figure 5-3 that you can use the Concurrency Scaling feature to automatically scale compute capacity to meet the requirements of your dynamic workloads. The workload concurrency tab provides metrics related to Concurrency Scaling and helps you understand the following:

- Analyze if enabling Concurrency Scaling will help reduce the number of queued queries by comparing the queued versus running queries in all WLM queues.

- View Concurrency Scaling activity in Concurrency Scaling clusters and determine if Concurrency Scaling is limited to the max_concurrency_scaling_clusters. This will give you an indication of whether you should choose to increase the max_concurrency_scaling_clusters in the parameter group for the cluster.

- View the total usage of Concurrency Scaling across all Concurrency Scaling clusters to determine the impact on cost of enabling Concurrency Scaling.

For serverless this happens automatically, and you need to analyze only the "compute capacity." The "query runtime breakdown" in serverless has query waiting metrics, which you can use to analyze if you have to increase the base RPU. We discuss some of the graphs available for monitoring impact of Concurrency Scaling next:

Queued versus Running queries on the cluster
> Figure 10-26 shows the number of queries running compared to the number of queries waiting in all WLM queues in the cluster. This metric includes all queries running in the main and the Concurrency Scaling cluster.

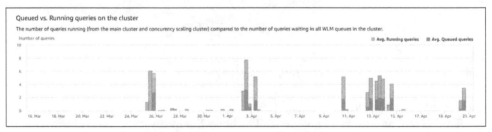

Figure 10-26. Queued versus Running queries on the cluster

Queued versus Running queries per queue
> Figure 10-27 shows the number of queries running compared to the number of queries waiting in each WLM queue.

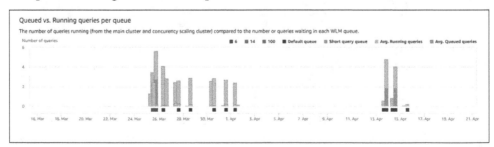

Figure 10-27. Queued versus Running queries per queue

Concurrency scaling activity

> Figure 10-28 shows the number of Concurrency Scaling clusters that are actively processing queries. You can use this metric to understand if you need to increase the number of Concurrency Scaling clusters or set any usage limit.

Figure 10-28. Concurrency scaling activity

Concurrency scaling usage

> Figure 10-29 shows the usage of Concurrency Scaling clusters that have active query processing activity.

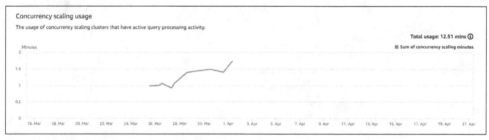

Figure 10-29. Concurrency scaling usage

Monitoring Queries and Loads Across Clusters

There is more than one way to monitor queries and loads in the console. To analyze queries and loads across clusters, you can select "Queries and loads" from the main Amazon Redshift console menu, as shown in Figure 10-30. Here you can analyze and view query details, which includes the query's completion status, duration, SQL statement, and whether it's a user query or one that was rewritten by Amazon Redshift.

A user query is a query submitted to Amazon Redshift either from an SQL client or generated by a BI tool. Amazon Redshift might rewrite the query to optimize it, and this can result in multiple rewritten queries. For example, with the Auto MV feature, when you write a query on the base tables, Redshift might create a materialized view and rewrite the query to run against the materialized view instead. Similarly, if you already have a materialized view and you have the query written on the base table, the query processor will rewrite the query to read from the existing materialized view.

You can view the rewritten queries on the query details page in the console along with the initial user query.

Monitoring queries and loads

In the screen shown in Figure 10-30, you can select the data warehouse for which to analyze the query workloads, and you can filter based on date/time range or status of queries. These filters can include top 100 queries, completed queries, and failed or stopped queries. The list of filters is also shown.

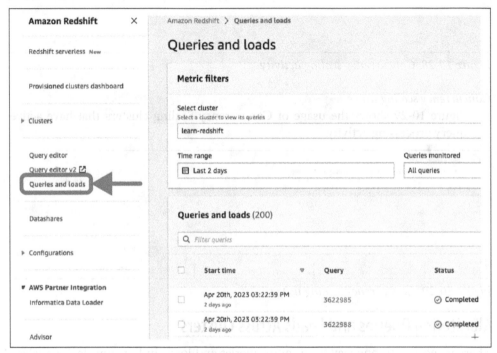

Figure 10-30. Monitoring queries and loads

The console allows you to drill down to the details of a specific query by clicking on the Query ID link. When Query ID and other properties are displayed in a row below the graph, then you can choose the query to see details like the query's SQL statement, execution details, and query plan, as shown in Figure 10-31. The "Query details" page shows you the parent query and all rewritten queries for read and write workloads for your analysis.

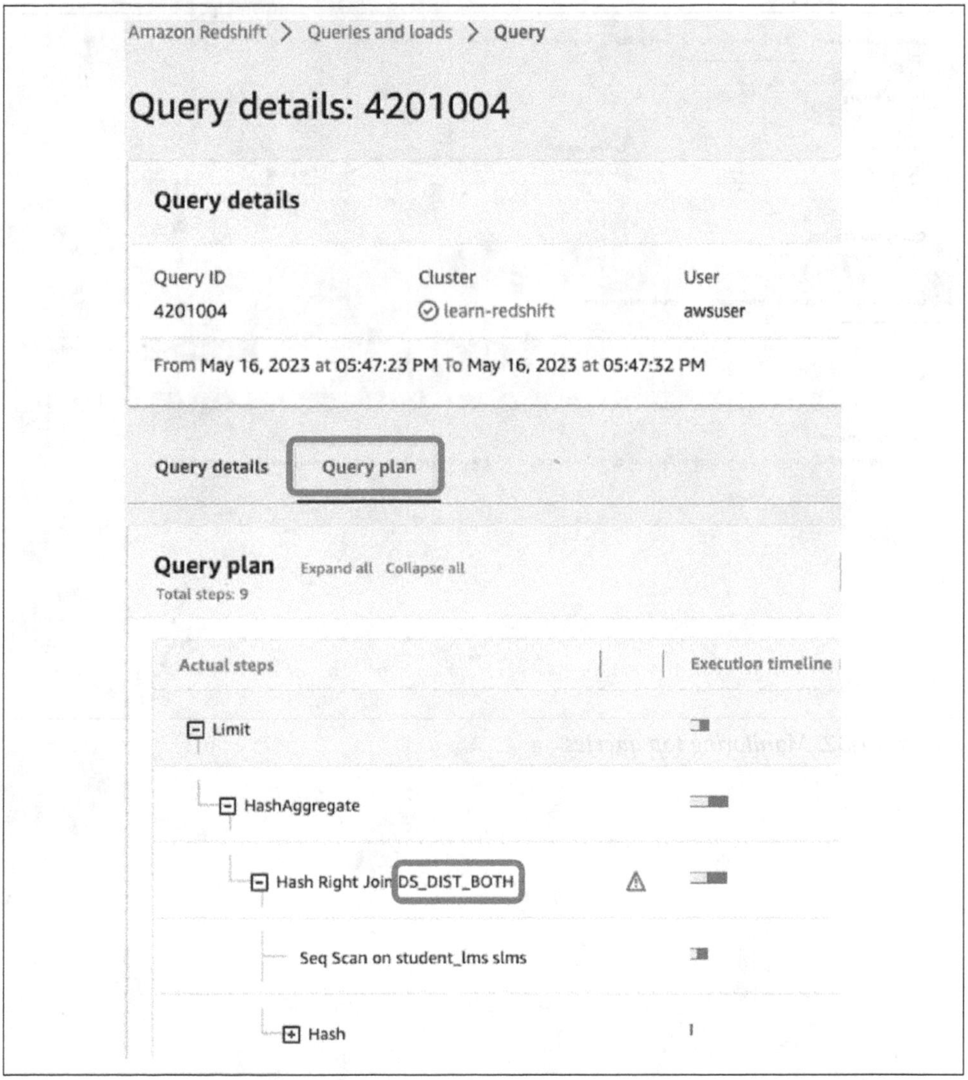

Figure 10-31. Monitoring query plan

Monitoring top queries

By default, the "Query monitoring" page shows the top 100 longest queries by runtime or duration for the selected time window. You can change the time window to view the top queries for that period (see Figure 10-32). The top queries also include completed queries and running queries. The completed queries are sorted by descending order of query runtime or duration.

Figure 10-32. Monitoring top queries

Identifying Systemic Query Performance Problems

Consider a scenario where many of your users are complaining about longer-than-normal query runtimes. You want to diagnose what is happening in your cluster. You can customize your time and switch to the graph view, which helps you correlate longer runtimes with what is happening in the cluster. As the Gantt chart and CPU utilization graph in Figure 10-33 show, many queries were running at the time when CPU utilization almost reached a peak of 25%.

Figure 10-33. Query duration

Monitoring Using Amazon CloudWatch

Amazon CloudWatch (*https://aws.amazon.com/cloudwatch*) is a monitoring service that monitors and captures alarms, logs, and events from various services in AWS. You can use Amazon CloudWatch to monitor and track various physical aspects of your cluster, such as CPU utilization, latency, and throughput of your resources and applications.

You can create a dashboard using the automatic templates available or create a custom dashboard with the metrics you want to monitor. There is an an automatic dashboard for Amazon Redshift that you can use as a template. Note that some performance metrics are displayed in different scaled units in CloudWatch compared to the console. For example, the WriteThroughput metric is displayed in GBs compared to bytes in CloudWatch, which is a more relevant unit for the typical storage space of a node.

You can create alarms to monitor metrics and send notifications when a limit or threshold is breached. You can also set up to automatically make changes to the resources based on a threshold; for example, you can monitor the CPU usage and query throughput or waiting in your Amazon Redshift data warehouse and then use that data to determine whether you should resize your cluster up or down. You can also use this data to pause or resize underutilized data warehouses to save money. With CloudWatch, you gain system-wide visibility into resource utilization, application performance, and operational health across all services. You can use CloudWatch to monitor metrics available in the console and additional metrics you want to monitor for Amazon Redshift provisioned clusters and serverless.

Using CloudWatch metrics for Amazon Redshift, you can get information about your overall cluster's health and performance or at individual node level. When working with these metrics, keep in mind that each metric has one or more dimensions associated with it. These dimensions tell you the scope of the metric and whether the metric is for the data warehouse or individual nodes:

- Metrics that have a NodeID dimension provide performance data for nodes of a cluster. This set of metrics includes leader and compute nodes. Examples of these metrics include CPUUtilization, ReadIOPS, and WriteIOPS.

- Metrics that have only a ClusterIdentifier dimension provide performance data for clusters. Examples of these metrics include HealthStatus and Maintenance-Mode.

Amazon Redshift CloudWatch Metrics

On the CloudWatch console, you have various dashboards available to view service dashboards, cross-service dashboards, billing dashboards, or recent alarms. Amazon Redshift metrics are collected under the `AWS/Redshift` namespace, and these metrics are collected at one-minute intervals. You can can choose "Service dashboards" and select "Redshift" to view the metrics captured in CloudWatch, as shown in Figure 10-34.

Figure 10-34. CloudWatch monitoring

As you can see in Figure 10-35, you can also search for any other specific service in the list. AWS has precreated automatic dashboards available with most commonly used metrics. In addition, if you want to create custom dashboards, you can create your own dashboards by selecting the "Custom dashboards" tab.

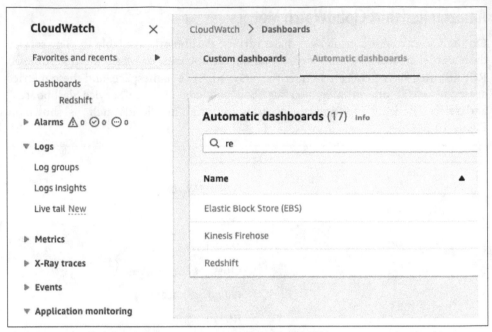

Figure 10-35. CloudWatch monitoring search for Redshift

The automatic dashboards have metrics like CPUUtilization, PercentageDiskSpaceUsed, DatabaseConnections, HealthStatus, and other metrics. If you want to add new metrics, you can use the "Add to dashboard" button as shown in Figure 10-36 to add the appropriate metrics to this dashboard, or you can create a new customer dashboard from the start.

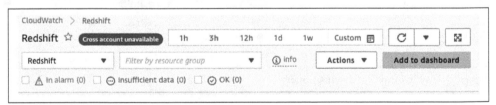

Figure 10-36. CloudWatch monitoring automatic add to dashboard

You can also override the period from default to any range from 1 second to 30 days. If there are any system-level alerts, the details are captured here, and you can filter to view only the alerts.

Figure 10-37 shows the default CloudWatch monitoring dashboard, which should satisfy most use cases. But you can also create a custom dashboard if required.

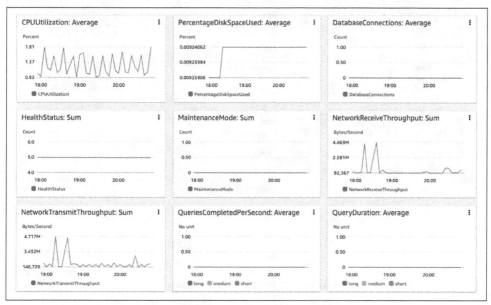

Figure 10-37. CloudWatch monitoring automatic dashboard

To create a custom dashboard, choose the "Custom dashboards" tab and click "Custom dashboards," as shown in Figure 10-39. You can choose the type of graph in the widget first, as shown in Figure 10-38, to create the custom dashboard.

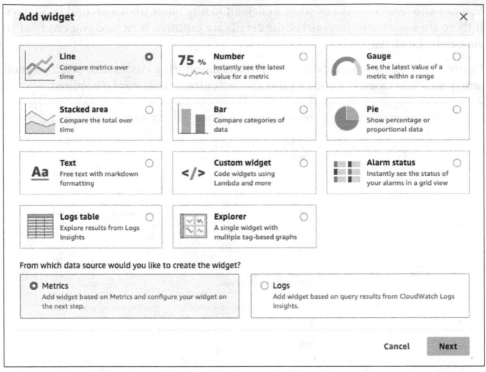

Figure 10-38. CloudWatch add widget to custom dashboard

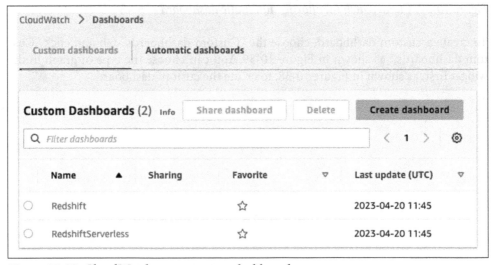

Figure 10-39. CloudWatch create custom dashboard

Here you can filter for Redshift-related metrics, and select any of the metrics available to create your own dashboard with the metrics relevant to your database or organization's monitoring requirements. You can also start with the default dashboard and customize it by adding new metrics to the dashboard using the "Add to dashboard" option. In Figure 10-40, you see the metrics like "By Resource Type," "Node Metrics," "Aggregated by Cluster," and other metrics related to WLM queues and queries.

Figure 10-40. CloudWatch monitoring custom dashboard

 In some cases, a cluster-specific metric represents an aggregation of node behavior. Some examples are HealthStatus and MaintenanceMode, where the interpretation of the metric value is aggregated of all compute nodes.

Monitoring Using System Tables and Views

Amazon Redshift stores various information about the data warehouse in system tables and views, and this information is useful to understand how the system is functioning. These tables are available as system views prefixed with letters STL, SVCS, STV, and SVV in the `pg_catalog` schema, and users who have permissions can query these system views directly to analyze database performance. This section explains key details stored in these system tables, with some sample system tables and queries. It also explains:

- How different types of system tables and views are generated
- What types of information you can obtain from these tables
- How to join Amazon Redshift system tables to catalog tables
- How to manage the growth of system table log files

Some system tables can be used only by AWS staff for diagnostic purposes. The following sections discuss the system tables that can be queried for useful information by system administrators or other database users.

There are several types of system tables and views:

STL system views

These are generated from logs that have been persisted to disk to provide a history of the system. These files reside on every node in the data warehouse cluster. The STL views take the information from the logs and format them into usable views for system administrators. STL system views retain seven days of log history. Log retention is guaranteed for all data warehouse sizes and node types, and it isn't affected by changes in data warehouse workload. Log retention also isn't affected by data warehouse status, such as when the data warehouse is paused. You have less than seven days of log history only in the case where the data warehouse is new. Retaining logs doesn't require any customer action, but if you want to store log data for more than seven days, you have to periodically copy it to other tables or unload it to Amazon S3. You can find the detailed list of views in STL views (*https://oreil.ly/O6n_N*).

STV tables

These are virtual system tables that contain snapshots of the current system data. They are based on transient in-memory data and are not persisted to disk-based logs or regular tables.

SVCS system views

The prefix *SVCS* provides details about queries on both the main and Concurrency Scaling clusters. The views are similar to the tables with the prefix *STL* except that the STL tables provide information only for queries run on the main cluster.

SVL views

These are system views in Amazon Redshift contain references to STL tables and logs for more detailed information. These views provide quicker and easier access to commonly queried data found in those tables.

SVV views

These system views in Amazon Redshift that contain references to STV tables and snapshots for more detailed information.

SYS views

These are system monitoring views used to monitor query and workload usage. These views are located in the `pg_catalog` schema. To display the information provided by these views, run SQL SELECT statements. SYS_SERVERLESS_USAGE gathers usage data for Amazon Redshift Serverless only.

> System tables are not included in automated or manual data warehouse backups (snapshots). The retention period for STL system views and log history is seven days. If you want to store log data for more than seven days, you have to periodically copy it to other tables or unload it to Amazon S3. You can write a stored procedure or use the Amazon Redshift System Object Persistence Utility (*https://oreil.ly/SeYIY*) to archive data from system tables.

There are two classes of visibility for data in system tables and views: visible to users and visible to superusers:

Superuser-visible views

Only users with superuser privileges can see the data in those tables that are in the superuser-visible category. Regular users can see data in the user-visible tables. To give a regular user access to superuser-visible tables, grant SELECT privilege on that table to the regular user (*https://oreil.ly/90LZA*).

User-visible views

By default, in most user-visible tables, rows generated by another user are invisible to a regular user. If a regular user is given unrestricted SYSLOG ACCESS, that user can see all rows in user-visible tables, including rows generated by another user. For more information, see information on how to alter a user (*https://oreil.ly/zbKCQ*) or create a user (*https://oreil.ly/Uiis9*).

> Giving a user unrestricted access to system tables gives the user visibility to data generated by other users. For example, STL_QUERY and STL_QUERY_TEXT contain the full text of INSERT, UPDATE, and DELETE statements, which might contain sensitive user-generated data.

Monitoring Serverless Using System Views

Monitoring views are system views in Amazon Redshift Serverless that are used to monitor query and workload usage. These views are located in the `pg_catalog` schema. The system views available have been designed to give you the information needed to monitor Amazon Redshift Serverless, which is much simpler than that needed for provisioned clusters. The SYS system views have been designed to work with Amazon Redshift Serverless. To display the information provided by these views, you can run SQL SELECT statements on any of these tables or views. For a comprehensive list of views, you can refer to documentation on system views (*https:// oreil.ly/CRJPa*).

System views are defined to support the following monitoring objectives. For a detailed list of all system views, you can refer to "Monitoring Queries and Workloads with Amazon Redshift Serverless" (*https://oreil.ly/gR8Y_*).

One of the views is SYS_SERVERLESS_USAGE, which has details on compute capacity and storage used with the charge seconds, and if there are any cross-region data transfer costs (see Figure 10-41). You can use the Query Editor V2 to query the data with a SELECT statement:

```
SELECT * FROM SYS_SERVERLESS_USAGE;
```

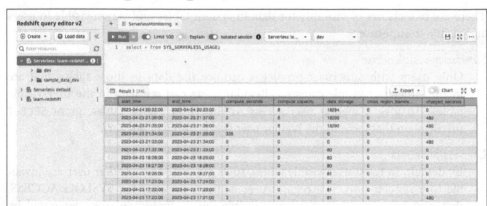

Figure 10-41. Serverless resource monitoring

The system views capture data to help you monitor various aspects of your data warehouse and the workloads you run. These views can be categorized as follows:

Workload monitoring
  You can monitor your query activities over time to understand workload patterns so you know what is normal (baseline) and what is within business SLAs. This will help you rapidly identify deviations from normal, which might be a transient issue or something that warrants further action. The views SVL_QUERY_SUMMARY, SYS_QUERY_HISTORY, and SYS_QUERY_DETAIL have details on the query workloads, and you can use these to monitor details of each step in query for runtime, blocks read, rows returned, and any alerts for the query.

Data load and unload monitoring
  To move data in and out of Amazon Redshift Serverless, you use COPY and UNLOAD commands to load or unload data. You can monitor progress of the

data load or unload closely in terms of bytes/rows transferred and files completed to track adherence to business SLAs. This is normally done by running system table queries frequently (that is, every minute) to track progress and raise alerts for investigation/corrective action if significant deviations are detected. The views SYS_LOAD_DETAIL, SYS_LOAD_HISTORY, SYS_LOAD_ERROR_DETAIL, and SYS_UNLOAD_HISTORY have details of rows, bytes, and any errors.

Failure and problem diagnostics

There are cases where you must take action for query or runtime failures. Developers rely on system tables to self-diagnose issues and determine correct remedies. The view STL_ALERT_EVENT_LOG has details on system-wide alerts, and the views STL_LOAD_ERRORS and SYS_LOAD_ERROR_DETAIL have details on errors for data loads using COPY commands.

Performance tuning

You might need to tune queries that are not meeting SLA requirements either from the start or have degraded over time. To tune, you must have runtime details including run plan, statistics, duration, and resource consumption. You need baseline data for offending queries to determine the cause for deviation and to guide you how to improve performance. Some of the key tables that can be used for user object monitoring are:

SYS_QUERY_HISTORY *and* SYS_QUERY_DETAIL

Use these views to analyze query and tune performance by checking if there is long queue_time, lock_wait_time, or planning_time. You can also look at the returned_rows to determine if you can filter selected data.

SVV_TABLE_INFO

This view include details on compression encoding, distribution keys, sort style, data distribution skew, table size, and statistics for a particular table. Using this, you can diagnose and address table design issues like distribution skew that can influence query performance.

User objects event monitoring

You need to monitor actions and activities on user objects, such as refreshing materialized views, vacuum, and analyze. This includes system-managed events like auto-refresh for materialized views. You want to monitor when an event ends if it is user-initiated, or the last successful run if system-initiated. Some of the key tables that can be used for user object monitoring are:

SVV_VACUUM_SUMMARY, STL_VACUUM, STL_SORT, *and* STL_ANALYZE

Summarize information about vacuum, sort and analyze operations logged by the system.

SVV_MV_INFO, SVL_MV_REFRESH_STATUS, *and* STL_MV_STATE
  Contains details on materialized view and refresh activity.

Usage tracking for billing
  You can monitor your usage trends over time to inform budget planning and business expansion estimates. You can also identify potential cost-saving opportunities like adjusting your max RPU or archiving cold data. The provisioned clusters are billed based on type and number of nodes provisioned. For serverless, SYS_SERVERLESS_USAGE system table tracks usage and gets the charges for queries. To track spectrum usage, you can use the SVL_S3QUERY_SUMMARY view.

> The SVL_QUERY_SUMMARY view contains only information about queries run by Amazon Redshift, not other utility and DDL commands. For a complete listing and information on all statements run by Amazon Redshift, including DDL and utility commands, you can query the SVL_STATEMENTTEXT view.

High Availability and Disaster Recovery

In an organization, some applications are categorized as mission critical and some not deemed as critical. The mission criticality of applications has a measurement you can use to identify how important a workload is.

Recovery Time Objective and Recovery Point Objective Considerations

Mission criticality of your applications or workloads is determined by two dimensions, and when designing a backup and recovery architecture for your production application, you have to consider these two factors:

- What is the acceptable time to recover from disaster recovery scenario? (Recovery Time Objective [RTO])

- What is the acceptable point in time in which all data ingested into the database will be consistent? (Recovery Point Objective [RPO])

Recovery Time Objective
  When using Amazon Redshift, your RTO is determined by the snapshot restore time. This is usually based on a volume of data in the data warehouse, node type, number of nodes, and the target restore data warehouse or serverless instance. You can test restoration from snapshots created on the production data warehouse to correctly determine RTO. It is also important that you retest the restore performance any time you resize the data warehouse or your data volume changes significantly. This determines what is considered an acceptable time window when service is unavailable. If you are using a

multiple Availability Zone (Multi-AZ) configuration, RTO is 0 because there are no snapshots to recover in a single-region strategy.

Recovery Point Objective

With Amazon Redshift, automated backups are triggered based on a threshold of blocks changed (5 GB) or after a certain amount of time (eight hours). For a data warehouse with minimal changes to data, a backup is taken after approximately every eight hours. For a data warehouse that churns a massive amount of data, backups can be taken several times per hour. If you find that your data churn rate isn't triggering automated backups at a frequency that satisfies your RPO, then you need to build custom solutions to guarantee the targeted RPO. This determines what is considered an acceptable loss of data between the last recovery point and the interruption of service.

Amazon Redshift supports Multi-AZ deployments for provisioned RA3 clusters. Multi-AZ deployments support running your data warehouse in multiple Availability Zones simultaneously and can continue operating in unforeseen failure scenarios. A Multi-AZ deployment is intended for customers with business-critical analytics applications that require the highest levels of availability and resiliency.

A Redshift Multi-AZ deployment leverages compute resources in two AZs to scale data warehouse workload processing. The Multi-AZ feature does round robin all the time, irrespective of high concurrency or low, to utilize all resources. It will automatically leverage the resources in both AZs to provide resiliency for read and write requests using active-active processing. For Multi-AZ, the recommendation from AWS is to have twice the number of nodes for good performance. So this costs twice the price but can be a compelling way to buy RIs for customers expecting heavy concurrency/burst, and you don't have to wait for burst cluster to become available.

Multi-AZ Compared to Single-AZ Deployment

In a Single-AZ deployment, Amazon Redshift requires a data warehouse subnet group to create a data warehouse in your VPC. The data warehouse subnet group includes information about the VPC ID and a list of subnets in your VPC. When you launch a cluster, Amazon Redshift either creates a default data warehouse subnet group automatically or you choose a data warehouse subnet group of your choice so that Amazon Redshift can provision your data warehouse in one of the subnets in the VPC. You can configure your data warehouse subnet group to add subnets from different Availability Zones that you want Amazon Redshift to use for data warehouse deployment.

All Amazon Redshift clusters today are created and situated in a particular Availability Zone within an AWS Region and thus called Single-AZ deployments. For a Single-AZ deployment, Amazon Redshift selects the subnet from one of the Availability Zones within a Region and deploys the data warehouse there.

On the other hand, a Multi-AZ deployment is provisioned in multiple Availability Zones simultaneously. For a Multi-AZ deployment, Amazon Redshift automatically selects two subnets from two different Availability Zones and deploys an equal number of compute nodes in each one. All these compute nodes across Availability Zones are utilized via a single endpoint as the nodes from both Availability Zones are used for workload processing.

As shown in Figure 10-42, Amazon Redshift deploys a data warehouse in a single Availability Zone for Single-AZ deployment and multiple Availability Zones for Multi-AZ deployment.

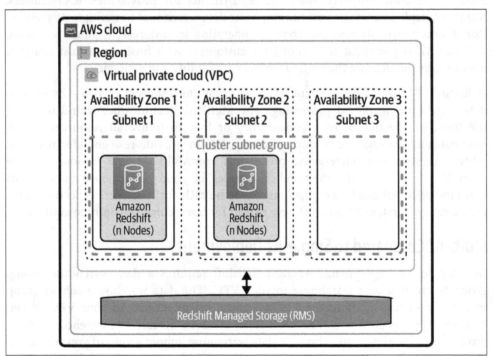

Figure 10-42. Multi-AZ compared to Single-AZ

Creating or Converting a Provisioned Data Warehouse with Multi-AZ Configuration

You can set up Amazon Redshift Multi-AZ deployment while creating a new provisioned cluster or migrate an existing Single-AZ cluster to a Multi-AZ configuration. In this section, we cover both options.

Creating a new data warehouse with Multi-AZ option

You can easily create a new Multi-AZ deployment through Amazon Redshift console. Amazon Redshift will deploy the same number of nodes in each of the two Availability Zones for a Multi-AZ deployment. All nodes of a Multi-AZ deployment can perform read and write workload processing during normal operation. Multi-AZ deployment is supported only for provisioned RA3 clusters. As shown in Figure 10-43, you select "Yes" for the Multi-AZ deployment option when creating a new cluster. This will deploy the cluster across two Availability Zones with twice the number of nodes entered.

To follow the detailed steps to create an Amazon Redshift provisioned data warehouse in multiple Availability Zones, refer to the blog post "Enable Multi-AZ Deployments for Your Amazon Redshift Data Warehouse" (*https://oreil.ly/GDTac*).

For Multi-AZ, when you select the number of nodes, you will be paying for four nodes, as two nodes each will be available in two Availability Zones. You can purchase reserved instances for all four nodes.

At the time of writing this book, the Multi-AZ feature (*https://oreil.ly/CypTq*) is in preview. Hence, you select "Preview track," shown in Figure 10-43, to create a cluster with Multi-AZ configuration. When the feature becomes generally available, you can choose the current track to enable this feature instead of "Preview track."

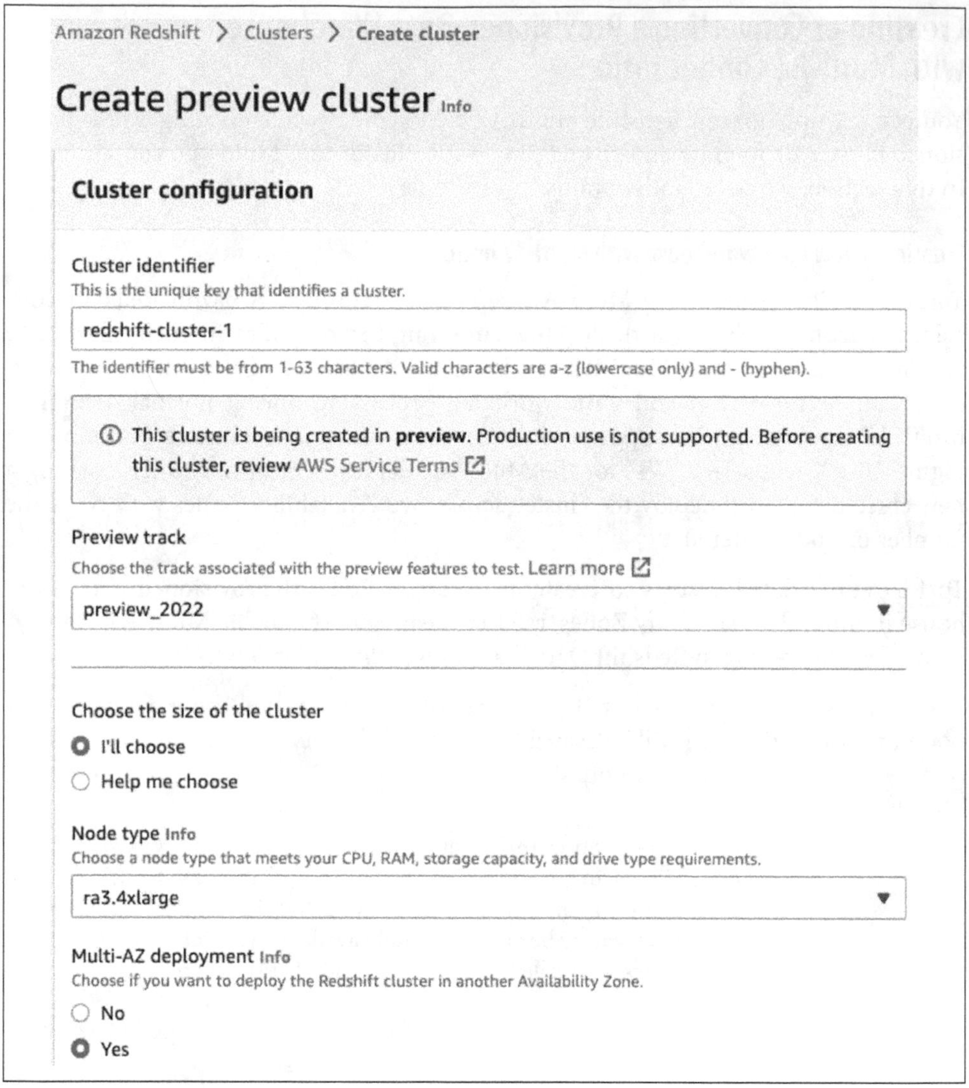

Figure 10-43. Create new data warehouse with Multi-AZ

Migrating an existing data warehouse from Single-AZ to Multi-AZ

If you have been running Amazon Redshift in your organization already, chances are it is not configured for Multi-AZ. To migrate this existing data warehouse to a Multi-AZ configuration, you can restore from a snapshot (see Figure 10-44) from the existing data warehouse and configure Multi-AZ. When migrating to a Multi-AZ deployment from an existing Single-AZ deployment, maintaining performance of a single query may require the same number of nodes used in the current Single-AZ deployment to be provisioned in both Availability Zones. This will result in doubling the amount of data warehouse nodes needed when migrating to Multi-AZ to ensure that single query performance is maintained. For example, if you have two nodes in Single-AZ, when you migrate to Multi-AZ, you need to maintain two nodes on each AZ for the same performance.

In the event of a failure in an Availability Zone, Amazon Redshift continues operating by using the resources in the remaining Availability Zone automatically. However, user connections might be lost and must be reestablished. In addition, queries that were running in the failed Availability Zone will be stopped. However, you can reconnect to your cluster and reschedule queries immediately. Amazon Redshift will process the rescheduled queries in the remaining Availability Zone. In the event that a query fails or a connection shuts down, Amazon Redshift retries the failed query or reestablishes connection immediately. Queries issued at or after a failure occurs might experience runtime delays while the Multi-AZ data warehouse is recovering.

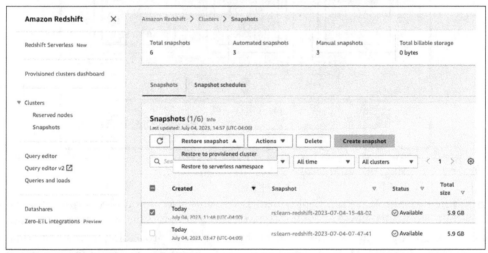

Figure 10-44. Convert existing data warehouse from Single-AZ to Multi-AZ

Auto Recovery of Multi-AZ Deployment

In the unlikely event of an Availability Zone failure, Amazon Redshift Multi-AZ deployments continue to serve your workloads by automatically using resources in the other Availability Zone. You are not required to make any application changes to maintain business continuity during unforeseen outages since a Multi-AZ deployment is accessed as a single data warehouse with one endpoint. Amazon Redshift Multi-AZ deployments are designed to ensure there is no data loss, and you can query all data committed up until the point of failure.

As shown in Figure 10-45, if there is an unlikely event that causes compute nodes in AZ1 to fail, then a Multi-AZ deployment automatically recovers to use compute resources in AZ2. Amazon Redshift will also automatically provision identical compute nodes in another Availability Zone (AZ3) to continue operating simultaneously in two Availability Zones (AZ2 and AZ3).

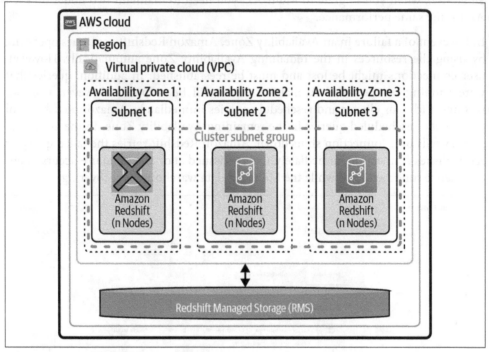

Figure 10-45. Multi-AZ auto recovery

Amazon Redshift Multi-AZ deployment is not only used for protection against the possibility of Availability Zone failures, but it can also maximize your data warehouse performance by automatically distributing workload processing across multiple Availability Zones. A Multi-AZ deployment will always process an individual query using compute resources only from one Availability Zone, but it can automatically distribute processing of multiple simultaneous queries to both Availability Zones to increase overall performance for high concurrency workloads.

It's a good practice to set up automatic retries in your ETL processes and dashboards so that they can be reissued and served by the data warehouse in the secondary Availability Zone when an unlikely failure happens in the primary Availability Zone. If a connection is dropped, it can then be retried or reestablished immediately. Only the active queries or loads at the time of failure will be aborted, and any new queries will be routed to the secondary AZ while the nodes in the failed AZ are restored into another AZ.

Snapshots, Backup, and Restore

Backup and restore operations are enabled through snapshots in Amazon Redshift. Snapshots are backups of a data warehouse or serverless that are taken point-in-time either automatically or manually.

Snapshots for Backup

Amazon Redshift stores these snapshots internally in Amazon S3 by using an encrypted Secure Sockets Layer (SSL) connection while writing to snapshots, and AWS KMS encryption for storage.

You can restore from a snapshot into a new data warehouse or serverless instance. When you restore from a snapshot, Amazon Redshift creates a new data warehouse and makes the new data warehouse available before all the data is loaded, so you can begin querying the new data warehouse immediately. The data warehouse streams data on demand from the snapshot in response to active queries, then loads the remaining data in the background. You can monitor the progress of snapshots by viewing the snapshot details in the AWS Management Console or by calling describe-cluster-snapshots in the CLI or the DescribeClusterSnapshots API action. For an in-progress snapshot, these display information such as the size of the incremental snapshot, the transfer rate, the elapsed time, and the estimated time remaining.

Amazon Redshift stores snapshots in an internally managed Amazon S3 bucket that is managed by Amazon Redshift, so it is always available. To manage storage charges, evaluate how many days you need to keep automated snapshots and configure their retention period accordingly. Delete any manual snapshots that you no longer need. For more information about the cost of backup storage, see the Amazon Redshift pricing page (*https://oreil.ly/6v1Pv*).

To manage cost, you can set a retention period for both automated and manual snapshots. You can change the default retention period for automated and manual snapshots by modifying the data warehouse or the time of creation.

Automated Snapshots

By default, automated snapshots is enabled and Amazon Redshift periodically takes snapshots for every eight hours or every 5 GB per node of data changes, whichever comes first. If your data is larger than 5 GB * the number of nodes, the shortest amount of time in between automated snapshot creation is 15 minutes. Alternatively, you can create a snapshot schedule to control when automated snapshots are taken. For custom schedules, the minimum amount of time between automated snapshots is one hour. As you can see in Figure 10-46, snapshots are taken periodically and spread across eight hours, as there is not a change in the total size.

Figure 10-46. Automatic snapshots

Automated snapshots are deleted at the end of a retention period and upon deletion of a cluster. If you are deleting a cluster, remember to take a manual snapshot for recovery. You can also schedule manual snapshots after daily loads to provide a recovery point in a disaster recovery situation.

Manual Snapshots

When you want to take a full backup of your database or need a longer retention period for the snapshot, you can create a manual snapshot at anytime. You can use the console or the CLI command `create-cluster-snapshot` to create a manual snapshot. In the console, after you select a cluster, under the Actions menu you choose "Create snapshot" to create the manual snapshot. For a manual snapshot, you can choose to retain indefinitely or a specific period of time using the retention period option, as shown in Figure 10-47. Manual snapshots are retained even when you delete the cluster. You can tag your manual snapshots with a date-timestamp to allow you to restore them to a previous state.

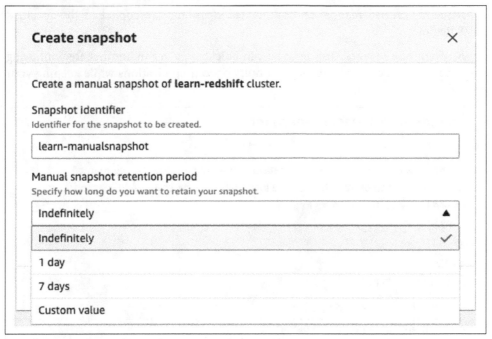

Create snapshot   ✕

Create a manual snapshot of **learn-redshift** cluster.

Snapshot identifier
Identifier for the snapshot to be created.

learn-manualsnapshot

Manual snapshot retention period
Specify how long do you want to retain your snapshot.

Indefinitely ▲

Indefinitely	✓
1 day	
7 days	
Custom value	

Figure 10-47. Manual snapshots

> To improve the performance of the restore snapshot process, you can create tables that do not require backup with the BACKUP NO option. This will also reduce the storage used for snapshots.

Disaster Recovery Using Cross-Region Snapshots

Disaster recovery (DR) has traditionally been important only for transactional applications. But recently, with the importance of data and analytics in decision making, data warehouse applications are becoming mission critical. Hence, DR has to be part of the architecture and strategy when you build a data warehouse application.

DR is about preparing for a disaster and having the ability to quickly recover your operations from another region in the event of an unforeseen outage in your primary region.

With Amazon Redshift, cross-region snapshots can be set up from the console. Select a cluster and you can use the Actions menu and choose "Configure cross-region snapshot" as shown in Figure 10-48 to set up cross-region snapshots to copy snapshots for a data warehouse to another AWS Region. You can configure where to copy snapshots and how long to keep copied automated or manual snapshots in the destination AWS Region. When cross-region copy is enabled for a cluster, all subsequently created manual and automated snapshots are copied to the specified AWS Region.

In the event of a regional disaster, you can quickly recover in another Region, using the snapshot, and ensure business continuity of your applications while keeping your costs down.

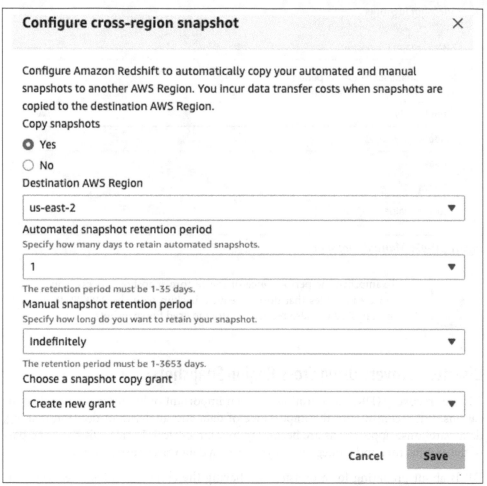

Figure 10-48. Cross-region snapshots for disaster recovery

For an active-active setup of Amazon Redshift across multiple Regions, you can use Amazon Route 53 (*https://oreil.ly/aBBbH*), a fully managed DNS service, to do latency-based or any rule-based routing to determine which cluster will be accessed by users. You can refer to this blog post: "Building Multi-AZ or Multi-Region Amazon Redshift Clusters" (*https://oreil.ly/AJ5Uc*).

Using Snapshots for Simple-Replay

For business-critical workloads that have to be available 24-7, testing different data model configurations or system configurations may not be possible on your production cluster. In these scenarios, you can use snapshots from a primary production data warehouse to create a test environment to test if the configuration changes meet your performance expectations. A Simple Replay Utility (*https://oreil.ly/Y0n3y*) is a tool that you can use to perform a what-if analysis to evaluate how your workload performs in different scenarios with different database configurations.

Monitoring Amazon Redshift Using CloudTrail

AWS CloudTrail (*https://aws.amazon.com/cloudtrail*) is a service that provides a record of actions taken by a user, role, or AWS service in Amazon Redshift. CloudTrail captures all API calls, including calls from the Redshift console and calls through code to the Redshift operations. Amazon Redshift data sharing, Amazon Redshift Serverless, Amazon Redshift Data API, and Query Editor V2 are all integrated with AWS CloudTrail and available under CloudTrail action categories, e.g., "Redshift," "Redshift-data," "sqlworkbench," and "Redshift-serverless."

The events captured in CloudTrail for Amazon Redshift are continuously delivered to an Amazon S3 bucket. If you don't configure a trail, you can still view the most recent events in the CloudTrail console in Event History. Using the information collected by CloudTrail, you can determine the request that was made to Redshift, the IP address from which the request was made, who made the request, when it was made, and the request parameters.

To monitor Amazon Redshift using CloudTrail, you can follow these steps:

Enable CloudTrail
> First, enable CloudTrail in your AWS account if you haven't already. CloudTrail logs AWS API calls and captures relevant events.

Configure Redshift Event Logging
> Enable event logging for your Amazon Redshift cluster. This will ensure that Redshift-related events are recorded in CloudTrail. You can enable event logging through the AWS Management Console or by using the AWS CLI.

Review CloudTrail Logs
> Once you have CloudTrail enabled and Redshift event logging configured, you can review the CloudTrail logs. These logs will contain information about Redshift API calls, such as cluster creation, modification, deletion, user activity, and more.

Set Up Monitoring and Alerts

Use AWS CloudWatch to set up monitoring and alerts for specific Redshift events. CloudWatch allows you to create custom metrics and define alarms based on specific thresholds or patterns in the logs. For example, you can set an alert when a cluster is modified or when a specific API call is made.

Analyze and Respond

Regularly review and analyze the CloudTrail logs and CloudWatch metrics to identify any suspicious activities or performance issues in your Amazon Redshift environment. Based on the findings, take appropriate actions to respond to the situation, such as investigating potential security breaches or optimizing query performance.

By monitoring Amazon Redshift using CloudTrail, you can gain insights into the activities and usage patterns of your Redshift cluster, which helps you maintain security, troubleshoot issues, and optimize performance. You should use CloudTrail in addition to Amazon Redshift database audit logging to get a complete picture of operational commands run both inside and outside the data warehouse.

Bring Your Own Visualization Tool to Monitor Amazon Redshift

In addition to using queries, the console, CloudWatch, or APIs to monitor your data warehouse, you can also use your own visualization tool of choice to analyze the metrics captured by Amazon Redshift. Amazon Redshift stores metrics about query, ingestion, userlogs, workload management and general system configuration, performance, and usage metrics in system tables, as discussed in "Monitoring Using System Tables and Views" on page 379. You can query these system tables and views the same way you would query any other database tables.

To make it easier to monitor the data warehouse using some specific insights you need from system tables, you can build your own dashboards using visualization tools like Amazon QuickSight and Grafana. You can use JDBC/ODBC connectivity to connect to the database from any front-end visualization tool and create your custom visualization based on the metrics that are important to your organization. We will look at how you can use your own tool of choice to build impactful dashboards with examples using AWS native visualization tool Amazon QuickSight and the Grafana plug-in for Amazon Managed Grafana.

Monitor Operational Metrics Using System Tables and Amazon QuickSight

With Amazon QuickSight, you can meet varying analytical needs from the same source of truth through modern interactive dashboards, paginated reports, embedded analytics, and natural language queries. You can connect to various databases including Amazon Redshift to create visualizations or reports. You can build your own monitoring dashboards by querying the system tables similar to the one shown in Figure 10-49.

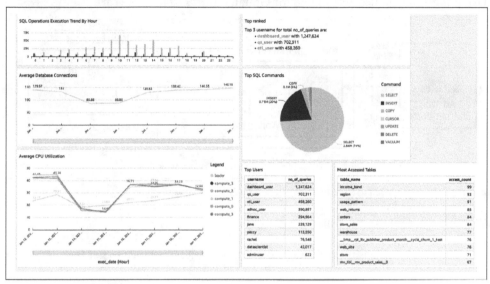

Figure 10-49. Create custom visualizations using QuickSight

Monitor Operational Metrics Using Grafana Plug-in for Amazon Redshift

Grafana is an interactive open source visualization tool by Grafana Labs to analyze and visualize data across one or many data sources. It is used in a variety of modern monitoring stacks, allowing you to have a common technical base and apply common monitoring practices across different systems. Amazon Managed Grafana developed by AWS is a fully managed service for Grafana that enables you to visualize alerts on your metrics, logs, and traces, as shown in Figure 10-50.

Grafana Reporting increases collaboration, transparency, and accountability while enhancing efficiency and visibility to operational metrics and trends. Using a tool like Grafana allows you to leverage the flexibility of using SQL to get insights about workloads. You can query system tables as discussed in "Monitoring Using System Tables and Views" on page 379.

Amazon Redshift supports a plug-in for Grafana with which you can build a consolidated dashboard that visualizes a set of curated operational metrics. This works on top of the Amazon Redshift Grafana data source, which you can add to an Amazon Managed Grafana workspace, as well as to any other Grafana deployments where the data source is installed.

For the step-by-step process to create an Amazon Managed Grafana workspace and configure an Amazon Redshift data warehouse with a Grafana data source, you can refer to the blog post "Query and Visualize Amazon Redshift Operational Metrics Using the Amazon Redshift Plugin for Grafana" (*https://oreil.ly/i2Yta*).

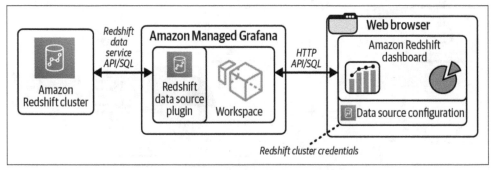

Figure 10-50. Create custom visualizations using Grafana

The solution includes the following components:

- The Amazon Redshift data warehouse or serverless instance to get the metrics to analyze.
- Amazon Managed Grafana, with the Amazon Redshift data source plug-in added to it. Amazon Managed Grafana communicates with the Amazon Redshift data warehouse via the Amazon Redshift Data Service API.
- The Grafana web UI, with the Amazon Redshift dashboard using the Amazon Redshift data warehouse as the data source. The web UI communicates with Amazon Managed Grafana via an HTTP API.

The dashboard, as shown in Figure 10-51, shows operational data from your cluster. When you add more clusters and create data sources for them in Grafana, you can choose them from the data source list on the dashboard.

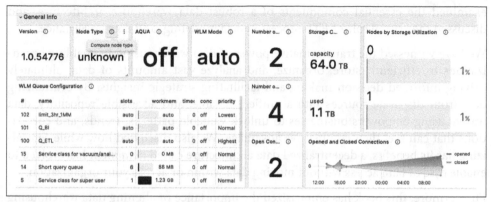

Figure 10-51. Create custom dashboard visualizations using Grafana

Because the Amazon Redshift data source plug-in for Grafana is an open source project, you can install it in any Grafana deployment, whether it's in the cloud, on premises, or even in a container running on your laptop. That allows you to seamlessly integrate Amazon Redshift monitoring into virtually all your existing Grafana-based monitoring stacks.

Summary

This chapter discussed different ways to monitor Amazon Redshift provisioned data warehouse and serverless. The Redshift console makes it easier for any administrator to view alerts on queries, ingestion workloads, or overall system resources. Since these statistics data are stored in physical tables, you have the flexibility to use your tool of choice to create alerts and monitor key metrics important for your workloads. We also covered how snapshots are a mechanism for backup and restore and the resiliency and disaster recovery options using the snapshots.

This also brings us to the end of the book. We have focused on discussing architecture patterns and real customer scenarios based on our experience and provided insights into when a particular feature of Amazon Redshift could manage your data better and provide better access to your customers. As you have seen, we have also provided references to online documentation and blogs throughout the book so you can refer to the latest updated documentation and best practices as more capabilities are added. Where required, we have dived deep into certain topics and explained the relevance of the features to business workloads with examples. We hope you find this book and the resources referenced here helpful to modernize your data workloads on the cloud.

This book has explored the world of data warehousing with Amazon Redshift, providing a comprehensive understanding of its concepts, methodologies, and practical applications. We have delved into the foundational principles of data warehousing, examined the essential components of a robust data warehouse architecture, and discussed the crucial role of ETL processes, data modeling, and data governance.

We have witnessed the transformative power of data warehousing in enabling organizations to efficiently store, organize, and analyze vast amounts of data, ultimately driving informed decision making and facilitating strategic insights. By centralizing data from disparate sources into a unified, reliable, and accessible repository, data warehousing empowers businesses to unlock valuable patterns, trends, and correlations that can fuel their competitive advantage. We also discussed how while centralizing has its benefits, a decentralized data architecture called *data mesh* has evolved to enable ease of data access without moving data within or across your organization.

Furthermore, this book has emphasized the importance of aligning data warehousing initiatives with business objectives, highlighting the significance of a well-defined data strategy, effective data governance frameworks, and robust data quality management practices. We have explored various data warehousing architectures, such as the traditional centralized data warehouse using star schema data model, as well as newer approaches including data lakes, data mesh, and data fabric and how you can build cloud-based solutions using Amazon Redshift. It is important for any data professional to recognize the evolving landscape and the need for adaptability to provide business insights to the key decision makers.

As we conclude this journey, it is essential to acknowledge that the field of data warehousing continues to evolve at a rapid pace, driven by advancements in technology, the proliferation of data sources, and evolving business needs. It is crucial for practitioners to stay abreast of emerging trends, such as generative AI, real-time data integration, big data analytics, and the integration of artificial intelligence and machine learning techniques into data warehousing processes.

Ultimately, this book has aimed to equip its readers with a solid foundation in data warehousing principles, techniques, and best practices, serving as a guide to navigate the complex realm of data management and analytics. By understanding the key concepts, challenges, and opportunities associated with data warehousing, readers can embark on their own transformative journeys, leveraging data as a strategic asset and unlocking the full potential of their organizations in an increasingly data-driven world.

Index

About the Authors

Rajesh Francis is a principal analytics specialist at AWS and works with strategic customers to help drive data strategy and deliver business outcomes. He has worked in various capacities over the last 25 years as a consultant, solutions architect, business development executive, and a leader in the data and analytics space with global organizations. He specializes in Amazon Redshift and is passionate about building scalable data architectures and working closely with customers and product teams to guide the direction of AWS Analytics Services. In prior roles, Rajesh led implementation of SAP analytics solutions for Fortune 500 corporations.

Rajiv Gupta is a manager of Amazon Redshift Specialist Solutions Architects who help customers design and build their data warehouse platforms. He is an AWS-certified SA Associate and an Analytics Specialty certification holder, based out of Lake Forest, California. Rajiv has been working in the data and analytics space for 20-plus years as a consultant, not only helping customers successfully implement their data warehouse implementations but also writing technical articles that educate his customers and colleagues and has managed teams of architects with the goal of producing positive customer outcomes.

Milind Oke is a senior Redshift specialist solutions architect who has worked at Amazon Web Services for three years. He is an AWS-certified SA Associate, Security Specialty and Analytics Specialty certification holder, based out of Queens, New York. In 1998, he started off as a database developer, developing analytical solutions on traditional database engines, and has gathered extensive experience in architecting and building data warehouse solutions for various banks and other Wall Street financial institutions. At AWS he works closely with Redshift engineers, product management, product marketing teams, and has authored several AWS Big Data blogs and actively answers question posted directly from customers on AWS re:Post.

Colophon

The animal on the cover of *Amazon Redshift: The Definitive Guide* is a scarlet tanager (*Piranga olivacea*), a medium-sized songbird that spends the majority of its time in North America and migrates to mature forests in northern and western South America during winter.

Male scarlet tanagers live up to their name during the breeding season, displaying bright, blood-red plumage on the majority of their body and black on their wings and tail. Once breeding season is over, they molt and appear similar to females, with a color transition to olive-yellow. Males retain their black tail and wings during this time, while females have dark, olive plumage on their wings and tail. Adult scarlet tanagers are between 16 and 17 centimeters long with wingspans between 25 and 29 centimeters, and they weigh between 0.8 and 1.3 ounces. They have stocky proportions and a thick, rounded bill that is perfect for catching insects and eating fruit.

Scarlet tanagers are primarily insectivorous during summer. They occasionally enjoy fruits, especially when scavenging for food in the winter. Berries, ants, butterflies, moths, spiders, earthworms, and snails are just a few components of their diet. They live high up in the forest canopy of mixed deciduous and evergreen tree forests, nesting in oak, hickory, beach, and the occasional aspen or birch tree. In the spring, they can be found snatching berries from gardens and parks.

While scarlet tanagers are designated as a species of least concern by the IUCN, they are impacted by habitat fragmentation. Additionally, scarlet tanager nests are at risk of being invaded by brown-headed cowbirds. If the tanagers are not vigilant, the cowbird will kick the tanager's eggs out of the nest and replace them with their own. The tanagers, unaware of this, will then hatch out the egg and raise the imposter baby with the rest of their brood, seemingly unaware of the difference. Many of the animals on O'Reilly covers are endangered; all of them are important to the world.

The cover illustration is by Karen Montgomery, based on an antique line engraving from Shaw's *Zoology*. The cover fonts are Gilroy Semibold and Guardian Sans. The text font is Adobe Minion Pro; the heading font is Adobe Myriad Condensed; and the code font is Dalton Maag's Ubuntu Mono.

O'REILLY®

Learn from experts.
Become one yourself.

Books | Live online courses
Instant answers | Virtual events
Videos | Interactive learning

Get started at oreilly.com.

Printed in the USA
CPSIA information can be obtained
at www.ICGtesting.com
JSHW050739141023
50189JS00006B/11